BARGAIN HUNTING

IN THE **BAY AREA**

BARGAIN HUNTING

IN THE **BAY AREA**

BY **SALLY SOCOLICH**

CHRONICLE BOOKS
SAN FRANCISCO

Copyright © 2000 by Sally Socolich.

Library of Congress Cataloging-in-Publication Data available.

Printed in the United States of America.

ISBN 0-8118-2617-1

Design by Tim Clark
Composition by Suzanne Scott

Distributed in Canada by Raincoast Books
8680 Cambie Street, Vancouver, British Columbia
V6P 6M9

10 9 8 7 6 5 4 3 2 1

Chronicle Books
85 Second Street
San Francisco, California 94105

www.chroniclebooks.com

Contents

How to Be a Bargain Hunter

It's 2000. Some things have changed and some haven't. The emergence of Internet commerce is changing the marketplace every day, in every way. Yet, not everyone has the inclination, the means, or the confidence in the system's integrity to go online. It's not my intention to cover bargain hunting on the Internet—but rather to serve the needs of shoppers who still want to engage in "hands-on" shopping. Online shopping has its place, but nothing can beat the adrenaline rush of pulling a super deal off the rack, shelf, or warehouse floor and the delight of telling friends and family of your coup.

Hunting for bargains is not nearly as black and white as it was twenty-five years ago. I used to climb three flights of stairs, undress between pipe racks, pay cash, and be made to feel like the owner was doing me a favor by letting me buy at a discount. Today I can drive to a regional outlet center and enjoy all the amenities of most full-service retail stores. Every strip center seems to be anchored by a big box discounter. Are there any challenges or mysteries remaining for bargain hunters? Yes! Now more than ever, this book is relevant. You need to know which retailers are doing what; are the bargains bogus or for real? You'll get the lowdown on who has the best deals and prices—and the best selection. This book will save you time because I've done the footwork and made the calls. As the evolution and revolution in off-price and outlet retailing continues on a very visible level, I've discovered and profiled new outlets that tend to keep an almost subterranean existence below the radar of most shoppers. They represent the best of what this book is all about.

The Bay Area has had its share of store openings, closings, expansions, contractions, and moves, all of which are reflected in this new edition. My standards haven't changed. Outlets and off-price stores must still measure up in price and integrity. Each store must offer greater savings than its competitors in the overall Bay Area retail marketplace. I'm not bothered by the lack of retail amenities found in many outlets or warehouse-style businesses, but I do try to warn you when this is the case so that you'll approach the business with the right expectations. It's not my intention to tell you what to buy (I leave that to product-buying guides like *Consumer Reports* and other publications). Rather, my mission is to direct you to those sources where, whatever you buy, you'll be getting the best value for the money you spend. Many of these stores and outlets are well known to consumers by now; others benefit from the high-profile brands they stock. In this new edition, I've limited or eliminated my comments regarding many of the well-known bargain sources, giving more space to those that are more obscure.

Remember that bargains are relative. Your income level, value system, and exposure to merchandise in all price ranges and qualities will provide you with your uniquely personal perception of a "bargain."

Bargain hunting appeals to shoppers at all income levels, but you must often think in terms of trade-offs. To capture savings, you may have to drive forty to ninety miles north or south to one of the outlet centers or to a community on another side of the Bay: is it worth it? At some stores and outlets, the hours may be inconvenient, the inventory unpredictable, the service indifferent, or the parking nonexistent. Only you can decide how much inconvenience equals the trade-off—saving money. Don't confuse "cheap" with "value." A $10,000 dining room suite purchased for $6,700 is as good a value as a $1,500 dining room suite purchased for $900. Likewise, a $300 cashmere sweater purchased for $150 is as good a value as a $40 cotton sweater purchased for $20. It's the savings that count, more than just the final price. And remember: nothing is a bargain if you don't need it. One of the biggest problems at outlets and discount stores is the compulsion to buy simply because everything seems so cheap. To truly save money, quit while you're ahead.

While I hope that this book will save you some time, comparison shopping can still be worth your while. It always helps to know your market. Timing, overhead, special promotions, stock liquidations, and other factors can be reflected in the prices offered by particular outlets. Please refer to the Glossary of Bargain-Hunting Terms on page 352 for a full explanation. It's time to admit that there's a lot of outlet merchandise being sold at phantom values—labels that once denoted quality are now trading on long-lost reputations. It appears that some manufacturers have a two-tiered distribution system: one quality for major full-price retailers, a knock-off and lesser quality for outlet stores. Those swayed by labels should know that by now labels do not necessarily indicate quality or value. Likewise, don't be fooled by "suggested retail prices"; some appear to have been arbitrarily chosen to create the illusion of a greater discount.

Fortunately, there are still many only-in-the-Bay-Area outlets that showcase the talents and diversity of local manufacturers and businesses. In addition, major companies (outside the Bay Area) have instituted outlet divisions, which has led to the factory stores that show up in regional outlet centers across the country. They may not always meet the

expectations of consumers who first cut their bargain-hunting teeth shopping at the original and unique factory outlets (many have vanished from the scene) that were profiled in earlier editions of this book. Yet, factory stores located far from the company's factory or distribution sites provide an opportunity to buy quality goods at modest to maximum discounts.

This edition of *Bargain Hunting in the Bay Area* includes more than 600 stores offering solid values. With few exceptions, I expect a store or outlet to offer at least 20% off the retail price, though most entries offer far greater reductions. When possible, I have quoted prices to indicate the kinds of bargains available at the various stores. These prices are based on research conducted in the spring and summer of 1999. This book is intended as a guide, not an endorsement of the stores listed. I have no affiliation with the stores reviewed; no one paid to be in this book; no printing charges were assessed (a practice sometimes utilized by other guidebooks); nor were my comments subject to store approval.

A Word of Warning Before You Set Out

Because store hours—and even locations—are subject to change, I recommend that you call those shops you intend to visit before driving miles across town. Addresses and phone numbers were correct at the time of publication, but these may change. Subsequent printings will include corrections, and readers are encouraged to notify me in care of the publisher of any such changes. Also, don't hesitate to let me know when a store doesn't measure up to my description. I want to know whether you were satisfied with the experience. Be fair—I need your name in case I have to contact you to establish that your letter is not an envious competitor's sour grapes. Be assured I will keep your name in confidence if I believe it's important to pass along your criticisms to the store involved. Your happy reports are appreciated, as well—I love them! And I would be delighted to hear from other bargain hunters regarding listings for future editions or other suggestions you may have. Please send any and all comments to my publisher:

Chronicle Books
85 Second Street, Sixth Floor
San Francisco, CA 94105

Happy hunting!
Sally Socolich

How to Use This Book

Bargain Hunting in the Bay Area is arranged by general merchandise category. Under each subject heading, store names are listed in alphabetical order. Some subjects, such as Apparel/Fashion, House and Home, and others, have been divided into subcategories. For each store, I give the address, phone number, Web site or e-mail when provided, hours, parking availability, and means of payment accepted (cash only, cash or check, and/or credit cards). If a store takes credit cards, it will also take checks unless otherwise noted. Credit card codes: MC—MasterCard, AE—American Express, DIS—Discovery, DC—Diners Club, CB—Carte Blanche, and VISA. Following this information, sometimes I'll list other outlet centers or other stores—that is, where branch stores or similar services are offered. For the exact street address, daily hours, and directions for stores located in outlet centers, refer to the appendix beginning on page 347.

Because many stores sell a wide variety of merchandise, I have made a limited number of cross-references that I thought would be helpful to a bargain hunter. These appear at the end of each section. And please consult the indexes at the end of the book: Store listings on 355, arranged alphabetically; Geographical listings on page 365, arranged by city; and Subject listings on page 381, arranged by product or service supplied.

An important note about phone numbers! Area codes throughout the Bay Area are subject to change. The area codes in this edition are correct as of September 1999. If an area code has changed and your call won't go through, call information for the new number.

Women's Apparel/Fashion

Rather than follow an alphabetical arrangement for all apparel, I've listed all categories in women's apparel first, followed by men's, then family, which includes children's. Next come fashion-related sections (cosmetics, jewelry, shoes, etc.). I've divided the women's apparel listings into several sections so that you can locate the resources that best meet your shopping needs. The first is devoted to the outlet and off-price stores in the South of Market and surrounding areas of San Francisco. It's a focal point for bargain hunters, so you can plan shopping days in the City by quickly perusing the listings. For special sizes, manufacturers' outlets elsewhere, and off-price, chain, and specialty stores, please refer to the sections that follow.

San Francisco's Factory Outlets and Off-Price Stores

Covering South of Market (SOMA), parts of the Mission and Potrero districts, and surrounding areas

The glory days of SOMA shopping are a thing of the past, but, fortunately, there are still some important outlets, and a few new outlets have opened. The biggest problem confronting SOMA shoppers is the dearth of parking. In the past few years, the area has been transformed into "media gulch" with the explosion of high-tech companies and pricey residential lofts proliferating in buildings formerly occupied by garment factories and small warehouse operations. The opening of the Pac Bell Stadium only compounds the parking problem. Your best bet is to shop on Saturdays (except Game Days) or be prepared to vigilantly feed the meters (metermaids will cut you no slack) or pay the high rates at parking lots. Call before making a long drive to visit any of these outlets. I wouldn't bet the farm that any of these outlets will survive the upheavals caused by new construction and freeway retrofitting scheduled to go on endlessly into the future.

Factory outlets: Many of the stores listed here and throughout the Apparel/Fashion chapter are factory stores or factory outlets, typically owned and operated by clothing manufacturers or importers, and often located on or near the manufacturers' plants. Some offer little in the way of retail store amenities; others have gone high tech. Some may not take credit cards, have unconventional hours, or have difficult parking resulting in very limited hours of operation. Be sure to call ahead to verify hours and addresses. I've noted in parentheses which stores are factory outlets.

BYER FACTORY OUTLET (FACTORY OUTLET)

1300 Bryant Street, San Francisco. (415) 626-1228.
W–Sat 10–5. MC, VISA. Parking: lot.
(Other outlets: BFO/Byer Factory Outlet,
Mervyn's Plaza, Santa Clara; Great Mall, Milpitas.)
Byer California manages to satisfy legions of
budget shoppers, many of whom consider regular
pilgrimages to its factory stores a must—most
prices at $8 to $49 are too hard for teens and their
moms to resist! At the outlet, discounts are usually
40–60% off original retail. These aren't seconds
but first quality. Younger working gals stretch
dollars on blouses, pants, and sophisticated coordinates or dresses; they can save on a New Year's
Eve knockout prior to the holidays. Byer offers
modestly priced lines of Junior, Misses, and Petite
dresses and related sets, jackets, and sportswear
(sizes 3–18); Large fashions (1X–3X); and Girls
sportswear and dresses (4–6X and 7–14). Some of
the labels you'll recognize: A. Byer, Byer Too, Byer
Studio, AGB, and Amy Too Amy. The Santa Clara
and Milpitas outlets are posh compared to the
San Francisco store and have a nicer selection and
more current fashions. No returns or exchanges
are allowed in San Francisco; 15-day exchange in
Santa Clara and Milpitas.

CHRISTINE FOLEY (FACTORY OUTLET)

430 Ninth Street, San Francisco. (415) 621-5212.
www.christinefoley.com. M–Sat 10–4. MC, VISA.
Parking: street.
Christine Foley's hand-loomed 100% cotton
sweaters are very special, offering whimsical
designs, bold colors, and real originality. Most
styles can be worn by girls or boys, women or
men. They're not cheap, and you're likely to find
them in elegant department stores or boutiques.
This colorful little outlet disposes of discontinued
styles, color imperfections, and seconds. Prepare
for the prices. Wholesale prices on children's
sweaters (sizes 2–12) range from $60 to $88;
adult sweaters (S, M, L) range from $138 to $166.
Retail prices are at least double. Seconds are
reduced the most, up to 70% off retail; stickers
reveal the defects.

CUT LOOSE FACTORY OUTLET
(FACTORY OUTLET)

*690 Third Street, San Francisco. (415) 495-4581.
M–Sat 10–5:30, Sun Noon–5. MC, VISA.
Parking: street. (Factory warehouse sales first
Thursday and Friday each month: 1780 Armstrong
Avenue, San Francisco.)*

You can have it two ways here: shop at the main
outlet for 50% savings and more on past- and
current-season overruns, or wait for the factory
warehouse sales, when seconds are sold at truly
skinflint prices. Cut Loose offers upscale designs
for weekday and weekend wear, garment-dyed
separates in distinctive fabrics—textured cottons,
crinkled rayons, washed linens, corduroys, silk-like
bembergs—and a wonderful variety of solid
colors. Prices range from $6 to $65 on separates:
pleated pants, leggings, assorted blouse and top
styles, skirts (straight, full, short, long), and many
styles of jackets—short and long to dramatic
oversized jackets. The cut is generous on most
styles—perfect for less-than-perfect bodies. Keep
it simple and basic, or show your fashion savvy by
choosing from sophisticated separates. Sizes:
XS–XL; Plus sizes 1X–3X. If you're on the mailing
list, you won't miss out on any sale opportunity at
either site. *Note: Cash only at factory sales.*

ESPRIT FACTORY OUTLET (FACTORY STORE)

*499 Illinois Street (at 16th Street), San Francisco.
(415) 957-2550. M–F 10–8, Sat 10–7, Sun 11–5.
Hours subject to change during special sales
and holiday season. MC, VISA, AE, DIS.
Parking: free lot.
(Other outlets: Gilroy, Napa centers.)*

The Esprit Outlet is more than an outlet, it's a
major tourist attraction. Whatever your age, Esprit
can cover you from head to toe. The outlet sells
seasonal overruns, returns, and samples. Its shoe
department is very popular. If you find the outlet
prices still too steep, your best strategy is to wait
for the fabulous sales, when prices may be reduced
an additional 30–40% off the lowest marked price.
Otherwise, check the bargain bins in the back.
You'll find everything Esprit, including the Dr. Seuss
collection for children and adults. Outdoor types
can check the bargains on high-end, high-tech
outdoor apparel, backpacks, sleeping bags, and
gear from Esprit's subsidiary, Moonstone Mountain
Equipment. Sizes range from Infant 12mos to

Toddler 36mos (boys, too) up to Junior 13/14 and Women's. Exchanges with receipt, within 14 days of purchase, for merchandise credit good for one year. Call for special sales and directions.

GEORGIOU FACTORY OUTLET (FACTORY OUTLET)

925 Bryant Street (bet. Seventh and Eighth streets), San Francisco. (415) 554-0150. M–Sat 10–6:30. Sun Noon–5. MC, VISA, AE, DIS. Parking: private rear lot, enter on Langston (alley next to store). (Other outlets: 579 Bridgeway, Sausalito; Milpitas, Vacaville centers.)

If you're dazzled by Georgiou's fashions, you'll be thrilled with its outlet's past-season overruns, overstocks, and missed shipments, and you'll probably get a buzz buying the "old stuff" on $1 to $9 racks. All Georgiou's fashions are made of natural fibers: wool, cashmere blends, silk, linen, rayon, and cotton, with each new color and print designed to coordinate with existing colors in its line. You can build a wardrobe of career separates piece by piece. Most styles qualify as contemporary classics—they'll remain au courant for seasons to come. Younger women especially love the detailing, buttons, and figure-flattering fit on many of the career suits. Holiday suits, ensembles, and dresses have real pizzazz. The colorful and fun cruise, leisure, and resort lines made from 100% cotton will survive many fashion seasons. Misses sizes 4–16. Prices are 50–80% off retail. Georgiou accessories at discount prices are just what you need to pull your outfit together. The outlet has a high-tech look, wonderful lighting, and an accommodating staff. Ask for a Club Georgiou card (for extra discounts) and don't miss Georgiou's special sales—one of my best buys in 1999 was a $280 dressy chic little suit marked down to $59. Wow!

ISDA & CO. OUTLET (FACTORY OUTLET)

29 South Park (bet. Bryant and Brannan, Second and Third streets), San Francisco. (415) 512-1610. M–Sat 10–5:30. MC, VISA. Parking: street.

Isda & Co. offers something that is often difficult to find when shopping South of Market: better quality and sophisticated styles for upscale shoppers. It has earned a Golden Shears Award and many articles in the fashion press with its clean, chic, well-tailored designs for women who have grown up and want high-quality clothes at afford-able prices. If you admire the Donna Karan line, you'll surely love Isda's designs. You can create your own ensemble from related separates: Combine a skirt (short or long), walking shorts, or pants with vest tops or hip-length, slimming jackets. You'll find elegant mercerized cotton knit T-shirts and fine-gauge mercerized sweater knits and vests. These tops are soft and lustrous and look very expensive. The fabrics are the best: quality rayon suitings, tropical weight wool, 100% cotton (in sophisticated white blouses), and rayon/linen blends. At the outlet, past-season groups are at least 50% off retail. That translates to about $146 for a jacket, about $70 for pants, or about $56 for a skirt, with even greater markdowns on way-past-season styles. It may become more diffi-cult to create ensembles as the season progresses and styles sell out. Women's sizes: 2–14 or S, M, L. Guys need to come in and check out the new line for men that conveys a very San Francisco image for dress Fridays or dining out on Saturday nights. Like the women's collections, great fabrics are the foundation of the line. Loved the men's sweater collection!

JEREMYS

2 South Park, San Francisco. (415) 882-4929.
M–F 11–7, Sat 11–6, Sun 11–5. MC, VISA, AE.
Parking: street.
(Other store: 2967 College Avenue, Berkeley.)
Jeremy, the hip young owner of this SOMA media-gulch lunchtime gathering place for fashion guys and gals, knows his customers. He buys popular lines of women's and men's contemporary sports-wear from status stores in New York. The labels will leave you agog! Some of these fashions are slightly irregular, some have been repaired (broken zippers, popped seams, missing buttons), but no one seems to mind. The men's department serves guys who want good deals on casual weekend separates, great ties, Saturday night out-to-dinner clothes, and trendier sportcoats and suits. The women's lines appeal to ladies who frequent contemporary sportswear departments of major stores or specialty shops. There's usually a collec-tion or two that's just right for the partying crowd and the SOMA club scene. Prices are generally 40–60% off original retail and often more (I spotted one status designer men's suit marked down from $1,800 to $425). Women's sizes 4–14. The College

Avenue location is classy too, to fit in with the Elmwood shopping district. Finally, Jeremys allows exchanges for store credit.

MARGUERITE RUBEL RAINCOATS/JACKETS (FACTORY OUTLET)

543 Howard Street, 2nd Floor, San Francisco. (415) 362-2626. www.rubel.citysearch.com. M–F 7–5, Sat 7–11:30. MC, VISA. Parking: street.
Marguerite Rubel can be unnerving for first-time shoppers; she is refreshingly honest, painfully direct at times, and altogether something of a character. Once you get past her gruff demeanor, you'll end up firm friends. Her World Map jackets worn by Ronald Reagan, George Bush, and Bill Clinton have garnered exceptional publicity. She enjoys a good reputation for the classic and innovative styling of her raincoats, blazers, jackets, coats, and sportswear. Velvets have always been a part of her line, and she keeps up-to-date by including poplins, silk-like polyesters, and other fabrics. Recently, her best-selling styles have included updated golf, tennis, or weekend jackets, some with appliqués or patchwork utilizing 200 squares in each jacket. Some of the inventory appears to have been around since the beginning of time, but retro-fashion buyers love it. You'll find many one-of-a-kind jackets, coats, and overruns from her sportswear. It's a grab bag of fashions with some real treasures; if you've ever wanted a dramatic velvet cape or wrap, this is your place. You can expect 40–50% savings, but not Nordstrom's service, and you're in for a scold if you don't handle the fashions with care. *Quilters note: Velvet scraps are sold in dozens of colors at $3/pound, with a 10-pound minimum. Some fun trimmings too!*

A MOTION STUDIO (FACTORY OUTLET)

440 Brannan Street, San Francisco. (415) 957-1411. M–F 11–6, Sat 11–4. MC, VISA. Parking: street.
If you're reconnoitering South of Market, you're likely to spot A Motion Studio, an outlet that may strike the staid and conventional shopper as bewildering. Yet, it's in sync with the urban hip, media-gulch crowd doing business in SOMA. The racks in this small outlet are filled with sportswear samples and (sometimes) cutting edge experimental fashions for men and women. Many outlet fashions result from the company's primary business as a product developer/pattern and

sample maker for designers and companies—
many that have glamorous appellations. Prices are
generally at a wholesale level. To experience this
outlet in its hippest element, stop in and unwind
after work the third Friday of every month for an
evening of cool music, snacks, wine, and a buy-
and-browse sortie through the racks of the
month's new fashions. Count on sportswear with
an edge or retro influence—body-conscious
silhouettes on women's sportswear, maybe some
$29 keep-warm-and-cozy Sherpa fleece tops, a
'50s retro simply styled mechanics jacket for $70,
men's sport shirts at $32, or $65 on a wear-any-
where Taslan fiber totally reversible zip jacket.
A Motion Studio outlet is bound to be a hit with
guys who never wear ties and women who wear
cargo pants; in other words, urban individualists
rather than mainstream fashion clones.

SIRI (FACTORY OUTLET)

540-D Barneveld Avenue, San Francisco.
(415) 431-8873. M–F 10–5, Sat by appointment.
MC, VISA. Parking: street.
An out-of-the-way location (behind Goodman
Lumber) for an out-of-the-ordinary collection of
feminine fashions. Siri's fashion studio is a combination retail boutique and outlet. Her elegant
collection of daytime and special occasion dresses
is sold to status stores and boutiques. Prices on
dresses range from $150 to $500. The styles are
timeless and classic, yet offer originality for those
who don't want to look like department store
clones. Women in their twenties, thirties, and
forties are prime targets for this sophisticated line.
Beautiful fabrics (many designed in-house), interesting textures, and distinctive colors are hallmarks
of each collection. Expect savings of 50–75% off
retail on past-season styles (many one-of-a-kind
beauties). Sign up for sale flyers announcing
quarterly "clear the racks" sales when prices take
a submarine dive. Sizes 2–12.

SUSAN LAWRENCE

*119 Sacramento Street, San Francisco.
(415) 399-0222. M–F 10–6, Sat 11–5. MC, VISA,
DIS, AE. Parking: pay lots.*

Executive women from the Financial District, their assistants, and recent college grads come here for the suits, dresses, and blouses that their jobs require, finding premium lines that are sold concurrently in downtown status stores. The more traditional labels include Jones New York, Evan Picone, Tahari, and Donna Ricco, starting at $169. Contemporary suits and dresses with European styling (fitted jackets and shorter yet businesslike skirts) from Expressions, Sunny Names, Ice Cube, View, Style, Mystery, Rina Rossi, and others are priced from $149 to $199. Pantsuits are back in the workplace in both contemporary and missy styles starting at $149, also lots of new business casual sets. Susan Lawrence offers discounts ranging from a modest 20% up to 35% (average about 25%). Sizes: 2–16. Alterations can be provided in-store. This shop offers a winning combination: good prices and professional and personal service.

WESTON WEAR BOUTIQUE & OUTLET

*3491 19th Street, San Francisco. (415) 695-2869.
www.westonwear.com. T–Sun 11–6. MC, VISA.
Parking: street.*

Weston Wear is innovative and sometimes strikingly avant-garde, but also practical and mainstream. Some dresses are high on the sex appeal quotient, perfect for women with a let's-have-fun attitude. Moms and daughters can enjoy exploring the racks; younger women will find festive Saturday night clothes (lots of slinky short dresses); mainstream moms can spruce up with contemporary separates or dresses. Many styles are body-hugging, figure-flattering designs—if you've got the figure. The fabrics are key to the line and fit—stretch knits with spandex or lycra, also slinky stretch velvets and laces, even sheer nylon mesh (with lining). The company's contemporary styling has made the cut and shows up at chic boutiques like Fred Segal in Santa Monica, and is worn by celebs on TV's *Melrose Place*, *Beverly Hills 90210*, and *General Hospital*. The company sells many of its styles under the private labels of department and specialty chain stores. Prices on current season collections are strictly retail—fortunately the $10 and $20 racks and $5 bargain bins will put new fashions in your closet for well below wholesale. These are discontinued styles, seconds, and samples. Expect to pay the going rate on vintage ceramics, purses, and on jewelry by local designers and others not so local. Sizes: 1, 2, 3 (fit 4–12). To be notified about the factory sales, call and have your name added to the outlet's mailing list. Postcards sent quarterly announce sale dates for three months at a time.

Also See

Under Active Sportswear:
EASY WEAR; SPORTS BASEMENT

Under Men's Suits:
SPACCIO

Famous Labels/Factory Stores

Factory stores: This is a designation I've given to stores owned by companies that have created a thriving and profitable side business by operating not just one, but dozens of factory-owned stores throughout the country. Major brands like Liz Claiborne, Jones New York, OshKosh B'Gosh, and Van Heusen go this route. This strategy makes sense in today's retail environment: in this way, clothesmakers are not entirely dependent on department stores, or subject to market forces over which they have little control. Factory stores usually offer more of a manufacturer's products or lines than any one retail or department store, and the prices and discounts can range from very modest (and disappointing) to quite impressive. To keep stores well stocked, many companies manufacture or buy merchandise specifically for their outlet divisions. I feel that often this "special" merchandise does not offer the same quality or value as the company's regular merchandise manufactured for full-price retailers. Modest discounts (25–30%) most often apply to current, first-quality merchandise.

Factory stores owned by major manufacturers are usually found in the outlet centers on the perimeter of the Bay Area. At times it seems like everyone in these areas is participating in an ongoing game of musical chairs as they hopscotch from one space to another, or move from one outlet center to another when leases come up for renewal.

In the following listings, very well known designers or brand names are afforded minimal space. I'm assuming the name will define the merchandise. However, the locations of the outlets and range of discounts are important in determining whether a trip is worthwhile. Many outlets offer extra-special promotions and discounts during national holidays—e.g., Martin Luther King's Birthday,

Presidents' Weekend, Labor Day, etc. These holidays are an especially good time to plan a visit to an outlet center. *For outlet addresses and daily hours, see the Appendix.*

ANN TAYLOR OUTLET & LOFT
Petaluma Village Premium Outlets, Petaluma. (707) 766-9592. Daily. MC, VISA, AE. Parking: lot. (Other stores: Marina Square, San Leandro; Gilroy, Napa centers.)
This Petaluma store has a dual personality: part Ann Taylor Outlet, part Ann Taylor Loft. About half the space is devoted to great past-season markdowns to 70% off retail. That's worth the trip to Petaluma. The other Loft stores are real crowd pleasers though I'm not sure about the bargain angle. Apparel sold in this Ann Taylor division is made specifically for Loft stores to address the budget needs of women who find its regular stores too pricey. The company chooses proven style winners from its retail division and manufactures knock-offs for the Loft stores. Jackets from coordinate groups ranged in price from $98 to $137 in early 1999; you can capture a professional look with a nice cotton or silk blouse—many styles are priced from $39 to $59, on average. The selection is always up-to-date. Count on an extensive sportswear category with lots of denims, knit tops, etc., a respectable shoe department, and, best of all, an extensive petite department. Sizes: Petite 2–12; Misses 2–14. Returns and refunds (except on Ann Taylor as-is or less than perfect merchandise in the Petaluma outlet).

ANNE KLEIN
Prime Outlets at Gilroy, Gilroy. (408) 842-7660. Daily. MC, VISA, AE, DIS. Parking: lot. (Other outlet: Pacific Grove center.)
Anne Klein is one of the best outlets for upscale fashions and really delivers on price, quality, and selection. Some style groups are from previous seasons, while the rest are current. Anne Klein II collections are the big attraction. Prices at the outlet are guaranteed to satisfy the savviest shopper. Solid 40% discounts are the norm on most groups, but look for extra specials. You'll also find modestly discounted Anne Klein accessories, including handbags, scarves, hats, fashion jewelry, and watches. Sizes: Petite 0–14; Misses 0–16. Exchanges accepted within seven days for store credit only.

BCBG

Napa Premium Outlets, Napa. (707) 254-7984.
Daily. MC, VISA, AE, DIS. Parking: lot.
(Other outlet: Great Mall, Milpitas.)
This line is a great favorite with the twenty-
something crowd. The body-conscious fashions
and contemporary styling add up to a collection of
trendy career and party clothes. There's an element
of retro in some of the styles, and the slinky little
dresses are perfect for Saturday night "club cruising." Skirts are slim and long or very, very short.
Lots of little jackets and career suits, but not much
in the way of casual weekend sportswear. Prices
range from $25 to $100 at an average 50% discount. New arrivals are marked down 30% and end
up at 70% off on final sale racks. The shoe racks
carry the same fashion-forward styling—a perfect
complement to the apparel collections. Sizes: 2–14.

CAROLE LITTLE OUTLET

Prime Outlets at Gilroy, Gilroy. (408) 847-4411.
Daily. MC, VISA, AE. Parking: lot.
(Other outlets: Napa, Pacific Grove centers.)
Carole Little is noted for "easy" clothing: mainstream yet chic, with contemporary and classic
career and weekend apparel. The related separates
are dramatic and make a statement, and on their
own they have a distinct character. Dresses and
sweaters are staples. Collections are priced from
40–75% off original retail. Each season's line of
color-themed styles offers tremendous versatility
for building an outfit. Sizes: 2–24. Plus gals love
the attention from the company's Carole Little II
Collection. Store exchanges within five days only.

CHICO'S FACTORY STORE

Factory Stores at Vacaville, Vacaville.
(707) 453-1336. Daily. MC, VISA, AE. Parking: lot.
I love leftovers! Especially Chico's distinctive
color-coordinated in-house-designed casual
clothing in 100% cotton, silk, and rayon. Loose
fitting and designed for easy care, these creative
designs feature attractive, bold colors in casual
contemporary motifs with just a hint of ethnic.
Combine pieces from the related separates for a
knockout ensemble! Save 25–50% off every day;
look for 50%-off promotions on discontinued
color groups. Sizes: 1, 2, 3 for women 7/8–14/16.
And you can't possibly leave without adding a
piece of dramatic fashion jewelry.

DONNA KARAN COMPANY STORE

St. Helena Premium Outlets, St. Helena.
(707) 963-8755. Daily. MC, VISA, AE.
Parking: lot.
(Other outlets: Folsom, Milpitas centers.)
Donna Karan's elegant, upscale St. Helena outlet is
equal to her reputation. Noted for her remarkable
sense of style and signature collections, her company store is merchandised with recent overruns as
well as past-season inventory. The 35–50% discounts
off retail on most everything make the trip worthwhile for a Donna Karan or DKNY customer, but the
apparel is still somewhat pricey. Retail prices on
many Donna Karan Collection pieces are often over
$1,000. DKNY and sportswear collections approach
affordability for most women. Lots of denim, classy
and elegant career silk blouses (many body-suit
styles), related separates, coats, handbags, belts,
sunglasses, fashion jewelry, scarves, and more. A
small men's boutique on the first floor has sportshirts, suits, sweaters, etc. The company offers a
14-day period for exchanges or merchandise credits.
The other outlets are smaller, with less emphasis
on the higher-priced collections. Full range of sizes
(some 2s–14), including Petites; Men's S–XXL.

ELLEN TRACY OUTLET

Napa Premium Outlets, Napa. (707) 226-2994.
Daily. MC, VISA, AE. Parking: lot.
From day one, this outlet has been drawing
hordes of women from all over the Bay Area.
Do yourself a favor and shop during the week to
avoid the long lines for dressing rooms on weekends. This is a four-star outlet offering Ellen
Tracy's sophisticated apparel from career, sportswear, and after-five collections. From the company's perspective, the collections sold in its
outlet are well past season, beyond the point
when local stores may still be selling the merchandise. Yet, because manufacturers and stores work
so far ahead of a season, almost everything in the
outlet is timely from a shopper's point of view.
Initially, new merchandise hits the outlet with
prices reduced 50% off original retail. February
and August are set aside for major end-of-season
sales. Sizes: Petite 0–14; Misses 2–16; Plus sizes
14–24. Refunds or exchanges within 14 days.

JONES NEW YORK COUNTRY

Napa Premium Outlets, Napa. (707) 226-7567.
Daily. MC, VISA. Parking: lot.
(Other outlets: Gilroy, Folsom centers.)
The orientation is dressier casual clothing and
ensembles and separates for business casual. The
image is classic, but not dull. Nice wool blazers,
more refined sweaters and vests, and traditional
slacks in winter and fall collections; linens, silks,
khaki, and dressy denims for spring and summer
collections. The quality is excellent both in fabric
and construction. Good values for the price—
although not greatly discounted. Sizes: 4–14.

JONES NEW YORK FACTORY FINALE & OUTLETS

Petaluma Village Premium Outlets, Petaluma.
(707) 766-8896. Daily. MC, VISA. Parking: lot.
(Other outlets: Gilroy, Napa, and Tracy centers;
Jones N.Y. Factory Finale, Pacific Grove center.)
Career women need no introduction to Jones
New York: beautifully made, simply designed
career apparel, a staple in department stores.
The Factory Finale stores in Petaluma and Pacific
Grove liquidate fashions from other factory stores

around the country. Discounts are an additional
40% on past season merchandise—some way
past season. Even so, the fashions fly out the door,
many selected to complete ensembles started
the year before. All sales are final at Finale stores.
Discounts at its other factory stores are 25–35%
off retail, not much better than a good department store sale, but the styles are all current, first
quality, and top of the line. For best buys, catch
the end-of-season sales. Lovely stores! Sizes:
Petite 2–14; Misses 4–16; Plus 14W–26W.

JONES NEW YORK SPORT

Napa Premium Outlets, Napa. (707) 224-7151.
Daily. MC, VISA. Parking: lot.
(Other outlet: Gilroy center.)
Just the ticket for your weekend unwind—
a collection of casual clothing that takes active
lifestyles into consideration. More laid back than
the country collection (listed above). Lots of
denim, knits, and linens. Sizes: 4–14 or S, M, L.

KAREN KANE

Napa Premium Outlets, Napa. (707) 254-8800.
Daily. MC, VISA, AE, DIS. Parking: lot.
Without a doubt, this was the best new women's
outlet to open in 1999. Karen Kane always offers
a very up-to-date collection of fashion groups that
are coveted by soccer moms, working women,
and anyone who likes a bit of a fashion edge. You'll
always find versions of long dresses for grocery
shopping or dressier parties; smaller groups of
career suitings; easy-wear basics and weekend
staples; updated denims (many softened with
tencel); twin sets; and travel-great dresses and
separates from rayon matte jerseys. Karen Kane's
detailing and superb fabric choices result in her
signature styles. Initial discounts in the outlet
average 40% off retail; progressive markdowns
end up at about 75% off retail. Check the back of
the store for racks of samples and seconds where
discounts start at 60% off retail. One Friday a
month, new racks of samples direct from the
factory prompt special visits by the faithful. Sizes:
Misses 4–14; Petites 4–12; Plus 1X–3X. No returns
or exchanges on merchandise marked as final sale.

KASPER A.S.L.

Prime Outlets at Gilroy, Gilroy. (408) 847-8157.
Daily. MC, VISA. Parking: lot.
(Other outlet: Folsom center.)
These are wonderful stores with collections of
feminine suits for women wearing Petite or Misses
sizes (some styles to 18). Prices on very current
inventory are 25–35% off major store retails, and
as the season progresses, markdowns reach 50%.
Kasper's suits and pantsuits have wonderful
detailing and there's styling for all "suit" occasions.
Pick an understated, traditional suit for executive
situations, or choose to emphasize your femininity
with suit jackets that nip in at the waist, that may
have dressier buttons, bolder colors, trim on the
lapels—items that allow one to feel dressed up for
weddings or other social and civic occasions.
Accessorize your suits with some elegant blouses
and dressy lightweight sweaters.

KORET OF CALIFORNIA FACTORY STORE

Prime Outlets at Gilroy, Gilroy. (408) 842-3900. www.koret.sf.com. Daily. MC, VISA, DIS. Parking: lot.

The Koret faithful will find 30–60% savings on current-season overruns, resulting in a $15 to $39.99 price range. You can put together a nice ensemble from the collections of related separates in mainstream styles. Many fabrics are washable, even the wool jackets/blazers. Collections are geared for the office and weekend, but some are fancy enough for dressy occasions. At the other end of the spectrum, Koret offers some very appealing and more contemporary sportswear groups. The size range is most accommodating: Petite 4–16; Women's 16–26/28; and Misses 8–18. Exchanges and returns within 30 days.

LIZ CLAIBORNE OUTLET

Prime Outlets at Gilroy, Gilroy. (408) 847-3883. Daily. MC, VISA, AE. Parking: lot. (Other outlets: Napa, Tracy centers.)

Everything Liz and more. A few other labels are taking up space: Russ Togs, Russ Sport, Crazy Horse, and Villager. About 60% of the inventory sold in the outlet is marked down 30% off retail, the rest 40–50% off. It's at least one season behind department stores and has already gone through one markdown cycle. In-season merchandise is usually excess from the year before; however, the stores are large and well stocked with Liz fashions for women and men. The handbag, hosiery, shoe, fragrance, and fashion jewelry departments are reasons to stop in if the apparel is not your preferred line. Petites are bound to be very pleased with their choices! I think the discounts are a little chintzy considering the status of the merchandise. Sizes: Petite 2–14; Women's 4–14; Large 14–22 (Elizabeth by Liz Claiborne).

LUCIA

Prime Outlets at Gilroy, Gilroy (408) 848-3877.
Daily. MC, VISA. Parking: lot.

This line resembles Villager, Country Suburban, Pendleton, and other somewhat conservative lines; it's sold through major stores under a private label and to specialty stores under the Lucia, That's Me, and TM Sport labels. Lots of nice suits, blazers, sweaters, pretty blouses, skirts, pants, etc., all very feminine in lovely colors combined with nice prints. These are mostly career clothes, along with festive and fancy sets for dressier needs and nice collections of sportswear for the weekend. Posted signs note each week's discount, usually 40–50% off the tagged price. Prices range from $20 to $50. Sizes: Petite 2–16; Misses 4–20; Women's 16–26.

MAX STUDIO OUTLET

Prime Outlets at Gilroy, Gilroy. (408) 842-3636.
Daily. MC, VISA, AE. Parking: lot.
(Other outlet: Napa center.)

The Max Studio Outlet is for those who don't conform or play it safe and want to stand out from the boring and blah. You'll find contemporary sportswear, sometimes avant-garde and updated groups of career, casual, and day-to-evening fashions. The fabrics make the difference: Lycra blends in body-hugging groups with short, short skirts or shorts, pants, and sassy jackets or tops; soft crepes or double knits resulting in figure-flattering styles. The career groups stand out. Some groups have flowing pants or longer skirts, but each group usually features a short skirt for the woman with great legs. Special Editions of its most popular styles are made for the outlet. Prices are reduced about half on all past-season styles, but look around for extra specials and additional 30% discounts. Sizes: XS–XL (fits 2–14). Exchanges within 10 days on non-sale merchandise for store credit only.

POLO JEANS COMPANY FACTORY STORE

Prime Outlets at Gilroy, Gilroy. (408) 848-5307.
Daily. MC, VISA, AE, DIS. Parking: lot.
The name says it all—a Polo company store
devoted to Polo jeans for a hip, younger fashion-
oriented customer (target market, 15 to 25 years
old). That's obvious with the pulse-pounding
high-tech music and video screens (it's a far cry
from Polo's classy grown-up outlets). Check for
Polo's interpretation of the latest new trends, but
count on lots of denim always, plus tops, T-shirts,
and other casual duds for guys and gals. If this is
your favorite fit and label, check it out.

ROBERT SCOTT & DAVID BROOKS

Napa Premium Outlets, Napa. (707) 253-7993.
Daily. MC, VISA. Parking: lot.
(Other outlet: Gilroy center.)
This company sells many groups under private
label to national catalog companies and upscale
specialty stores around the country, including
Talbots. Most of the clothing is current season,
sold at a 30% discount (end-of-season closeouts
usually 60% off on final markdowns). The look is
classic, tasteful, and updated. The quality of
fabrics and manufacture is first rate, accounting
for the slightly higher prices than at many other
factory stores. Spring blazers may be about $114,
shorts about $42, and blouses $36. I love the
career groups, casual coordinates, and extensive
sweater collection. Other cottons in very appealing cardigan and pullover styles have designs and
contrasting trims to coordinate with sportswear
groups. Limited dress selection. Sizes: Misses
4–18 or S–XL; Petites 2–16. This store rates high
for its beautiful, timely fashions and immaculate
merchandising.

ST. JOHN

Great Mall of the Bay Area, Milpitas.
(408) 942-0440. Daily. MC, VISA. Parking: lot.
This maker's enduring styles in wrinkleproof knits travel beautifully—one reason why so many women consider them to be wardrobe treasures. Discriminating shoppers don't flinch at the prices. Even at an average of 50% off original retail on past-season collections, those unfamiliar with the line may be stunned. Don't expect to find St. John's basic styles—they're never discontinued. Seasonal collections (including some dazzling holiday), cotton sport, accessories (jewelry, scarves, belts, handbags), and some shoes to match color collections get the spotlight. Sizes: Misses 2–16. *Note: Located near the Great Auto Court's entrance.*

TSE CASHMERE

Napa Premium Outlets, Napa. (707) 259-9444.
Daily. MC, VISA, AE. Parking: lot.
Expect to find TSE's ultraluxurious classic and fashion-oriented cashmere sweaters and sportswear for women and men at 33% discounts every day, or wait for end-of-season markdowns at 75% off. Holiday weekends are always celebrated with extraspecial sales and markdowns. Anything that might show up in the company's collections may show up in the outlet. Some cashmere silk and linen blends, plus very delicate, superfine knits distinguish the summer collections. Fall collections include cashmere knits, wovens, meltons, wool crepe, and superfine wool. Some Infants and Children's sizes; even blankets, throws, etc. from the home collections show up from time to time. *Note: TSE is pronounced "say."*

VERSACE

Prime Outlets at Gilroy, Gilroy. (408) 842-8509.
E-mail: versacegilroy@hotmail.com. Daily.
MC, VISA, AE, DIS, DC. Parking: lot.
Devotees of Versace will appreciate the markdowns here—others won't get it. Even at half off,
a T-shirt may still be $46 and a slinky party dress
may be over $1000. Men's and women's collec-
tions are sold at 40–50% markdowns and sometimes up to 75% off original retails on special
markdowns. In the outlet, you'll find in-season
fashion groups from the previous year—culled
from Versace boutiques around the country. At
discount prices, men's suits and sportcoats are
priced from $400 to $1200; Women's career suits
are about $800; and couture jeans might be $78.
Survey the store's inventory and you'll find formal
and semi-formal fashions, sportswear (jeans, tops,
sweaters, etc.), outerwear, career and dressier
women's suitings, fashion accessories (sunglasses,
handbags, some belts), and a few items from its
home accessory collections. Keep "in the know"
by putting your name down on the preferred
client list for calls and announcements of special
sales and shipments.

Also See

Under San Francisco's Factory Outlets
and Off-Price Stores:
BYER FACTORY OUTLET; ESPRIT;
GEORGIOU FACTORY OUTLET

Under Men's Sportswear:
MOST LISTINGS

Under Family, Men's & Women's,
General Clothing:
DOCKERS; EDDIE BAUER; GAP; GUESS?;
J. CREW; LEVI'S; POLO/RALPH LAUREN

Under Shoes:
BASS; TIMBERLAND

Bay Area Manufacturers' Factory Outlets

The following outlets are owned and operated by Bay Area manufacturers or importers. We're lucky to have them; most are treasures, and they reflect both the originality and diversity of the local apparel industry. They're true to the original concept of "factory outlet"—what outlets were before major companies hijacked the terminology and applied it to their "outlet divisions." As time allows, try to visit as many as you can to identify which outlets are going to come through with bargains in your personal style. In addition to each outlet's ongoing business, most have very special sales during the year for mailing list customers. To reach the backstreet locations of some outlets, you may need a map of the area. The hours may be limited (and often change), so do call ahead before venturing miles out of your way. In addition to these, you'll find other factory outlets listed throughout the apparel chapters.

BEBE OUTLET

Great Mall of the Bay Area, Milpitas.
(408) 263-BEBE. Daily. MC, VISA. Parking: lot.
Bebe's retail stores are popular with younger career women. The collections of chic and updated career suits and separates in distinct fabrics, with elegant European tailoring and subtle shaping, are stylish enough to go straight from the office to a dinner date. Retail may not accommodate the just-getting-started career woman; at the outlet at 30–70% off, past-season fashions are within reach. (At retail most fall jackets range from $169 to $189; at the outlet they sell from $80 to $132. Most pants retail from $78 to $124; they sell from $62 to $87 at the outlet.) Women who don't have the legs for the 17-inch skirts may opt for pants to coordinate with the jackets. Love the weekend collections, too! Sizes: 0–12.

DESIGNER OUTERWEAR OUTLET

*525 Center Street, Rheem Shopping Center,
Moraga. (925) 631-6877.*
E-mail: sales@mycrapac.com.
M, W, F 1–4. MC, VISA. Parking: lot.
This old Bank of America building is an unlikely
place to find a fast-growing company of stylish all-
weather apparel. You can buy Mycra Pac coats
and jackets at Harrods in London and in status
stores around the country. The fashion-forward
designs are hot sellers in many upscale catalogs.
They're made from high-performance fabrics that
are treated with Dupont Teflon to be water- and
wrinkle-resistant, and they're low maintenance
too. About 80% of the coats are designed to be
reversible—there may be a subtle and sophisticated animal print on one side, a rich solid color
on the other. Many styles have a daytime to
evening option—like black velvet reversing to a
bronzed high-tech fabric. Most coats have collars
that pull up into rain hoods. Even better, most
coats or jackets come in their own carrying case,
usually a cleverly designed compact handbag-
styled pouch that gives no clue to the coat con-
tained inside. Needless to say, they're simply

great coats for women on the go and fashion-
conscious world travelers. The coats and jackets
(really two coats or jackets in one) are priced from
$200 to $350 at retail. At the company's elegant
little outlet, prices are reduced about 50% (sometimes more) on discontinued styles, production
samples, and occasional seconds. At any one time
there'll be about six or seven racks of Mycra Pac
fashions; enough to make a trip worthwhile. Lucky
Lamorinda ladies are close at hand for frequent
sorties to the outlet to get the first crack when
"new" discontinued styles are put out on the racks.
This outlet bears watching; the company continues
to push the envelope with new fabrics, designs,
and fabrications, and inevitably these will end up
in the outlet. Whatever you buy, you're likely to
consider it a wardrobe treasure, good for many
seasons to come. Sizes: 0, 1, 2 (fits Petite through
Medium/Large). *Note: The building stands alone
in the middle of the shopping center parking lot
near T.J. Maxx.*

EDDER SWAY (FACTORY OUTLET)

2618 Eighth Street, Berkeley. (510) 704-9992.
M–F 8:30–6, Sat 11–3. MC, VISA.
Parking: street.

I suspect that not too many go out of their way
to check out this outlet, and that's too bad. This
outlet is stocked with choice goods. You'll find
mostly women's sweaters/knit dressing and a
limited number of very special men's sweaters.
The sweaters are fully fashioned, knit to shape
and size before the sides and sleeves are stitched
together—the way all quality sweaters should be
made. Most of the sweaters are made under private
labels for designers, fashion houses, department
stores, or catalog companies, which accounts for
the fashion styling and the wonderful textures and
yarns (cashmere, mohair, cotton, and silk). A
special "Corrie & Deanna for Edder Sway" label
has been created for the company's own line that
sells in boutiques around the country. Prices hover
around wholesale, with greater discounts on
prototype samples. Prices range from $35 to $150.

EMERYVILLE OUTLET

1467 Park Avenue, Emeryville. (510) 655-9578.
M, T, F 10–4. Cash/Check. Parking: street.

You can call these fashions shifts, floats, dresses,
sundresses, caftans, patiowear, cruisewear, or
casualwear—anything but muumuus! You've seen
this line in better specialty and department stores,
and in many major catalogs catering to mature
women. Outlet prices from $35 to $45 reflect an
average of 50% or more off retail. The comfortable,
loose garments combine fabrics, ribbon, and
corded trims, use of patchwork, insets, bands, and
borders in 100% cotton and better cotton blends.
Styles with elegant gold trims and dramatic prints
are dressy enough for entertaining, other styles are
casual and chic for sunning on the deck of a cruise
ship, and many styles are perfect for around the
house. Check out the racks of "seconds" (minor
flaws) where prices dive to $10 to $30. Sizes: Petite
through 3X (4–26). Sew-it-yourselfers will love the
selection of leftover fabrics in prints, stripes, and
solids, in 45- and 60-inch widths, priced at $2 to
$5/yard. All sales final. *Directions: Take the Powell
Street exit east from Highway 80, turn right at Hollis
Street. Follow Hollis to Park Avenue, turn right.*

LAFA KNIT CORPORATION OUTLET

291 Utah Avenue (at Littlefield Avenue),
South San Francisco. (650) 875-1989. M–F 10–5,
occasional Sat. MC, VISA. Parking: street/lot.
You can't be expected to recognize this name because the company is primarily a private label sweater manufacturer for many stores and designer collections. Its outlet is where surplus inventory and samples are sold without any fanfare or obvious effort to showcase the sweaters. Removed from a retail store's careful merchandising, closer scrutiny is required to appreciate and liberate the many better-quality sweaters. There's not a lot of any one style or group—which lends a somewhat hodgepodge aspect to the selection. There are lots of fine-gauge flat knits, merino wool knits, chenille knits, rib knits, cotton, and cotton/lycra blends. You'll find tricot knits in the body hugging sweater tops, as well as cropped styles, vests, and some more mainstream styling in the cardigans and jackets (sometimes with coordinating skirts and pants), assorted pullover styles, and sweater dresses. A smaller selection of men's sweaters is also sold. Prices are reduced at minimum of 50% off store retails—during end-of-season sales the prices are reduced to an almost ridiculous level (the best time to replenish your sweater wardrobe). If you're cruising through this industrial area, give yourself an extra few minutes to case the outlet. Sizes: S–L.

LAS MANOS

6948 Sebastopol Avenue, Sebastopol.
(707) 829-9245. M–Sat 10:30–6, Sun 11–5.
MC, VISA. Parking: lot.
Take time out from apple picking to check out Las Manos in Sebastopol where the company showcases its apparel line and furniture collection imported from Indonesia (armoires, chests, etc.). If you're a fan of contemporary, casual clothing with a somewhat ethnic orientation, you'll hit paydirt if you keep to the outlet section—about a third of the store. The company has ten local specialty boutiques and ships its line to specialty stores in Sun Belt states and resorts everywhere. The clothes are made in Bali or in Guatemala from distinctive fabrics. Lots of batiks, ikats, and wrinkle-resisting crinkle fabrics in cottons and rayons. At the outlet, prices are reduced 30–70% off store retails on the dresses and related separates.

Other retail store clearance inventory shows up—some great fashion jewelry, hats, and shoes add to the selection of seconds and past-season merchandise. Also, Guatemalan fabric is well priced at $5.95 to $6.59 per yard. Sizes: Petite to XL. All sales final. Located just a few blocks from the downtown square.

M.A.C. SPORT OUTLET

*7049 Redwood Boulevard #104, Novato.
(415) 898-1622. T–F 10–6, Sat 10–5.
MC, VISA, DIS, AE. Parking: lot.*
M.A.C. Sport's line consists of preshrunk custom-dyed apparel, most in 100% cotton knits and wovens. Past-season styles are reduced about 50% below normal retail, with added discounts on seconds. These are California casual, related components designed for women seeking weekend or updated business wear. Collections appearing throughout the year include long slim or tie-back dresses and jumpers, more structured weekend outdoor clothes in corduroys and twills, soft coordinates in cotton or rayon knits, classic contemporary styles in washed linen, and more. You have options whether your look is loose and drapey, or whether you like something with a little cinching to flatter the figure. Many styles are designed and made just for the outlet; others are seconds and overruns. At any one time, you'll have about eight different exciting colors to work with. You can mix and match from its one-size-fits-all in most tops, or S, M, L in other styles. You may not find every element of a complete ensemble. Fashions are priced $5 to $55. *Directions: From 101 North, take the Rowland Avenue exit, go west across overpass, turn right at first set of stoplights onto Redwood Road. Turn left at Lamont (look for Redwood Chevrolet) and left again onto the frontage road. Drive to end of cul-de-sac.*

MISHI

*801 Delaware Street, Berkeley. (510) 525-1075.
M–Sat 10–6, Sun 11–5. MC, VISA, DIS. Parking: lot.
(Other outlet: 201 Western, Petaluma.)*
Mishi is known for its contemporary, natural-fiber, garment-dyed sportswear line: "lifestyle" clothing that escapes being trendy without being dull. It's popular with sophisticated women who appreciate styles that camouflage midlife figure imperfections. The colors in the line change every season,

providing the faithful with an excuse to buy something up-to-date. Mishi's stores devote half their space to showcasing current and recent styles at full retail prices, while the outlet half offers past-season closeouts and samples. Outlet inventory at 40–75% off is priced at $15 to $60. The moderately priced fashion accessories sold here are not discounted but are carefully selected to go with the apparel. Sizes: S, M, L (4–14), and some XL (16).

NORTHCOAST INDUSTRIES
WAREHOUSE SALES

10 Liberty Ship Way, #130, Sausalito.
(415) 331-7150 ext 402. Fri–Sat 9–4 on
announced dates only. Cash/Check. Parking: lot.
This line is a great favorite with women—young moms to motor home mamas who want updated styles that offer comfort (elastic waistbands) and easy care. There's no room for fellas to hang around at these sales when this manufacturer of women's casual sportswear trims prices 50–70% off retail on collections of discontinued fashion groups. Sale prices generally range from $18 to $30. There's a fit for just about everyone who puts on size Petite, Missy, or Large fashions (to 3X).

Everyday and weekend fashions come in coordinates with tops, jackets, and pants in poly/cotton or 100% cotton knit fabrications (seasonal velours and fleece fabrications). Each sale features new colors, great detailing, and clever combinations of fabrics. A caveat: Not all styles or colors, in all sizes. Call the number and extension above to get sale dates (several times a year) and directions.

PJ'S 2 GO

1361 Main Street, Montara. (650) 728-1759.
M–F 9–5, Sat–Sun 10:30–5:30. MC, VISA.
Parking: street.
Take a scenic drive down the coast to Montara, and your reward is significant savings off PJ'S 2 GO—a designer line of pajamas and loungewear worn by the rich and famous. You'll find full retail prices on current-season goods in the company's charming home store and retail boutique, but check the closet-sized bargain room and you're likely to find 50% off and more on discontinued styles. The company's concept is a simple one—comfortable, loose-fitting pants with drawstring waists and basic tops—but with a quality of workmanship and uniqueness of fabrics that set the

line apart from the rest of the crowd. Cotton, silk, velvet, and rayon pajamas are sold in long and short sets, and each pair comes inside a drawstring bag made of the same fabric. Designed in "one size" to fit women 4–14 and most men. The line is expanding to include wrap robes, slippers, one-size nightshirts, and a bedding line. Prices at retail range from $110 to $350; for past-season leftovers, you'll pay more like $55 to $175. Celebs like Demi Moore, Emma Thompson, Meg Ryan, Barbra Streisand, Nicole Kidman, Robin Williams, Nicolas Cage, Danny Glover, Tom Cruise, Arnold Schwarzenegger, and other headliners have been pictured in PJ'S 2 GO in national magazines, major movies, and on TV. Hollywood types don them to tool around town, but first and foremost, these are pajamas sought by upscale customers who are looking for something special to wear around the house. If you're on the mailing list, you'll be the first to know when the company's semiannual warehouse sales occur with can't-stop-buying-prices.

PAPY BOEZ OUTLET
1041 Murray Street, Berkeley. (510) 849-2856. www.papyboez.com. M–Sat 10–6, Sun Noon–5.

MC, VISA, AE, ATM. Parking: street.
(Other outlet: 2109 University Avenue, Berkeley.)
Papy Boez and Harvest are two very popular labels for women and children that show up in national catalogs and boutiques around the country. Designed locally and made in India, China, and Lithuania, Papy Boez uses a variety of fabrics including natural cottons, rayons, 100% linen and linen blends, fleece, chenille, velour, and velvet. This line is charming and timeless with a contemporary flavor. Word has it Papy Boez' dresses, jumpers, blouses, and separates are being worn by Hollywood favorites these days on television and in popular films. At the same time, I can picture this creative clothing on moms, teachers, and anyone who has an appreciation for art and the unusual. The line is set apart by its detailing (blanket stitching, appliqués, pattern mixing, embroidery, etc.), original hand-painted or hand-blocked printed fabrics, and vegetable-dyed fabrics. New collections reflect updated and contemporary styling in corduroy, cotton knits, rayon crepe (coordinating jackets, vests, skirts, shirts, and pants), and some wonderfully textured and embroidered chenille sweaters. During quarterly

sales usually held in April, July, August (back-to-school), and for the holidays (Thanksgiving to Christmas), past-season styles and slightly imperfect fashions are priced 60–75% off retail. Prices range from $7 for blouses to $75 for linen collections. Sizes: Small/Medium or Medium/Large. *Directions: Murray is a small side street that angles off from the intersection of Seventh Street and Ashby. Outlet is midblock between Seventh and San Pablo Avenue.*

TOM TOM FACTORY OUTLET

1716-B Fourth Street, Berkeley. (510) 559-7033. M–Sat 10–6, Sun 11–6. MC, VISA, DIS. Parking: street.

Tom Tom makes a line of garment-dyed clothes that are easy to wear and easy to care for. The company has been around for years, but it has left its funky image behind and grown up with its customers. These are typically women in the workforce who want contemporary clothing that's unstructured and comfortable—they're not dressing as accountants or courtroom lawyers with stiff, conservative, and usually predictable suitings. The Tom Tom look works well on the job, around

town, and for Saturday night occasions—such as when you want something with a little pizzazz for restaurant dining or socializing with friends. Styles are accommodating: take your pick from form-fitting styles or those designed to flow around the body and cover up all one's imperfections. At the outlet, you save 50% off retail prices on the company's first-quality overruns or past-season fashions. Natural fibers like linen, rayon, flax, cotton, and blends are fabricated in a new palette of colors each season. An extra dimension is achieved with the textures and weaves of many fabrics. Prices generally range from $20 to $70 on jackets, big coats, jumpers, dresses, skirts, pants, etc. Everything is washable and all shrinkage has been eliminated in the dyeing process. Sizes are simple—X-Small, Small, Medium, and Large—and they easily accommodate women in sizes 4–14.

V. C. TORIAS THE OUTLET

783 Rio del Mar Boulevard #47, Aptos. (831) 687-0744. Sun–M 9:30–4:30, T–F 10–6, Sat 9:30–5:30. MC, VISA. Parking: lot.

Aptos is a bit of a drive, but worth the trek if you want bold, bright, casualwear that qualifies as wearable art. The owner/artist/designer has created this eye-catching line for women who don't want to conform to the standard fashion-page image. These women may not have perfect bodies; they may, in fact, go up and down in size with frustrating regularity. Working in high-quality rayon, linen, cotton knit, and washable velvet, the basic silhouettes—dresses, pants, shorts, shirts, and jackets—are transformed with hand-painting and appliqué. These distinctive fashions have been worn by Rue McClanahan on *Golden Girls*, and by the cast of *Sisters*. No two pieces are exactly alike. Other benefits: garments need no ironing, and they wash and travel well. One-size labels can accommodate women from sizes 2 to 22 (certain styles are more flattering to particular sizes). Sold at retail at better boutiques and resorts, at the outlet, overruns, design samples, and outdated styles are discounted 25–50% off original retails. Tops and bottoms range from $25 to $100 ($98 to $175 retail); dresses from $75 to $200 ($150 to $300 retail). *Directions: Take Hwy. 1 south to Aptos. Take the Rio del Mar exit and head west. Located on the second floor of the Deer Park Marketplace.*

WE BE BOP

1380 Tenth Street, Berkeley. (510) 528-0761. www.webebop.com. M–F 10–5, Sat 10–6, Sun Noon–5. MC, VISA. Parking: street.
We Be Bop fashions have pizzazz! They're made from natural fibers, usually cotton or rayon. The batik fabrics are distinctive, an interplay of prints and patterns combined in most garments using unique colors. The owners develop the designs in collaboration with Balinese craftspeople. Some garments are straightforward, others so clever you almost need a manual to figure out how to tie or wrap them. In any case, women with an individual-istic sense of style embrace the look. Large-sized women are not overlooked and can wear the styles with great panache. Prices are discounted 30–50% off retail (ranging from $20 to $80), sometimes more on way-past-season closeouts. As offbeat as this line may sound, it shows up in some pretty mainstream stores. Sizes: S, M, L; one-size-fits-all; Large sizes to 5X.

Bay Area Off-Price/Chain Discount Stores

Many of the chain off-price stores have been around so long and are so familiar that Bay Area shoppers hardly need any introduction to them. They consistently offer a good product mix for consumers who appreciate shopping close to home. Before seeking out a specialty discount boutique, call first to make sure it's still in business at the same address with the same hours (they are an endangered retail species). *For outlet addresses and daily hours, see Appendix.*

CASUAL CORNER OUTLETS

Great Mall of the Bay Area, Milpitas.
(408) 956-9640. Daily. MC, VISA, AE, DIS.
Parking: lot.
(Other outlets: Folsom, Gilroy, Petaluma, Tracy, Vacaville centers.)
The "outlets" (dozens around the country) carry the same categories of merchandise that one might find at full-priced mall stores, but there is a difference. The outlet division has its own buyers committed to finding merchandise that conveys the "Casual Corner" image, but at a more afford-able price. You won't find anything originally sold through its regular stores. Even so, women seem to appreciate the prices on all the casual weekend apparel groups, career and soft dresses, related separates, suits, blouses, outerwear, and some very special fashion sweaters. Everything is first quality and in-season. In spring '99, linen blend blazers from $39 to $59 and linen-rayon blend pants from $29 to $39 were great buys. Sizes: 4–16.

DESIGNER LABELS FOR LESS

929 and 931 Market Street, San Francisco.
(415) 512-1057. M–Sat 10–6, Sun 11–6.
MC, VISA, AE, DIS. Parking: pay lots.
(Other stores: South Shore Center, 2216 South Shore Drive, Alameda; Westgate Shopping Center, 1600 Saratoga Avenue, San Jose.)

Designer Labels for Less is true to its name. If names like Ellen Tracy, Donna Karan, Jones New York, Emmanuel Ungaro, Eileen Fisher, Nicole Miller, Ralph Lauren, Polo, Karen Kane, Tommy Hilfiger, Nautica, and many others give you an adrenaline rush, stop in at one of its stores. One of the original pioneers of off-price retailing, it has become an institution for bargain hunters in Southern California. With 33 stores and growing, their volume allows the company to buy directly from manufacturers as well as other department stores. The San Francisco store with three levels and more than 20,000 square feet of fashions offers the biggest selection of its three Bay Area stores. It has a lower-level men's department with suits, sportcoats, slacks, and casual sportswear. Expect some Plus sizes for women, and a limited selection of Petites mixed in with the Misses career, casual, and after-five selections. Best buys: The large Lily of France lingerie department with everyday markdowns at 50% off original retail on bras, panties, camisoles, daywear, sleepwear, etc. A caveat: many fashion groups and styles are from collections that have come and gone from retail stores—a season or more past, to more than a

year ago. Not every fashion group hits the mark; colors may seem out-of-date and styles too removed for mainstream shoppers. However, this is a great resource for latching onto a designer label that's otherwise out of reach, or for gathering pieces—a blouse, skirt, or pants to match apparel at home in your closet. Successful shoppers stop by weekly to cull the best styles from weekly shipments at all three stores.

DRESS BARN

*1670 S. Bascom Avenue, Hamilton Plaza, Campbell. (408) 377-7544. M–F 10–9, Sat 10–6, Sun Noon–5. MC, VISA. Parking: lot.
(Other stores: fourteen in greater Bay Area—refer to Geographical Index for location nearest you.)*

The selection here is dedicated to a clearly defined target customer (career women aged 18–45). Besides career apparel, you'll find a very nice dress line, suits, separates, activewear, coats, and accessories. Sizes: 4–14. Most discounts are approximately 25–35% off department store prices; clearances and special promotions up to 60% off.

GROUP USA

Great Mall of the Bay Area, Milpitas.
(408) 935-8787. www.group-usa.com. Daily.
MC, VISA, AE, DIS. Parking: lot.
This outfit refined its concept operating eighteen East Coast outlets before launching this first West Coast store. Practice makes perfect. This store is a boon to career women with its offerings of current collections of apparel from brand-name companies usually associated with major department stores. Kenar, Expressions, Rina Rossi, Saville, Jones New York, Michael, Bicci, Dani Max, Albert Nipon, David Bijoux, and Larry Levine were some of the labels on spring '97 fashions. The career selection (primarily suits) is evenly balanced between contemporary styling for a more fashion-forward customer and updated classic (more mainstream) styling for traditionalists. Discounts start at 30% off regular retail and are often much greater. The social dressing and after-five department is one of the best around with some real dazzlers for cruises, proms, and elegant black-tie affairs. The handbag and shoe departments offer the "look" of more expensive lines. Faux leathers keep prices for handbags under $40. A nice blouse selection, coat department, some dresses and coordinated sets, a decent Petite department, scarves, and fashion jewelry complete the picture. Sizes: Missy/Petite 2–14.

HIT OR MISS

4130 Mowry Avenue, Fremont Hub, Fremont.
(510) 794-5607. M–F 10–9, Sat 10–6, Sun 11–5.
MC, VISA, AE, DIS. Parking: pay garage.
(Other stores: Thirteen in greater Bay Area—refer to Geographical Index for location nearest you.)
Hit or Miss sells stylish work and weekend apparel at value prices. You'll find an in-depth selection of dresses, weekend sportswear, related separates, all-weather and wool coats, suits, dresses, blouses, jackets, and fashion accessories. Savings usually 20–50% off retail; sizes 3/4–13/14 (rarely 16s). Good service, good savings, tasteful merchandising, and convenience—a winning combination. Refunds and exchanges.

INGA'S/CASUAL ELEGANCE

*504 Sycamore Valley Road West, Danville Livery
Mercantile, Danville. (925) 837-1123.
M–Sat 10–5:30. MC, VISA, AE. Parking: lot.*
Inga, a former model who knows the fashion biz
inside and out, buys all her fashions in New
York—from showrooms, manufacturers, and reps.
Dealing with smaller designers and companies
with names you may or may not know, she chooses
styles that are up-to-date without being trendy,
styles that appeal to sophisticated women with
multifaceted lifestyles and that address the relaxed
side of glamour. This is a great place to shop for a
sophisticated cruise wardrobe. Quality combined
with value are Inga's goals. There's a little of
everything: after-five (some mother-of-the-bride
dresses), elegant daytime, some weekend and
casual sportswear, star-status sweaters, and a few
career suits. Buying right allows her to pass along
savings that average 40% off retail on current-
season merchandise. Most suits or two- or three-
piece ensembles range from $159 to $279. I
coveted the silk blazers marked down to $245
from $395. Inga's can't be all things to all people,
but the woman who resists being a department
store clone will love this place. Inga's service—
akin to that of a personal shopper—is thrown in
for free. Sizes: 4–14 (some 16s).

LOEHMANN'S

*222 Sutter Street, San Francisco. (415) 982-3215.
www.loehmanns.com. M–F 9–8, Sat 9:30–8,
Sun 11–6. MC, VISA. Parking: pay lots.
(Other stores: Sacramento, San Ramon, Sunnyvale.)*
Loehmann's is the original off-price fashion store,
with a solid reputation for designer and couture
lines at discount prices, covering all the basics
and then some: cocktail, dressy, fine furs, in-
between, career apparel, coats, lingerie, hosiery,
fragrances, swimsuits, activewear, sportswear,
shoes, and accessories. If you can spot designer
clothes without a label, you'll recognize fashions
from many status designers. Prices are guaranteed at least 33% off retail, and there is a reliable
quantity always priced at 50% off. The San
Francisco store excels in its selection of career
apparel. Exchanges for store credit within seven
days. Sizes: 4–16 with a few racks of Plus sizes and
a fair selection of Petites.

RAGSMATAZZ

2021 Broadway, Oakland. (510) 763-3735.
M–F 10–6, Sat 11–5. MC, VISA. Parking: street.
(Other stores: South Shore Center, Alameda;
622 Clement Street, San Francisco.)
Ragsmatazz provides a fun, colorful, fairly current
selection of junior-oriented and contemporary
fashions (including some surprising labels like
XoXo and Rampage). Fashion shoes, purses,
wallets, and backpacks from a leading manufacturer are very popular with shoppers. Discounts
are 40–60% off retail. If you love trendy junior
styles, you'll want to check out the new shipments
frequently. Moms and sisters can buy clever and
cute sportswear from Spumoni for younger girls
(sizes 12mos to Girls 14—best selection at Clement
Street store). Sizes: Junior 1–13; Women's 4–16.
Exchanges are allowed up to seven days after
purchase with receipt.

RUE 21 COMPANY STORE

Factory Stores at Vacaville, Vacaville.
(707) 469-0152. Daily. MC, VISA, AE, DIS.
Parking: lot.
(Other store: Gilroy center.)

These direct-to-consumer discount stores are
proof positive that teens can buy up-to-date
clothes with babysitting dollars. Nothing's over
$14.99 and actually most of the casual fashions
and basics are less—$4.99, $6.99, $9.99. Teens
like the cutting-edge styles, but grown-ups have
no problem picking up pants and tops. Sizes:
Girls 7–16, S–XL Junior, Women's, and Men's.

SANDY'S—THE UNIQUE BOUTIQUE

3569 Mt. Diablo Boulevard, Lafayette.
(925) 284-2653. M–F 10–6, Sat 10–5:30.
MC, VISA, AE. Parking: lot.
If I had a star rating system, Sandy's would get
four stars. Without a doubt it's the best off-price
boutique in the Bay Area. Sandy has the magic
touch at selecting upscale, intriguing women's
apparel for discriminating customers. This has
been a secret source for many local women. The
store is so beautiful, you'll feel that you're shopping in a very special boutique and once initiated,
you'll return again and again. Although Sandy's
caters to the up-to-date mature woman, younger
women will find fancier dresses for parties, proms,
and weddings. Regulars grab the Tadashi, Wild

Rose, Laundry, Nina Picalino, SAII, Sisters, Gerties, Faith, and other lesser-known but intriguing lines of dresses, related separates, sportswear, and jumpsuits. Sandy buys lots of wonderful fashion jewelry, watches, hats, and handbags so no one leaves the store unfinished. You'll see discounts of 30–50% off retail, and everything is current. Sizes: 2–18 (a few 20s). If you're willing to go a little out of your way to seek out Sandy's (next to the chic Postino restaurant), you won't be disappointed.

SPECIALTEES OUTLET

572 Center Street, Rheem Shopping Center, Moraga. (925) 376-8337. M–F 10-6, Sat 10–5:30. MC, VISA. Parking: lot.

Flax fans are finding their way to Moraga to get a crack at the 50% discounts on Flax overruns at the SpecialTees outlet. Ladies who know labels will glom onto the Kiko coordinates, Stephanie Schuster, and Duma sweaters and other lines, also reduced a minimum of 50% off original retails. SpecialTees, with two popular women's fashion boutiques in Lafayette and Montclair, and the Erin Paige boutique on San Francisco's trendy Union Street, is sending clearance inventory from its three full-price stores to its Moraga outlet. Additionally, first-quality overruns are being shipped directly from the warehouses of its most popular manufacturers. SpecialTees has garnered a loyal following of suburban women. Some may have relinquished their chic executive wardrobes to the back of the closet to be stay-at-home moms, but they haven't lost their sense of style. Others no longer have the figure for trendier, body-conscious fashions they wore as twenty-somethings. Clothes are the exception in every way at SpecialTees boutiques and at the outlet. Most everything is relaxed and comfortable but with contemporary panache! In the selection of coordinated separates, sweaters, and dresses, you'll find both great Saturday night restaurant clothes and outfits just perfect for sideline duty at the kids' sporting events—and everything in between. Sizes range from 4 to 16. And while you're in the neighborhood, do yourself a favor and stop in at the Designer Outerwear Outlet (page 29). It's about 100 feet away in a converted bank building in the middle of the center's parking lot.

WESTPORT LTD.

Factory Stores at Vacaville, Vacaville.
(707) 449-0833. Daily. MC, VISA, AE, DIS.
Parking: lot.
(Other outlets: Anderson/Shasta, Folsom,
Lathrop, Milpitas, Pacific Grove centers.)
Westport Ltd. offers a well-rounded, always-
current selection: Ascending in quality and price,
you'll find career suits, lovely daytime go-to-
lunch-or-meeting dresses, sophisticated career
dresses, and separates. Discounts are 20–50%
off, maybe more on frequent in-store unadver-
tised specials. Sizes: 4–16. Returns, exchanges,
and refunds.

Women's Accessories

LISA VIOLETTO ACCESSORIES
425 Brannan Street, San Francisco. (415) 543-6261.
M–F 11–5, Sat 11–4. MC, VISA. Parking: street.
If you love fashion accessories and wonderfully
unique jewelry, you'll want to sashay in here and
spend some time. Lisa Violetto is a local designer
and manufacturer of fashion jewelry and accessories. Her line of necklaces, earrings, and jacket
clips is sold to boutiques and major stores. The
line is constantly evolving, from Austrian crystal
beads and vintage-inspired designs made with
antique gold or silver plating to the popular
Y-necks and new hair accessories. Prices at the
outlet are reduced 40–50% off original retails on
the leftovers—surplus inventory, samples, discontinued styles, etc. In addition, Lisa makes some
wonderful hats, scarves, and—using beautiful
fabrics—velvet throws for home or body, Victorian
evening bags, and decorative pillows. To balance
out the selection, other fashion jewelry and home

accessory designers are sending both new and
current designs at mini 10–20% discounts, and
discontinued pieces and samples at maxi discounts. Many of the small designers sell "under
the glass" and to posh stores. This is a charming
outlet, organized like a classy upscale boutique
yet offering downscale pricing.

1928 DESIGNER BRANDS/ACCESSORIES
Prime Outlets at Gilroy, Gilroy. (408) 842-3790.
Daily. MC, VISA. Parking: lot.
(Other outlets: Folsom, Pacific Grove,
Vacaville centers.)
Stop in for the "extras" to fill the spaces in your
jewelry chest and dresser drawers. You'll save a
minimum of 40–50% every day on costume
jewelry from the 1928 Jewelry Co. (including the
Aurora collection), Kenneth Jay Lane, and Jody
Coyote. Look for famous-maker handbags and
small leather goods; 1928, Pulsar, Citizen, Gucci,

Anne Klein, Liz, Bulova, and Seiko watches to 50% off; sunglasses; Buxton wallets; men's jewelry; scarves; hair accessories; jewelry boxes; picture frames; and more. Solid discounts on Italian sterling silver.

SOCKS GALORE & MORE

Factory Stores at Vacaville, Vacaville.
(707) 448-2420. Daily. MC, VISA, DIS. Parking: lot.
(Other outlets: Gilroy, Folsom centers.)
You want socks, you got socks! You'll find socks for everyone in the family. Over 60,000 pairs of designer brand socks (with and without labels) are sold for 20–80% off retail. Whatever your size or needs, you've got options. Money-back guarantee.

SUCCESSORIES

152 Reina Del Mar (on Highway 1), Pacifica.
(650) 359-0260. Fri–Sun 11–5. Cash/Check.
Parking: street.
This eclectic selection of fashion jewelry, belts, hats, handbags, hair accessories, clothing, scarves, and other fancies showcased by Bay Area designer sales rep Pamela Winston-Charbonneau is worth the trip. Most jewelry pieces are contemporary,

collectible, and qualify as artwork. The prices are surprisingly affordable ($6 to $150), especially at the 30–60% discount offered here. The artists/designers include Famous Melissa (jewelry made from computer chips and components), Broken Bottles (jewelry and housewares made from recycled glass), Cute As a Button (rings made from antique buttons set in silver), Spinoso (scarves), and several others. It's artistic and unusual. Look for the little red caboose that houses this gem on Hwy. 1.

SUNGLASS CITY

623 San Anselmo Avenue, San Anselmo.
(415) 456-7297. M–Sat 10–5:30, Sun 10–5.
MC, VISA, AE. Parking: street.
If you're serious about sunglasses, Sunglass City is the place to go. The folks here are specialists who can give you all the technical information you need to make an intelligent choice. You'll find top brands like Ray-Ban, Vuarnet, Revo, Serengeti, Armani, Persol, Hobie, Timberland, Smith, and Maui Jim at 15–40% off retail. Ray-Bans are always 30% off list. Vuarnets are discounted 15–20%. If you're like me and only buy glasses you can afford to lose, check the inexpensive lines, $3.95 to $20.

TOTES FACTORY STORE
Factory Stores at Vacaville, Vacaville.
(707) 449-9022. Daily. MC, VISA. Parking: lot.
(Other outlets: Anderson/Shasta, Pacific
Grove centers.)
Women and men can poke around here and
come up with treasures so inventive, clever, and
practical that it's hard to leave without a tote of
some kind. Check the selection of rainwear for
women, children, and men, ranging from lightweight to heavyweight. Plus there are umbrellas
in all configurations, duffel bags, lightweight
luggage, sunglasses, portfolios, notebooks, and
more goodies to solve many gift-giving dilemmas.
A universally popular store!

Also See

Under Women's Apparel/Fashion:
ALL SECTIONS

Under Cosmetics and Fragrances:
ALL LISTINGS

Under Handbags and Luggage:
ALL LISTINGS

Under Shoes:
ALL LISTINGS

Under Family, Men's & Women's,
General Clothing:
THE BIG FOUR

Large Sizes

ALL THE MORE TO LOVE (CONSIGNMENT)
1355 Park Street, Alameda. (510) 521-6206.
M–Sat 10–6. MC, VISA. Parking: street.
A consignment shop where some better-quality
like-new dresses or ensembles show up.
Otherwise, it's a mixed bag of apparel for large-
size women in all categories. Good prospects for
women in transition up or down the scale. Shoes,
accessories, and jewelry too.

CASUAL CORNER WOMAN
Great Mall of the Bay Area, Milpitas.
(408) 934-9788. Daily. MC, VISA, AE, DIS.
Parking: lot.
(Other outlet: Gilroy center.)
Just like the Petites who shop Casual Corner's
Petite Sophisticate Outlets or the Misses-size
women who shop Casual Corner Outlets, women
sized 14–24 can find well-priced collections of
casual sportswear and career apparel at Casual
Corner Woman. The company does a very nice
job of selecting stylish, mainstream fashions that
are appropriately in season. Ensembles, related
separates, sweaters, some dresses, and small
groups of extra-fancy special-occasion fashions
are ready for the taking.

DRESS BARN WOMAN/WESTPORT WOMAN
1650 S. Bascom Avenue, Hamilton Plaza,
Campbell. (408) 371-7730. M–F 10–9, Sat 10–8,
Sun 11–6. MC, VISA, AE, DIS. Parking: lot.
(Other Westport Woman outlets: Folsom, Gilroy,
Milpitas, Vacaville centers.)
Dress Barn Woman and Westport Woman (same
ownership) are worthwhile destinations for all
large-size ladies. Their selection of large-size
fashions at 20–50% off retail is impressive. In
December, you'll find dazzling holiday dresses; in
summer, vacationwear. Everything—coats, jackets,
swimwear, sweaters, casual weekend garb, active-

wear, and accessories—appears very current. Sizes: 14–24 (a few 26s), or 1X–3X. Exchanges and cash refunds are available within 14 days. How nice!

FULL SIZE FASHIONS

Factory Stores at Vacaville, Vacaville.
(707) 447-9505. Daily. MC, VISA, DIS. Parking: lot.
(Other outlet: Anderson/Redding center.)
Because Full Size Fashions is dedicated to addressing the "whole woman," you'll find lingerie (panties), sleepwear, bathing suits, coordinated groups of sportswear and career fashions, dresses, separates (jeans, sweaters, tops, etc.), and cover-ups, all discounted 30–50% off original retail. This isn't a resource for expensive designer label apparel at discount; its lines are moderately priced at retail. Young women, career women, and even silver-haired senior ladies can find fashions for their lifestyles. Sizes: dresses 16–38; tops 36–58; bottoms 30–52. Exchanges only within two weeks.

HARPER GREER

580 Fourth Street, San Francisco. (415) 543-4066.
www.harpergreer.com. M–Sat 10–6, Sun Noon–6.
MC, VISA, AE, DIS. Parking: street.

Large-size career women will find better quality and good design at Harper Greer. Since 1989 it has sold all its designs exclusively through its company store; it delivers sophisticated clothing in silk, wool, cotton, and better synthetics in chic and updated styles. Career coordinates, dresses, and a tempting selection of separates for workdays and weekends will keep you going in and out of the dressing rooms. Dresses range in price from $69 to $249 (executive boardroom dress); jackets in several lengths and career blazers range from $96 to $379. Obviously, the higher prices are for fine-quality wool, silk, or linen. Sizes: 14–28 (depending on style or cut, many fit larger sizes). Tailor on premises for quick alterations; many may be free.

MAKING IT BIG SPECIALTY STORE AND OUTLET

135 Southwest Boulevard, Rohnert Park.
(707) 795-6861. M–Sat 10–6, Sun Noon–5.
MC, VISA, AE, DIS. Parking: lot.
Catalog requests to: 501 Aaron Street, Cotati,
CA, 94931 or call (707) 795-1995.
This company fills a special niche in the large-size marketplace. It manufactures garment-dyed cottons (both wovens and knits), washable rayons,

and ethnic prints. Cotton dresses and sportswear are made in sizes 32–72. Catalog prices usually range from $30 to $60 on its sportswear separates. It's a crossover line, going from work to weekend wear. Its new and expanded store is equally divided into a retail boutique showcasing the full-price current-season merchandise, and an outlet for all its catalog overruns, past-season merchandise, seconds, and sale markdowns. Outlet discounts range 20–70% off retail. Get on the mailing list for its semiannual blowout sales.

SEAMS TO FIT

6527 Telegraph Avenue (between Alcatraz and Ashby), Oakland. (510) 428-9463. www.sayswho.com. M–F 11–6, Sat 10–6, Sun Noon–4. MC, VISA, DIS. Parking: street. Seams to Fit is the clearance rack for Says Who?, a large-size specialty store that manufactures a line of natural fiber clothes. Seams to Fit is also a consignment store for clothes with a history. The racks are filled with great deals and some steals and outfits that appeal. This is a store for shoppers. If you're planning a career change but can't afford a new wardrobe, if your body size has changed, or if you just want to buy clothing at affordable prices, you'll want to pick through the racks. Regulars check in weekly because consigned beauties move so fast. Keep an eye out for other off-price clothing brands like Vikki Vi, Liz & Jane, and Jumping Joy, plus any and all major brands on consignment.

SIZES UNLIMITED

1809 Willow Pass Road (Park and Shop Center), Concord. (510) 825-2022. M–F 10–9, Sat 10–7, Sun Noon–5. MC, VISA, AE. Parking: lot. (More than twenty Northern California stores.) Sizes Unlimited has updated and improved all its full-size fashions. Women of all ages find attractive sportswear, career apparel, lingerie, sleepwear, and outerwear at pleasing prices. Nice selection of wide-width shoes. Weekly promotions keep bargain hunters happy and card holders get special discount coupons. Sizes: 14–32. Returns and refunds allowed.

Also See

Under San Francisco's Factory Outlets
and Off-Price Stores:
BYER FACTORY OUTLET; CUT LOOSE

Under Famous Labels/Factory Stores:
**CAROLE LITTLE; ELLEN TRACY; KAREN KANE;
KASPER A.S.L; KORET; LIZ CLAIBORNE; LUCIA**

Under Bay Area Manufacturers' Factory Outlets:
**EMERYVILLE OUTLET; NORTHCOAST
INDUSTRIES; V. C. TORIAS; WE BE BOP**

Under Bay Area Off-Price/Chain Discount Stores:
DESIGNER LABELS FOR LESS

Under Wedding and Formal Wear:
GUNNE SAX/JESSICA MCCLINTOCK

Under Family, Men's & Women's,
General Clothing:
THE BIG FOUR

Under Clearance Centers:
NORDSTROM RACK; TALBOTS

Lingerie, Sleepwear, and Robes

FARR*WEST FACTORY OUTLET

294 Anna Street, Watsonville. (831) 728-0880, (800) 848-7891. M–F 10–4. MC, VISA. Parking: lot.
It may be a drive, but once there you'll find 60–90% reductions on tap pants, petti pants, half slips, full slips, camisoles, and chemises. These are samples, discontinued styles, and irregulars priced from $3 to $23 at 60–90% off retail. Farr*West produces fine lingerie collections in woven goods: polyester "taffecrepe," crepe georgette, cotton batiste, and a very high quality noncling woven polyester charmeuse. Sizes: P–XL, slips 32–40, and 1X–4X. *Directions: Take the Airport exit from Highway 1. The first street is Westgate, turn right, then left on Anna.*

JOSEF ROBE OUTLET

2525 16th Street, Second floor, San Francisco. (415) 252-5522. M–F 9–5. MC, VISA. Parking: street.
This is for those who have no qualms about spending a little more for quality. Josef Robe makes luxury robes for hotels and for the general public. Retail robes are sized by height and circumference to ensure a proper fit for all body types. There are numerous styles, including both wrap robes and pullover robes in 100% cotton in basic white or fashion colors. These are expensive for velour or terry cloth robes, often selling at retail for $100 and up. First-quality robes are sold for a 20% discount, but pick up a second and you'll save at least 50%—that means as little as $40 on a short white kimono-style terry robe, or about $55 on a logo robe from the Post Resort or the Inn at Spanish Bay. Many seconds priced from $40 to $80. More discounts will be found in

corners of the outlet that showcase Early Gilbert's boutique line of form-fitting lingerie in stretch laces and fabrics; Parks for Recreation's line of men's body-conscious underwear and workout wear; and Barbara Hume's samples from her fine line of handwoven (and expensive at retail) classic apparel (jackets and vests) and coordinating sportswear separates. Closed holidays.

L'EGGS, HANES & BALI

Petaluma Village Premium Outlets, Petaluma. (707) 778-1056. Daily. MC, VISA, AE, DIS. Parking: lot.
(Other outlets: Folsom, Gilroy, Milpitas, Pacific Grove, Vacaville centers.)
From the name you can assume that you'll find pantyhose, knee highs, lingerie, men's underwear, Isotoner gloves, thermal underwear, socks, and children's underwear and socks. These are close-outs or slightly imperfect goods (usually noncon-forming colors). Sizes to 50DD bras for women and undershirts in XXL and Tall for men. The variety in Bali lingerie is gratifying. Larger gals will be particularly pleased with the panty selection that goes to size 13. You'll also find other interesting

labels and merchandise like Playtex maternity bras and gowns; a spiffy selection of Champion activewear and sport underwear for men and women; and Ralph Lauren's intimate wear and sleepwear. Savings 20–60% off original pricing. Returns and refunds.

MAIDENFORM OUTLET

Prime Outlets at Gilroy, Gilroy. (408) 848-4233. Daily. MC, VISA, AE. Parking: lot.
(Other outlets: Milpitas, Pacific Grove centers.)
At Maidenform you'll find bras (32A–42DDD, also full-figure), camisoles, tap pants, full slips, bustiers, half slips, garter belts, sleepwear, and loungewear in Regular and Queen sizes. The lingerie ranges from basic to elegant in fashion colors and dependable neutrals; also sleepwear and robes designed for good-looking comfort. Discounts are 25–60% off.

OLGA/WARNER'S OUTLETS
Prime Outlets at Gilroy, Gilroy. (408) 842-3799.
Daily. MC, VISA, AE, DIS. Parking: lot.
(Other outlets: Folsom, Petaluma centers.)
The selection of Olga and Warner's styles in
sleepwear, controlwear, panties (sizes 4–10), bras
(sizes 32AA–42DDD), slips, camisoles, bodysuits,
and swimwear (seasonal) is very impressive. The
discounts on the overruns and discontinued styles
range from very modest to sensational. Speedo
swimsuits and an impressive collection of Calvin
Klein intimate wear for women and pajamas and
boxers for men are nice extras. The staff is always
ready to assist with measurements and fitting if
requested.

Also See

Under Bay Area Off-Price/
Chain Discount Stores:
DESIGNER LABELS FOR LESS;
LOEHMANN'S

Under Cosmetics and Fragances:
CRABTREE & EVELYN, LTD. OUTLET

Under Clearance Centers:
ALL LISTINGS

Under Fabrics:
THAI SILKS

Maternity

FASHION AFTER PASSION (CONSIGNMENT)

1211 Park Street, Alameda. (510) 769-MOMS. E-mail: MajMomUnit@aol.com. W–Sat 10:30–6, Sun 11–4. MC, VISA, DIS, AE. Parking: street.

To add a few pieces to your temporary maternity wardrobe, Fashion After Passion offers good buys; it's packed with sportswear and separates, nursing garments, and in-and-out-of season maternity apparel, undergarments, hose, and career apparel. Better dresses and career apparel are in short supply and don't stay in the store long. All sizes in lines that were originally moderately priced. The full line of undergarments and bras are in good supply but not discounted. A consignment children's department (to Junior sizes) allows moms to get a head start on baby's wardrobe. This six-year-old mom-to-mom store offers a helpful staff (they're all moms) and breast pump rentals. In addition to store-wide credits (at 60%), consignments (at 50/50) are available for maternity/nursing items and most children's equipment.

MATERNITY WORKS

Prime Outlets at Gilroy, Gilroy. (408) 847-7560. Daily. MC, VISA, AE. Parking: lot. (Other outlets: Great Mall, Milpitas; Petaluma center.)

If you're set on maintaining a professional image and putting on the ritz through the ninth month, or if you just want to look your best when your waist grows to 44 inches, then make the trek to Maternity Works. Owned by the Mothers Work (a company that's brought the Mimi specialty retail chain, the Pea in the Pod and Motherhood stores, and Maternité catalog into its fold), this is the best maternity outlet I've found yet, with satisfying discounts and markdowns (30–75% off), a stylish selection of apparel for all occasions, and quality that should meet the requirements of the most discriminating shopper. About 50% of the merchandise is past-season closeout inventory from its regular stores, and the remaining selection is a collection designed for its outlet division offered at special value pricing. The private label outlet merchandise measures up in every way to the regular lines. The company designs and manufactures almost everything in the United States, but a few outside lines are carried (bras, panties, pantyhose, etc.). This is a great resource for professional women! I loved the many styles of jumpsuits, dresses, knit tops and pants, and many nursing style fashions. Overall, a nice mix of traditional and contemporary fashions (under the Mimi label). Sizes: Petite to XL. *Note: The current season "basics," a few rounds at the front of the outlets, are always priced at regular retail.*

MOM (MATERNITY OF MARIN)

874 Fourth Street, San Rafael. (415) 457-4955. E-mail: Rkaderali@aol.com. M–Sat 10:30–5. MC, VISA, DIS. Parking: private lot.
You'll want to hit the racks here for consignment clothing that encompasses all categories of maternity apparel. Don't miss the new apparel

(past-season overruns) at nicely discounted prices. Good selection of necessities for the nursing mom. Consignments accepted anytime!

MOTHERHOOD MATERNITY OUTLET

Factory Stores at Vacaville, Vacaville. (707) 446-4792. Daily. MC, VISA, AE. Parking: lot. (Other outlet: Shasta/Anderson center.)
Motherhood Maternity's leftover and surplus inventory from its 200 stores is very current and beautifully displayed. The modest 20% discounts on very current fashions are better than none at all, but you'll have to watch for end-of-season markdowns to get gratifying 50% discounts. The selection reflects the complete "cover" Motherhood offers for expectant moms: lingerie, sleepwear, swimsuits, sweaters, sportswear, dresses (career and dressy), jumpsuits, pantyhose, etc. Sizes: S, M, L (occasionally some XS and XL).

NATURAL RESOURCES

1307 Castro Street, San Francisco. (415) 550-2611. M–F 10:30–6, Sat 11–5. MC, VISA. Parking: street.
As a resource center for pregnant women and new families, Natural Resources offers classes, a

reference library, health-care products, breast-feeding supplies, and more. You'll also find close-outs and overruns of new maternity fashions and consignment maternity apparel. Nice discounts on the new merchandise; consignment prices for shoestring budgets.

Also See

Under Family, Men's & Women's, General Clothing:
THE BIG FOUR; JOCKEY; VF FACTORY OUTLET

Petites

Many stores in all clothing categories may have a small selection of Petite sizes; you can find them at Loehmann's, Marshall's, Dress Barn, Anne Klein, Donna Karan, Koret Factory Stores, Lucia, Liz Claiborne, Karen Kane, Jones New York (all divisions), Westport Ltd., Carole Little, Robert Scott & David Brooks, Ross Dress for Less, T.J. Maxx, Burlington Coat Outlet, Nordstrom Rack, Off Fifth, Talbots, Group USA, Mondi, Ellen Tracy, Evan Picone, Kasper A.S.L, and St. John. The selections range from two to three racks to whole sections of a store or outlet specifically devoted to Petite customers. Check the Store Index for the page numbers of these stores.

PETITE SOPHISTICATE OUTLET
Petaluma Village Premium Outlets, Petaluma.
(707) 763-8097. Daily. MC, VISA, AE, DIS.
Parking: lot.
(Other outlets: Gilroy, Milpitas, Vacaville centers.)
There's a slew of terrific fashions to cover all a Petite needs. Career suits, activewear (or spectator), casual weekend collections, dresses, related separates, sweaters, and accessories. A division of Casual Corner, these specialty stores have won a loyal following of diminutive women. While the merchandise in the outlets does not come from its full-price retail division, the same image is conveyed. Discounts are 20–50% off retail on comparable merchandise, averaging about 40%. Fashions are in season and first quality. Make a splash with less cash if you're 5 feet 4 inches or under and wear sizes 2–16. Refunds and exchanges.

Wedding and Formal Wear

BRIDAL IMAGE

*586 Sixth Street (near Brannan), San Francisco.
(415) 861-4696. www.bridalimage-sf.com.
M–F 10–5, Sat 10–6, Sun 11–5. MC, VISA.
Parking: street.*

Bridal Image has come a long way since it first
opened its doors. The new two-story location
across the street from the Flower Market is posh
compared to its former site. Even better, there are
more designer labels in the custom-order selection
and a wide range of choices for every budget.
The styles are au courant—lots of simple understated designs, but still some gowns in synthetic
fabrics, heavily beaded, and very ornate in both
full and sheath styles for those wanting more
embellishment. Prices range from $99 to $2,000
with a good mid-priced range from $500 to $1000.
Check the second floor for a buy-today-for-week-
end-wedding selection. Many gowns are available
for purchase off the rack. Sizes: 4–30 in stock in
upstairs off-the-rack selections; any size for custom
orders. Bridesmaid dresses are 15% off when at
least three are ordered. Check the racks for prom
dresses and good values on beaded mother-of-
the-bride dresses.

DISCOUNT BRIDAL OUTLET

*300 Brannan Street (bet. Second and Third streets),
San Francisco. (415) 495-7922. M–Sat 10–5,
Sun 11–5. MC, VISA. Parking: street.*

You won't find the elegant salon feeling of most
bridal shops here; its no-frills, no-glamour, close-
to-tacky decor keeps prices down. But if you covet
gowns in the $250 to $1,000 range at retail, you're
a good candidate for the selection. Of course,
dresses at more modest prices are available, too.
Discounts are about 20% off retail, but may be
more because many salons take a higher markup.
You can buy right off the rack for a wedding
on Saturday. Other dresses may be ordered for

delivery in a week or two, or at most two to four months. Discontinued styles may be discounted as much as 50% off retail, while fluffy petticoats are 20–30% less than salon prices. I spotted a few dogs, but in order to get the best styles, the owner sometimes has to take a loser. The same discounts apply to gowns for bridesmaids and flower girls, or a dress for a prom or a *quinciñera*. Large selection of gowns in sizes 4–42 (off the rack or special order).

GUNNE SAX/JESSICA MCCLINTOCK OUTLETS (FACTORY OUTLET)

494 Forbes Boulevard, South San Francisco. (415) 553-8390. M–Sat 9:30–5, Sun 11–5. MC, VISA, AE. Parking: lot.
The Gunne Sax outlet is supermarket-sized! It's the Bay Area's resource for prom and party dresses, wonderful if you're enchanted with the feminine, romantic Jessica McClintock look or excited by the more contemporary Scott McClintock line. Suits, skirts, and dresses come in a wide variety of fabrics for daytime or evening occasions. Many brides and bridesmaids have found beautiful dresses here that would have been off-limits at full retail prices. Prom-trotters and GenXers can find slinky, saucy,

and fun party fashions, long or short. There are also infant christening gowns and First Communion dresses. Except for a few samples and irregulars, most of the inventory is past season. Discounts are 50–80% off retail. The prices are tempting, but take care to scrutinize for flaws, which are easily acquired on delicate fabrics. Sizes: Junior 3–13; Women's 4–16; Plus 14W–24W (Scott McClintock only); Girls dresses in 2–4T (very limited), 4–6X, 7–14; Preteen 6–14. All sales are final. Fellas appreciate the "waiting room" next to the outlet. Leftover fabric from factory production is sold at the outlet, plus laces, beaded trims, and appliqués, at prices that make home sewing worth the effort.

NEW THINGS WEST

350 South Winchester Boulevard (off Stevens Creek), Second floor, San Jose. (408) 241-8136. M–F 11–8, Sat 10–6, Sun 1–5. MC, VISA, AE, DIS. Parking: lot.
New Things West has multiple personalities. First, retired samples of bridal, bridesmaid, formal wear, and some MOBs from its first floor main store (Bay Area Bridals) are sold at modest to maximum discounts. Bridesmaid dresses start at $19.99,

bridal gowns at $99, and prom dresses generally range from $19 to $79. Clearance racks of formal wear (some mother-of-the-bride and cocktail dresses) are always reduced a minimum of 60%, many 80%. Naturally, you'll find some forlorn fashions on the racks, but also some real beauties. The "new" bridal department at New Things West covers the spectrum, with gowns priced for every budget. The owner utilizes his connections to buy special closeouts and factory overstocks. These are discounted a minimum of 20% off regular retail and some styles can be special ordered. There are gowns available off the rack in sizes 4–44. Any sample is available as a special order. A nice dressy shoe clearance department offers outstanding values. If you strike out in the clearance depart-ment, don't leave without checking out the first floor full-service salon. *Note: Before driving miles, call first. Renovations to the shopping center may force a move to another location in the area.*

TRADITIONAL WHITE & BRIDAL VEIL OUTLET
11 Duncan Street (at Valencia), San Francisco.
(415) 255-6192. By appointment only.
Cash/Check. Parking: pay lots.
Here you'll save at least 20–50% off retail on samples and discontinued headpieces and veils for brides and bridesmaids from this bridal veil manufacturer. Prices range from $45 to $145, while retail prices would be more like $150 to $300. You'll find veils in informal to cathedral lengths, and headpieces in tiara, crown, bandeau, juliet, wreath, pillbox, and other styles. Many have exquisite beading and appliqués on fabrics that include silk shantung and satin. Special orders and custom designs are available, but at strictly "custom" prices. The bridal gown selection with an emphasis on a mid-price range is lovely, alas not discounted.

Rental, Previously Worn, and Vintage

AGES AHEAD

524 Bryant Street, Palo Alto. (650) 327-4480. T–Sat 11:30–4. MC, VISA, AE. Parking: street, pay lots.

Past-the-ingenue-stage brides (first and second weddings) seek out this charming shop for dresses that are bridal, special, but also feel appropriate for their stage in life. That's the appeal of the hundreds of vintage gowns gathered by the owner in her scouting trips around the country. About 90% of the older gowns are in sizes 6 to 8, so brides needing larger sizes scout through the more recent versions from the '50s and '60s, or they have a gown made from some of the vintage fabrics that are available. The average price on gowns is around $500. Everything is cleaned and restored; in-house alterations save headaches. The very personal service includes free hugs and hankies for when moms and daughters get weepy after finding the perfect dress.

CHERISHED

2635 North Main, Walnut Creek. (925) 280-0128. www.cherishedweddinggowns.com. T–Th 11–7, Fri–Sat 10–5. MC, VISA, AE. Parking: street.

Consignment shopping for wedding gowns makes sense when you're trying to trim wedding costs. The owner brings her special understanding and expertise to the business—for many years she owned an upscale bridal salon. Whether you're hoping to spend a modest $200 or ready to pay more than $1,000 for a gown that may have been worn at an elegant country club reception, chances are you'll find many to consider within your budget. The gowns are in excellent condition, a requirement for consignment. Prices are approximately half off the original price. The styles reflect anything that may have been shown in bridal magazines from the past few years. Some gowns are new—retired try-on samples or canceled orders from the inventory of other bridal salons. These are also reduced in price from 40–75% off original retail. Some labels you'll find on the racks: Vera Wang, Richard Glasgow, Badgley Mishka, Amsale, Helen Morley, Manale, and others. Sizes generally range from 4–38.

Bridal veils available too. If you're retiring a gown, bring it in—you'll split the selling price 50/50 with the owner.

FORMAL RENDEZVOUS

118 South Boulevard (south end of B Street), San Mateo. (650) 345-4302. By appointment. T–F 12:30–6:30, Sat 11–5. MC, VISA, AE. Parking: street.
At this boutique-style salon crammed with beautiful fashions, those needing a wedding, cocktail party, formal, or semiformal dress have a good chance of finding a real dazzler. It may be a show-stopping beaded and sequined formal, tea-length cocktail dress, even a chic black cocktail dress. The selection provides options for women of varying ages and style orientations, in sizes 4–20. Most designer dresses and bridal gowns come with well-known labels like Bob Mackie, Sho Max, Oleg Cassini, Demetrios, and Victor Costa. You have two options: buy the dress outright, or rent it just for the event. The owner handpicks the latest fashion gowns each season to keep the inventory up-to-date. To allow the staff time to give you the personal service and attention you may require, appointments are essential.

THIRD HAND STORE

1839 Divisadero Street, San Francisco. (415) 567-7332. M–Sat Noon–6. MC, VISA, AE. Parking: street.
Many love the vintage and antique collection of bridal gowns sold at this unique establishment, in business since 1967, but for those who prefer a fresh start, there are always racks of new, discontinued sample wedding gowns priced for the most straitened budget (lots under $200). The samples may be somewhat shopworn; they're sent over from the company's bridal salon in San Anselmo. On racks of preowned or vintage gowns you may find a beauty (probably in a tiny size) from the 1870s or more recent gowns from the '30s, '40s, up to the '80s. Make it a tandem shopping excursion; grooms can rent a vintage tux, tails, or really gallant-looking morning coat (from the 1900s to the 1960s) and ensure a truly charming wedding picture.

WEDDING STORE & MORE

1419 Burlingame Avenue, Suite O
(in the Fox Mall), Burlingame. (650) 347-3250.
M–Sat 9:30–6. MC, VISA, AE.
Parking: street or lots.

No appointments required, plus the owner's personal and friendly service at this small consignment boutique, add up to a hassle-free shopping expedition. It's worth a shot for the opportunity to save 50–65% off the original prices on these worn-once consignment gowns and never-worn discontinued sample gowns. If you've studied bridal magazines you'll recognize the labels— Demetrios, Bianchi, Marissa, Galina, Eden, Jasmine, Venus, Diamond Collection, and many others. You can find some gowns for second weddings, occasionally MOB's and more informal gowns for simple affairs, plus new veils and headpieces. Check for accessories. Sizes depend on what's come in, but count on a reasonable selection in 4 to 16, larger sizes often available although they go out pretty fast. Referrals for alteration services. Check here too for 25% discounts on your invitations, wedding-related stationery, and other paper goods available by special order from about 20 books (the same popular books shown at most stores). Brides: call for the particulars of selling your gown after the wedding.

Also See

Under San Francisco's Factory Outlets
and Off-Price Stores:
GEORGIOU

Under Famous Labels/Factory Stores:
ELLEN TRACY; MONDI; ST. JOHN

Under Bay Area Off-Price/Chain Discount Stores:
GROUP USA; LOEHMANN'S

Under Family, Men's & Women's,
General Clothing:
BURLINGTON COAT FACTORY

Under Clearance Centers:
ALL LISTINGS

Men's Sportswear

CALIFORNIA BIG & TALL

625 Howard Street (at New Montgomery),
San Francisco. (415) 495-4484. T–Sat 9–5:30.
MC, VISA. Parking: Fifth and Mission Garage (pay).
Everything sent to California Big & Tall from the
17 Rochester Big & Tall stores is initially marked
down at least 20–40% off retail; some racks add
up to 60% and more. The bargains are usually
past-season styles and include suits, sportcoats,
sportshirts, sweaters, wool and poly/wool slacks
for workday and weekend clothing. Some basics
like underwear and belts are not discounted.
Sizes: suits 46–60 Reg, Long, and Extra Long;
shirts to 20-inch neck, 38-inch sleeve. A small
shoe selection to 17 Medium, 15 Wide. As at
most clearance centers, not everything is wonderful, but there are many good-quality buys.
Alterations extra.

G.HQ. OUTLET

Great Mall of the Bay Area, Milpitas.
(408) 263-8571. Daily. MC, VISA, AE. Parking: lot.
Part showcase for its current collections and part
clearance center for its eight Southern California
stores, G.Hq. is popular with twenty-somethings
and men who are not afraid to be on the forefront
of fashion trends. Most of the selection is geared
toward "dress casual"—shirts, sweaters, slacks,
sportcoats, and suits that fit right into the Saturday
night club scene, have a little extra pizzazz for
dates and restaurant dining, or are more relaxed
for Friday casual days at the office. The clearance
inventory in the back half of the store is marked
down 25–50% off original retail, because this
merchandise is slightly past season. Sizes in
European-styled sportcoats are S–XL; pants from
waist sizes 29–38.

GREG NORMAN

Prime Outlets at Gilroy, Gilroy. (408) 848-8835.
Daily. MC, VISA, AE, DIS. Parking: lot.
Maybe Greg Norman finds winning the "big one" elusive, but he's got a winner with his collection of sport and golf apparel. Watch any tournament he's playing in, and you've got a preview of what you'll find in this outlet (attached to the Rockport/Reebok Outlets). There's some pretty classy duds with a masculine design sense so guys can play like a gentleman, but dress to kill. Count on some golf shirts in the softest, smoothest mercerized cotton knit priced at $94 ($125 retail); classic cotton polos at $51 (retail $65 to $70); GQ-standard print sportshirts in soft tencel fabrics at $98 (retail $130); and anyone-can-afford T-shirts at $15. Also shorts, slacks, swimwear, jackets, and accessories. Look for the super deals on special markdown displays.

HAGGAR CLOTHING CO.

Prime Outlets at Gilroy, Gilroy. (408) 842-4983.
Daily. MC, VISA, AE, DIS. Parking: lot.
(Other outlet: Vacaville center.)
Taking the coordinate concept used in selling women's clothing, Haggar sells suit jackets and suit pants separately. The pants are sold in finished lengths in waist sizes 30–44; jackets sizes 38–44 in Short, Medium, and Long. Some suit fabrics are labeled "washable." This is a moderately priced line sold in many major national chain stores. Prices are reduced 25–50% off major store retails. There's also a nice selection of casual sportswear and pants (waist sizes 30–44) in a variety of styles and fabrics that he can wear while he's doing whatever!

IZOD FACTORY STORE

Prime Outlets at Gilroy, Gilroy. (408) 842-3696.
Daily. MC, VISA, AE, DIS. Parking: lot.
(Other outlets: Truckee, Vacaville centers.)
It's been years since the Izod logo set you apart, but the line is still appealing and much desired. Golfers in particular love the Izod Factory Store, where I spotted the classic "links" cardigan and many styles of pullovers, twill and cotton/linen slacks, shorts, shirts for any weather or season, and accessories, all at 20–50% discounts. Izod's smaller sportswear collection for women particularly appeals to a more mature and mainstream customer. Sizes: S–XXL, some Big and Tall sizes. Refunds and exchanges within 60 days.

JONES NEW YORK MEN

Napa Premium Outlets, Napa. (707) 265-0272. Daily. MC, VISA, AE, DIS. Parking: lot.

Preferred customers on the store's mailing list will get advance notice of new shipments and special discounts. That's the best way to get real values from this spiffy store. Otherwise, everyday markdowns on the fairly current merchandise is a modest 25% off retail. The Jones New York Men's collections are perfect for corporate types shopping for classy duds for casual dress Fridays at work or on the weekend. Sportcoats and suits; resort collections; coordinated collections of pants, shirts, and sweaters; and accessories for head-to-toe coverage make shopping easy for men without a fashion degree. There are some special markdown groups all the time. Loved winter's wool sportcoats marked down to $99 from $249 in June. Sizes: S-XL; sportcoats and suits 28R–48R or 40L to 48L; waists 32–40.

NAUTICA OUTLET

Napa Premium Outlets, Napa. (707) 252-3992. Daily. MC, VISA, AE, DIS. Parking: lot. (Other outlet: Gilroy center.)

This is the consummate headquarters for the sailing crowd. It's true that some men may find Nautica's prices steep at retail, but that's directly related to the quality of its well-made line and the quality of its fabrics. You'll get some price relief with discounts that average about 35% off retail. A $76 sweatshirt that looks as good a year later as the day you bought it will set you back about $48; a casual $300 jacket (perfect for cold days out on the Bay) may be reduced to $200 or $149 on special end-of-season racks. The store is done up with taste and style, the better to showcase the classic, clean lines of Nautica's first-quality pants, shorts, shirts, sweaters, jackets, sweats, and all the other bits and pieces. Sizes: S–XXL (with accommodating athletic cut).

ROBERT TALBOTT FACTORY OUTLET

The Village Center, Carmel Valley.
(831) 659-4540. M–Sat 10–5, Sun Noon–5.
MC, VISA, AE. Parking: lot.
The next time you're visiting Carmel, take a ride out to the Robert Talbott Factory Outlet. You'll save 50–80% on fine ties that typically retail for $42 to $100. Many have minute to major flaws like slubs in the fabric, wrinkles, and pulled threads. Prices are discounted accordingly. Frequent in-store specials feature ties as low as $5. Also, fabulous buys on elegant discontinued fabrics such as silks (all types), wool challis, and fine cottons. The shirt selection has been expanded. Both the shirts and shirt fabrics are in demand because of the superior quality of the cotton fabric and the high thread count. Don't overlook the good deals on bow ties, cummerbunds, and pocket squares. Quilters make the pilgrimage just to pick up the special grab bags of silk remnants. *Directions: From Highway 1, take Carmel Valley Road 13 miles to the Village Center; turn right at the Texaco station.*

TOMMY HILFIGER OUTLET STORE

Napa Premium Outlets, Napa. (707) 224-4299.
Daily. MC, VISA, AE. Parking: lot.
Mailing-list customers get cards three to four times a year offering additional discounts during extra special sales. Altogether, the savings reach sublime levels ($65 sportshirts reduced to $24.99). At any other time, the savings are modest—25–35% off retail on average. Even so, business is brisk, as fans of this line relish the opportunity to buy current and past-season overruns. Tourists can load up and have the sportswear shipped home via UPS.

VAN HEUSEN DIRECT

601 Mission Street, San Francisco. (415) 243-0750.
M–Sat 9–6, Sun 11–5. MC, VISA, DIS.
Parking: street.
(Other outlets: Folsom, Gilroy, Milpitas, Vacaville centers.)
The Van Heusen Factory Group comprises over 400 off-price stores selling Van Heusen and other labels directly to the consumer. You can always find dress shirts in dozens of fabrications in regular and European (slim) fits, sizes 15–18½.

You'll also want to browse through racks of casual sportswear for both men and women, geared for traditional tastes.

Also See

Under San Francisco's Factory Outlets and Off-Price Stores:
CHRISTINE FOLEY; JEREMYS

Under Bay Area Manufacturers' Factory Outlets:
EDDER SWAY

Under Famous Labels/Factory Stores:
DONNA KARAN; LIZ CLAIBORNE; TSE; VERSACE

Under Bay Area Off-Price/ Chain Discount Stores:
DESIGNER LABELS FOR LESS

Under Family, Men's & Women's, General Clothing:
ALL LISTINGS

Under Active Sportswear:
FILA FACTORY OUTLET; URBAN ATHLETIC

Under Children's Clothing:
BUGLE BOY

Under Shoes:
TIMBERLAND

Under Sporting Goods:
ALL LISTINGS

Men's Suits

AFTERWARDS

1159 El Camino Real (at Santa Cruz), Menlo Park.
(650) 324-2377. M–Sat 10–6, Th until 8.
MC, VISA, AE. Parking: street.
Afterwards is a consignment store offering an
intriguing selection of new and used men's suits
from upscale stores: you'll always find some Polo
by Ralph Lauren and occasionally status labels
like Brioni, Mani, or Armani. Because the owners
have good industry connections, men will find
new "samples" from Robert Talbott and Ferrell
Reed (ties), Alexander Julian, Trafalgar (belts),
J. Abboud (sweaters), Tommy Bahama, Ermene
Gildo Zegna, Polo, and others. Afterwards also
takes new excess inventory on consignment. New
merchandise is marked at about 50% off retail;
consignment inventory is about 75% off original
retail. Prices are $100 to $400 plus. The women's
half of the store is equally impressive, with better
labels. These folks obviously refuse more than
they accept for consignment. To see the whole
Afterwards empire on this block, stop in at 1137
to see consignment kids, maternity, and bridal, or
at 1153 for upscale home furnishings.

BROOKS BROTHERS FACTORY STORES

Prime Outlets at Gilroy, Gilroy. (408) 847-3440.
Daily. MC, VISA, AE. Parking: lot.
(Other outlets: Petaluma, St. Helena centers.)
Brooks Brothers career clothing appeals equally
to men and women, with dependable basics and
fine quality. Prices are discounted about 30% on
average, with extra point-of-purchase markdowns
to 50% off on selected groups every day. The
company has expanded its sportswear: casual
slacks, shirts, and sweaters. Pick up some essentials—ties, pajamas, socks, belts, and more. Sizes
for men: 36 Short to 48 Long and Extra Long;
dress shirts from 15 (32-inch sleeve) to 18 (36-inch
sleeve). I loved the women's career clothing—

suits, separates, and silk sets and dresses, and great weekend sportswear collections. Returns anytime. No alterations.

CLOTHING BROKER

5327 Jacuzzi Street, Richmond. (510) 528-2196. MC, VISA. F 10–7, Sat 10–6, Sun 11–5. Parking: lot. (Other stores: 300 Alemany Blvd., San Francisco, 415/642-8034; 3280 Victor Street, Santa Clara, 408/748-7637.)

The Clothing Broker stores are located in industrial parks, are open only three days a week, and use minimal advertising: a successful formula for very low pricing. Each store is well stocked with suits and sportcoats in sizes 36S to 60 Regular. Summer 1999 navy blue blazers were $109; most suits ranged from $99 to $179 (international collections from Zanetti, Lebus, and others to $299). All-wool tuxedos were $169. The company buys directly from manufacturers or manufacturers' reps and occasionally buys closeouts. There is an extensive selection in Big and Tall from 40 Portly to 60 Long to a 22-inch neck in shirts. Dress shirts were priced from $12.99 to $32.99. Ties from $7.99 to $19.99. A separate vendor maintains a very nice shoe department with styles from Johnston & Murphy, Florsheim, Stuart James, Bally, and others for $54 to $119. Most slacks were priced $39 to $44. This is a pipe-rack operation but nicely presented; all in all, I think Clothing Broker does a very good job, satisfying all but the most elite shoppers. Alterations done on site for a fee. Returns, exchanges, and refunds. Call for directions.

GOOD BYES

3464 Sacramento Street, San Francisco. (415) 346-6388. E-mail: goodbyes@aol.com. M–Sat 10–6, Th until 8, Sun 11–5. MC, VISA, DIS. Parking: street.

Good Byes offers cut-above consignment men's apparel. In labels, you'll find everything from Gap to Gucci. You'll find prices starting at $50, averaging about $125, and topping out at about $300. Sizes usually 36–46. Good selection of slacks, dress shirts, ties (many new), belts, and shoes. The owner has a pipeline to an upscale line of men's sportswear, resulting in new merchandise (mostly samples) in all categories of men's apparel. Go to the women's side and the sister store next door for tempting buys in women's apparel.

PRESIDENT TUXEDO OUTLET

2527 El Camino Real, Redwood City.
(650) 299-0555. www.prestux.com.
M–W 10–6, Th–F 10–9, Sat 10–6, Sun 11–4.
MC, VISA, AE. Parking: lot.

If you've added up the cost of renting a tuxedo and accessories, you'll find that buying used equals about two rental charges, maybe less, and the tux will be in the closet for future use. Most used wool-blend jackets at the President Tuxedo Outlet are priced at about $110; pants range from $40 to $50. You can buy used or new shirts and accessories. The retired rental inventory in the clearance section reflects the selection found at its twenty-six regular stores. You'll find new tuxedos (all wool or wool blend) that are priced reasonably. Alterations are extra. Sizes for everyone, including a few boys' sizes.

SPACCIO

645 Howard Street (at New Montgomery),
San Francisco. (415) 777-9797. M–Sat 9–7.
MC, VISA, AE, DIS, CB, DC. Parking: free garage
on Hawthorne side of building.

This major Italian manufacturer sells direct at consumer-friendly prices. Bottom line: savings of 30–40% off other store retails. Spaccio makes Italian suits in four different cuts (including one that comes close to the American traditional fit), plus new cuts in suits and sportcoats to reflect the new trends for the younger generation. Italian suits use very fine fabrics like lighter-weight merino wool or wool gabardine (rather than the worsted wool used by most American manufacturers). You'll find somber and dignified fabric suitings along with standout bold colors appealing to a younger fashion-liberated customer. Sizes 36S to 50XL. Prices range from $299 to $699 every day; during special sales prices dive for drop-dead deals. Alterations can be done on the premises for a modest fee. Completing the selection: sportcoats, full-length topcoats, lightweight contemporary fashion sweaters, well-made and elegant slacks, 100% silk Italian ties, dress shirts of fine 100% Egyptian and Swiss cotton, shoes, belts, and other accessories. Spaccio also manufactures and carries a line of sportswear and outerwear—Blouson jackets, coats, and leather and suede jackets come in lightweight and heavyweight versions depending on the season.

Also See

Under Famous Labels/Factory Stores:
DONNA KARAN; VERSACE

Under Family, Men's & Women's,
General Clothing:
**BURLINGTON COAT FACTORY;
POLO/RALPH LAUREN**

Under Clearance Centers:
NORDSTROM; OFF FIFTH

Men's Suits

73

Family, Men's & Women's, General Clothing

The Big Four:
Ross Dress for Less, Marshall's, T.J. Maxx, Burlington Coat Factory

Think of these stores as your "four best friends": Ross, Marshall's, T.J. Maxx, and Burlington Coat Factory do an admirable job of providing solid discounts and a head-to-toe selection of apparel, accessories, and shoes for each family member. Each store has its own personality and slight differences in merchandising. In my comparison surveys, I've often found that prices on many brand names at these four stores are significantly lower than those found at the factory stores or outlets.

Highlights: Burlington Coat Factory has the best selection of coats and outerwear (some skiwear) in all sizes and styles for adults and children of any Bay Area store. Its men's and young men's departments are the best of the four—Big and

Tall sizes, too! Also great home and kitchen accessories, shoes, linens, and, at some stores, baby furniture. T.J. Maxx comes up with surprising status labels in women's apparel and has a discriminating selection of giftware, designer bed and bath linens, a satisfying shoe department, and good Petite- and Plus-size selections. Ross, with 60 Northern California stores (some just humongous), offers moderately priced fashions (selected stores receive upscale labels), plus shoes, fragrances, giftwares, linens and domestics, picture frames, handbags, and body and bath products. Marshall's captures occasional groups of better women's apparel. Check in for fragrances, jewelry, giftware, and linens.

Women's Petite and Plus fashions get respectable rack space at all four stores, and men's and children's selections are generally excellent. Each company's stores are stocked according to the customer base of their area. If you feel your store doesn't have enough "good stuff," try another location. These stores are consumer-friendly, allowing returns, exchanges, and refunds. For the Marshall's nearest you, call (800) MARSHALL (627-7425); for Ross (800) 945-ROSS (945-7677); T.J. Maxx (800) 2TJ-MAXX (285-6299); Burlington Coat Factory (415) 495-7234.

Other Stores

ASHWORTH

Factory Stores at Vacaville, Vacaville.
(707) 447-0237. Daily. MC, VISA, AE, DIS.
Parking: lot.
Ashworth sportswear, designed as a golf collection, goes just about anywhere. At pro shops, prices are a lot higher; here they're just about right. PGA tour star Freddy Couples endorses Ashworth. Women have a few racks to call their own, but men's sweaters, slacks, shorts, tops, and jackets from about $15 to $59 get the spotlight.

BIG DOG SPORTSWEAR

1299 Marina Boulevard, Marina Square,
San Leandro. (510) 895-1510. Daily.
MC, VISA, AE, DIS. Parking: lot.
(Other outlets: Folsom, Gilroy, Milpitas, Napa,
Pacific Grove, Petaluma, Tracy, Vacaville centers.)
Reflecting the Southern California lifestyle and a sense of whimsy with its St. Bernard logos, Big Dog sportswear for men, women, and kids is great fun. Savings are about 25–40% off on sweats, T-shirts, graphic ties, shorts, pants, shirts, jackets, and beach towels. Sizes from 6mos to 5X (real big and real tall!). Great for lighthearted gifts. For a warm and fuzzy gift, pick up an adorable stuffed "big dog" with ageless appeal.

CALVIN KLEIN OUTLET STORE

Prime Outlets at Gilroy, Gilroy. (408) 847-7889.
Daily. MC, VISA, AE, DIS. Parking: lot.
(Other outlets: Great Mall, Milpitas; Napa center.)
Don't let money come between you and your Calvins! Shop at the outlet and you'll save 30–50% on average on a great selection of first-quality sportswear for men, women, and children. Denim fashions are always in evidence—you'll save about

$20 on basic jeans that retail for about $54. There are smaller sections with 40% discounts on average devoted to Calvin's bridge collections—some career separates and casual clothing for women; dressier slacks and shirts for dress-down Fridays. T-shirts go with every fashion category in the store, and you'll also find belts, underwear, caps, etc. One of the better designer outlets. Sizes: Boys 8–20; Girls 7–16; Men's S–XL, waists 28–40, length 30–34; Women's 2–14; Juniors 1–13. Exchange and refunds within 14 days.

DKNY JEANS

Napa Premium Outlets, Napa. (707) 226-3853. Daily. MC, VISA, AE, DIS. Parking: lot.
Jeans in basic and trendy styles, T-shirts, and some weekend casual clothes fill the displays here. If this is your label, there's a pair of jeans waiting for your visit. Hope you'll be satisfied with the less than pulse-pounding discounts (average price on jeans $39), 20–25% off retail except for selected groups with markdowns to 50% off. Sizes: Men's waist 28–42, lengths 30–32 or 34; Women's 2–14 (some short and longs).

DOCKERS

Napa Premium Outlets, Napa. (707) 252-7526. Daily. MC, VISA, AE, DIS. Parking: lot.
A prominent sign in the store reads "Quality control experts never miss a thing. If there's a blemish in the fabric, a shade off color, or a variance in size, the merchandise is labeled as irregular." Even so, you'll be challenged trying to identify the imperfections on merchandise that accounts for about half the inventory in the outlet. It's well stocked with fashions from the entire Dockers collection of casual clothing for men, women, and children. Men can pick up pants from the Slate collection, golf shirts, sweaters, ties, and just about anything else in the men's Dockers line. Prices are reduced 25–35% on average, up to 50% on some displays.

EDDIE BAUER OUTLET STORE

1295 Marina Boulevard, Marina Square, San Leandro. (510) 895-1484. M–F 10–9, Sat 10–7, Sun 11–6. MC, VISA, AE, DIS. Parking: lot. (Other stores/outlets: Sunrise Shopping Center, Citrus Heights; Hilltop Mall, Richmond; Gilroy center.)

Eddie Bauer's outlets emphasize its casual apparel and outerwear for men and women: pants, shirts, dresses, sweaters, and jackets. You'll also find some shoes, socks, backpacks, luggage, watches, sunglasses, and small accessory items. Catalog overstocks, discontinued products, surplus from its retail store division, and some apparel made specifically for its outlet stores make up the selection. Prices are reduced 40–70% off original. Exchanges or cash refunds with receipt.

GAP OUTLET

Great Mall of the Bay Area, Milpitas.
(408) 946-1760. Daily. MC, VISA, AE, DIS.
Parking: lot.
(Other outlets: Gilroy, Petaluma, Vacaville centers.)
Gap heaven for the faithful. The outlets are just as tempting as the regular stores. The difference? Large quantities of slightly irregular merchandise at about 50% off retail pricing, plus first-quality past-season merchandise at 25–40% reductions. Shop the outlet as a family—men, women, teens, and tots can load up. Some Banana Republic and Old Navy labels show up on the racks.

GEOFFREY BEENE

Factory Stores at Vacaville, Vacaville.
(707) 452-0603. Daily. MC, VISA. Parking: lot.
(Other outlets: Folsom, Gilroy centers.)
Geoffrey Beene factory stores are stocked with an impressive array of men's fashions. Everything is very current and stylish, and priced an average 25–50% off. A versatile array of sportshirts, occasional sportcoats, slacks, lots of denim pants and shirts, activewear, robes, gorgeous ties, and a posh stock of dress shirts make it possible for a fella to build a wardrobe that everyone will admire. Most stores have a split personality, devoting about half the space to a well-designed collection of women's sportswear. Refunds and exchanges allowed.

GUESS? OUTLET

Prime Outlets at Gilroy, Gilroy. (408) 847-3400.
www.guess.com. Daily. MC, VISA, AE, DIS.
Parking: lot.
A little of everything Guess? for teens and adults: discontinued, seconds, and irregulars, resulting in 30–70% discounts. You'll find great buys on Guess? shoes designed to complement its apparel:

Western boots, clogs, and clunky street shoes for women and men. Large store, lots of energy: Guess? heaven for the faithful.

J. CREW

Prime Outlets at Gilroy, Gilroy. (408) 848-1633. Daily. MC, VISA, AE. Parking: lot. (Other outlet: Napa center.)
A mixed bag of bargains, with some discounts so chintzy you'll wonder if the company realizes that consumers expect savings—other pricing and markdowns so good that they prompt a grab-it-and-go response. All the merchandise at these outlets is from J. Crew's catalog division, lagging behind by about two catalog cycles. Discounts 20–70% off original catalog retails. The women's and men's selections are equally balanced, with a little of everything originally offered in the catalog. Attentive staff and beautiful merchandising make shopping a pleasure. You've got 10 days for exchanges or cash refunds.

JOCKEY

Factory Stores at Vacaville, Vacaville. (707) 451-8119. Daily. MC, VISA, AE, DIS. Parking: lot. (Other outlets: Folsom, Gilroy centers.)
There's a lot more to Jockey than men's briefs: you'll find underwear for women and children, casual shirts, pantyhose, tank tops, etc. Sizes for all dimensions. All first-quality goods at average 30% off retail.

LEVI'S OUTLET

Napa Premium Outlets, Napa. (707) 252-6926. Daily. MC, VISA, AE, DIS. Parking: lot.
This outlet is the real thing. Owned by Levi Strauss, it is accordingly well stocked with jeans of every description for men, women, and children. All your favorite styles are priced 30% off retail, on average. Also, shirts, jackets, and other Levi's sportswear to make sure you're covered head to toe before leaving.

LEVI'S OUTLET BY MOST

Factory Stores at Vacaville, Vacaville.
(707) 451-0155. Daily. MC, VISA, AE, DIS.
Parking: lot.
(Other outlets: Anderson/Redding, Folsom,
Gilroy, Milpitas, Petaluma, Tracy centers.)
This company sells Levi's irregulars and closeouts.
In some instances the flaws were obvious, like
small spots from sewing machine oil or unequal
fading on stonewashed jeans, but most of the
time I was at a loss to find anything wrong with the
apparel. You'll find all the Levi's labels: Dockers
for women and men (men's pants usually at $19.99
to $29.99); popular pants styles from the 501, 540,
550, and 560 collections; even Slates at $19.99 to
$39.99; many styles for students, girls, and boys
(all sizes covered), all at about 50% discounts! Plus
shirts in an endless selection, casual tops, belts,
socks, and a little bit of everything Levi's. Children's
wear discounts are modest—about 25% off original
retail. Great store, great selection, great bargains!

LONDON FOG FACTORY STORES

Factory Stores at Vacaville, Vacaville.
(707) 447-1196. Daily. MC, VISA, AE, DIS.
Parking: lot.
(Other outlets: Folsom, Gilroy, Pacific Grove,
Petaluma, St. Helena, South Lake Tahoe centers.)
This is London Fog's headquarters for outerwear
and rainwear for men and women. It's all quite
nice, and nicely discounted. The factory stores
primarily showcase men's and women's raincoats,
all-weather coats (many with zip-out linings),
jackets, and heavyweight down jackets (for the
slopes), all with water-repellent fabrics, at 50%
discounts. Sizes: Petite 2–20; Misses 2–26½;
Men's 36–52 in Short, Regular, and Long. Some
children's outerwear, too! Returns anytime—no
problem! *Note: Due to company reorganization
in late 1999, many stores may close. Call first.*

PANGEA OUTLET

110 Howard Street, Petaluma. (707) 778-0110.
First Sat of each month 10–2. Cash/Check.
Parking: street.
Pangea screenprints and embroiders messages on
T-shirts, jackets, sweatshirts, and other garments

on which customers may want their message or logo. Flawed merchandise and test prints are tossed into the reject box, where you can hunt for T-shirts, all for $2. About 70% of the merchandise is first-quality, the remaining irregulars have minor flaws. Seconds in T-shirts are priced $3 to $4, firsts $6 to $9; seconds in sweatshirts $5 to $12, firsts $8 to $12. Sizes for the whole family.

POLO/RALPH LAUREN FACTORY STORE

Prime Outlets at Anderson, Anderson.
(530) 365-1090. Daily. MC, VISA, AE, DIS.
Parking: lot.
(Other outlets: Atascadero, Barstow, Gilroy
[opening April 2000], Mammoth Lakes centers.)
Good news! About April 2000, you'll find a big, new Polo/Ralph Lauren Factory Store at the Prime Outlets at Gilroy. Like the other factory stores in more remote locations, discounts are 30–50 % off original retail, 30% on current-season overruns, while greater discounts apply to merchandise that may be one or two years old or irregular. About 95% of the merchandise is first-quality; the remaining irregulars have minor flaws. If you time your visit right, you'll catch additional markdowns on the already well-priced merchandise (get on the mailing list!). Polo's "designer collections" aren't stocked, but you'll find just about everything else in its extensive line, including men's and women's apparel from the classic collection, boy's clothing, and homewares (towels, duvets, comforters, sheets, bed skirts, and rugs). Refunds (usually a MC, VISA, or AE credit) on merchandise returned within seven days in person or by mail. Exchanges for credit are accepted up to 30 days after purchase.

QUIKSILVER FACTORY STORES

Napa Premium Outlets, Napa. (707) 256-3526.
Daily. MC, VISA, DIS. Parking: lot.
This is a cool outlet for teens, but it's also a line that expresses a certain attitude that's not limited to any age group. It's required wear for board sports, i.e., surfers and windsurfers, wakeboarders, skateboarders, snowboarders, and wanna-bes. Originally known for wacky print shorts, the line now includes shirts, jeans, jackets, hats, and swimwear. Teen girls love the Roxy line (sizes 1–13). Prices hover at 40–50% off on past-season collections. Sizes: X–XL; Boys 4–7, 8–20.

REEL STUDIO STORE

Prime Outlets at Gilroy, Gilroy. (408) 842-9393.
Daily. MC, VISA. Parking: lot.
(Other outlet: Great Mall, Milpitas.)
A captivating store for cartoon and movie buffs.
Most merchandise is related to major studios
(Walt Disney, Looney Tunes/Warner Bros., etc.) or
cultural icons like Barbie, Betty Boop, Hello Kitty,
and Sanrio. The manufacturer makes clothing under
licensing agreements for sale to mass merchandisers and sells its leftovers through the outlet.
Sweaters, sweatshirts, T-shirts, overalls, underwear,
and more are available for men, women, tots, and
teens. Much of the merchandise is unisex—just
zero in on a favorite character represented with
a whimsical image. There's a small selection of
accessories, too (caps, tote bags, stuffed animals).
Prices reduced 20–40% off original retail.

ROYAL ROBBINS FACTORY OUTLET

841-A Gilman Street, Berkeley. (510) 527-1961.
www.royalrobbins.com. M–F 10–6, Sat 10–5,
Sun 11–5 (extended summer hours).
MC, VISA, DIS. Parking: lot.
(Other outlets: 1508 Tenth Street, Modesto;
Loehmann's Plaza, Sacramento.)
Royal Robbins classic clothing for outdoor—and
indoor—living is sold nationally through well-
known mail-order companies and stores specializing in men's and women's outdoor wear. At the
outlets you'll find seconds (very small flaws) on
current collections and overruns from preceding
seasons. The clothing is transitional for year-round
use and is designed to wash and dry easily—a
boon for adventure travelers. Many collections are
made from 100% cotton or other natural fibers in
distinctive patterns and weaves; other fabrications
are in Italian fleece—microfibers with moisture
transport systems that make wear and care a
snap. Many styles are unisex. Prices at the outlets
are 35–70% off retail. The line includes sweaters,
belts, hats, skirts, pants, shorts, dresses, shirts,
and tops. The outlets are nicely stocked and a
pleasure to shop. Exchanges and credits are
allowed, but no cash refunds.

THE SWEATSHIRT COMPANY

Factory Stores at Vacaville, Vacaville.
(707) 451-0307. Daily. MC, VISA. Parking: lot.
(Other outlets: Folsom, Gilroy centers.)
The Sweatshirt Company sells crewneck sweatshirts, track pants, and hooded sweatshirt jackets in sizes ranging from Infant to Adult XXXL and some Talls. All its first-quality goods are sold for 30% off full retail. Also, sweatshirts with college logos or unique pocket treatments and printed T-shirts. Prices range from $6.99 to $25.

VF FACTORY OUTLETS

Factory Stores at Vacaville, Vacaville. (707) 451-1990. Daily. MC, VISA, AE, DIS. Parking: lot.
(Other outlet: Gilroy center.)
The VF Factory Outlet offers a wealth of merchandise and good values for the whole family. You'll find fashions sporting labels from Healthtex (newborn to teenagers), Jantzen and JanSport (sportswear and swimsuits), Vanity Fair (intimate, daywear, and sleepwear), Wrangler, and Lee (men's, women's, and youth fashions—jeans, shirts, shorts, and jackets). These are first-quality fashions, plus irregulars and way-past-season

merchandise marked down substantially. Overall discounts are 50% off every day. Sizes for everyone: women's fashions from Junior size 1 to Women's 26; men's pants to waist sizes 44, lengths to 36. If you need special sizes they can be ordered, along with just about anything else in these brands. Returns and refunds okay.

WOOLRICH

Prime Outlets at Gilroy, Gilroy. (408) 847-9088.
Daily. MC, VISA, DIS. Parking: lot.
(Other outlet: Pacific Grove center.)
One glance at the apparel at Woolrich and you'll think of weekends in the country. The store showcases far more of its sportswear and outerwear collections for men and women than you'll ever see in any one store. Rugged, warm, and weatherproof outerwear (jackets, coats, windbreakers, parkas), fishing vests with dozens of pockets, warm bulky sweaters, plus pants, skirts, shirts, hats, caps, packs, and slippers, prove there's lots more to the line than you might have imagined. There are the enduring, classic Woolrich styles and some groups designed with more fashion. The women's groups offer some surprises—charming prints,

novelty fabrics, and chic jackets and coats. Wool-rich blankets (often tagged as seconds) are good buys, too. Expect to save 20–60% off retail on past-season overruns and seconds. A very nice store for traditionalists.

Also See

Under Famous Labels/Factory Stores:
POLO JEANS COMPANY FACTORY STORE

Under Clearance Centers:
ALL LISTINGS

Under Active Sportswear:
ALL LISTINGS

Under General Merchandise—Discount Stores, Warehouse Clubs:
COSTCO; WAL-MART

Active Sportswear

Aerobics, Camping, Dance, Exercise, Golf, Skiing, Tennis, etc.

BODY BODY

224 Greenfield Avenue, San Anselmo.
(415) 459-2336. M–F 9–8, Sat 9–6. MC, VISA.
Parking: street.
Body Body offers a collection of bodywear at modest discounts: past-season apparel 20–40% off and some current styles at minimal 10% discounts. Racks are jammed with brand-name apparel devoted to the workout crowd, plus a nice collection of active sportswear. Sizes 4–14; small selection of XL to fit up to size 18. Leotards and tights for kids at 20–33% off retail.

DANSKIN

Factory Stores at Vacaville, Vacaville. (707)
448-9313. Daily. MC, VISA, AE, DIS. Parking: lot.
(Other outlets: Folsom, Gilroy, Pacific Grove
centers.)
Whatever your size, Danskin has got you covered. Dancewear, aerobic wear, Petites, Danskin Plus (sizes 14–24), and Danskin Pro (for heavy use by serious athletes involved in daily training) are reduced 30–50%. Great colors, prints, and styles add up to a sizzling selection. Girls can get ready for the gym or dance studio with Danskin's collection in sizes 2T–14.

EASY WEAR FACTORY OUTLET

685 Third Street, San Francisco. (415) 778-6313.
Daily 10–6. MC, VISA. Parking: street.
You don't have to wear the same few outfits to the gym—not if you stop by the Easy Wear Outlet for a workout wardrobe update. This private label manufacturer of aerobic/active sportswear and anything that goes to the gym sells the "leftovers" at well below wholesale from a cubby-hole-sized outlet. The company makes apparel under many different labels and celebrity names for various stores and brand name collections. It also applies its own "Easy Wear" labels to many overruns. Pick

up a new leotard and tights for about $17. With frequent infusions of new inventory from the factory, every day there are racks of shorts, tights, and bike shorts priced at $10 each, or more likely 2 for $9.95. Bra tops priced at $24.99 to $34 at retail (depending on the label) are typically $10. A long zip-top jacket with hood is usually about $15 ($29 to $39 at retail); leotards usually hover around $10. Many styles are made from 100% cotton or cotton/lycra blends. Women's apparel takes up the most rack space; however, there are always a few racks of girls' and men's clothing. If you can shop without ambiance or fanfare and don't mind digging through jam-packed racks, stop by!

FILA TRADING, INC. FACTORY STORE

Prime Outlets at Gilroy, Gilroy. (408) 848-3452.
Daily. MC, VISA, AE. Parking: lot.
(Other outlet: Tracy center.)

Fila has gone way past ski and tennis apparel. You can get all togged out for just about any active sport in Fila style. If wearing expensive tennis (or any sport) clothes might improve your game, consider the bargains on past-season merchandise, samples, and overruns. Prices are reduced approximately 40%, more affordable but still not inexpensive. Current merchandise is discounted a minimum of 40%. Although limited in style and size, the selection of tennis skirts, golf/warm-up suits, ski vests, sweaters, bathing suits, shorts, shoes, footwear, and sports gear (including baseball mitts) changes frequently. Fila uses quality fabric, resulting in clothes that are made well to wear well. Sizes: Women's 4–14, Women's shoes 5½–10; Men's 44½–56, Men's shoes 6½–13. Exchanges only within 30 days.

SPORTS BASEMENT

1301 16th Street (off Third Street), San Francisco.
(415) 437-0100. www.sportsbasement.com.
Daily 10–6. MC, VISA, AE, DIS. Parking: lot.
Stop by and you'll understand the reasons for the
success and low pricing at Sports Basement—
an offbeat location not far from PacBell Stadium
and a spartan warehouse set-up. Markdowns at
30–60% are a sure bet on all the high performance
sports apparel and shoes. Everything is a first-
quality closeout or sample of some sort—from
high-end big name companies to smaller niche
manufacturers that are too small to have outlets of
their own. What's your sport? Cycling, snowboarding, skiing, tennis, golf, swimming, running,
soccer, aerobics, working out? You're covered!
You'll find racks and displays with labels that are
familiar (and usually expensive) to those serious
about their gear. Along with all the high-tech stuff,
there are loads of great fashions for spectators
and outerwear for outdoor recreation, for men and
women. Check your label IQ against this partial
roster of names: Helly Hansen, Sportif, Airwalk,
Kombi, Manzella, Duofold, and Moonstone for
snowboarding and skiing; Pearl Izumi, Bellwether,
Cannondale, Zoic, and Koulius Zaard for cyclists;
New Balance, Saucony, Etonic, In Sport, Moving
Comfort for runners; and New Balance, Saucony,
Brooks, Etonic, Teva, Asolo, Hi-Tech, Merrill,
Airwalk, Ripzone, and Nike (samples) for shoes.
Surprisingly, the 30-day exchange and refund
policy is absolutely first class. Can't get into the
City, shop online through their Web site.

TENNIS EXPRESS

2175 N. California Boulevard #205-A,
Tishman Center, Walnut Creek. (925) 937-0232.
E-mail: texp@mindspring.com. M–F 8–5.
MC, VISA, AE, DIS. Parking: lot (validated).
(Other store: Lafayette Tennis Club.)
Tennis Express is located on the mezzanine of an office building in Walnut Creek's "golden triangle" next to BART (until they relocate mid-2000). It's convenient for all the office workers in the area and is a source of discount prices on everything tennis. The focus is on top name brand tennis rackets, apparel, footwear, and accessories for men, women, and children. Its clientele is the serious club and junior tournament player. Everyday low prices are 15 to 20% off the latest, newest merchandise (Wilson, Head, Prince, K-Swiss, Adidas, Reebok, Yonex, Volkl, and Tail), the models usually not found at major sporting goods stores. Bigger markdowns can be found on the clearance racks. Also, golf apparel shows up on the racks from time to time. In the real world, this outfit is a major wholesaler of sports apparel, footwear, and equipment to big sports retailers and discounters. Its industry connections lead to the good stuff, stuff not typical of their wholesale business, but reflecting the owner's passion for tennis, service, and knowledge of the latest equipment.

URBAN ATHLETIC

434 Ninth Street, San Francisco. (415) 255-8881.
M–F 9–5, Sat 10–4. Cash/Check. Parking: street.
The Urban Athletic outlet is the place for active-wear and comfortable weekend separates when comfort is key. Take your pick from leggings, crop tops, leotards, bike shorts, hooded tops, baggy shorts, and T-shirts in cotton/lycra blends or French terry, fleece, thermal knits, and sports rib fabrics. Many fabrications are in classic neutrals—beige, gray, cream, and white. Thermal knits are prewashed and preshrunk. Prices range from $5 to $24 (wholesale prices on samples, discontinued patterns, and overruns). Sizes: S, M, L (fits 4–14). Exchanges and/or store credit.

Also See

Under Women's Apparel/Fashion:
MOST LISTINGS

Under Men's Apparel:
ALL LISTINGS

Under Family, Men's & Women's,
General Clothing:
ALL LISTINGS

Under Clearance Centers:
ALL LISTINGS

Under Shoes:
**ADIDAS; NIKE FACTORY STORE;
REEBOK FACTORY STORE**

Under Sporting Goods:
OUTDOOR OUTLET BY ANY MOUNTAIN

Children's Clothing

BUGLE BOY OUTLET
Factory Stores at Vacaville, Vacaville. (707) 446-9297. Daily. MC, VISA, AE. Parking: lot. (Other outlets: Anderson/Redding, Folsom, Gilroy.)
Boys, teens, and young men can have it any way they want at Bugle Boy. Racks are jammed with pants and shorts in all sizes. Generally, the discounts are 22–30% on current-season merchandise and get better during the frequent in-store promotions. Girls, teens, and women get a little rack space, too. Sizes: Girls 4 to Women's 16/18; Boys 4 to Men's 40; decent selection of Boys Huskies 8–16; Infants and Toddlers sizes. No cash or credit card refunds. Exchanges only within 30 days.

CARTER'S CHILDRENSWEAR
Factory Stores at Vacaville, Vacaville. (707) 446-9297. Daily. MC, VISA, AE, DIS. Parking: lot. (Other outlets: Folsom, Gilroy, Milpitas, and Pacific Grove centers.)

Carter's is well stocked with everything Carter's makes. Great selection of playwear, sleepwear, and layettes. Everyday discounts are 30% off retail. There are lots of irregulars in the layette, sleepwear, and playwear selection, but they're clearly marked and in no way less desirable. Carter's also makes clothing exclusively for its own stores, and prices are quite pleasing. Sizes: Preemie to 6X for girls; to 7 for boys.

CHICKEN NOODLE OUTLET
605 Addison Street, Berkeley. (510) 848-8880. April–June, Oct–Dec M–F 10–5. MC, VISA. Parking: lot.
Chicken Noodle children's playwear is every bit as cute as the name would imply—wonderful prints and practicality along with clever and engaging design details. The 100% cotton fabrics in wovens or knits predominate. Deck out your boys from a small selection of sizes Infant to 7; your girls in

Infant to 14. Prices are reduced 40–70% off retail on past-season overruns, ranging from $5 to $28 (special dresses); seconds (very small quantities) are marked way down. The accessories caught my eye: hair bows, scrunchies, socks, and hats, plus short sets, jumpers, and the new polar fleece swing coats. Bundled remnants of fabric are priced $3 to $4/yard. *Directions: From 80 take the University Avenue exit east, turn right at Sixth Street. Go one block to Addison, turn right, and drive to end of street (toward Aquatic Park). Building and parking are on right. The outlet is sometimes closed during heavy shipping periods—call ahead.*

FLAPDOODLES

Prime Outlets at Gilroy, Gilroy. (408) 842-3081. Daily. MC, VISA, AE, DIS. Parking: lot.
Working mothers must love this line. No ironing required! The 100% garment-dyed (eliminates any shrinkage) cotton play clothes come in a spirited selection of colors. The style is relaxed and contemporary, which means everything runs a little big. Mix and match for creative outfitting and functional fun: tops, bottoms, socks, T-shirts, leggings, hair accessories, jumpers, rompers, swimwear, outer-

wear, and more. An added plus—the Marisa Christina sweaters for children. Save 25–50% off retail prices on sizes Layette through 14.

KIDS R US

220 Walnut Street, Mervyn's Plaza, Redwood City. (650) 367-6005. M–Sat 10–9, Sun 11–6. MC, VISA, AE, DIS. Parking: lot. (Other stores: Colma, Newark, Sunnyvale.)
Kudos to Kids R Us for providing a one-stop resource for busy parents seeking solid values, name brands, good selection, and maximum convenience when shopping for their children (ages newborn to about 13). From no-nonsense basics to accommodating a child with a penchant for trendy styles, you'll shop with success! And every-day discounts average about 30% off retail, even more on end-of-season specials or promotions.

OSHKOSH B'GOSH

Prime Outlets at Gilroy, Gilroy. (408) 842-3280.
Daily. MC, VISA, AE, DIS. Parking: lot.
(Other outlets: Napa, Pacific Grove, Petaluma,
Vacaville centers.)
For the best deals at these large and colorful
factory stores, look for special promotions on
targeted racks and rounds for additional 30–50%
markdowns. Otherwise, discounts are modest—
averaging about 25% off retail. Sizes: Girls to 14;
Boys to 16; plus a few rounds of adult-sized overalls for men. While discounts are sometimes
disappointing, I have no quibble with the adorable
quotient on everything OshKosh.

REBECCA RAGGS, INC. OUTLET

10200 Imperial Avenue, Cupertino.
(408) 257-7884. M–F 9–4:30 (some Sats, call first).
MC, VISA. Parking: lot.
Rebecca Raggs makes a charming line of children's
clothing! Many of its styles are made from lovely
velours in vibrant colors, others in soft flannels or
cotton knits. Rebecca Raggs designs are appealing, with unique appliqués on the dresses,
jumpers, and warm-up suits in sizes 6mos to 14.

The quality is excellent. Ruff! Raggs is a boys' line
that moms will love. The outlet is jammed with
end-of-season overruns, seconds, and production
samples. Prices are 20% above wholesale, much
less if the item is damaged or way past season.
Moms make time to line up for the fabulous winter sale that starts every year the Wednesday
following Thanksgiving. Exchanges only on first-
quality goods, no exchanges on seconds.

SARA'S PRINTS (FACTORY OUTLET)

3018-A Alvarado Street, San Leandro. (510) 352-
6060. Quarterly sales. MC, VISA. Parking: lot.
Sara's Prints are made in Israel from fine Egyptian
or Israeli cotton, the softest fabric imaginable.
The colorful and whimsical prints are highlighted
against the fresh white background of all garments.
The line consists of layettes, rompers, diaper sets,
coveralls, playsuits, polo-style shirts, dresses, turtlenecks, boys' undershirts and briefs, girls' panties
and camisoles, long underwear sets, pajamas,
nightgowns, and playsets for boys and girls. Soft
and cuddly Polar-Tech jackets, coats, snowsuits,
buntings, and mittens from its pricier American
Widgeon division (staple items in popular catalogs)

are much more affordable during quarterly sales. Retail prices on Sara's Prints are moderate depending on your budget. During quarterly one- to two-week factory sale events, past-season merchandise and seconds are sold for a minimum 50% off retail. A phone call will get your name added to Sara's mailing list.

SWEET POTATOES FACTORY OUTLET

1799-A Fourth Street, Berkeley. (510) 527-5852. M–Sat 10–6, Sun 11–6. MC, VISA, DIS. Parking: lot.
Bummer! Regulars are in for a shock at Sweet Potatoes' chic new location. The bargains are accorded just a small section in the rear of the store as the spotlight is put on the full-priced new collections at the front. That said, you'll find sec- onds, overruns, samples, and past-season styles discounted 30–60%. The active sportswear featur- ing bright colors, prints, plaids, and fun details hasn't changed; it's still grandma bait. Dresses, overalls, shirts, jog sets, jumpsuits, tights, leggings, socks, skirts, hats, suspenders, and turtlenecks add up to many options when outfitting the kids. You'll love the whimsical Yazoo line for girls in sizes 4–14; Spuds for boys in sizes 12mos–7;

Sweet Potatoes for Infants to 10; New Potato and Marimekko for Layette to Toddler; and the new Ruth Hornbein sweaters, Claude Vell with sophis- ticated French styling, and Big Fish swimwear collections. Make sure you're on the mailing list for occasional sales at the factory just a few blocks away—you may recapture the bliss of yesteryear's fabulous sale blowouts.

TRUMPETTE OUTLET

108 Kentucky Street, Petaluma. (707) 769-1173. M–Sat 10–5, Sun Noon–5. MC, VISA. Parking: street.
Maybe you've seen the adorable infant and toddler suits with "Got Milk?" or "Automatic Sprinkler" or "Tax Deduction" emblazoned across the front. If you've been captivated by these whimsical outfits, this is the company you want to connect with. Those sayings may no longer be available, but you can be sure that equally clever and appealing quotes or phrases will have been created. Original and fun silk-screened graphics (critters, fruits, veg- gies, etc.) adorn the front of many other outfits, all made from 100% garment-dyed cotton. Jumpers, potty pants, big pants, dresses, jackets, and Henley

T-shirts are staples of the line. You'll want to buy one or several of these outfits if there are any kids in your sphere or if gift-giving is on the horizon—many items are packaged in clever pouches or boxes for adorable gifts. You'll save about 40% off original retails on the first-quality overruns and past-season collections. A typical infant jumper goes for about $22.50 at the outlet. Sizes: 0 (infant) to 7. No doubt you'll be charmed by the supporting cast of gift-oriented merchandise, alas sold at full retail—books, baby toiletries, plush, critters and more—an out-of-the-ordinary selection!

Also See

Under San Francisco's Factory Outlets and Off-Price Stores:
BYER FACTORY OUTLETS; CHRISTINE FOLEY; ESPRIT

Under Bay Area Manufacturers' Outlets:
PAPY BOEZ

Under Wedding and Formal Wear:
GUNNE SAX/JESSICA MCCLINTOCK

Under Family, Men's & Women's, General Clothing:
MOST LISTINGS

Under Clearance Centers:
ALL LISTINGS

Under Furniture and Home Accessories—Baby and Juvenile Furniture/Equipment:
ALL LISTINGS

Under General Merchandise—Warehouse Clubs:
COSTCO

Clearance Centers

For Major Department Stores, Catalog Companies, and Retail Chains

NORDSTROM RACK

81 Colma Boulevard, 280 Metro Center, Colma.
(650) 755-1444. M–Sat 10–9, Sun 11–7.
Nordstrom Card, MC, VISA, AE. Parking: lot.
(Other stores: Marina Square, San Leandro;
Howe Bout Arden Center, Sacramento.)
The Rack's inventory consists of clearance and
out-of-season fashions from the main Nordstrom
stores, as well as special purchases from regular
Nordstrom manufacturers (easy to spot because
some of this stuff would never be selected for the
stores). Expect to save 30–70% off Nordstrom's
original retail, and 30–50% on special purchases.
I think some of the best buys and quality are
found in the men's department. The emphasis at
the Rack is on apparel and shoes for the entire
family. Exchanges, refunds, and Nordstrom's
unconditional guarantee.

OFF FIFTH (SAKS FIFTH AVENUE OUTLET)

Great Mall of the Bay Area, Milpitas.
(408) 945-9650. Daily. MC, VISA. Parking: lot.
(Other outlet: Petaluma center.)
Saks has opened so many Off Fifth stores around
the country that my worst fears have been
realized—a decline in the overall quality of the
inventory and more and more special-purchase
fashions just for the Off Fifth division. Some very
high-profile designer names that were evident
during the first year of operation are now harder
to find. However, I still recommend scouring the
racks for the real deals: merchandise that previously graced the racks of Saks Fifth Avenue stores
or was destined for the Folio catalogs. Discriminating shoppers can cull through the career suits
and coordinates (including Petite sizes), casual
sportswear, dresses, coats, footwear, and accessories and leave with satisfying bargains. I do like
the men's department! Men's suits, sportcoats,

sportswear, furnishings, outerwear, and footwear should prompt many couples to plan tandem shopping sprees. Prices range 40–75% below original Saks Fifth Avenue prices.

TALBOTS OUTLET

1235 Marina Boulevard, Marina Square, San Leandro. (510) 614-1090. M–F 10–9, Sat 10–7, Sun 11–6. MC, VISA, AE. Parking: lot.
I have friends that arrive at the Oakland Airport and insist on a ten-minute detour down the freeway to the Talbots Outlet before going anyplace else. That's because Talbots really comes through with quality goods and solid discounts (30–60% off). It's a great favorite—drawing women from all over Northern California. Year-round, you're likely to find "nice" dresses for special occasions, some with extra dazzle for the holidays. There's a small children's department with worth-the-trip bargains. Extras include career and casual shoes, lingerie and loungewear, bathing suits, and fashion accessories. I liked the career and dress departments best of all. Savvy shoppers, don't ignore the postcards announcing special sale events. Talbots rewards petite ladies with a very extensive selec-

tion of fashions and has a better-than-average inventory of clothing for that often-neglected 14- to 20-size woman. Kudos to the staff for their gracious service. Sizes: Petite 2–16; Misses 4–20. Refunds and exchanges.

TRAVELSMITH OUTLET

Napa Premium Outlets, Napa. (707) 257-5250. www.travelsmith.com. MC, VISA, AE, DIS. Parking: street/lot.
The TravelSmith Outlet is a must for folks who rely on the popular catalog for duds and accessories for their travels. Expect 20–70% off catalog retails on returned catalog merchandise (classified as seconds), samples, and catalog overstock inventory. Apparel constitutes 80–90% of the outlet's inventory, with the rest encompassing gadgets, accessories, and luggage oriented toward the needs of world travelers. TravelSmith has garnered a loyal following of catalog shoppers who appreciate apparel for men and women that addresses the special concerns of travelers trying to pack a carry-on case with enough clothing to see them through weeks of touring. You'll find apparel with a range of useful attributes, including light weight,

wrinkle resistance, heat defiance, easy care, fast drying, convertible styling (like pants with legs that zip off to become shorts), and more. Many jacket, vest, and pant styles have security pockets or multiple compartments (like the photojournalist's vest). The overall catalog collection provides styles that work whether you're going on a back-road trek, visiting a museum, or daytripping from a cruise ship. Shoes are also a big catalog item, and you can see some of the best buys here on catalog returns.

Leather Apparel

LEATHER FACTORY OUTLET

950 Detroit Avenue #14, Concord. (925) 687-8883.
F–Sun Noon–5 (or by appointment).
MC, VISA, DIS. Parking: lot.
The Leather Factory Outlet sells leather fashions (lamb, calf, cowhide, wild boar) from better U.S. companies. The outlet is small but versatile. Men can opt for bomber styles, motorcycle jackets, blazers, flight jackets, trench coats, and long fingertip jackets, some with zip-out inserts for warmth. Women will find racks of chic butter-soft jackets and some fringed jackets. Prices are around wholesale. Most men's jackets are $99 to $289 in sizes 36–64; women's $79 to $269 in sizes XS–XXL (5/6–20).

LEATHER TO GO/GOLDEN BEAR SPORTSWEAR

200 Potrero Avenue, San Francisco. (415) 863-6171.
M–F 9–4. MC, VISA, AE. Parking: street.
The jackets from this local company are a source of much pride and satisfaction—you've seen presidents from Reagan to Clinton in casual modes sporting Leather to Go's favorite brown cowhide jacket. Buy this jacket and others at Leather to Go's factory showroom, where samples, imperfects, closeouts, and first-quality overruns are 40% off retail. If approximately $100 to $400 sounds like a good price range for better-quality leather jackets in bomber, Western, and blazer styles, or suede and shearling outerwear, you'll be right at home here. The company sells through fine stores, specialty shops, and catalogs in the United States, Europe, and Asia. Jackets with some famous labels show up on the racks. These are often production samples made for private label collections sold by well-known designers or status brands. It also

makes jackets for law enforcement agencies, athletic teams, etc. Sizes: Men's 36–46 or S–XXL; Women's 6–16.

LEATHERMODE OUTLETS

Great Mall of the Bay Area, Milpitas.
(408) 956-1899. Daily. MC, VISA, AE, DIS.
Parking: lot.
(Other outlets: Gilroy, Tracy centers.)
Leathermode is well known in Southern California with its fifteen retail stores. Excess inventory, past-season styles, and closeouts on apparel, casual luggage, handbags, executive cases, and accessories keep this outlet well stocked. First-quality fashions with labels from Kenneth Cole, Michael Lawrence, Nicole Miller, Luis Alvear, and more are reduced 20–60% off original retail. Couples can find cowhide or brushed-leather bombers, motorcycle jackets, men's full-length coats, or three-quarter-length lambskin ladies' jackets. Leather portfolios, attachés, and similar goods are all very nicely priced. Men's jackets range from $89 to $399; women's from $79 to $499. Sizes: Men's to XXL; Women's to XL. A very good leather source!

WILSONS LEATHER OUTLET

Great Mall of the Bay Area, Milpitas.
(408) 934-9095. Daily. MC, VISA, AE, DIS.
Parking: street.
Whatever your leather fantasy, they've got it here. Of course the company has the right pipeline to the goods. Men and women can buy jackets, coats, pants, vests, hats, whatever! Basics, classics, and some real high-fashion contemporary styles are in the mix. Prices reduced 20–40%.

Also See

Under Famous Labels/Factory Stores:
ANNE KLEIN; ELLEN TRACY; DONNA KARAN; MONDI

Under Bay Area Off-Price/Chain Discount Stores:
GROUP USA; LOEHMANN'S

Under Men's Apparel:
CLOTHING BROKER; G.HQ. OUTLET

Under Family, Men's & Women's,
General Clothing:
**J. CREW; LONDON FOG;
POLO/RALPH LAUREN; WOOLRICH**

Under Clearance Centers:
ALL LISTINGS

Under Handbags and Luggage:
LEATHER LOFT

Recycled Apparel

Consignment, Resale, and Thrift Shops

In today's politically correct environment there's a certain cachet to buying resale. Consumers from all income and education levels enjoy the pursuit and pleasure of finding great buys from resale, consignment, and thrift shops. A consignment shop is where one is likely to find the best quality. Usually their prices are higher than thrift shops. The affluent use these shops as a discreet way to recycle their clothing and recoup some of the original cost. Most resale shops operate on a consignment basis. Usually the potential seller brings in any items she wants to dispose of, and the store agrees to try to sell them for her for a certain percentage of the price. Other stores agree on the price the item will go for (the amount depending on the item's condition and age), and this is split fifty-fifty with the shop owner. Strictly resale shops buy outright. Either way, it's a winning proposition for everyone involved: The original owner makes a profit, the store owner makes a profit, and customers are able to buy clothes that might otherwise be out of reach. Expect to save 50–70% buying this way; when you pay $40 for a dress, it probably cost about $200 new.

At many shops, you'll find some very sophisticated clothes with designer labels. Often clothing may be as good as new—an indication that the original owner may never have worn the item. Even the best of us make mistakes with our purchases: we buy a garment that's a tad too tight and then never quite get our weight down to wearable size, or the color or style seems all wrong after consideration (and returning the merchandise to the store is no longer an option). Finding these shops is not difficult. Many advertise in community newspapers, while a quick perusal of the Yellow Pages of your phone book under "Clothing: Used" will provide a list of shops closest to you. Some shoppers "follow the money" by choosing shops in areas that are obviously supplied by an affluent clientele.

There are hundreds of resale shops around the Bay Area, and it may take time to find the ones that suit your fashion personality. Stores do vary, particularly in the standards applied to the merchandise they accept. The most discerning resale shops accept only recent fashions, in like-new condition, with recognized labels that denote quality. Some feature vintage or retro clothing, and prices may be based more on the collectible status of the goods. Always ask if there's more to see, because some shops keep the best merchandise in the back room for their regulars. As you begin your explorations, be prepared to see some stores that will leave you cold, with merchandise that's out-of-date, too tired, and presented in such a hodgepodge fashion that you can't generate any enthusiasm for shopping. If the store smells like old clothes and sweat, just leave and keep on trekking; there's a store somewhere that's perfect for you. Resale stores specializing in children's clothing are a boon to budget-pressed parents. Fortunately, there are several free publications that focus on the services, concerns, and interests of parents and their children. *Parents' Press, Bay Parent, Bay Area Baby, Valley Parent, Peninsula Parent,* and others are widely distributed at places where children and parents congregate: preschools, clinics, doctors' offices, supermarkets, and children's toy, apparel, and specialty stores. These publications are filled with advertising from children's resale and consignment stores. Many of these children's shops are also very good sources for used shoes, toys, baby equipment, books, and maternity clothing.

Cosmetics and Fragrances

In almost every shopping center around the Bay Area, you'll find a beauty supply store that offers more merchandise than you'll find in most drugstores and supermarkets. Even though the selection of hair-care, nail, and, sometimes, skin-care and beauty aids is extensive, prices all around are pretty competitive. Often these stores offer incentives for return visits, such as a card to tote up cumulative totals in purchases leading to rebates or extra discounts. It pays to stick with one store if this is the case.

CALIFORNIA THEATRICAL SUPPLY

132 Ninth Street, Second Floor, San Francisco.
(415) 863-9684. M–F 9–4. MC, VISA.
Parking: street (until 4 p.m.).
This company deals mainly with local and national television personalities, theater and opera stars, and performing troupes. The shelves offer a rainbow collection of cosmetics that fill the requirements of stage and studio. Geared for the pros, the staff is not equipped to spend time giving makeup lessons or helping you make decisions. Kryolan, Dermacolor, Mehron, and Ben Nye are the professional lines offered, along with some generic products in lipsticks, eyeshadows, foundations, pancakes, powders, blushes, mascaras, pencils, and a baffling array of brushes. Professionals buy nose putty, eyelashes, moustaches, wigs, feathers, and other tricks of the theatrical trade. Plastic surgeons refer patients here for the store's line of camouflage makeup. Planning a face-painting party for kids or fund-raisers? This is where to buy the makeup/paints that are guaranteed to wash off. Prices, while not discounted, are substantially lower than on comparable lines in department stores. You'll also see many products no longer found in department store selections.

THE COSMETIC COMPANY STORE

Napa Premium Outlets, Napa. (707) 226-3025.
Daily. MC, VISA. Parking: lot.
(Other outlet: Gilroy center.)

The company likes to keep a low profile but
I can't help sharing. If Clinique, Prescriptives,
Origins, Estée Lauder, and Bobbie Brown are
your preferred cosmetic and skin-care lines, you
can buy up a stash if you can find your particular
product—and that's the problem. Because the
inventory consists of packaging changes, discontinued colors and products, seasonal promotional sets, as-is, and overstocks, it's like roulette.
From time to time, I've been lucky to find just the
right shade of foundation, powder, or lipstick,
and have appreciated the 25 to 50% reductions.
Other times, I'm out of luck and settle for a good
buy on fragrances or various lotions, potions,
and bath products.

CRABTREE & EVELYN, LTD. OUTLET

Prime Outlets at Gilroy, Gilroy. (408) 846-9447.
www.crabtree-evelyn.com. Daily.
MC, VISA, AE, DIS. Parking: lot.

You'd be hard pressed to discern that this is a
company outlet rather than one of its very charming
retail boutiques. Same fragrant ambiance, lovely
displays, and oh-so-appealing products. The difference: discounts of 25 to 70% on discontinued
products, packaging changes, seasonal closeouts,
and surplus inventory. If you're a fan, you won't
leave without buying something—toiletries, candles,
paper goods, gourmet edibles, bath and body
products, and gifties. Occasionally, you'll find some
of the company's very feminine and fine quality
sleep and loungewear at wonderful markdowns.
Also, just to keep the inventory balanced, there
are some "favorites" carried at full retail prices.

PERFUMANIA

359 Grant Avenue, San Francisco. (415) 956-1229.
M–Sat 10–7, Sun 11–6. MC, VISA, DIS.
Parking: pay lots.
(Other stores/outlets: Anderson/Redding,
Concord, Daly City, Folsom, Gilroy, Milpitas,
Petaluma, Pleasanton, Richmond, Tracy, Vacaville.)

The first thing to do when stopping in is to pick up
the monthly flyer that highlights selected fragrance
specials: great savings on promotional merchandise, unboxed products, miniatures, testers, and

other brand-name products. Your best bet?
Special boxed gift sets. Overall, 20–60% off on
your favorite fragrances for women or men.

Also See

Under Family, Men's & Women's,
General Clothing:
ROSS; MARSHALLS; T.J. MAXX

Handbags and Luggage

BORSA FINE LEATHERS

Great Mall of the Bay Area, Milpitas.
(408) 263-9867. Daily. MC, VISA, AE, DIS.
Parking: lot.
Borsa was created by an Italian manufacturer as a store name because the manufacturer was reluctant to draw too much attention to the label on its leather goods, which are well known in Europe and Japan. In the United States much of what it makes is sold under private label by other well-known companies or designers. The label Castello may not be a household word, but that takes nothing away from the very fine quality of all of its leather handbags, wallets, and professional cases. Made to the company's specifications in China from Italian top-grain leathers, the line is very European in style and definitely classy. Prices on its handbags generally range from $100 to $200 at discount; small leather goods and wallets from $9 to $50; and document cases/totes from $200 to $300. Other better quality and fine handbag lines are also carried: Kenneth Cole, Liz Claiborne, Perlina, Valentino, Romeo (from Italy), and others are discounted at least 20% off—and usually more. Look for designated weekly specials of another 20% off. Returns and refunds up to five days, returns up to fourteen days. Close to the Airplane Court entrance at the mall.

BRIGGS & RILEY TRAVELWARE OUTLET

850 Airport Street (behind Half Moon Bay airport), Moss Beach. (650) 728-6155. www.briggs-riley.com.
M–F 8:30–4:30. MC, VISA. AE. Parking: lot.
It's a lovely and scenic drive down to this outlet, a trade-off for the extra time and mileage invested in tracking down luggage bargains. Briggs & Riley is a specialty maker of travel bags. It offers one of the best warranties in the business on first-quality merchandise purchased from a retailer—free repairs on any problem, even if caused by the

airline. This doesn't apply to discontinued styles, seconds, samples, and refurbished travel bags and luggage sold at the outlet every day at 50–60% off original retails. Briggs & Riley's five collections are made from tough, wear-resistant, water-repellent, ballistic nylon. Every detail—from form to seam to zipper—has been carefully crafted for easy functionality and unparalleled durability. Look for pieces from the BRX Collection for a diverse assortment of casual bags or to the Baseline Collection for the most bag choices. Overall, you'll find uprights, garment bags, backpacks, travel bags, business cases, totes, carry-ons, and accessories. Examples of 1999 outlet pricing: dye imperfections on a group of 26-inch wide verticals with garment carriers were priced at $216 (retail when perfect $557). A discontinued style of a 21-inch vertical carry-on with garment carrier was $125 (originally $325). Seconds of a 17-inch tote bag in black or olive were $65 (retail $170 if perfect).

CALIFORNIA LUGGAGE OUTLET

Premium Outlets at Napa, Napa. (707) 259-1146. www.california-luggage.com. Daily. MC, VISA, AE, DIS. Parking: lot.

(Other outlet: Vacaville center.)
You have to wonder if anyone buys luggage at retail anymore. This store is owned by El Portal Luggage & Leather Goods, usually found in shopping malls. It's capturing some business from bargain hunters by offering 20–50% discounts on major brands: Tumi, Samsonite, Delsey, Skyway, Travelpro, and Lark. All types of luggage, plus backpacks, soft weekend bags, travel accessories, games, and more.

CHOICE LUGGAGE

1742 El Camino Real, Mountain View. (650) 968-3479. M–F 10–7:30, Sat 10–6. MC, VISA, AE. Parking: lot.
Choice offers bargain prices on an extensive inventory of brand-name garment bags, carry-on luggage, and tote bags from moderate to top-of-the-line companies. You'll find Briggs & Riley, Skyway, Samsonite, Atlantic, Halliburton, Andiamo, Travelpro, Delsey, Eagle Creek, and others. It also stocks small travel accessories, men's over-the-shoulder pouches, fine leather wallets, and attachés. Exchanges allowed only within 30 days of purchase.

THE COACH STORE

St. Helena Premium Outlets, St. Helena.
(707) 963-7272. Daily. MC, VISA, AE.
Parking: street.
(Other store: Carmel.)

At Coach stores, everything is "value priced,"
20–50% off retail. The leathers may have surface
flaws, but usually the merchandise is simply
discontinued. Travelers might consider its leather
duffels, carry-ons, and totes. Men should stop in
for an executive case, belt, wallet, or travel kit,
and examine its handsome line of ties. Ladies
will naturally zero in on the handbags that constitute about 75% of the store's overall selection.
Anything made by Coach might be available,
including pocket diaries or organizers. Prices
average 26% off original retail; 50% discounts can
be found on the special sale tables. All merchandise bears a discreet mark inside noting that the
item was purchased from a Coach value-priced
store. This should not deter you from buying any
item as a gift.

EDWARDS LUGGAGE OUTLET

Great Mall of the Bay Area, Milpitas.
(408) 934-9559. Daily. MC, VISA, AE, DIS.
Parking: lot.

Edwards puts on a new personality with this
clearance outlet, a fun, high-energy store in keeping with the Great Mall's orientation. Customers
love the mock airline cabin with seats and overhead bins. The focus is on travel everything: a
variety of luggage, attachés, travel aids (security,
passport cases, personal accessories, etc.),
games, maps, and books. Discontinued inventory
from its posh full-price stores—agendas, business
cases, computer bags, and women's small leather
goods—are sold at 20–50% off original retail.
Better brands of luggage such as Hartmann, Tumi,
Lark, and Samsonite are 30–50% off retail on
seconds, overruns, and discontinued colors.

GLASER DESIGNS

*32 Otis Street (at S. Van Ness and Mission),
San Francisco. (415) 552-3188.
M–F 9:30–5:30, Sat Noon–5. MC, VISA.
Parking: street/pay lot off Brady Alley.*

The emphasis here is on high-end, long-lasting handmade travel gear that costs a lot, but less than comparable lines sold in status stores. Glaser's handsome travel and custom-finished leather/fabric garment and stadium bags cost $500 to $700; packing cases are in the $400 to $500 range. Customers have inspired innovations like the "insiders"—stretch-proof nylon mesh containers to organize travel goods. Business travelers also appreciate its Traveler's briefcases, which double as computer bags ($700 to $800). Garment bags are designed to "stand" when folded so that they won't collapse on your garments. You'll find a few seconds year-round, but most customers are willing to pay premium prices for the regular merchandise and feel the quality/price/value ratio is reasonable.

HANDBAG FACTORY OUTLET

*2100 Fifth Street, Berkeley. (510) 843-6022.
M–F 8:30–5, Sat 10–4:30. MC, VISA. Parking: lot.*

You'll bag some great buys here, even though the prices are not cheap. This anonymous outfit manufactures a moderate- to high-priced line (retail $36 to $200). The handbags have casual inclinations, but they're classy enough for executive dressing. You'll find discontinued items, samples, and seconds with minor flaws for 30–60% off retail. All its bags are made from superior-grade leathers. You'll have your choice of style with compartments and pockets. Expect to spend about $80 for a midsized bag. The color range is very good, with all the basics and some fashion hues. Fanny packs, backpacks, and wallets are also popular here; the wallets and belts at discount are from other manufacturers.

HCL HANDBAG AND LEATHER GOODS OUTLET

1111 East Francisco Boulevard, Suite B,
San Rafael. (415) 458-8228. M–F 10–4. MC, VISA.
Parking: lot.

If you have no qualms about spending over $100, $200, or $400 for a memorable status handbag, at 40–60% off original retails, you'll have a field day here. HCL, a European-based company, makes a status, high-end, and expensive line of handbags, small leather goods, and luggage. Handbags most often sell "under the glass" at status stores. Discontinued styles and colors, seconds, samples, and returned goods are available at the company's small clearance outlet. All HCL items are made of the finest topgrain cowhide with a pig-suede lining. Hardware is goldplated. The lines are available in two different collections: Signature (its well-known logo print) and Vintage (nonprinted leather). Choose from classic neutrals or fashion colors. Latch onto some small leather goods that include wallets, credit card holders, eyeglass cases, pill boxes, key chains, sewing kits, etc. They make classy little gifts. Just to keep everything on the up and up, each handbag or luggage piece bears an interior mark denoting the item was purchased at the outlet; however, gift buyers won't find the marks a deterrent.

LEATHER LOFT

Factory Stores at Vacaville, Vacaville.
(707) 446-7262. Daily. MC, VISA, AE, DIS.
Parking: lot.
(Other outlets: Folsom, Gilroy, Milpitas,
Pacific Grove, Petaluma centers.)

Leather Loft stocks its 200-plus factory stores with handbags, belts, wallets, briefcases, travel and desk accessories, gifts, designer accessories, and a small array of leather jackets. The selection includes timeless classic styles as well as the latest color or design. You'll find first-quality merchandise and closeouts. Discounts are 25–60% off retail. Handbags for every budget from $25 to $225. The leather jackets deserve a close look!

LUGGAGE CENTER

828 Mission Street (across from Fifth and Mission
Garage), San Francisco. (415) 543-3771. M–F
8:30–6, Sat 10–5, Sun 11:30–5. MC, VISA, AE, DIS.
Parking: street/pay lots.
(Other stores: Berkeley, Burlingame, Cupertino,

Daly City, Dublin, Emeryville, Los Gatos, Mountain View, Pleasant Hill, Redwood City, Sacramento, San Jose, San Rafael, Vacaville, Walnut Creek. See Geographical Index.)

The Luggage Center offers solid discounts to first-class as well as economy-minded travelers. The luggage is first-line merchandise, open stock, and special purchases from companies like Skyway, Samsonite, Eagle Creek, Delsey, Travelpro, Halliburton, and others. There are no seconds. Savings are 20–50%. The inventory includes all types of luggage and a wide variety of travel accessories, totes, attachés, and wallets. Exchanges and refunds within 30 days with receipt.

LUGGAGE TO GO

75 Bellam Boulevard, Marin Square, San Rafael. (415) 459-5167. M–Sat 10–6, Sun Noon–5. MC, VISA, AE. Parking: lot.

This store's discounts are 20–60% off retail on luggage (many current styles and fabrications), plus bonus pricing on special manufacturers' promotions, factory purchases, and leftovers from the owner's Beverly Hills store. Attachés, luggage, and almost anything required for carrying goodies on a trip are stocked. The selection is particularly choice for those wanting better lines not often found at discount. You'll like these labels: Samsonite, Lark, Delsey, Halliburton, Travelpro, Hartmann, the French Co., and more. The beautiful Italian leather collection is for the very chic. Monogramming is free—how nice!

MALM WAREHOUSE & REPAIR

1429 Burlingame Avenue, Burlingame. (650) 343-0990. M–F 9–6, Sat 10–6, Sun Noon–5. MC, VISA, AE, DIS. Parking: street.

Malm offers new suitcases, carry-ons, garment bags, and more from its inventory of discontinued and slightly irregular luggage. Hartmann, Tumi, Lark, Delsey, and Samsonite are some of the brands you'll find at 25–50% markdowns. Take care of details with a discounted portfolio, attaché, toiletry kit, business case, agenda, or small leather goods. Repairs, too—a complete service for luggage and attachés. Free monogramming.

ROCKRIDGE LUGGAGE & LEATHER GOODS

5816 College Avenue, Oakland. (510) 428-2247.
M–F 10–7, Sat 10–6. MC, VISA, AE.
Parking: underground garage.
This company manages to cram an extensive
selection of luggage from many recognized companies into its small space: Tumi, Briggs & Riley,
Atlantic, Samsonite, Travelpro, Andiamo, Eagle
Creek, Jansport, and others. Discounts every day
are 20–40% off retail. Students will have any number of choices when it comes to choosing a pack
to tote heavy textbooks, while executives can find
a leather attaché, portfolio, or briefcase in just the
right configuration and size. Travel carts, small
leather goods, gift items, and pens are the right
price for gift givers.

SAMSONITE COMPANY STORE

Great Mall of the Bay Area, Milpitas.
(408) 946-7785. Daily. MC, VISA, AE, DIS.
Parking: lot.
(Other outlets: Folsom, Gilroy, Pacific Grove,
Tracy, Vacaville centers.)
Samsonite seems to own it all—American
Tourister, Lark, and many other companies. Its
company stores are well stocked with molded and
soft-sided luggage, along with sport bags, backpacks, handbags, Buxton wallets, travel accessories, and business cases. These are closeouts
and irregulars with minor cosmetic flaws. You'll
also find a fair amount of first-quality merchandise.
Discounts overall are 40–70% off retail. Same
discounts apply on the U.S. Luggage, Jansport,
LaSalle, and Jourdan collections of luggage,
duffels, totes, and travel accessories.

SVEN DESIGN

2301 Fourth Street, Berkeley. (510) 848-7836.
M–F 10–5, Sat 1–5. MC, VISA. Parking: street.
Sven's outlet showcases its line, which it sells
primarily through craft shows and boutiques,
although selected styles show up in status department stores. About 75% of the selection here is
current season offered at 20% discount. Handbag
prices are $22 to $100; you'll find deeper discounts (40–50% off retail) only on closeouts and
discontinued styles. Its drum-dyed leather requires
skilled artisanship (which means higher prices).
Fine-quality construction features suit the most
exacting requirements. Handbags come in neu-

trals and fashion colors, plus a few styles in exotic leathers or tapestry fabrics, serving traditional and contemporary tastes. You'll also find totes, book bags, fanny packs, and minibags/wallets with detachable straps. The handbags here are not inexpensive, but if quality is your concern and you feel that a little saving is better than none, you'll be very pleased.

THE WALLET WORKS

Pacific West Outlet Center, Gilroy. (408) 842-7488. Daily. MC, VISA, DIS. Parking: street/pay lots. (Other outlets: Napa, Pacific Grove, Petaluma centers.)

The Wallet Works is perhaps known best for its wallets, available in department stores around the country. Think of a leather item in any configuration made to hold money, credit cards, or passports, and it'll be here, plus portfolios, soft luggage, fanny packs, daily organizers, tote bags, and portable coolers. The handbag selection is tempting, too. The few seconds are clearly marked, with extra discounts as the tradeoff. Discounts range from a modest 20 to 60% off retail.

Also See

Under Women's Apparel/Fashion:
ALL LISTINGS

Under Family, Men's & Women's, General Clothing:
ALL LISTINGS

Under Shoes:
ETIENNE AIGNER; TIMBERLAND

Under General Merchandise—Discount Stores, Warehouse Clubs:
ALL LISTINGS

Jewelry and Watches

Fine and Costume Jewelry, Diamonds, and Watches

Some ABCs on Buying Fine Jewelry

If you're buying fine jewelry for the first time, you're probably quite wary, because diamonds, gemstones, and gold don't come with labels and brands that make comparison shopping easy. You may feel ill-equipped to determine quality and value, to be sure that you're buying at a fair price, or know if you're paying more than you have to. If you are armed with some basics about buying jewelry—using common sense, taking time, asking questions, and, above all, comparison shopping—you need not hesitate to venture out of malls or high-profile jewelers to make your purchase.

A word about diamonds: Two diamonds that look alike at first may be very different, and two diamonds of equal size can have very unequal values. Because no two diamonds are alike, experts use four criteria to determine a diamond's value: the "Four Cs"—carat, color, clarity, and cut. The different combinations of all these characteristics determine the quality and value of a diamond.

AZEVEDO JEWELERS & GEMOLOGISTS, INC.

210 Post Street, Third Floor, Suite 321, San Francisco. (415) 781-0063. T–Sat 10:30–5. MC, VISA. Parking: pay lots.
Azevedo offers a beautiful selection of diamonds, colored stones, gold jewelry, and cultured pearls at substantial savings; its success is due to low overhead, careful buying, and referrals from satisfied customers. Appraisals are done by graduate gemologists. Its showroom is very classy, but most of the jewels are kept under wraps for obvious security reasons. Azevedo features jewelry designed by Oscar Heyman & Bros. at the lowest prices you'll find in the Bay Area. This is one of six American Gem Society stores in San Francisco.

BARBINI STUDIO OUTLET

*2599 Eighth Street #41, Berkeley. (888) 704-0203.
M–F 10–5, (most) Sat 11–5. MC, VISA.
Parking: street.*

For some very original fashion jewelry, take a peek into this boutique-sized outlet. Maybe you'll recognize the line—"People Pins" with over 60 familiar faces engaged in various activities, including sports, hobbies, and professions. They're fabricated from 24K gold and rhodium-plated metals. They're fun and almost guaranteed to grab a smile. Free up your hands with a necklace pouch. These are elegantly designed, in various sizes, to hold eyeglasses, cell phones, credit cards, keys or cosmetics. The lambskin pouches hang from metal chains decorated with swirls, beads, and other adornments. The contemporary, mixed metal earrings and pins are usually spotted under the glass in museum gift shops around the country. Buy any of the leftovers from these three collections and you'll save about half off retail. Prices range from $5 (bargain baskets) to about $30.

BEADCO/SMALL THINGS COMPANY

*760 Market Street (Phelan Building), Suite 860,
San Francisco. (415) 397-0110. M–F 10–4, other
hours and Sat by appointment. Cash/Check, VISA.
Parking: pay lots.*

This company's talent lies in finding maximum value for the best price, using connections developed over the years. If you're interested in a special gift—pearls, lapis, jade, diamonds, precious gemstones, gold, or silver—Beadco probably has it in stock, or can find it, usually at a price 30–60% lower than conventional retailers. Contact Beadco if you need pearls restrung, plating, jewelry repaired (including sterling silver and costume jewelry) or remodeled, a custom design, or an appraisal. Creating innovative wedding rings is the store's special pleasure. Unless you're coming in for repairs, it's essential to call for an appointment.

BRODER JEWELRY COMPANY

*210 Post Street, Room 611, San Francisco.
(415) 421-9313. Tues–F 9:30–3:30, Sat by
appointment. Cash/Check. Parking: pay lots.*
Mr. Broder does custom design, appraisals, and repair work for many of San Francisco's finest

jewelry stores and works closely with a private clientele, creating special pieces like rings, pendants, and bracelets. However, he does not sell watches or other items usually found in jewelry stores. His closet-sized office has no stock on hand, so this is definitely not a store for casual browsing. If you have a picture of a design, bring it in, or Mr. Broder can create one. His low overhead accounts for the low prices on diamonds and colored stones and on anything he can special-order from a large number of manufacturers and their catalogs. Naturally, if you need a ring sized, repaired, or reset, his talents are at your disposal. One of the few jewelers who works in platinum. A 50% deposit is required before custom orders are started.

CRESALIA JEWELERS DIAMOND EXPERTISE

111 Sutter Street (at Montgomery), San Francisco.
(415) 781-7371 or (800) 781-7371.
www.cresaliajewelers.com. M–Sat 9:30–5:30.
MC, VISA, AE, DIS. Parking: validated parking
in garage next block.
Cresalia displays an extensive selection of diamond rings, fine jewels, and watches. It designs and manufactures its own rings and carries well-known brands as well. You'll recognize the companies in its selection: Artcarved, Italiano gold, Kobe pearls, Krementz, Gorham, Reed & Barton, Lunt, Wallace, Ballou, Sheffield, Kirk, and Cross pens just for starters. Prices are guaranteed to be 25–50% below regular retail prices. Cresalia has a staff of graduate gemologists from the Gemological Institute of America to help you choose a diamond or gem, and to grade and appraise jewelry you own. If you're shopping for elegant gifts, you'll appreciate the extensive array of silverware, crystal, clocks, hollowware, china, and dinner accessories that can be wrapped and shipped UPS if requested.

DESIGNER ACCESSORIES OUTLET

2660 Harrison Street, San Francisco.
(415) 821-9971. Sat 10–4. Cash/Check.
Parking: street.
A woman can never have too many earrings, or pins, or pendants, or belts. That's never more evident than when trying to choose just a few pieces to buy at this outlet for a local manufacturer of mixed-metal jewelry collections. The line is sold by many famous stores and well-known fashion

mail-order catalogs. The leftovers—samples and discontinued collections—are reduced to about half off wholesale in the outlet. Although designs are contemporary, there are earrings understated enough for corporate boardrooms and earrings that dangle for expressing one's liberation on Saturday nights. Both clip and post styles are available. Clip-earring wearers can afford to buy a spare pair to make up for the inevitable lost earring. Average pricing at retail: Earrings range from $30 to $60; necklaces/pendants $30 to $70; belts $60 to $120; bracelets $18 to $50; and pins $20 to $40. It's possible to match up earrings, pins, or necklaces for a very nice gift set. Your biggest challenge? Resisting the temptation to go overboard and buy, buy, buy! *Note: The hours for the outlet are still being fine-tuned, so a call ahead might be prudent.*

DOROTHY BAUER DESIGNS

1015 Camelia Street (one block south of Gilman), Berkeley. (510) 527-2431. M–F Noon–6, Sat 10–4. MC, VISA. Parking: street.

This company manufactures a somewhat esoteric (to my mind) line of funky, novelty, whimsical, and appealing rhinestone jewelry. Collectors buy some very special Dorothy Bauer pieces under the glass at better stores. Prices are half off wholesale. Most pins are $7.50 to $30 (some can go as high as $100); earrings $10 to $40. Some themes: sports, wildlife, domestic pets, Christmas, patriotic symbols, flowers, recreational activities, and words and expressions (like one that I should have: "I Love to Shop"). These are all discontinued, prototypes, samples, mistakes, and occasional seconds. A popular store for collectors of rhinestone jewelry.

THE FENTON COMPANY

210 Post Street, Suite 203, San Francisco. (415) 563-0258. By appointment. Cash/Check. Parking: pay lots.

Joan Fenton serves as a personal jewelry shopper. In her twelve and a half years in business, Joan has helped many brides, professional women, and "awfully smart men." She keeps no inventory, and her low overhead lets her pass on good prices to her discriminating clientele. She knows how to get things done and brings a sense of style and charm along with her expertise to her business. Call for an appointment to assess your needs. When Joan knows what you want, she can present choices that meet the specifications of size and price that you've requested. Using her trade resources, she'll either find it for you or have it custom-designed at wholesale prices plus a slight markup, generally 10–20%.

FOSSIL

Prime Outlets at Gilroy, Gilroy. (408) 848-2709. Daily. MC, VISA, AE, DIS. Parking: lot.
Fossil achieved fame with its fashion watches, popular with a younger and hipper crowd. It didn't take long before the company was expanding into sunglasses, belts, ties, sweatshirts, women's handbags, and fashion jewelry. All these things are sold at about 30% off original retail. There's usually a $19.99 watch or sunglasses special on selected styles. Look for other exceptional savings on closeouts and discontinued styles.

GOLDEN K FINE JEWELRY

2229 Bunker Hill Drive (off Hwy. 280), San Mateo. (650) 349-2912. M–Sat by appointment. Cash/Check. Parking: street.
If you have old jewelry tucked away and you'd like to have it updated, reset, or repaired, this company can do the job. For years Golden K has worked with prominent jewelry stores creating custom designs and repairing gold, platinum, and precious stones. It has also created replacement jewelry for insurance claims. You can bring in stones for setting, or stones can be purchased for you if you know what you want. No inventory is kept on the premises. If you want a wedding set, ring, or piece designed, you can browse through wholesale catalogs, or you can bring in a picture. When updating jewelry, the gold or platinum in your jewelry can be reused. (No work is done with sterling silver jewelry.) Although this small studio is not a conventional retail setting, I think customers will feel very comfortable here. However, it's important to schedule an appointment, because Golden K is not set up for walk-in business. I think you'll find the savings very worthwhile, and the work is done to the highest standards.

GUARDIAN INTERNATIONAL

150 Bellam Boulevard, Suite 240, San Rafael.
(415) 258-0601. M–F 9–5, Sat by appointment.
MC, VISA. Parking: street.

Guardian International has solid credentials. When buying directly from this source, you'll save about 35% off the "major store price." If you need something fast, you'll be able to find something that's just right. Guardian provides extraordinary quality in original custom designs, and special orders are its forte. It keeps a good inventory of diamonds up to one carat and can readily provide larger sizes upon request. If you're in the market for a status watch (most priced over $1,000 at retail) such as Bertolucci, Omega, Cartier, Rolex, and many more, you can pick a style from a notebook full of catalogs, and on most lines you'll pay just 10% over Guardian's cost. Don't come in expecting to see several cases of fine jewelry. It's more of an office serving its private clientele (the public) on an appointment basis.

HOCHERMAN & SON JEWELERS

760 Market Street, Suites 346–348, San Francisco.
(415) 986-4066. www.irahocherman.com.
M–F 8:30–4:30 by appointment. MC, VISA.
Parking: pay garages.

"Bargain" is a relative term. Even at great values, a fine piece of jewelry purchased at Hocherman & Son may still be quite expensive depending on your perspective and budget. It's not set up for casual browsing, because most of its work is done on a custom-design basis. Many couples come here seeking unusual settings (true works of art) for wedding rings and will spend $6,000 to $8,000 for a ring that would cost $12,000 to $14,000 at a Union Square jeweler. Of course, other customers spend much less, especially on wedding bands, gemstone jewelry or pearls, or jewelry resetting. If you'd like estate jewelry reset or want to rework original wedding sets into something more up-to-date, consider this resource. The company keeps an extensive selection of loose diamonds and gemstones on hand and works with you to develop a design for your jewelry piece. There are modest charges for designing the model and renderings, and work proceeds with a 50% deposit.

MOVADO COMPANY STORE

St. Helena Premium Outlets, St. Helena.
(707) 967-0738. Daily. MC, VISA, AE. Parking: lot.
Upscale buyers are very impressed by the watches
they see under lock and key at Movado. Some are
seconds with small cosmetic surface imperfections.
Others are discontinued styles. Whatever the
"flaw," the movements inside are perfect and the
watches are under full warranty. You don't have to
be rich to shop here, because you can find many
styles priced $100 to $300. On the other hand,
you can buy Concord watches, solid gold pieces
with diamonds, solid gold pieces with leather
straps and also two-tone gold and stainless steel
starting at $400. Movado's 14K solid-gold watches
are priced at $400 and up, while its sportier
Esquire line goes for $30 to $300. The new Coach
collection watches range from $125 to $350.
Overall discounts are 20–70% off original retail.
Buy with care because there are no refunds;
exchanges only within 10 days with receipt for an
item of equal or higher value. This elegant store
hardly seems to fit the term "bargain," but you
will be surprised.

TAYLOR & JACOBSON

1475 N. Broadway (Lincoln Broadway Building),
Suite 490, Walnut Creek. (925) 937-9570. M–F 9–6
by appointment. MC, VISA. Parking: garage
across street.
The best values are often found in the least likely
locations. This company does most of its business
with stores that use its custom fabricating,
diamond-setting, and repair service. Essentially a
wholesaler, it also works directly with local
consumers.

It doesn't claim to sell at wholesale prices (how
refreshing!), but it certainly offers substantial
savings. It has a display case with many dazzling
rings; however, most of its available settings are
kept in trays or are represented in wax patterns
that you can try on. Engagement rings and
wedding sets are a specialty. Services include
repair, remounts, sizing, repronging, reshanking,
and polishing. You can choose from loose stones
including diamonds, jade, lapis lazuli, pearls,
and other precious and semiprecious beauties.
Appointments are essential to get through the
locked doors.

ZWILLINGER & CO.

*760 Market Street (Phelan Building), Suite 800,
San Francisco. (415) 392-4086. www.citysearch.com
/sfo/zwillinger. T–Sat 9:30–5. MC, VISA, AE, DIS.
Parking: downtown pay garages.*

You'll feel more comfortable if you wear your
Sunday best before entering the vaultlike security
doors of this firm, which has been in the same
location for the past fifty years. For those great
occasions in life—engagements, anniversaries,
graduations—when you desire a very special
memento, a piece of fine jewelry can be purchased
here at considerable savings (20–50% off retail).
Prices on 14K and 18K gold and platinum jewelry,
watches, and diamond rings are very impressive.
You can create your own wedding set by selecting
a mounting with or without stone, and then pick a
center diamond of the size and quality to fit your
budget. The selection of loose diamonds is breathtaking! Discriminating women and men appreciate
the large array of fashion jewelry from such noted
designers as Charles Garnier, Winward, Judith
Conway, Garaveli Aldo, Gemveto, and others
usually seen advertised in *Architectural Digest,
Connoisseur, Town & Country,* et al. If Zwillinger
doesn't have a particular piece in stock, bring in a
picture; chances are the piece can be ordered or
custom-made for you. Watches from Omega,
Movado, Seiko, and other status brands ($3,000-
plus range) are available. Graduates from the
Gemological Institute of America are on staff.
Appraisals and full jewelry repairs are done.
Zwillinger buys diamonds and replacement jewelry for several large insurance companies. First-
time jewelry buyers will be in good hands.

Also See

Under Women's Accessories:
ALL LISTINGS

Under Giftware and Home Decor:
ALL LISTINGS

Under General Merchandise:
ALL LISTINGS

Shoes

ADIDAS

Prime Outlets at Gilroy, Gilroy. (408) 842-1638. Daily. MC, VISA, AE, DIS. Parking: lot. (Other outlet: Vacaville center.)

If the company's advertising campaigns are on target, Adidas needs no introduction. Count on shoes for active sports—basketball, soccer, running, and training. Discounts range from 30–50% on average, up to 75% off on the these-have-got-to-go special markdowns. Shoes may have small cosmetic blemishes or be discontinued styles. Sizes: Men's 6½–15; Women's 5–10; Youth 8½–6; Children 4–8. All sales final. An extra—Adidas nylon jogging sets priced at $59.

ATHLETE'S FOOT OUTLET

1237 Marina Boulevard, Marina Square (next to Talbots), San Leandro. (510) 895-9738. M–F 10–9, Sat 10–7, Sun 11–6. MC, VISA, AE, DIS. Parking: lot. (Other outlet: Great Mall, Milpitas.)

Most parents cringe at the prospect of outfitting their children with new shoes, especially the Nike, Reebok, and Adidas types. Athlete's Foot Outlets carry the major high-profile brands of shoes for crosstraining, tennis, soccer, football, basketball, aerobics, running, track, and all-around everyday wear. Prices at this self-service store are reduced 15–60% off retail, averaging about 30% off retail, plus occasional super markdowns. Sizes for the whole family start with Infant 0–8; Children's 1½–6; Youth 10½–13; Women's 5½–11; Men's 6½–15. Also, T-shirts, shorts, sweats, and warm-ups. Refunds or exchanges within 30 days with receipt.

BANISTER SHOE STUDIO

Great Mall of the Bay Area, Milpitas.
(408) 956-9928. Daily. MC, VISA, AE, DIS.
Parking: lot.
(Other outlets: Folsom, Gilroy, Pacific Grove
centers.)

These outlets are part of the Nine West Group
and showcase all its labels. Women's fashion shoe
collections from Calico, Bandolino, Easy Spirit,
Evan-Picone, Amalfi, Pappagallo, and others are
moderately discounted every day. Prices are more
enticing during special sale times. The shoes are
nicely displayed in sizes 6–10 (a few 11s).

BASS SHOE OUTLET

Prime Outlets at Gilroy, Gilroy. (408) 842-3632.
Daily. MC, VISA, DIS. Parking: lot.
(Other outlets: Lake Tahoe, Pacific Grove,
Petaluma, Truckee, Vacaville centers.)

Finding the perfect vacation walking shoe is
difficult, especially if you're trying to find a style
that won't get you arrested by the fashion police.
Bass provides the comfort and style to take you
through hours of museums and miles of city
streets. You'll find the original Bass Weejuns,
Sunjuns, and Saddles, as well as the latest fashion
footwear to take you from the beach to the
boardroom. Prices reflect 15–30% discounts on
most styles and up to 50% discounts on some
seconds. Also, belts, duffels, totes, wallets,
shoelaces, mink oil, and more at discount prices.
A few stores showcase Bass's weekend sportswear
lines for men, women, and kids. If you'd like, they
offer free shipping to your home on special offers.

BIRKENSTOCK FOOTPRINT

Prime Outlets at Gilroy, Gilroy. (408) 848-1602.
Daily. MC, VISA, AE. Parking: lot.

Those funny-looking shoes are no longer considered funky. Mainstream America has embraced
the comfort of the contoured footbed. It helps
that Birkenstock now makes so many styles that
there's one for every personality and situation.
There are Birkenstocks to slip on, buckle up, or
lace, with open or closed heels and toes. You'll
find styles for beachcombing or for wearing into
the office on dress-down Fridays, and you'll find
"professionals"—shoes for those who stand on
their feet or walk on the job. This is the only outlet
in the country, and here prices are reduced

30–50% off original retail on discontinued styles or seconds. (The seconds have cosmetic imperfections.) All shoes in European sizing—refer to wall charts for translation. American sizes: Men's 5–17½; Women's 4–13½; Kids 7–3. Options are expanded with the unisex styling of many shoes.

BOOT & SHOE OUTLET

2810 Bay Road, Redwood City. (650) 369-5615.
M–F 11–7, Sat 11–5. MC, VISA.
Parking: street or lot.
I'm sworn to secrecy on this brand name. One hint I can give you, people come from miles around to buy this line. You won't be disappointed if comfort, quality, style, and price are your hallmarks of a savvy buy. Prices at 50–70% off original retails are posted on discontinued styles, colors, and blems (usually minor imperfections on the leather). The great looking collection of shoes and boots (for working hard or just loafing and looking chic) are destined to become classic wardrobe favorites. The boots have an advanced design that ensures stability, support, and comfort. The footbed provides exceptional internal cushioning. Gel inserts at the forefoot and heel cushion and protect small bones and nerves. These same technical advances have been incorporated into a collection of "lifestyle" shoes that are showing up in the shoe departments of status stores. Sandals, slip-on loafers, slides, classic oxfords, and half boots are some of the shoe styles geared for casual wear. Men's sizes 7–13; Women's sizes 5½–11½ (occasional 12s). A caveat: don't expect complete size or color ranges in any particular style. During one visit, everyone except those wearing size 10 had to pass up a fabulous $200-plus boot marked down to $49 (no other sizes were available). This situation repeats itself in some version or the other throughout the outlet's inventory; however from what I've observed at the outlet, no one leaves empty-handed.

BOOT FACTORY

Factory Stores at Vacaville, Vacaville.
(707) 449-6429. Daily. MC, VISA, AE, DIS.
Parking: lot.
(Other outlets: Gilroy, Shasta/Anderson centers.)
Take the whole family up to the Boot Factory for rompin', stompin' Western-style boots, and serious work and outdoor boots. You'll find cosmetic

irregulars or discontinued styles from a famous Texas-based maker of traditional boots and its Western-inspired, more contemporary label. Prices $40 to $400; most average $75 to $100. About half the shelf space is devoted to sturdy and heavy casual boots; insulated, waterproof, and leather hiking boots; and some steel-toe work boots for men. Catch these labels: Wolverine, Doc Martens, and Caterpillar in steel or nonsteel toes. Take a hike in Hi-Tec, HH, Texan Boot, J. Chisholm, Yukon, and Brown. Kids love the cowboy/cowgirl boots! Sizes: Women's 5–11; Men's 7–13; some wide widths for men and women. Most boots appear discounted about 35–40% off original retail (during special sales prices to 60% off).

BROWN BROS. SHOES

848 Lincoln Avenue (at Ninth Street), Alameda. (510) 865-3701. M–Sat 9:30–6. MC, VISA. Parking: street.
Brown Bros.' shoes are all first quality, in up-to-date styles from Florsheim, Kenneth Cole, Stacy Adams, Dexter, and Rockport. It's strictly a men's shoe store with sizes 6–15 to EEE widths. It sells athletic shoes for solid discount prices and has

some of the lowest-priced work boots that I've found, which is why so many hardworking fellas come here from miles around. You'll always find a good shoe at a reasonable price, usually 25–35% off retail. Exchanges and refunds allowed.

CAROLE'S SHOE RACK

851 Cherry Avenue, San Bruno. (650) 869-5300. M–F 10–7, Sat 10–6, Sun 11–5. MC, VISA, AE, DIS. Parking: lot.
Carole's is a self-service operation displaying an intriguing selection of shoes warehouse-style. There are funky, fashion, conventional, and sporty styles—occasionally including a few dogs. Buying liquidations, overruns, and clearance inventories yields an extensive variety of dress heels (including chic imports from Italy and Spain), boots, and casuals. Men can buy nice Italian dress and casual shoes (average price $40 to $80). Savings 30–60% off retail (average discount 40–50% off). Sizes: Women's 5½–12; Men's, a few 5s to 13. The racks of women's apparel offer some unpredictable and surprisingly good buys—worth a peek.

COLE-HAAN

Napa Premium Outlets, Napa. (707) 258-0898.
Daily. MC, VISA, AE, DIS. Parking: lot.
If you love Cole-Haan shoes but hate the price tags, you'll find a measure of savings at its elegant factory store. Collections of shoes for women and men are about one season behind and priced 20–50% off retail. In addition to its signature shoe styles, Cole-Haan stocks nicely executed luggage, handbags, belts, and small leather goods. Those seeking shoes in narrow or wide widths, small or extra-large sizes, will want to splurge when they find these shoes available—an unpredictable occurrence. Those wearing medium or narrow widths have the most options when shopping. Sizes: Women's 5–11 AAAA–W; Men's 7–15 B–D (a few Es).

DEXTER FACTORY SHOES

Petaluma Village Premium Outlets, Petaluma.
(707) 773-3802. www.dexterfactorystores.com.
Daily. MC, VISA, AE, DIS. Parking: lot.
(Other outlets: Folsom, Gilroy centers.)
If you're a "Buy American" consumer, then head to this Maine-based manufacturer (one of the few American shoe manufacturers left) to get fitted for work and casual shoes. Dexter concentrates on the classics in casual and conservative dressier shoes and leaves the trendy stuff to others. Expect comfort footwear (hiking, golf, and bowling shoes, too) in a wide range of sizes that includes a double-wide. Keep an eye peeled for color-coded tags leading to extra 20–50% discounts off everyday discount prices. Sizes: Men's 7–14; Women's 5–11.

EASY SPIRIT

1253 Marina Boulevard, Marina Square,
San Leandro. (510) 352-8804. Daily. MC, VISA,
AE, DIS. Parking: lot.
(Other outlets: Gilroy, Vacaville.)
If you're standing on your feet all day, in uniform or out, then comfy shoes are essential. Easy Spirit shoes have gained great popularity for their comfort-enhancing features. At the outlet you'll find serious work, dress, and casual styles, flats and heels, reduced about 20–30% every day with frequent promotions that bring prices down even more. I also spotted a few Selby, Capezio, and Amalfi labels in the selection. Sizes: Women's 4½–12 (occasionally 13s), widths AA–EE.

ENZO ANGIOLINI

Great Mall of the Bay Area, Milpitas.
(408) 934-1349. Daily. MC, VISA, AE, DIS.
Parking: lot.

This label is made by Nine West. It's a more expensive line for women, European-inspired, featuring Italian leathers in a more tailored collection of shoe styles. Retail prices range from $68 to $150; at this outlet you'll save 20–40% every day. The shoe styles convey classic silhouettes with contemporary fluidity and they're destined to outlast the season. Casual boots, booties, flats and loafers, daytime heels (in beautiful leathers and nubuck), fabric shoes (for evening), and a few metallics define the collection. The store is pretty posh—complementing this quality selection nicely. Sizes: Women's Medium width 5–11, Narrow and Wide 7–10. Returns and refunds.

ETIENNE AIGNER

Factory Stores at Vacaville, Vacaville.
(707) 452-1385. Daily. MC, VISA, AE. Parking: lot.
(Other outlet: Gilroy center.)

This is a real winner for women's shoes, an elegant factory store beautifully merchandised with upscale-quality shoes, handbags, leather accessories, gloves, and leather jackets. Those familiar with this line will not be disappointed with the extensive selection of classic, tailored, and dress shoes. Sizes: Women's 5½–10 (a few 5s and 11s); widths: Narrow to Wide. Prices on handbags (all leather) vary from $39 to $110, with the average price nesting at $63. Discounts are 33% off retail across the board. During special sale promotions many groups are posted with additional 20% markdowns. Add your name to the mailing list; it's your only pipeline to special promotions and discount coupons. Exchanges only allowed within 14 days with receipt.

FAMOUS FOOTWEAR/FACTORY BRAND SHOES

1600 Saratoga Avenue, Westgate Mall, San Jose.
(408) 378-5064. M–F 10–9, Sat 10–7, Sun 11–6.
MC, VISA. Parking: lot.
(Other stores: Anderson/Redding, Carmichael, Fremont, Gilroy, Milpitas, Monterey, Newark, Roseville, Sacramento, San Jose, Stockton, Tracy, Vacaville.)

Famous Footwear and Factory Brand Shoes offers a full selection of moderately priced brand-name shoes, discounted a minimum of 10% to a maximum of 40% off retail. Its strength lies in the selection of what I call family basics and "sensible" shoes for women. Expect a complete range of sizes and styles for the whole family.

FLORSHEIM FACTORY OUTLET

Factory Stores at Vacaville, Vacaville.
(707) 453-1552. Daily. MC, VISA, AE, DIS.
Parking: lot.
(Other outlets: Gilroy, Petaluma centers.)
This well-known company now offers 20–50% discounts on overruns, closeouts, and slightly blemished (surfaces only) shoes. Men can revel in the selection of everything Florsheim: dress shoes and boots (including the top-of-the-line Royal Imperial group), casual street and outdoor shoes, Comfortech styles, tennis shoes, and slippers during the holidays. Sizes: Men's 6–15, A–EEE. Refunds or exchange on unworn shoes.

FOOTLOCKER/FOOTQUARTERS OUTLETS

Great Mall of the Bay Area, Milpitas. (408) 946-0408. Daily. MC, VISA. Parking: lot.
(Other outlets: Gilroy, Vacaville centers.)
Selling both new shoes at full retail and discontinued styles from famous makers like Adidas, Nike, Vuarnet, and Reebok, the Footlocker and Footquarters outlets function as clearance centers for the company's retail stores. Clearance inventory yields savings of 25–60% off retail.

HUSH PUPPIES FACTORY OUTLET

Prime Outlets at Gilroy, Gilroy. (408) 848-1180.
Daily. MC, VISA, AE, DIS. Parking: lot.
(Other outlet: Folsom center.)
Hush Puppies have taken on a whole new personality. The classic suede styles remain, but the company has added fashion colors, canvas, and new leathers in its new collections. Savings are 10–50% off retail on the outlet's first-quality selection. Styles for the whole family. Sizes: Women's 4–12 Narrow–XW; Men's 6–16 Narrow–XXW. Other brands from the company's family— Wolverine, Harley Davidson, and Merrill boots and shoes, Cat footwear.

JOAN & DAVID

Petaluma Village Premium Outlets, Petaluma.
(707) 763-7109. Daily. MC, VISA. Parking: lot.
(Other outlets: Milpitas, Pacific Grove, St. Helena centers.)

Most Joan & David loyalists buy these shoes as an investment. The line's popularity is due in part to its classic styling, even though each season "the classics" reflect a new interpretation of fashion trends and colors. The prices are higher than other outlet stores that focus on American brands. You'll usually save 40–50% off original retail. Expect to pay at least $79 to $89, up to $169 (original retail $325). Boots are $129 to $269 (original retail to $450). Sizes: Women's 5–10 (occasionally larger sizes and some Narrows are available). Handbags and belts are an extra plus. At outlet center stores, discriminating shoppers appreciate the exquisitely made updated sportswear collection from Joan & David. Beautiful fabrics and quality construction justify the high prices on this line.

JOHNSTON & MURPHY FACTORY STORE

Factory Stores at Vacaville, Vacaville.
(707) 446-4652. Daily. MC, VISA, AE, DIS.
Parking: lot.
(Other outlet: Napa center.)

A 25% discount off a $10 item isn't much, but 25% off $200 is $50, an entirely different prospect. So I'm satisfied with the 20–40% discounts here. You'll find discontinued styles, past-season shoes, and occasional slight imperfects, plus markdowns on current-season men's shoes. Johnston & Murphy's quality is a given in its lines of classic dress, dress casuals, comfort dress, modern classic (more Italian), or athletic casuals. Expect classic wingtips retail-priced at $195 to be about $129, or golf shoes at $170 to be $139. Sizes: Men's 7–15 A–EEE. Sign up for mailing-list specials. No-hassle refunds and exchanges.

KENNETH COLE

Prime Outlets at Gilroy, Gilroy. (408) 848-2026.
www.kencole.com. Daily. MC, VISA, AE.
No checks. Parking: lot.
(Other outlet: Napa center.)

I love this line of footwear for men and women. Its best customers are 20- to 30-year-olds who seek comfort, plus some flash, glamour, and sexiness in their lives. Kenneth Cole's line is a forerunner of fashion and trends—the line is trendy without being extreme. The quality is great. Many women's shoes are menswear-influenced (oxfords, chukka boots, ghillie-laced shoes, and kiltie shoes), yet there are more feminine styles. At retail the shoes are usually priced from $89 to $160. Good selection of men's shoes. I wish the company would be more aggressive with its discounts. Discounts of 18–30% are unlikely to increase the pulse rate of seasoned bargain hunters, but a few shelves post 40%-off specials. Look for mailings announcing annual sales when prices are 50% off outlet prices. Men's ties, hosiery, luggage, briefcases, small leather goods, eyeglasses, and handbags add spice to the shoe collection. Sizes: Women's 5½–12; Men's 7–13 (some Wide).

LIZ CLAIBORNE SHOE OUTLET

Factory Stores at Vacaville, Vacaville. (707) 446-7112. Daily. MC, VISA, AE, DIS. Parking: lot.
(Other outlet: Gilroy center.)

Think of all the shoes you see in department stores and specialty shoe stores with the Liz label and you'll have a fair idea of what to expect. True, the shoes are not current with retail stores, but they're not far behind. Discounts start at about 25% off original retails, and dive from there as the season's progress. Very nice stores with a first-class selection!

NATURALIZER OUTLET

Factory Stores at Vacaville, Vacaville.
(707) 452-1083. Daily. MC, VISA, DIS. Parking: lot.
(Other outlets: Milpitas, Gilroy centers.)

If Naturalizer, Life Stride, Connie, or Natural Sport are your brands, then stop in for 30–50% discounts on a wide selection for women of all ages. Lots of no-nonsense comfort shoes! Very good choices of in-season styles; great markdowns on slightly past-season goods. Sizes: Women's 5–11 (some 4s and 12s); widths: Slim (AAA) to Wide (WW) in some styles.

NIKE FACTORY STORE

Prime Outlets at Gilroy, Gilroy. (408) 847-4300.
Daily. MC, VISA, AE. Parking: lot.
(Other outlet: Folsom, Vacaville centers.)
You won't find the latest, hippest, or hottest styles
from Nike here. However, you may find fairly
recent popular styles priced about 30% off retail
as blems. The selection of blems, closeouts, and
discontinued styles covers just about all of Nike's
sport shoes. Sizes: Infant 2–8; Preschool 8½–13;
Girls 1–6; Boys 1–6; Women's 5–12; Men's 6–15.
Discounts are 20–40% off retail. Half of the store
is devoted to many styles of first-quality discontinued apparel for active sports or simple leisure for
men, women, and children. Discounts average
30% off retail. Exchanges only; no cash refunds.

NINE WEST FACTORY STORE

1251 Marina Boulevard, Marina Square,
San Leandro. (510) 614-0758. M–F 10–9,
Sat 10–7, Sun 11–6. MC, VISA. Parking: lot.
(Other outlets: Folsom, Gilroy, Milpitas,
Petaluma, Tracy, Vacaville centers.)
Nine West offers a mixed bag of bargains, from
hardly worth noting to dazzling. You'll save just $5
on some current women's styles, but more like
30–60% on last season's regular prices. The selection covers a little of everything Nine West. Look
for two-for-one price offers on absolutely going,
going, gone past-season styles! Sizes: Women's
5½–10 (a few 5s and 11s). The outlets accept
returns and give refunds within 21 days on unworn
shoes with receipt.

REEBOK FACTORY STORE

Factory Stores at Vacaville, Vacaville.
(707) 452-0235. Daily. MC, VISA, AE. Parking: lot.
(Other outlets: Gilroy, Pacific Grove, Petaluma,
Tracy centers.)
The Reebok stores are upbeat and energizing, but
for me that doesn't make up for the fact that the
discounts are often downright chintzy. However,
you may find a shoe that addresses your needs on
the more deeply discounted closeout tables.
If you're lucky you'll find a special promotion like
the frequent "buy one, get a second pair at half
off." The stores also carry Reebok activewear for
the whole family. Shoes in sizes for tiny tots, kids,
teens, women, and up to great big lugs (Men's
sizes 15–16).

ROCKPORT OUTLET

Prime Outlets at Gilroy, Gilroy. (408) 848-8837.
Daily. MC, VISA, AE. Parking: lot.
(Other outlets: Pacific Grove, Tracy, Vacaville
centers.)
If this is your label, then this is the place to shop.
You'll find a combination of discontinued styles,
current overruns, and some blems (cosmetic only)
sold at average 30% discounts. Not all sizes
available in each style. *Note: Vacaville's Reebok*
Outlet has a respectable Rockport selection.
Sizes: Women's 5–11; Men's 7–15.

SAS FACTORY SHOE STORE

Prime Outlets at Gilroy, Gilroy. (408) 842-2185.
Daily. MC, VISA, DIS. Parking: lot.
If you spend hours on your feet each day, the
prospect of so many comfort-oriented shoes will
be exciting. If you're a true bargain hunter, you'll
be a little disappointed at the discounts that
range from a teensy 10% to a maximum of 25%
off retail. Most SAS shoppers find compensation
in the depth of the first-quality selection and
extensive size range. Sizes: Women's 4–12
Slim–WW; Men's 6–15 Slim–DD.

SHOE DEPOT

280 Metro Center, 43 Colma Boulevard, Colma.
(650) 755-0556. M–F 10–9, Sat–Sun 10–6.
MC, VISA. Parking: lot.
When a steel-toe boot or heavy work shoe is
necessary for OSHA's safety requirements on the
job, Shoe Depot is the place; it has more work
shoes than I've seen anywhere, starting at hard-
to-find small sizes (6) and going up to 14, in
widths D–EEE. The discounts are decent. You'll
also find athletic-style, casual, dress comfort, and
traditional dress shoes. Some famous brands:
Nunn Bush, Stacy Adams, Florsheim, Rockport,
Dexter, Gorilla, Wolverine, and Georgia. Also, you
can pick up some everyday duds, work wear from
brands like Carhartt and Ben Davis.

SHOE PAVILION

899 Howard Street, Yerba Buena Square (at Fifth
Street), San Francisco. (415) 974-1821. Daily.
MC, VISA, AE, DIS. Parking: street/pay lots.
(Other stores/outlet centers: Eighteen Bay Area
stores; see Geographical Index.)
Shoe Pavilion describes itself as the "leading off-
price retailer of quality brand-name footwear on

the West Coast," offering women's shoes with 30–70% discounts daily on major brands. Although I feel the rapid expansion of this company has led to a decrease in the selection of "better" shoe brands, for the most part, the styles are very current and service is very accommodating. Prices range from $10 to $89 for shoes. Most discounts on current styles are in the 35% range. Check the displays that highlight the latest arrivals in full size ranges. Even shoes on the self-serve racks are often backed by additional sizes in the stockroom, so don't hesitate to ask for your size. Good selection of men's shoes, too!

SKECHERS

Great Mall of the Bay Area, Milpitas.
(408) 719-8155. www.skechers.com. Daily.
MC, VISA, AE, DIS. Parking: lot.
(Other outlet: Gilroy center.)
Skechers caught the attention of the MTV generation and teen fashion hounds with its platform sandals and sneakers. Skechers, now mainstream and emulated by almost every shoe manufacturer, has expanded its line to offer shoe styles for guys and gals in versions that look for inspiration in

everything from classic oxfords to space age footwear. Save 15–50% on current- and past-season styles on Men's sizes 6½ to 13; Women's sizes 5 to 11; and 5 Toddler to 4 in Girls, to 6 in Boys.

STRIDE-RITE

Prime Outlets at Gilroy, Gilroy. (408) 842-1011.
Daily. MC, VISA. Parking: lot.
Closeouts, slight irregulars, and past-season styles from Stride-Rite's shoe divisions are offered at 30% off every day. Specials on the "dump" tables take discounts down to 50–60% off retail. Sperry Top-Siders, Keds, and Stride-Rite shoes come in all sizes for everyone in the family.

TIMBERLAND

Napa Premium Outlets, Napa. (707) 259-1191.
Daily. MC, VISA, AE. Parking: lot.
(Other outlet: Gilroy center.)
Timberland has been a rising star in the shoe industry. Its rugged outdoor shoes have become as fashionable as everyday streetwear. With success comes excess, and that leads to outlet stores. Discontinued styles and factory blems (cosmetic flaws) are discounted 30–50% off retail.

There's a little of everything made by Timberland in the selection and it's all guaranteed. Sizes: Women's 5–10; Men's 7–13. About half the space at Timberland's outlets is devoted to its apparel (sportswear and outerwear) and accessory divisions for men and women. Just like the shoes, many styles of its weathergear are waterproof. Handbags, backpacks, duffel bags, gloves, and caps provide customers with head-to-toe cover options.

VANS

Factory Stores at Vacaville, Vacaville.
(707) 447-8368. Daily. MC, VISA.
Parking: lot.
(Other outlets: Anderson/Redding, Folsom, Gilroy, Petaluma, Tracy centers.)
Vans updates the classic canvas boat shoe with bold colors and prints. Entire families can choose comfortable fun shoes at this outlet; irregulars and discontinued styles keep the racks well stocked. Both lace-up and slip-on styles are available, plus some in suede. Vans fills a special niche with its snowboots and skateboarding shoes. Because the styles are more or less unisex, you can purchase by fit, or stick to Toddler 5–10½; Boys 2½–6;

Youth 11–3; Women's 4–10; Men's 6½–13. Discounts 30–65% off original retail.

WALKING CO./MEPHISTO OUTLET

Great Mall of the Bay Area, Milpitas.
(408) 262-5105. Daily. MC, VISA, AE, DIS.
Parking: lot.
Before going on vacation, stop by this outlet, which is owned by the reliable Walking Company specialty shoe chain (eighteen retail stores). The Mephisto brand is the headliner here, with discount prices (30–50% off) on men's and women's discontinued styles and surplus inventory. These shoes are noted for the durability, comfort, support, and breathability of the natural materials used in each handmade pair of shoes. Other popular brands of walking shoes are carried: Rockport, Teva, Clark's, Ecco, Rieker, and Timberland at closeout prices. Sizes: Women's 5–11½; Men's 5½–13½.

Also See

Under Famous Labels/Factory Stores:
ANN TAYLOR LOFT; LIZ CLAIBORNE

Under Bay Area Off-Price/
Chain Discount Stores:
GROUP USA; LOEHMANN'S

Under Family, Men's & Women's,
General Clothing:
**BURLINGTON COAT FACTORY; GUESS?;
J. CREW; MARSHALLS; T.J. MAXX**

Under Active Sportswear:
SPORTS BASEMENT, TENNIS EXPRESS

Under Children's Clothing:
KIDS R US

Under Clearance Centers:
NORDSTROM RACK; OFF FIFTH; TALBOTS

Appliances, Electronics, and Home Entertainment

The superchains dominate the Bay Area appliance and home electronics market. Their volume purchasing power gives them a price advantage, but if you read the want ads, you'll see that they pay their sales "counselors" hefty commissions. These stores are careful to avoid blatant bait-and-switch tactics, but you can be sure that a salesperson is motivated to trade you up to models or brands that offer a larger commission and/or greater profits. In my opinion, most chains offer a "price guarantee" that is almost worthless. Each store appears to carry many exclusive models (known as "derivatives"). Typically the only difference between models at competing stores are in exterior color, finish, or other minor cosmetic or technical features. Good luck comparison shopping on the basis of model numbers! Because the numbers differ, it's very hard to meet the requirements for the price guarantee. Instead, you must note the features in detail to get a feel for comparative pricing. And when the salesperson starts pushing an extended service warranty, remember that stores consider such a warranty the best way to increase profits in times of intense competition for market share, which otherwise keeps profit margins low. These stores have driven many smaller operations out of business, but independents survive who operate with small margins, no commissions, and without the high overhead of the superchains. Shop smart! Take careful measurements of the existing space or cavity in your home for a replacement appliance so you don't spin your wheels selecting something that doesn't fit. Standard sizes of twenty years ago are not the standard anymore.

ABC APPLIANCE SERVICE

*2050 Taraval Street (at 31st Avenue),
San Francisco. (415) 564-8166, (800) 942-1242.
M–Sat 9–4, Sun 10–1. MC, VISA, DIS.
Parking: street.*

ABC's modest store lacks razzle-dazzle merchandising glamour. Its secret for low prices on major
brands of kitchen and laundry appliances is volume
purchasing. Most built-in appliances on display
are connected to gas, water, or electricity, allowing
for working demonstrations. That's convenient!
Check out the new displays of imported kitchen
sinks and faucets. ABC can provide immediate
delivery on most of the lines it carries. Phone
quotes are given (sometimes grudgingly when
busy). Delivery charges vary with the size of your
order and distance involved.

AIRPORT APPLIANCES

*20286 Hesperian Boulevard, Hayward.
(510) 783-3494. M–F 9–8, Sat–Sun 10–6.
MC, VISA, DIS. Parking: lot.*

The selection of major brands in laundry
and kitchen appliances includes high-tech lines
like Bosch, Best Hoods, Thermador, Dacor,
Gaggenau, Frigidaire, GE, Kitchen Aid, Viking, and
Wolf, which are popular with remodelers. Designer
faucets, sinks, and custom-made countertops
in Corian or laminates are offered at very competitive prices. Its kitchen remodeling center offers
semicustom European-style cabinets. Delivery to
almost anywhere (evening delivery and installation); extra charges for installations and hook-ups.
Aggressive pricing keeps this Mom, Pop, and
Daughter shop going.

APPLIANCE SALES & SERVICE

*840 Folsom Street, San Francisco. (415) 362-7195.
M–F 8:30–5:30, Sat 9–5. MC, VISA, AE, DIS.
Parking: street/pay lot.*

Bargain hunters will really appreciate the selection
of as-is blems and factory seconds on many brands
of small appliances here. These were once display
models, samples, discontinued styles, or closeouts; all pieces are mechanically perfect and carry
a manufacturer's warranty. All accessories and
parts are carried for these lines, which include air
purifiers, espresso makers, water filtration units,
pressure cookers, and electric shavers. There are
also hard-to-find appliances such as egg cookers,

large juicers, and meat grinders. Brands include Braun, Cuisinart, Rowenta, Oster, Sunbeam, Krups, Bionaire, West Bend, and KitchenAid, all at competitive prices. The store will special order any new item and can provide or order any replacement part or accessory for small appliances. And it ships anywhere via UPS.

BEST BUY
3620 Buskirk Avenue, Pleasant Hill. (925) 988-0256. M–Sat 10–9, Sun 11–6. MC, VISA, AE, DIS. Parking: lot.
(Other stores: Dublin, Milpitas, Pinole, San Carlos.)
If you can plug it in or if it runs on batteries, you can probably find it at Best Buy and at a price that's kept its competitors on edge since its West Coast invasion in Fall 1999. The stores are more self-service oriented than the other major retailers and discounters and, as with the warehouse clubs, Best Buy's no-frills stores feature shopping carts and large displays of bulk product. A non-commissioned sales staff eliminates some of the aggressive sales pitches for things like extended service plans. Shop here for consumer electronics products (geared for the masses rather than the

elite high-end niches), personal computers, appliances, home-office machines, and entertainment software like music CDs.

BOSE FACTORY STORE
Prime Outlets at Gilroy, Gilroy. (408) 842-2541. www.bose.com. Daily. MC, VISA, AE, DIS. Parking: lot.
(Other outlet: Petaluma center.)
If your curiosity has been piqued by national radio commentator Paul Harvey's testimonials on Bose products, a trip to the Bose Factory Store will allow you to hear first-hand what all the fuss is about. For the uninitiated, Bose is an American electronics manufacturing corporation with worldwide distribution. It's also the largest speaker and amplifier manufacturer in the world—the Bose stereo system is factory-installed in Mercedes-Benz and many top domestic car models. Although some of the Bose audio products are sold through retail outlets, others, like the WAVE radio and Acoustic Wave Music System, are sold only on a mail-order basis or through one of the company's nineteen factory stores in outlet centers around the country. The factory stores also sell "factory

renewed" Bose products at minimal to modest savings (10–30%). When a product is returned for any reason, it may eventually qualify as a "factory renewed" product (a special seal is displayed on the item). Before it can be resold, the item goes through a rigorous retesting and remanufacturing process at Bose. The performance of a renewed product is the same as a factory-new product; both are subjected to the same testing and quality standards and have identical warranties. At the outlet, the WAVE radio sells for $349 new, and $299 renewed; the Acoustic Wave Music System with built-in CD is $1079 new and $899 renewed. Take a seat in the separate Bose Music Theater inside the outlet for a thirty-minute audiovisual Bose product demonstration.

CALIFORNIA AUDIO & VIDEO

9550 Main Street, Penngrove. (707) 795-9065, (800) 866-1222. M–F 10–7, Sat 10–6, Sun 11–5. MC, VISA, AE. Parking: lot.

You'll feel right at home here with the wide range of audio and video products. VCRs, TVs, stereo components, car stereos, telephones, answering machines, video cameras, and most other high-tech gadgets can be ordered if they're not in stock. Lines represented include Acurus, Aragon, B & K, JVC, Panasonic, Hitachi, Harmon/Kardon, Onkyo, Kenwood, JBL, Polk, Denon, Carver, Nakamichi, NHT, Infinity, Yamaha, Pioneer, Paradigm, Quasar, Technics, and Energy. Prices are very good every day and try to beat any advertised special sale price. The folks who work here do their best to provide all the attention and help you need, especially if you've driven a distance to do business with them. You'll get a sound perspective when buying a fine audio/video system after spending time in the comfortable environment of the home theater room. You can get phone quotes from the free 800 number and have articles shipped anywhere. *Directions: Take 101 to the Penngrove exit, go right on Old Redwood Highway one and a half miles, then right on Main.*

CAMBRIDGE SOUNDWORKS
CLEARANCE CENTER

702 Dubuque Avenue, South San Francisco. (650) 225-9500. M–Sat 10–7, Sun Noon–6. MC, VISA, AE, DIS. Parking: lot.

Cambridge is not giving away the store here—instead, it's mostly small change. Located in front of Cambridge's distribution warehouse, this center sells discontinued models, refurbished or returned products, and out-of-box or open box speakers and electronics for discounted prices. Most of the time you're saving a teensy 10–20% off the regular or sale prices of its other Bay Area store; more rarely, you'll save 25–40% on a close-out model. Anything that's carried by Cambridge may be found here: CD players, receivers, VCRs from JVC, Sony cassette decks, etc. Everything is fully warranted with a 30-day return or exchange policy. Its location on a frontage road north of the San Francisco airport makes the Cambridge Soundworks Clearance Center convenient for a quick stop to prospect for bargains.

CHERIN'S

727 Valencia Street, San Francisco. (415) 864-2111. M–F 9:30–5:30, Sat 10–5. Cash/Check. Parking: private lot at 18th and Valencia.

They must be doing something right—they've been in business since 1892 (the decor hasn't changed much since then). This is a great source for home appliances: refrigerators, freezers, washers, dryers, ranges, and microwave ovens. Remodelers can find esoteric brands like Wolf, Viking Range, Bosch, Garland, Fisher Paykel, Asko, Miele, Sub-Zero, U.S. Range, Gaggenau, and Traulsen. If you're updating or upgrading and covet European-style appliances, you'll have plenty of options here. Cherin's also sells mainstream brands like GE, Maytag, Amana, Thermador, Dacor, and KitchenAid. It specializes in built-in appliances. Contractor prices prevail for everyone. Its business is mostly referral because it rarely advertises, and its low prices reflect a minimal markup. No price quotes over the phone. Delivery is free within the Bay Area.

FILCO

1433 Fulton Avenue, Filco Plaza, Sacramento. (916) 483-4526. www.filcoinc.com. M–F 10–7, Sat 10–6, Sun 11–5. MC, VISA, DIS. Parking: lot. (Other stores: Chico, Citrus Heights, Folsom, Lodi.) Filco offers an extensive selection in cameras, appliances, home entertainment, and electronics at minimal markup. Prices on cellular phones keep competitors steaming, but consumers have no complaints. Most major brands of 35mm cameras, accessories, and instant cameras are in stock at terrific prices. Kodak film is sold at cost. Filco's on-site processing is its loss leader. Jenn-Air, KitchenAid, Panasonic, Whirlpool, Amana, Sony, GE, Sub-Zero, Mitsubishi, Hitachi, Quasar, RCA, Onkyo, and Bose are a few of the major brands found in appliances and home entertainment.

FRIEDMAN'S MICROWAVE

2301 Broadway, Oakland. (510) 444-1119. M–F 10–5:30, Sat 10–5. VISA, AE, DIS. Parking: street. (Other stores: Hayward, Palo Alto, Pleasant Hill, San Francisco, San Rafael.) I approach the purchase of a new appliance as if I were planning the invasion of Normandy. Enter Friedman's Microwave. It sells a full range of microwaves from the most basic and inexpensive models up to top-of-the-line types. The prices are competitive with superstores. Thanks to a price guarantee, weekly free classes in microwave cooking, trade-in allowance, and 20% discounts on accessories (including carts) bought with the microwave (10% thereafter), you come out the winner. Most of all, you'll appreciate the information provided by the staff in a sane, no-pressure atmosphere. The Oakland store is also an "as is" center for GE microwaves.

FRY'S ELECTRONICS

1077 E. Arques Avenue, Sunnyvale. (408) 617-1300. M–F 8–9, Sat 9–8, Sun 9–7. MC, VISA. Parking: lot. (Other stores: Campbell, Fremont, Milpitas, Palo Alto.) Fry's is well established with tech types for computers and related products. Also home and office electronics, high-tech toys and gadgets, TVs, boom boxes, cordless phones, speakers, CD players, cassette players, satellite dishes, and fax machines—enough to keep you wandering the aisles for hours. Very competitive prices!

HOUSE OF LOUIE

1045 Bryant Street (at Ninth Street), San Francisco. (415) 621-7100, (800) 99-LOUIE. M–Sat 8–6, Sun 10–5. MC, VISA, DIS. Parking: small side lot; street.

House of Louie offers aggressive pricing on kitchen and laundry appliances, televisions, VCRs, and bedding. Its bilingual staff is appreciated by many consumers. It's also very sharp on prices! It can't always beat loss-leader "door buster" prices, but what you want usually isn't the "door buster" anyway. House of Louie offers an everyday and upscale selection of brands, including Wolf, Viking, and Thermador ranges and cooktops, Bosch and Asko dishwashers, KitchenAid, Amana, GE, Whirlpool, Sub-Zero, Jenn-Air, etc. You'll see Sony and Panasonic TVs from small "spare room" sets up to huge 61-inch Videoscope units; the more expensive the model, the greater the savings are likely to be. You can also resort to catalogs. Upstairs is a room full of mattress sets from Simmons, Beautyrest, BackCare, and Maxipedic at solid discounts.

ORION TELESCOPE & BINOCULARS CENTER

3609 Buchanan Street, San Francisco. (415) 931-9966; catalog requests (800) 447-1001. T–Sun 10–5:30. MC, VISA. Parking: lot. (Other stores: Cupertino, Watsonville.)

Orion is the largest telescope firm in North America; its catalog is very helpful to consumers in the prepurchase stage. Get set to view celestial wonders by doing your homework, then contact the Orion Telescope Center. If you know what you want, you can order over the phone by credit card. Or you can stop by and pick the brains of the pros on the staff. You can gaze through models from Celestron, Pentax, Edmund Scientific, Orion, and Televue. Naturally, all the esoteric accessories you haven't even thought of buying, but will eventually, are available. Orion also sells binoculars, spotting scopes, photographic accessories, and telescope-making parts. And you're going to save 10–30% on anything you buy!

REED SUPPLY

*1328 Fruitvale Avenue, Oakland. (510) 436-7171.
M–Sat 9:30–5. MC, VISA. Parking: lot.*
You'll be surprised at the selection of kitchen
and laundry appliances that can be crammed into
this relatively small space. Major brands, including
status lines popular with architects and kitchen
planners, are sold at very good prices. If you have
special installation problems, you'll be referred to
someone who can do the job. Reed also sells
kitchen cabinets (Omega, Westwood, Mid Conti-
nent), bathroom vanities, custom countertops
(including Corian, marble, and maple), greenhouse
windows, water heaters, shower doors, wall heaters,
Cadillac lines of faucets, and more. Something
really esoteric on your list? You can special order
from catalogs. Working on a low markup, Reed
essentially sells to everyone at contractors' prices.
Beware: At times the staff is stretched too thin
for prompt service. Delivery charges relate to
distance involved.

REMINGTON SALES & SERVICE

*86 Second Street, San Francisco. (415) 495-7060.
M–F 8:30–5:30, Sat 9–5. MC, VISA, AE, DIS.
Parking: lot.
(Other stores/outlets: Gilroy, Milpitas,
Vacaville centers.)*
At the Remington store you'll obviously find
shavers and trimmers of all description for men
and women (face, leg, nose, ear, mustache, etc.),
as well as parts and accessories. But that's not
all. There are knives for every use: Swiss Army
knives, cutlery sets and kitchen knives, Henckels,
Buck knives, and other knives I'm not sure how to
describe except that some looked fairly menacing
(the Fury Scimitar, for example). A good selection
of flashlights, Maglights, knife sharpeners, whet-
stones, manicure sets, scissors (all uses), and travel
aids complete the inventory. Discounts from
minimal to fairly good. Service done on shavers
at San Francisco store only.

SAN JOSE HONDA ELECTRONICS

1610 S. First Street, San Jose. (408) 294-6632.
M–F 10–8, Sat 9–5:30, Sun 11–5. MC, VISA, DIS.
Parking: lot.

San Jose Honda is hard to beat with Sony devotees. An authorized dealer, its focus is on volume sales at discount prices, and it monitors the competition closely to make sure it beats everyone. TVs in all configurations and sizes including big screen. VCRs, 8mm camcorders, DVD's, satellite dishes, home theater systems, telephones, minirack stereo systems, and audio components at good prices, too. Although Sony is the primary emphasis, other brands like Panasonic, Monster Cable, and Onkyo get the same price trimming. The showroom is filled with boxed units ready for your car trunk. The store can provide setup and delivery for a reasonable price. The bilingual staff addresses the needs of San Jose's diverse community.

SEARS FURNITURE & APPLIANCE OUTLET

1936 West Avenue at 140th, San Leandro.
(510) 895-0546. M–F 10–8, Saturday 9–6, Sun 11–5.
MC, VISA, AE, DIS, Sears charge. Parking: lot.

If you're not adverse to a dent or scratch somewhere on the surface of a refrigerator, washer, range, freezer, or water heater, then the mammoth Sears Outlet in San Leandro may be just the place to go when you need an immediate replacement. The appliances are out of carton and may be categorized as discontinued, previously used, and/or reconditioned. Outlet merchandise may be reduced 20–60% percent off original retail; however the average appliance markdown is 20–40% percent. These are worthwhile savings given the slim profit margins in this competitive category of the marketplace. The selection includes any of the major appliances that may have been sold at a regular Sears store, from top-of-the-line to the most basic level. Each item is tagged and noted with an explanation of its status—used, reconditioned, damaged, discontinued, etc. "Used" applies to anything that was delivered to a customer and then returned whether there was any actual use or not. The Sears Outlet also has many larger-size televisions (27-inch to over 60-inch screens) at good markdowns. A 52-inch RCA model (used, damaged, and reconditioned) was marked down to $1,339 from $1,999; a 50-inch Hitachi was $1,499 from $2,799 (also used, damaged, and reconditioned); and a 35-inch RCA Proscan was $1,299 from $1,999. About half the 70,000-square-foot warehouse is filled with furniture from Sears' Northern California furniture departments and individual HomeLife stores. Upholstered pieces, formal and casual dining room sets, bedroom sets, occasional pieces, mattress sets, and lots of one-of-a-kinds and odd pieces fill the space. All products are fully warranted functionally. No warranty on cosmetic damages. All sales are covered by a 30-day return policy—return for any reason with sales receipt and accessories included. Not to worry, all the operating manuals are available, and essential operating parts are included. No delivery or installation is offered; instead, referrals are provided to local services/individuals. Typically, there are independent delivery trucks and personnel on-site ready to give immediate service. Merchandise can be held for three days while arrangements are made.

Directions: From Highway 880, take Marina exit heading west. Turn left at Merced, right at West Avenue to 140th Street.

SONY OUTLET

Prime Outlets at Tracy, Tracy. (209) 832-3440. Daily. MC, VISA, AE, DIS. Parking: lot.

Even with fierce competition from big box retailers, the Sony Outlet more than holds its own. One of twelve factory stores around the country, this is where discontinued models, refurbished products, and display samples spend their last days. Refurbished products may have failed in initial use, but once factory overhauled and repackaged the products are given a full factory warranty. There are many first-quality products, usually discontinued, but sometimes just overstocks. Consider your choices: TVs (up to 60 inches), Web TVs, VCRs, camcorders, still-image digital cameras, home and car stereos, radios, telephone products, boom boxes, short wave radios, video editing equipment, CD players, and altogether just about anything from Sony's consumer products division. Don't hesitate when you spot an I-can't-believe-this-price item; if you do, it may not be there when you

return. Some of the best deals are one-shot shipments. If you've never been to the Tracy outlet
center, this is all the reason you need. All sales are
final, but a 30-day exchange period is allowed for
products found initially defective.

SUNBEAM & OSTER OUTLET

Great Mall of the Bay Area, Milpitas.
(408) 263-3155. Daily. MC, VISA, AE, DIS.
Parking: lot.
(Other outlet: Vacaville center.)
The two brands have been around forever, but
at the company's outlet stores you'll find more of
everything it makes than you'll find anyplace
else—more choices in models, price, and features.
Plain white boxes contain refurbished products
with a one-year warranty (new models have 2-year
warranties). Unless you happen on a loss-leader
promotion at another retailer, you'll probably pay
the lowest price too. Shop for irons, blenders, bar-
becue grills, slow cookers, toasters, coffee makers,
bread makers, processors, warming blankets and
mattress pads, vaporizers, and more. Parts, attach-
ments, and accessories are a welcome sight!

TELECENTER APPLIANCES—TV—VIDEO

1830 S. Delaware Street, San Mateo.
(650) 341-5804. www.telecenterappliances.com.
M, W, F 9–6, T, Th 9–8, Sat 9–5, Sun Noon–5.
MC, VISA, DIS. Parking: lot.
Telecenter's prices are very competitive with other
stores and superstores. Telecenter carries brand
names in kitchen and laundry appliances (popular
new high-end appliances for remodeling projects),
plus TVs, video equipment, stereos, and more.
There's no aggressive sales bafflegab here. If you're
working with a contractor, you'll get a contractor's
discount if you can provide their name and license
number. Modest delivery charges.

VIDEO ONLY

24040 Hesperian Boulevard, Hayward.
(510) 785-1470. M–F 10–9, Sat 10–7, Sun 11–6.
MC, VISA, AE, DIS. Parking: lot.
(Other stores: Dublin, San Francisco, San Mateo.)
They keep it simple and specialize in selling TVs,
VCRs, camcorders, and home theater audio. All
the leading brands, too: Quasar, Panasonic,
Toshiba, Hitachi, Sony, JVC, RCA, Infinity, Sharp,
Samsung, Sound Dynamics, Yamaha, Technics,

and more. Prices are very competitive with the big guys around town, and the service and pace of business is more consumer friendly. Keep track of local ads and you can hold them to their "double your money" low-price guarantee—though I doubt very many buyers have ever needed to.

Also See

Under Cameras:
SAN JOSE CAMERA & VIDEO

Under Furniture and Home Accessories—
Catalog Discounters:
DAVID MORRIS CO.; DEOVLET & SONS; GIORGI BROS.; MILLBRAE FURNITURE COMPANY

Under General Merchandise—
Membership Warehouse Clubs:
COSTCO; SAM'S CLUB

Cameras and Photography

If you're looking for a camera that requires no fancy accessories or particular savvy, you're probably in the market for something under $100—a basic point-and-shoot, no-hassle model. Your best bet is to rely on local superstores, which frequently offer promotional pricing on these cameras. Check ads for Kmart, Target, Wal-Mart, Best Buy and Circuit City, or visit Costco or Sam's Club. On the other hand, if you're serious about your photography and investing in esoteric camera equipment, look in on the local resources listed below or consider the many mail-order companies that advertise extensively in publications like *Popular Photography*. Ordering by mail, especially when dealing with brand-name products, can be a time- and money-saving option if you've done your homework and follow sensible consumer guidelines. The trade-off for mail-order savings? You forgo the personal service and technical support that local camera shops offer. I've listed two mail-order companies that my shutterbug friends consistently recommend for price and reliability. One other essential is required before tackling the advertisements, which can cover many pages: a magnifying glass!

B & H PHOTO–VIDEO–PRO-AUDIO (MAIL ORDER)

420 Ninth Avenue, New York, NY, 10011. Orders: (800) 947-7785 (photo), (800) 947-1186 (video), (800) 357-1999 (imaging), (800) 859-5252 (Pro-Audio). Fax (800) 947-7008. Information: (212) 444-6670. www.bhphotovideo.com. MC, VISA, DIS. Serious amateurs and professionals make pilgrimages here when visiting the Big Apple to make a connection to this community of like-minded people. B & H covers all aspects of its technical empire—from basic point-and-shoot cameras to the most esoteric equipment and supplies known only to professionals. Camcorders, VCRs, video monitors, videotape, printers, microphones, editing equipment, lighting, photographic paper, and other essentials for professionals fill this company's ad pages. Ordinary folks will zero in on binoculars, cameras, lenses, film, and accessories. The multilingual international staff is an asset for many shoppers.

CAMBRIDGE CAMERA EXCHANGE, INC. (MAIL ORDER)

119 W. 17th Street, New York, NY, 10011. Orders: (800) 221-2253. 24-hour fax order line: (212) 463-0093. Information: (212) 675-8600. Customer relations: (212) 255-3744. MC, VISA, DIS, C.O.D.

A good resource for amateurs and professionals—you could set up your own studio and darkroom by ordering from Cambridge. Some video cameras, camcorders, telephones, radios; accessories for all categories, too. Used department to sell and trade. Write for free Cambridge Camera catalog.

L. Z. PREMIUMS

241 E. Campbell Avenue, Campbell. (408) 374-3838. T–Sat 10–6. MC, VISA, and financing. Parking: lot.

L.Z. has a loyal shutterbug following for its prices on cameras, accessories, and developing equipment. Kodak film is sold at dealer's cost; Kodak processing is 30% off. Major appliances, electronics (VCRs, faxes, beepers, home and car stereos), cameras (new and used), camera gear, and cellular phones are also sold. The floor selection is very limited, but their large catalog library extends your options. Prices reflect a modest markup, and delivery charges are reasonable. Forget hype and hustle; the staff is knowledgeable and low-pressure. No phone quotes.

PHOTO SUPPLY

436 Bryant Street, San Francisco. (415) 495-8640. M–F 9–6: Sat 10–5. MC, VISA, DIS. Parking: garage at 435 Bryant.

This company serves the professional photographers and graphic arts firms that are concentrated in the SOMA area. The emphasis is on supplying products for mounting, storage, and presentation—allowing for direct purchase of many items that must often be bought through mail-order companies. Except for some very esoteric items, everything is discounted. Photography students, hobbyists, and other consumers seek out this resource to purchase albums, mount board, foam core, and archival papers for mats. All too often when one needs mat board for mounting, it can only be purchased in large sheets. Sizes here start at 8 by 10. You can also buy film, paper, and chemicals in quantity at discount prices. Everything for the darkroom too. Feel secure with its roster of brands: Kodak, Fuji, Agfa, and Ilford films and papers for starters. Check the bargain tables for "whatever."

SAN JOSE CAMERA & VIDEO

1600 Winchester Boulevard, Campbell. (408) 374-1880. M–Sat 10–6, Th until 8, Sun Noon–5. MC, VISA, DIS. Parking: lot.
Photo buffs looking for sophisticated and usually expensive cameras and accessories will feel right at home here. Most major brands are on hand: Canon, Nikon, Olympus, Vivitar, Minolta, Pentax, Hasselblad, Mamiya, Leica, Gitzo, Yashica, Ricoh, Fuji, Bogen, Kodak, Metz and Beseler enlargers,

Kodak carousel projectors, and Gossen exposure meters. Keeping up with the market, a full line of advanced photo system cameras are carried, as well as an expanded selection of digital cameras, scanners, and printers. This shop aggressively discounts video cameras from Canon, Sony, and RCA, ruffling the feathers of other dealers by not playing ball and offering products at higher prices, as they do. This place is a hero to consumers. For a close-up look at the world, check out the binocular department. You'll probably get the lowest price in the Bay Area by shopping here. Save gas if you're out of the area; order by phone and have it shipped UPS.

Also See

Under Appliances, Electronics, and Home Entertainment:
FILCO

Under General Merchandise:
MEMBERSHIP WAREHOUSE CLUBS

Computers

The Bay Area abounds with computer stores. Trying to pick just a few and applying the label "bargain" is extremely difficult. Prices, products, locations, and the marketing direction of various stores tend to change so often I'm wary about making recommendations. There are so many variables to this market—whether you're buying a brand product or a clone, which system you're buying, whether you're trying to build one yourself, etc.—that it can hardly be covered with a few recommendations. Choosing a store on the basis of price alone may lead to nothing but frustration if the service and support you need is not part of the price. When canvassing other computer users, I find that their advice is most often based on a special relationship they have developed with a particular store or dealer, though some choose stores based on price rather than support. Some hard cases think the best way to spend a day off is perusing the esoterica of the computer market at someplace like Fry's Electronics or Comp USA, while novices will undoubtedly end up on sensory overload and feel like their brains have been scrambled. Price buyers tend to be folks who can whip off the top of their system unit, pull a screwdriver out of their pocket, and add new chips, cards, drives, or other hardware without any apprehension at all.

I suggest networking with high-tech friends or user groups to lead you to businesses with a reputation for good prices and support. Your local user group is hands-down your best resource for all kinds of information, shopping recommendations, and free public-domain software. Finding a dealer in the Bay Area is not difficult. After you've passed the novice stage, you'll find bargain-priced resources for software and add-on hardware (memory, modems, boards, et al.) located all over the Bay Area, particularly in Silicon Valley.

Two valuable Bay Area publications for information on microcomputers are *Computer Currents* and *MicroTimes*. They provide practical computer information for businesses, professionals, serious home users, and absolute novices. They have question-and-answer columns, let you know what's available in the Bay Area, and list services and products, events and classes to attend, and organizations and user groups to join. *Computer Currents* and *MicroTimes* are distributed from hundreds of locations in seven counties around the Bay. You're most likely to find them in local libraries, colleges, adult education facilities, record stores, video and electronic stores, and anyplace where high-tech people are likely to hang out. If you can't find one, call their offices 9–5. See below for information about where to find copies.

COMPUTER CURRENTS
(510) 527-0333 to find local distribution points or for subscription information.

MICROTIMES
(510) 768-1200 to find local distribution points or for subscription information.

Art, Craft, and Hobby Supplies

AMSTERDAM ART

1007 University Avenue, Berkeley. (510) 649-4800.
M–Sat 9:30–6, Th until 8, Sun 11–6.
MC, VISA, AE, DIS. Parking: lot.
(Other stores: 1013 University Avenue, Berkeley;
5251 Broadway, Oakland; 5424 Geary Blvd., San
Francisco; 1279 Boulevard Way, Walnut Creek.)
Discounts at its four retail stores have always been
gratifying, but the new warehouse outlet next door
to its Berkeley site is where you'll find Amsterdam's
best deals. This is where overstocks, closeouts,
and special purchases of paints, brushes, easels,
pads, canvas, and more end up at 50% discounts
and higher. It's geared towards volume buyers
with many products packaged in multiples or sold
by the dozen (aka Costco). Savvy art students
combine purchases to get the deals, while teachers
stretch budgets with the bulk buys. From time to
time, special purchases allow for some out-of-the-
ordinary buys. Summer 99's creative activity kits
for kids at 50% off must have provided vacation
entertainment for legions of kids. Any heavy-duty
user of art materials should keep a close eye on
this outlet. Amsterdam's four other stores (discounts of 20–40% off) offer a much broader array
of supplies, materials, graphic, architectural, and
engineering resources. Amsterdam's fine paper
department offers more than 700 types of papers.
Fine writing instruments from Montblanc, Parker,
Waterman, Sheaffer, Aurora, Tombow, and Lamy
are all sold at 10–20% discounts. Amsterdam has
a good selection of prefab frames at solid discount prices; precut mats, discounts on glass, and
framing sections for the do-it-yourselfer; and in-
house custom frame orders competitively priced
with other frame shops.

ANGRAY FANTASTICO

559 Sixth Street, San Francisco. (415) 982-0680.
M–F 7–5, Sat 8:30–4. Cash/Check.
Parking: street/lot.

Fantastico's warehouse has just about everything for craft-oriented people. It stocks an extensive selection of dried and silk flowers (exotic specimens you see beautifully arranged in fancy stores), plus all the makings to put them together: tapes, wires, ribbons, foam, etc. My favorite is florist ribbon in rolls for gift wrapping at one-third the cost of the Hallmark kind. Its aisle of ribbons is unsurpassed. Come here for holiday decorations and ideas. It also has baskets, plastic flowers and fruits, dollhouses, ceramics, garden statuary, and many accessory items. Prices to the general public are usually 10–30% lower than stores closer to home, except for paper party supplies, which are competitive with all the other party discount stores. Nice wedding department, and 10% off on wedding and party invitations from several books.

ART EXCHANGE

77 Geary Boulevard, Second Floor, San Francisco.
(415) 956-5750. E-mail: Artxchng1@aol.com.
T–Sat 11:30–5:30. Cash/Check. Parking: street.

The Art Exchange is a wonderful resource for those who have art that no longer fits their lifestyles. Perhaps they've moved, gone through a divorce, inherited art that doesn't suit their decor or taste, or redecorated. The gallery resells artwork, including paintings, sculpture, prints, and other objets d'art. The only requirement is that it be original: no reproductions like posters or photographs. The emphasis is on contemporary art. There are watercolors, monoprints, woodcuts, sculptures, carvings, etchings, oils, and more, at prices ranging from $300 to $30,000 and including the works of famous artists like Henrietta Berk, Gary Bukovnik, Richard Diebenkorn, David Hockney, Roy Lichtenstein, Joan Miró, and Robert Motherwell alongside those of lesser-known talents. Before you bring your art in, call the owner to discuss what you'd like to place on consignment and its price. When the work is sold, the gallery gets one-third of the selling price. Documentation about the artist or the work is especially desirable.

ARTS & CRAFT SUPPLIES OUTLET

41 14th Street, San Francisco. (415) 431-7122.
M–F 9–4. MC, VISA. Parking: street.
(Other store: Annex, 50 13th Street,
San Francisco. Sat only 10–5.)
Arts & Craft Supplies is an outlet for an importer
and distributor of many of the categories of merchandise you find in major arts and crafts supply
stores: painting supplies, acrylic paints, pens, glues,
lace, transfer type, paper goods, beads (lots and
lots!), macramé, inks, brushes, basketry, doll parts
and accessories, craft patterns and magazines,
jewelry findings, jute, oil paints, floral supplies,
wedding and shower favors, and more. Organiza-
tion may not be the outlet's strong suit, but keeping such a convoluted inventory in order would
defy all but the pathologically organized. Most
folks like the mess—it seems more in keeping with
one's expectation of an outlet. Pick up a shopping
basket—I guarantee you'll find goodies you didn't
know you wanted as you stroll along the long
wall, with its merchandise dangling off pegboards
and stashed on shelves. Discontinued or surplus
merchandise is usually at least 50% off original
retail. (Expect some surprises—the company picks
up some very interesting inventory, buying up
entire booths at trade shows.) Small craft manufacturers or anyone else interested in volume purchases may have access to additional discounts.
Inquire! Shop on Saturdays at the company's
annex, located a block away.

BEESWAX CANDL'ART OUTLET

1501 Powell Street, Suite A, Emeryville.
(510) 547-8469. www.shendls.com. W only
Noon–5:30 (or by appointment). MC, VISA, DIS.
Parking: street.
Make sure it's Wednesday (or call for an appointment) before setting out to replenish your candle
stock. This outlet sells two lines of candles: one
specifically for Jewish holidays—shendl's candls—
the other perfect for any time lovely candles are
appropriate. All candles are made of pure beeswax: in honeycomb, smooth finish, or solid. Most
candles are sold in boxes or in pairs and priced
30–50% below retail as seconds or overruns. A
12-inch pair of dinner candles at retail runs about
$10; for overruns you'll pay about $6. Pillars,
fluted tapers, chime, and birthday candles in
gorgeous colors add beauty to entertaining and

special holiday occasions. The Shabbat, Chanukah, and Havdalah candles are dripless, virtually smokeless, and emit a fresh honey scent. Make your own candles after buying sheets of honeycomb beeswax and the candlemaking kits that are sold here. Beeswax candles in all shapes and sizes work especially well with rustic accessories and decorations that are popular now—the new natural look sweeping the home accessories industry. An unusual selection of candleholders are priced at $2.50 to $150. Add your name to the mailing list for invitations to special sales prior to Chanukah and Christmas. *Note: The outlet is located under the Powell Street overpass with its entrance on Landregan, next to the accommodating Amtrak parking lot.*

THE CANDLE FACTORY

60 Galli Drive (Bel Marin Keys business park), Novato. (415) 883-7220. M–F 9–5, Sat 11–5. MC, VISA. Parking: lot.
Increase your stash of candles by stopping by the Candle Factory, where you'll find your senses overpowered by the combined fragrances used in candlemaking here. Because the candles are made on the premises, you can buy at reduced prices (sometimes just very minimal savings). These dripless and smokeless candles are made of organic domestic ingredients, and it's claimed they outburn imported ones. Occasionally you'll find specials when a wheel runs off color or a tint proves unpopular. Seeking wellness? Then you'll appreciate the line of holistic healing candles.

CANDLE OUTLET

1223 Donnelly Avenue, Burlingame. (650) 343-0804. T–Sat 10–7. Sun 11–6. MC, VISA, DIS. Parking: city lots.
At this fragrant and charming outlet tucked inside a vintage cottage behind the big Pottery Barn on Burlingame Avenue, discontinued candles, seconds, and occasional surplus candles are reduced in price at least 50% off original retails. The manufacturer keeps some very high profile company: it supplies gift candles and other candle accessories to trendsetting lifestyle stores, major department stores, and upscale gift stores and provides candles under private labels for famous collections. All the candles are scented with fragrances made exclusively in France (vanilla,

cedar, bergamot, ylang-ylang, exotic woods, melon/cucumber, etc.). Aromatherapy candles with 100% essential oils are in the collection. The candles are distinctive—rounds in several sizes have inset designs around the sides of the candles, including flowers, herbs, leaves, starfish, cinnamon sticks, hot red peppers, stars, and even dressmaker buttons (in silver or gold). The patterns are illuminated as the candles burn down through the center (no drips over the sides). Plain candle rounds come in a crayon-box range of colors. Assume anything wrapped in cellophane is first quality; other "bare" candles are usually seconds.

The candle beauties are pricey at retail—a 3-by-3-inch round $12 to $14 at retail is at least half off as discontinued, up to 80% off as a second. Ditto for first-quality 4-by-6-inch rounds at $28 to $34 at retail. Discontinued and seconds of three- to five-wick candles range from $20 to $30; plain (but fragrant) 3-by-9-inch columns hover around $8; and square-shaped aromatherapy candles are $5 or less. Lots of little candle accessories are left over—flat bases (tiles, recycled glass, slate) to protect furniture, plus vases, soaps, and other gift items recently part of the company's line. Locals stop in frequently to scout for bimonthly special promotions. Expanded hours between Thanksgiving and Christmas.

CHEAP PETE'S FRAME FACTORY OUTLET

4249 Geary Boulevard, San Francisco.
(415) 221-4720. M–Sat 10–6, W–Th until 8,
Sun Noon–5. MC, VISA, DIS. Parking: street.
(Other stores: 11 East Fourth Avenue, San Mateo;
Montecito Plaza, San Rafael; 1666 Locust Street,
Walnut Creek.)

If you have travel posters, prints, and family photos languishing in your closets and drawers because the cost of framing far exceeds the price of the picture, Cheap Pete's comes to the rescue with more than 10,000 ready-made frames in sizes ranging from 3-by-5-inch to 30-by-40-inch, including hard-to-find 4-by-6 and 5-by-5. The frames, available in metal, Plexiglas, and wood (styles for all decors), are wonderfully discounted. Also tabletop, collage, and frames for gift giving. You'll achieve maximum savings (20–60% off) if you select a ready-made frame; on custom framing expect savings of 20–40% off pricey frame shops. Labor costs and overhead are kept down by doing custom work on a production-line basis. Also, volume purchasing of frames and using leftover materials result in the discount prices.

COLLECTOR'S CORNER ART GALLERY

2441 San Ramon Valley Boulevard #4,
Diablo Plaza, San Ramon. (925) 829-3428.
M–Sat 10–6, Sun Noon–5. MC, VISA. Parking: lot.
Collector's Corner sells original art—numbered and limited editions—at nicely discounted prices. Its inventory is quite eclectic, ranging from very modest prints to more expensive (investment) pieces priced in the hundreds and even thousands. By far the largest part of the selection is in the middle range of framed pieces selling for $195 to $350. Markdowns on designated pieces can reach 30–40% off comparable prices at other galleries. Those able to spend big bucks (thousands) might be able to order a piece of art that they have seen in another fine art gallery and save 20–40% on the framed piece. The selection will appeal to the sophisticated connoisseur as well as those who simply want an affordable lithograph. Written certification on everything guarantees

authenticity. Artists in the collection include Thomas Pradzynski, Eidenberger, Viktor Shvaiko, Buckles, Thomas Kinkade, Mark King, Barbara Wood, S. Sam Parks, Sabzi, Royo, G. Gordon, Don Hatfield, Kati Roberts, Ming Feng, Jim Buckles, Fairchild, and many others. Framing prices are about 20–30% below typical frame shops.

DHARMA TRADING CO.

1604 Fourth Street (corner of F Street), San Rafael.
(415) 456-1211. www.dharmatrading.com.
M–Sat 10–6. MC, VISA, DIS. Parking: lot.
If the textile artist in you needs an avenue for expression, Dharma Trading can provide the essentials for you to paint your wardrobe. It carries dyes and coloring agents for fabric painting, silk-screening, batiking, etc. The company provides excellent information and how-to advice. It also offers a wide range of cotton and silk fabrics ready for dyeing. Even better, each piece in its extensive inventory of ready-made clothing for babies, children, and adults in "naked white" cotton and silk needs only a dip in the dye or a brush stroke before it's transformed into an original creation. Apparel includes baby sets, basic T-shirts, body-

wear, dresses, jumpers, scarf blanks, rompers, and other styles. The store's yarn brings in many women, who carefully check for special markdowns on this out-of-the-ordinary selection. Dharma satisfies the needs of "cottage industry" apparel manufacturers as well as just plain folks. To get the full picture, write or call for a catalog: P.O. Box 150916, San Rafael, CA 94915, or (800) 542-5227.

ELITE PICTURE FRAMES (MAIL ORDER)

1547 Jayken Way #B, Chula Vista, CA, 91911. (800) 854-6606. M–F 7–3:30. MC, VISA.
This mail-order company specializes in preassembled frames and wood sectionals for assembling your own frames at home. Many preassembled frames come complete with linen liners (some with gold or wood lips) in many different finishes: antique white, Renaissance gold, walnut, driftwood, cherry, oak, pewter, etc. Prices are good: a 12-by-16-inch frame ranges from $12.50 to $29.50. Custom wood sectionals are sold by the pair. The framing finishes available offer lots of design choices—traditional, ornate, contemporary, or natural, in widths ranging from ¾ to 2½ inches. Order two pairs for a frame and you'll receive four miter clips for easy joining. No special tools are needed, although wood glue is recommended for more secure joining. (Glue and hangers are not included.) To finish the project you may have to go to a local resource for mats and glass. Nielsen metal sectionals, linen liners, Fredrix stretched canvas, and oval stretched canvas are also available. The catalog features color pictures of its frames, but if you're still not certain about a particular framing finish, you can order samples for a small charge (to cover shipping). Call for a catalog and join all the corporations, schools, and galleries that have discovered this money-saving option for framing.

FRAMERS WORKSHOP

156 Russ Street, San Francisco. (415) 621-4226. M–F 9–5:30, Sat 9–2. MC, VISA. Parking: limited street (two spaces marked Tenant Only).
This business is not paying a high-priced rent in a commercial district, and it passes the savings on to its customers through lower prices. It's a do-it-yourself frame shop only if you buy all the materials and assemble them at home, an option for artists who find that the $6.39 to $13.50 assembly charge

adds up when they're framing many pictures for exhibit or sale. Aluminum framing and custom wood frames are available. You can select budget-priced materials to frame an inexpensive picture or print, or go first class with museum-quality materials for conservation mounting of fine artworks. Prices on aluminum frames are often lower than at do-it-yourself frame shops, even when all the work is done for you. Prices on basic conservation matting are also lower, but on the more elaborate fabric and French detail mats, Framers is competitive.

GENERAL BEAD

637 Minna Street, San Francisco. (415) 621-8187. T–Sat 10–5, Th until 7, Sun 1–4. VISA, MC, DIS. Parking: street.

The General Bead store in San Francisco is a serious bead wholesaler and the largest bead retailer in Northern California. Anyone willing to meet wholesale minimums (which vary from item to item) can buy at wholesale. However, those without resale numbers will have to pay appropriate taxes. Those interested in buying in smaller quantities will be charged retail prices. The store's strength is its high-fashion beads for the style-conscious client. Its main focus is on glass beads and on Austrian crystal pieces. The beads, in all varieties (ethnic, glass, bone, shell, pearl, antique, sterling, crystal, ceramic, brass, etc.) from around the world, are not readily available anyplace else. With two floors and 25,000 items in inventory, General Bead also offers artists metal studs, sequins, and rhinestones, plus such "tools and fixin's" as jewelry findings and much more. Be warned: The staff is geared toward working with professionals, and there's no time for counter seminars for novices about the esoterics of making jewelry.

GRAPHIK DIMENSIONS LTD. (MAIL ORDER)

2103 Brentwood Street, High Point, NC 27263. Catalog requests and orders (800) 221-0262. www.graphikdimensions.com. Daily 24 hours. MC, VISA, DIS.

Graphik Dimensions Ltd. is a mail-order company that publishes a catalog for consumers and volume frame users, including smaller frame shops. Its prices are the result of volume buying of framing materials. Most small frame shops pay a premium price to keep a wide variety of wood molding and aluminum framing on hand. Graphik offers preassembled frames in 5-by-7 to 14-by-18 inches (some to 24-by-30 inches), with prices ranging from $9.95 to $43.95. Several styles have linen liners. Sectional metal/aluminum or lacquer-finished frames are easy to assemble, with the hardware, hangers, and spring clips provided. Custom-made frames are just that—assembled at the factory and shipped to you. Frames larger than 50 inches are shipped in sections with an easy assembly kit. Turn page after page in the catalog and you'll see that almost every style of frame molding is available, whether you want an ornate gold-finished carved frame, a faux stone finish, burled wood, hand-lacquered, contemporary wood, touches of silver or gold, or a frame with a linen liner or antique brass corners. You don't have to buy blind. You can order a free sample of the metal or custom-made wood moldings. Precut acid-free mats, glass, and nonglare plastic in standard sizes are also available. Service is another point of pride for the company. Most orders are shipped within forty-eight hours. Shipping costs in many cases are offset by the fact that no sales tax is charged.

HANG

565 Sutter Street, San Francisco. (415) 434-4264. www.hangart.com. M–Sat 10–6, Sun Noon–5. MC, VISA, AE, DIS. Parking: pay lots.

If you're ready to upgrade from college era posters to real adult art, but not yet ready to spend the big bucks on fine art displayed by most of the galleries in the heart of San Francisco, there's hope to be found at Hang. Its mission is to provide high-quality art at affordable prices; its motto is "emerging artists for emerging collectors." The 4,000 square feet of Hang features the works of approximately 40 emerging artists at any one time who are working to gain exposure and build a collector base. The majority of work in a wide variety of contemporary styles and media sells for under $2,000. Hang's approach is to make neophytes comfortable (no snooty here), with artist biographies posted by the work so visitors can get some immediate insight into a particular artist's background, motivation, and process. As an alternative to purchasing, Hang offers a rental program that allows customers to either evaluate a piece before purchasing or simply refresh their surroundings by rotating their art.

Art, Craft, and Hobby Supplies

163

LEESEN INC.

New San Francisco address pending.
(415) 703-0086. www.leesen.com. Hours pending.
MC, VISA. Parking: lot.

Leesen will be at a new location by January 2000. It must leave its SOMA location so the building can be converted to a high-tech facility. Its Web site is probably the best way to keep in touch if you're looking for a dramatic gold-finished frame for a picture or mirror. Leesen frames are made out of a hardwood from China called "cham," which is used in construction, being especially good for lintels and other load-bearing applications. Most Leesen frames have handcrafted corner ornaments that are made from a chip-resistant resin compound. (This compound is different from the easily chipped plaster that some framers use.) Unlike most machine-made soft wood molding frames with exposed seams, Leesen's corner ornaments are made to discreetly cover the seams of the joints. The detailed designs give the frames an elegant (sometimes ornate) look without being overpowering or overdone, making them suitable accents for many rooms. The frames are hand-finished with gold leaf that will not dull or tarnish over time. Leesen is not a custom frame shop; the frames are fully assembled in popular sizes from 8-by-10 inches to 30-by-40 inches. Those who have shopped around will find that the frame prices are substantially lower than the prices on comparable frames—even on many look-alike frames made from softer woods like pine (often imported from Mexico). Taking the savings even further, the company's prices on plain or beveled mirrors are lower, and there's no charge for mirror assembly. Any way you look at it, these frames and framed mirrors offer a good value/quality/price ratio.

MITCHELL'S BEESWAX CANDLES

Factory Stores at Vacaville, Vacaville.
(707) 446-6448. Daily. MC, VISA. Parking: lot.

Beeswax candles are virtually drip-free, burn smoke-free, and last longer than petroleum-based candles. Mitchell's Beeswax Candles are expensive—some would say extravagant—and are sold in gift stores around the globe. A pair of 10-inch silhouette tapers may be priced $20 to $25 at these stores; but at the factory store you'll pay about $17. The store offers a complete range of pillars and tapers in a setting that's hard to resist.

SAN FRANCISCO MUSEUM OF MODERN ART RENTAL GALLERY

Building A, Fort Mason Center (at Buchanan and Marina), San Francisco. (415) 441-4777. T–Sat 11:30–5:30; closed August. MC, VISA. Parking: lot.
This gallery's goal is to give new artists exposure; you get an excellent chance to take part in the beginning of an artist's career at a very low cost. You can rent a painting, sculpture, or photograph for a two-month period, with the option of renting for another two months. If you decide to buy, half the rental fee applies toward the purchase price. Rental fees vary: an artwork with a purchase price of $300 to $399 rents for $44 for two months, while an $800 to $900 work would rent for $72. Many corporate offices, restaurants, and film companies come here for fine art to display. A suggestion: When selling your home, rent a dramatic piece of art to increase the buyer appeal. Regulars anticipate the gallery's major museum fund-raiser held each June. The fund-raiser consists of a special sale at which artists donate their works to be sold at 50% off regular prices. All proceeds go to the San Francisco Museum of Modern Art.

SAN FRANCISCO WOMEN ARTISTS GALLERY

370 Hayes Street, San Francisco. (415) 552-7392. T–Sat 11–6, Th until 8. MC, VISA. Parking: street.
This group has been around since women wore long skirts and wide-brimmed hats as they did their plein-air sketching in the fields near San Francisco—in other words, more than 100 years. The gallery is staffed by its members and volunteers (many past members have acquired fame and fortune). Members' exhibits change every month and the expressions are diverse—abstractionists, realists, expressionists, landscapists; painters, etchers, sculptors, etc. There is a rental gallery allowing art lovers to acquire an original piece on a payment plan, to take it home for a trial period before making a permanent buying decision, or just to borrow one for a limited period to brighten up a room for a particular occasion. In the gallery stands, many smaller works of art are available at reasonable prices, a good starting place for beginning collectors.

STAMPER'S WAREHOUSE

12147 Alcosta Boulevard, San Ramon.
(925) 833-8764. M–F 11–5:30, Th 10–9, Sat
9:30–5:30, Sun Noon–5. MC, VISA. Parking: lot.
If you think a little savings is better than none at all, you'll be satisfied with the 20% discounts reflected on the marked prices on stamps and papers from 300 companies. This modest operation shows just how popular stamping and creating scrapbooks has become. Customers are stamping papers (invitations, giftwrap, stationery, etc.), fabrics, lamp shades, and sundry other items. The costs on the paraphernalia can add up for the enthusiastic stamp/book crafter—stamps, stamp pads, inks, glitter, papers, stickers, and more. The warehouse offers more than 1,000 stamp images displayed along two walls of the outlet. Check the center tables for extra-special closeouts. The faithful look forward to special paper sales in March and October, and clearance sales in August and December. *Directions: From Highway 680, take the Bollinger Canyon exit east. Turn right on Alcosta. Located in the Country Faire Shopping Center.*

STRAW INTO GOLD

3006 San Pablo Avenue (corner of Ashby),
Berkeley. www.straw.com. (510) 548-5247.
T–F Noon–5:30, Sat 10–5:30. MC, VISA.
Parking: street.
If your pleasure comes from knitting or crocheting a fine-quality treasure, you'll want to use a natural fiber commensurate with the time you're going to spend making it. Straw Into Gold's customers approach this store as if making a pilgrimage to a religious shrine. Its attraction? One of the most impressive selections of fibers on the West Coast. This company serves a clientele of weavers, machine knitters, stores, and the public. The bargains are in the center aisle's baskets of closeout yarns and in the "cone" selection. It's much cheaper to buy off the cone, priced by the pound. You can save about 30% if you buy a whole cone (unused portions can be returned within six months for a refund). You'll also find notions, supplies, wonderful buttons, and more. Inquire about receiving a catalog and price list for mail orders.

UP AGAINST THE WALL

3400-D De La Cruz Boulevard, Santa Clara.
(408) 727-1995. M–F 9–4:30, Sat by appointment
only. MC, VISA. Parking: lot.

Catering to artists, galleries, and interior designers, Up Against the Wall primarily uses aluminum frames, as well as lovely wood framing materials, at prices about 15% below standard frame shops (higher discounts on quantity orders). If you have works to frame, you have two options: You can have the work done here from start to finish, or you can do it yourself at home, after purchasing the materials. This is a time-saver of special value to artists who may be framing a number of pieces at once for a show or fair. Many rely on this outfit to locate poster art that's not readily available in the mall stores. Call for directions.

VALLEY ART GALLERY

1661 Botelho Drive, Suite 110, Walnut Creek.
(925) 935-4311. T–Sat 11–5. MC, VISA. Parking: lot.
Valley Art exhibits, sells, and rents the work of established and emerging artists. Artists submit work to a jury of professionals for inclusion in its sales and rental program. There's a nice selection of original canvases priced $150 to $3,000. More than 200 artists are represented. The gallery also sells fine crafts, jewelry, and sculpture by talented local artisans. Rental periods extend for three months starting at $10/month.

Also See

Under Food and Drink:
SAN FRANCISCO HERB CO.

Fabrics

General Fabrics

BOLT'S END
2743 Castro Valley Boulevard (behind Burger King), Castro Valley. (510) 537-1684. T–Sat 10–5, Th until 8. MC, VISA. Parking: lot.
Bolt's End is overloaded with fabrics, lace, and trims, plus buttons, linings, and other paraphernalia, leftovers from apparel manufacturers. Prices are very good. The selection is always interesting, although somewhat eclectic. Check the bridal department for laces, headpieces, and some fabrics. Gussy up your home quilting cottons with home-decorating fabrics—cottons, brocades, tapestries, laces, and trims (fringe, gimp, piping, etc.). The clever owners have added a section of military surplus with mosquito netting, camouflage rip-stop and mesh, black vinyls, burlap, fishnetting, nonslip rubber matting, nylon cord, belting, and a grey wool from 1950 Swiss Army uniforms.

Discounts are 20–70% off retail. Good resource for buttons.

BRITEX FABRICS
146 Geary Street; 147 Maiden Lane, San Francisco. (415) 392-2910. M–Sat 9:30–6, Th until 8. MC, VISA, AE. Parking: lot.
Britex is an institution, its four floors stocked to the ceilings with a most distinctive selection of fabrics. It's the place of last resort, where you go when you can't find a particular fabric anyplace else. Now there is a bargain angle: on the third floor, you'll see remnants and end cuts at drastic reductions. Additionally, each floor has a sale table. I won't claim that the trims, tassels, wonderful selection of buttons (about 30,000), bridal, and jewelry findings are bargain priced, but just learning what is available makes most people happy. The store's expanded home-decorating department offers many distinctive and well-

priced fabrics that are more typical of those associated with restricted designer showrooms.

DISCOUNT FABRICS

501 Third Street (at Bryant), San Francisco.
(415) 495-4201. M–F 10:30–5:30, Sat 10:30–3:30.
MC, VISA, ATM. Parking: street.
(Other store: 1600 Harrison Street, Oakland.)
The goal at Discount Fabrics' warehouse is to sell fabric by the bolt, but you can buy in any quantity you want. This outfit buys from a variety of sources, resulting in many terrific buys and some fabrics that are hard to picture in any application. Yet there are times when one wants inexpensive fabric of any kind for utility without regard to quality, color, or pattern—to protect plants from frost, cover furniture, provide insulation, use as drop cloths, whatever. There's a little of everything: merino wool knits and an extensive selection of velvet, felt, drapery yardage, sheers, raw silk, dupioni silks, flannel, printed rayon, muslin, Lycra, vinyl, woven prints, knits (jersey and interlock), an expanded selection of home-decorating fabrics (upholstery, drapery, linings), and more. Small craft makers don't have to worry about minimums and can utilize the full library of fabric catalogs from Eastern and New York suppliers to find what they need. Check for notions: excellent prices on bulk buttons, zippers, Velcro, etc. Special-order bridal fabrics at discount prices, too! Prices seemed very good across the board.

FABRIX

835 Fourth Street, San Rafael. (415) 257-8811.
M–Sat 10–7, Sun 11–6. MC, VISA. Parking: lot.
(Other stores: Fabric Outlets, 101 Clement Street
at Second Avenue, San Francisco; 320 Gellert
Boulevard, Daly City.)
Fabrix has a split personality. Its two Fabric Outlet stores in San Francisco and Daly City may look like poor cousins when compared to the newer, more elegant Marin City store, but the selection is much the same. Most of the fabrics are purchased directly from manufacturers as roll balances, end rolls, discontinued goods, off dye lots, etc. These are the leftovers from upholstery, home decorating, and apparel manufacturers, and that's the appeal. You can recognize some fabrics as the same ones you've seen on furniture, accessories, or apparel in the retail marketplace. Home decorating fabrics

generally range in price from $3.99 to $19.99 a yard on rolls that may have 10 to 300 yards. New infusions of fabrics are added to the store's selection about twice a week, and generally you'll find a little of every category of home decorating fabric—jacquards, tapestries, drapery sheers, prints, solids, chenilles, etc. The most appealing fabrics don't gather any dust. If there is not enough fabric on any one bolt, don't hesitate to inquire if additional fabric may be available from the company's warehouse or other two stores. There's a designer corner where fabrics from apparel manufacturers like Calvin Klein, DKNY, Dana Buchman, and others are showcased. This dovetails nicely with the recent crossover trend of using fabrics from the apparel sector in upholstery or home-decorating applications—like decorative pillows or slipcovers from fleece, flannel, or worsted wools. Some colorful Jeanne Marc remnant rolls were marked at 30% off the $4.99 sale price. The Marin City Fabrix store has a couple of other niches worth noting. One corner is taken up with ready-made tab curtains—the same or very similar to those sold by many popular lifestyle stores. It's strictly a selection of what-you-see-is-what-you-get. No special orders because these

are manufacturers' closeouts and overruns. A very nice assortment of trims and tassels were well priced (with some priced substantially below competitors' pricing). Buttons sold individually at 25 cents each; 12 for $2; or 100 for $10. Don't count on the store for pattern books or patterns—there are just a few available for reference. Referrals to custom workrooms, custom sewing, and alterations provided. Overall, Fabrix may not have the depth of inventory that specialty fabric stores provide, but it has treasures just waiting to be unearthed throughout the selection.

SILKROAD FABRIC
811 Broadway, Oakland. (510) 763-1688. M–Th 10–7, F–Sat 10–8, Sun 11–6. MC, VISA. Parking: street.
It's hard to peg this fabric store. There's a smattering of everything—apparel, home-decorating, craft, and a few really yucky fabrics, plus some really wonderful silks (from a tie manufacturer). Many fabrics come from local manufacturers or contractors, which accounts for unusual selection. It's worth a visit if you're one not to leave any fabric source unexplored.

STONEMOUNTAIN & DAUGHTER

2518 Shattuck Avenue, Berkeley. (510) 845-6106.
M–F 9:30–6:30, Sat 10–6, Sun 11–5:30.
MC, VISA, AE. Parking: street.

The owners of this shop have long-established connections with the apparel industries in Los Angeles and New York. They combine quality with modest to maximum discounts in purchasing and pass on savings of 10–60% to their customers. They bring in leftover designer wools and silks from Calvin Klein, Donna Karan, Ellen Tracy, Liz Claiborne, and others. Along with some ordinary fabrics, there's a superior selection of quality, (relatively) bargain-priced wool, silk, cotton, and rayon blends that are really quite special—the fabrics are much more elegant than the store. Love the bridal fabrics and accessories, French reem-broidered lace with coordinating trims, the hand-selected bulk buttons to match with fashion fabrics, expanded selection of cotton for quilters, and patterns in stock always discounted 20%. To keep up with the latest sewing trends, more home-decorating fabrics are stocked or can be special ordered, alas at only modest discounts. Discriminating customers seeking fabric for sophisticated apparel rarely leave disappointed and look forward to discount coupons sent throughout the year to mailing-list customers.

THAI SILKS

252 State Street, Los Altos. (650) 948-8611.
www.thaisilks.com. M–Sat 9–5:30. MC, VISA, AE.
Parking: street.

Thai Silks is the retail division of Exotic Silks, an importer whose materials are used by artists, decorators, designers, yardage shops, quilters, and home sewers. Thai Silks has an extensive inventory of white and natural silks, hand-hemmed scarf blanks, and other items for artists to paint and dye, including ties, Christmas ornaments, and fashion accessories. There are exclusive prints, a dazzling array of fashion and bridal silks, velvets, and cut velvets. The prices are 20–40% off regular retail. La Soie lingerie is also available in a wide range of styles, fabrics, and prints. The first-quality silk gowns, chemises, kimono robes, teddies, cami-sole and tap pants sets, nightshirts, and pajamas are the most popular styles sold. Silk boxers for men in sizes 32–44. Women's sizes: P–XL. Prices are well below regular retail of specialty shops.

Home-Decorating Fabrics

ALAMEDA UPHOLSTERY SHOP

859 W. San Carlos Street, San Jose.
(408) 295-7885. M–F 9–5:30. MC, VISA, AE, DIS.
Parking: street/back lot.

This shop caters to do-it-yourselfers, with its huge selection of upholstery fabrics, plus fabrics that can be ordered from most major manufacturers, including Waverly, Schumacher, Pacific Hide & Leather, Barrow Industries, and many others at a 25% discount. Draperies, vertical blinds, pleated shades, and miniblinds are sold for a 25–50% discount when customers measure and hang their own. Foam rubber is cut to order.

CALICO CORNERS

1100 Howard Avenue, Burlingame.
(650) 558-1070. M–Sat 10–6, Sun Noon–5.
MC, VISA, DIS. Parking: lot.
(Other stores: Greenbrae, Los Altos, Pleasant Hill,
Sacramento, San Jose, Santa Rosa.)

The real bargains are not actually calico, but beautiful imported and domestic fabrics for upholstery, draperies, and slipcovers at 20–50% off regular retail. The emphasis is on first-quality fabrics, but you will find occasional seconds. Sample books and hanging swatches further extend the selection with discount pricing. Capture the look of hot new trends with specialty rods, finials, home-decorating books, and publications. Calico Corners now has its own workrooms, if you can't do it yourself. To keep everything in the corporate family, it now sells a complete line of upholstered furniture—pick a frame, pick a fabric, and in a few months your rooms are transformed. With reasonable, sometimes exceptional prices (during sales and on remnants), beautiful displays, and helpful clerks, these stores are an absolute pleasure to shop in.

D & S DISCOUNT FABRICS

1000 15th Street (at Bryant), Second Floor, San Francisco. (415) 522-1098. M–Sat 10–5. MC, VISA. Parking: street.

D & S Discount Fabrics, near Showplace Square, is a warehouse-styled showroom that's well organized and stocked with several categories of home-decorating fabrics. Some of the best buys are showcased in a side sale room where prices start at $3/yard on short end rolls and remnants. Those wanting recent or current fabrics for pillow making can consider hundreds of 24-inch pillow halves with finished edges at $3 each, or 24-inch and larger fabric pieces at $1.50 each. These are sample cuts from major fabric houses typically used in trade showrooms or by fabric reps. Larger, 1- to 4-yard pieces (often wing-display samples from trade showrooms) are priced well below wholesale. A large sample swatch gallery from several fabric distributors provides more options. Prices on custom-order fabrics vary from minimal to heart-stopping depending on the particular source or channel of distribution. Other fabrics (surplus yardage from local fabric suppliers and fabric distributors) are available from large bolts piled on tables. The outlet is strong on multipurpose fabrics that can be used for window coverings, bedding treatments, upholstery, etc. Vintage trims and fabrics (velvets from the 1920s, needlepoints, brocades, and tapestries from the 1930s and 1940s) occupy a few tables and satisfy purists renovating upholstered pieces or making decorative pillows. Many trims, while new, replicate vintage trims. Individually priced vintage bed linens and tablecloths (from old estate homes in Europe) add to this unusual selection. Discount-priced Dacron or goose-down pillow fillers are for sale. If you're talented enough to take on a drapery or slipcover project, you'll love the selection of workroom supplies and notions (heading tapes, drapery pins, welting, etc.), and trims, tassels, and tiebacks.

FABRICS & MORE

*460 Montgomery Street, The Marketplace,
San Ramon. (925) 277-1783. M–Sat 10–6,
Sun Noon–5. MC, VISA. Parking: lot.*
Fabrics & More is stocked with the latest home-decorating fabrics: lovely tapestries, chintz, jacquards, velvet, neutral cotton upholstery, sheers, and more. Overstocks offer the lowest pricing: $5/yard in the clearance corner, while prices on roll displays start at $15. Discounts are 20–60% off retail. Special orders at discount pricing are offered (buy more, save more). You'll find fabric from Braemore, Cyrus Clark, Waverly, Robert Allen, Harris, P. Kaufman, Bloomcraft, and many others. Need rods? There's the standard selection in stock, with more choices available from catalogs, at modest discounts. You can order elegant trims and tiebacks or pick up a tapestry pillow square. The staff is very knowledgeable, and advice is freely given. There is a $75 one-time charge for home visits. Once you have the fabric, the staff will arrange for labor. *Directions: From Highway 680, take Bolinger Canyon Road east to Alcosta. Turn right one block to Montgomery/ The Marketplace.*

FURBELOWS

*170-D Alamo Plaza, Alamo. (925) 837-8579.
M–F 10–5:30, Th until 8, Sat 10–5. MC, VISA.
Parking: lot.
(Other stores: 6050-A Johnson Drive, Suite A,
Pleasanton, 510/463-0242; 506 East El Camino
Real, Sunnyvale, 408/733-5797.)*
Fur•be•low (noun) 1. A ruffle or flounce on a garment; 2. a piece of showy ornamentation. This fabric chainlet is aptly named, with its selection of trims, fabrics, and wallpapers. It offers an upscale selection at downscale prices. On wallpaper books from most well-known companies you'll save 30% on papers, 20% on companion fabrics. Other fabrics are sold for 50–70% discounts off bolts nicely arrayed around the store. These are up-to-date home-decorating fabrics geared primarily to contemporary and traditional decors. You can always spend time looking through sample fabric books and special order what you need for a 20% discount; on large quantities, you may save even more. Check the sample selection of expensive, elegant decorator trims offered at a 20% discount by special order.

Furbelows is also spreading its wings with the addition of two major North Carolina–based upholstery and furniture lines offered at nicely discounted pricing. The aim? To increase its fabric sales. Customers who do not find the fabric they like in the selection offered by the furniture manufacturer can order the upholstered piece on a COM basis (customer's own material) and choose the fabric from Furbelows' inventory. Furbelows then ships its fabric to the company. Either way, Furbelows makes a sale. Because space is limited in the stores, only a few sample pieces from each company are on the floor for a look, sit, and feel evaluation. Catalogs reveal all the other styles available. Three types of pricing are involved: a straight 35% off manufacturer's list price on upholstery order (using manufacturer's fabric); 40% off on a COM basis (Furbelows fabric extra); ask about a slipcover option.

Often pictured in full-page glossy ads in many magazines, the extensive casegoods line is offered at the lowest markdowns allowed by the manufacturer (35–40% off). It's a mid- to-higher priced line with many style choices (very little contemporary). Catalog pages offer many choices in bedroom, dining, accent, and occasional living room pieces and groupings. Keep decorating with the 25–35% discounts off an extensive selection of wallpaper books, and nicely discounted prices on two lamp lines. The best bargain of all is the free decorating assistance by the talented staff members and March month-long sales for extra discounts of 10–30% off all in-stock fabric inventory. *Note: The Pleasanton and Sunnyvale stores need to expand to larger spaces. Call (925) 803-4136 for information on possible new locations.*

KAY CHESTERFIELD MFG. CO.
6365 Coliseum Way, Oakland. (510) 533-5565. M–F 8:30–5, Sat 9–1. MC, VISA. Parking: lot.
The Kay Chesterfield Mfg. Co. specializes in reupholstering furniture for residential and commercial clients around the Bay Area; to serve its clientele, it maintains an extensive in-stock inventory of fabrics. Bargains come into play when the bolts are sold down to a relatively small amount of yardage. Additionally, the owners buy roll balances and discontinued fabrics from mills and often find deals that are too good to pass up.

The deepest discounts are on small pieces, 1 to 8 yards. In any case, the minimum you'll save is about 50% off retail. Because fabrics can cost up to $50 to $100/yard wholesale, some prices may be unnerving. The greater part of the selection falls in the $10 to $30 price range. Many people who come in are making handbags, place mats, teddy bears, art, or craft projects. Very little in the way of drapery or bedspread materials. *Directions: Take 66th Avenue exit from Highway 880 to first light, and turn left (near Coliseum parking lot).*

LAURA & KIRAN WAREHOUSE SALES
2542 Tenth Street (between Dwight and Parker), Berkeley. (510) 647-1493, Fax (510) 647-1490. MC, VISA. Parking: lot.
Laura and Kiran Singh are a Bay Area couple who have been designing fabrics from India for eighteen years. Originally clothing designers, they have expanded into designing fabrics for home furnishings. They work directly with master weavers in India to create contemporary fabrics by traditional hand techniques. They wholesale their upholstery and drapery fabrics nationwide to furniture manufacturers and major fabric houses.

Four times a year, the colorful collection is sold to the public through highly anticipated warehouse sales. Their line offers a rich selection of coordinated color groupings—striking reds, deep indigoes, warm earthtones, crisp blacks and whites, breezy blues and greens, subtle neutrals, and luminous golds. All fabrics are 100% natural fiber, from rustic cottons to lustrous silks to textured linens. The wide selection ranges from their signature hand-dyed ikats, handloomed cotton solids, stripes, checks, and plaids to jewel-tone dupioni silks and hand-cut silk jacquard sari fabrics which have been turned into sheers for window treatments. In addition to fabrics, the warehouse sales also feature unique handmade items for the home. These vary from sale to sale, ranging from hand block-printed table linens and cushion covers in a bright array of colors to antique Indian textile pieces which can beautifully accent any decor. Warehouse sale savings range from as much as 75% off on fabric overruns, discontinued designs, and remnants to 50% off on table linens to 25% off on the entire current fabric stock. Seconds (dye imperfections) when available are sometimes priced as low as $3.95. Referrals can be made for custom sewing services. To be notified of warehouse sales (spring, summer, fall, and holiday season), fax or send a postcard with your name and address to Laura and Kiran to get on their mailing list.

MYUNG JIN STUDIO OUTLET

10 Liberty Ship Way #370 (Schoonmaker Building), Sausalito. (415) 331-8011. F only 10–4 (or by appointment). MC, VISA. Parking: lot.
Myung Jin Studio Outlet is top-notch for beautiful home-decorating fabrics. The owners design them in-house and have them made in India or the United States. These exclusive and expensive fabrics are sold to the design trade, and discontinued fabrics and mill ends await you at the studio. There are two primary fabric collections. First, the 54-inch heavy cottons in both subtle and crisp colorations (stripes, checks), ikat prints, contemporary textures, and solids to be used on leaning-toward-contemporary/informal furnishings. They also make great slipcovers. These are outlet-priced at $8 to $12/yard. Next, the exquisite rayon chenilles in unique weaves for more elegant and traditional applications are priced $35 to $45/yard.

Some fabrics are available in small quantities; others (mostly cottons) can easily accommodate any yardage requirements. Creative sewers with upscale inclinations will see many possibilities in the luxurious chenilles for making apparel. There's a small selection of beautiful silks. Finally, cones of chenille yarn (discontinued dye lots) are sold by the pound (about $15/pound)—of interest to weavers or knitters. Chenille throws and scarves, pillows, and sturdy tote bags are ready to go for those without time to sew.

NORMAN S. BERNIE CO.

1135 N. Amphlett Boulevard, San Mateo. (650) 342-8586. M, W, F 8–4:30 T, Th 9–5:30, first Sat every month 10–2. MC, VISA. Parking: street.
Psst! Many in-the-know designers slip in to buy bargain-priced fabrics here. The founder of this company is a fabric man from way back, selling mill ends to fabric retailers and dyeing and printing "naked" fabrics for manufacturers. You'll find full bolts of 60-inch denim (many types of stripes, plus solids in various weights); muslin (all weights and widths); cotton duck; sheeting; canvas; marine fabrics; drapery fabrics; scrims (gauzelike);

occasionally luxury and liner furs by the pound or yard; chintz; raw silk; and lots more. In the upstairs gallery you'll find full bolts of better-quality home-decorating and craft fabrics. The decorators and wanna-bes waste no time in snatching up yards of laundered jacquard for "shabby chic" treatments, washed chenilles, tapestries, and elegant damasks, with most priced at $22.50/yard. Bernie also buys leftover current patterns of upholstery fabrics and other home-decorating and special-use fabrics. Often there are only 6 to 9 yards left on a bolt, not enough to cover a sofa, but maybe enough to cover dining room chairs, a small chair, or pillows. Warning: Bernie's prices and selection can be addictive. Loved the sign on the door: "She who dies with the most fabric wins!" Located between Peninsula Avenue and Broadway exits off Hwy. 101. Outlet faces highway.

POPPY FABRICS

5151 Broadway (near 51st Street), Oakland. (510) 655-5151. M–F 9:30–8, Sat 9:30–5:30, Sun 11–5:30. MC, VISA. Parking: lot.
Poppy Fabrics excels in its selection of upscale and distinctive fabrics for sophisticated shoppers. Many fabrics are just not found in the typical store's selection of home-decorating fabrics. P. Kaufman, Covington, Collins, and Aikman are a few of its lines from major U.S. mills (some fabrics are exclusive imports). Create a *House Beautiful* result working with one of Poppy's unique French provincial fabrics, or choose an Italian tapestry—then embellish with a distinctive ribbon or braid from the trim department. A beautiful store, Poppy offers a nice level of customer support with knowledgeable staff, how-to books, and all the paraphernalia one needs to see a project from start to finish. Prices are discounted a little to a lot (20–60% off retail). Utilize Poppy's custom work-room and design services if you're too timid to go the do-it-yourself route.

RODOLPH FABRIC FACTORY OUTLET

989 West Spain Street, Sonoma. (707) 935-0316. W & Th 11–2, or by appointment. Hours subject to change during holidays. MC, VISA. Parking: lot.
This outlet focuses on unusual dye lots and remnants of fabrics traditionally sold only through interior designers. Fabrics normally priced from $80 to $120/yard at retail are offered via the outlet at $15 to $30/yard. There are beautiful colors and textures in a selection of silks, wools, and cottons found in contemporary and classical motifs. A great resource for those trying to capture that *Architectural Digest* image in their decorating projects, as well as a unique source for quilters and crafters. Also available, for $5 to $10/yard, is a selection of Jim Thompson Thai apparel silks. Call or sign up so you won't miss Rodolph's 3-day factory sale events every spring and fall.

S. BERESSI FABRIC SALES

1504 Bryant Street, Second Floor, San Francisco. (415) 861-5004. M–Sat 10–5. MC, VISA. Parking: lot.
S. Beressi, a local fabric wholesaler, gives the public a chance to buy a huge variety of first-quality leftover and discontinued fabric, thread, polyester fiberfill, and bedspreads from his upstairs warehouse. Prices are below wholesale to encourage fast sales and speedy removal. These materials are used not only for bedspreads, but for draperies, upholstery, slipcovers, costumes, apparel, and crafts. Fabrics purchased from mills on buying trips around the world include exquisite velvets, 120-inch drapery sheers, and silk damasks from Europe. Regulars at the outlet will recognize the almost prehistoric fabrics that get cheaper and cheaper every year. Special sale periods that usually start in mid-April and mid-October are prime-time shopping periods that yield extra discounts. Rely on Mr. Beressi for workroom referrals to suit your pocketbook—budget to best and priced accordingly. He's been around long enough to know everyone in the business.

THE SILK TRADING COMPANY

1616-A 16th Street (at Rhode Island), San Francisco. (415) 282-5574. M–F 9–5, Sat 10–5. MC, VISA. Parking: private lot.

There's one fabric showroom near the San Francisco Design Center that offers access to the public, good value, and a high level of personal service, unlike other "to the trade only" showrooms that occupy most Design Center buildings. The Silk Trading Company has recreated its successful Los Angeles home fabric emporium that has been profiled in *Elle Decor*, and has had its fabrics featured in *Martha Stewart Living*, *Metropolitan Home*, *Home*, and others. The company's specialty is silk fabric in every form, but that's not to say that you won't find other natural fibers and blends in velvets, chenilles, linens, and Egyptian cottons. The owners own fabric mills around the world. This allows them to eliminate the costs of a middleman/distributor and sell directly to the public. They also sell their own exclusive label (Zimmer & Koplavitch), drapery hardware, handmade Egyptian trims and tassels (designed to match their fabric), and more.

There is one price for everyone, designer or consumer. Prices on most fabrics are significantly less than comparable fabrics sold through the area's designer trade showrooms; they are still not inexpensive. The Como silk (an upgraded dupioni often used in drapery fabrications) is available in 60 colors. A consumer may end up paying as much as $40 to $60 in a trade showroom; here it's $22 per yard. Prices on the wide variety of silk fabrics, 54 inches to 60 inches wide, range from $20 to $85 a yard. The fabric orientation is sophisticated, luxurious, and very upscale. You won't find any chintz or cotton country plaids and florals. Minimum fabric purchase is one half yard. Swatches are provided for matching. Unlike restricted trade showrooms, there are bolts of fabrics beautifully displayed and ready for cutting, eliminating any delay in buying and acquiring the fabric. This is a real benefit for designers or anyone trying to complete a project quickly. Many fabrics work beautifully for apparel or bridal patterns.

The Silk Trading Company is more than a fabric store. You can buy fabrics, then have them made to order into whatever you want: bed linens (duvets, shams, bedskirts), lampshades, chair upholsteries, draperies, or Roman shades from the company's own workrooms. The company has developed a substantial mail-order department for fabrics and custom draperies. Six different drapery styles are offered with labor costs for drapery, lining, or interlining ranging from $65 to $140 per fabric width (fabrics not included). Count on three weeks for delivery. You can rely on the impressive full-size drapery display models to bring the fabrications into focus. The staff is accommodating and knowledgeable; referrals can be made to design professionals for those who need more than a little help; and best of all, you can walk out the door with your fabric knowing you've paid a fair price.

Also See

Under Bay Area Manufacturers' Factory Outlets:
EMERYVILLE OUTLET; LAS MANOS

Under Wedding and Formal Wear:
GUNNE SAX/JESSICA MCCLINTOCK

Under Children's Clothing:
CHICKEN NOODLE; SWEET POTATOES

Under Art, Craft, and Hobby Supplies:
DHARMA TRADING CO.

Under Draperies and Window Coverings:
ALL LISTINGS

Under Furniture and Home Accessories—Catalog Discounters:
ALL LISTINGS

Under Giftware and Home Decor:
CRATE AND BARREL OUTLET

Office Supplies

Three mammoth stores with locations all over the Bay Area dominate the office supply market. Office-Max, Office Depot, and Staples are self-service operations selling a complete selection of basic office necessities. Prices are very competitive—each claims discounts of 30–70% off retail—and usually much lower than at other office supply stores.

ARVEY PAPER CO.

2275 Alameda Street (at Potrero), San Francisco.
(415) 863-3664. M–F 8–5:30, Sat 10–4.
MC, VISA. Parking: street/lot.
(Other stores: Oakland, Redwood City, San Jose.)
Arvey offers the best selection of printers' supplies and papers of every description, plus graphic supplies, light printing equipment, etc. It caters to small to midsize businesses; the average consumer gets a fair shake, too! Arvey sells business machines, pens, janitorial needs, and lots more. If you're a big user of stationery supplies, get on its mailing list.

KELLY PAPER

1375 Howard Street, San Francisco.
(415) 522-0420. M–F 7:30–5, Sat 9–1.
MC, VISA, AE, DIS. Parking: lot.
(Other stores: Concord, Hayward, Oakland, Palo Alto, San Carlos, South San Francisco.)
This company is handy if you've started producing your own letterhead, flyers, reports, or whatever, using the newer, more affordable laser or ink jet printers. Kelly's mission in life has been to supply the various print shops and offices with all their needs, but do-it-yourselfers can also stop in to shop and lay in a supply of papers. As paper specialists, Kelly offers a better range of quality, finishes, weights, and color. For fun, take a look at all the laser printer papers with designs for invitations, announcements, holiday cards, and envelopes to match. Mailing-list customers get the word on specials for stocking up and extra savings.

Stationery and Party Supplies

Party supply stores have proliferated all around the Bay Area. Select the store that is closest to you, but note that particular stores may have something extra to offer. Here's the general profile that applies to the stores in this section: They all have a good selection of paper party products; paper plates, napkins, plastic utensils, table covers, and paper place mats are typically about 25% less than at well-known specialty stores. You'll frequently find lots of extras: bibs, crystal (plastic) hostess or caterers' trays and punch bowls, regular and helium balloons, party hats, favors, carnival-type toys for children, and more. Most stores have good buys on giftwrap; some also carry craft supplies, silk flowers, and baskets.

BOSWELL'S DISCOUNT PARTY SUPPLIES
1901 Camino Ramon, Danville. (925) 866-1644.
M–Sat 9–6:30, Sun 10–5. MC, VISA, DIS.
Parking: lot.
(Other stores: 5759 Pacheco Boulevard,
Pacheco; 3483 Mt. Diablo Boulevard, Lafayette;
Rosewood Pavilion Center, Pleasanton.)
Boswell's has wonderful gifts, gags, etc. Great selection of paper products in fabulous colors discounted 30%. Everything for weddings and parties for all ages and occasions. Trophy ribbons, stocking stuffers, jokes, toys, gag gifts, wedding and shower accessories, bandannas, inexpensive hats, and scads more. Depending on the size of your order, you can save up to 25% on wedding invitations. Craft and educational supplies, too! Individual store hours may vary.

THE CARD AND PARTY DISCOUNT OUTLETS

1880 Alum Rock Avenue, San Jose.
(408) 254-7060. M–F 9:30–7, Sat–Sun 10–5.
MC, VISA. Parking: lot.
(Other stores: 562 E. El Camino Real,
Pavlina Plaza, Sunnyvale; 545 Meridian Avenue,
Suite F, San Jose.)
For help planning for a big event, you've come
to the right place. Not only will you find all paper
goods at 50% off, you'll also scoop up wrappings
and ribbons at minimum 20% discount and
catering supplies at 30–50% off. Greeting cards
are always 50% off retail, while the intriguing
collection of closeout giftware (including stuffed
animals, ceramics, rubber stamps, stamping
accessories, and frames) is also discounted 30–50%.
Lots of little goodies for tots, hats for grown-ups,
piñatas, and balloons complete the picture.
Also, wedding invitations at modest discounts.
Those with resale numbers can shop at its Cash
& Carry warehouse at 143 E. Virginia Street in
San Jose, (408) 287-3177.

CASH & CARRY WAREHOUSE

1201 Andersen Drive, San Rafael. (415) 457-1040.
M–F 8:30–5, Sat 8:30–3. Cash/Check. Parking: lot.
If you're cooking for a crowd or planning a big
party, the Cash & Carry Warehouse may make
your preparations easier. The paper and party
products selection is as complete as most party
supply stores throughout this chapter, plus there
is a good selection of janitorial products. Food
too—they offer institutional products used by
restaurants, catering services, and schools.

CRAIG'S WAREHOUSE

15 Dodie Street, San Rafael. (415) 456-5090.
M–Sat 10–6, Sun 11–5. MC, VISA. Parking: lot.
A local favorite for party paper goods, favors,
party paraphernalia, and balloons on a budget.
Although I can shop much closer to home, I whiz
off the freeway to check out the "specials"—
including items like sun glasses and readers at $4
to $6 (so I can really stock up) and lots of other
little surprises. The store is a bit of a mess, but
that appeals to bargain hunters.

CURRENT FACTORY STORE

190 Golf Club Road, Pleasant Hill. (925) 602-0644.
M–F 10–7, Sat 10–6, Sun 11–5.
MC, VISA, AE, DIS. Parking: lot.

I'd speculate that anyone involved with fund-raising efforts over the years has come across the Current company. The outlet is where overstock and discontinued merchandise is sold at modest to very gratifying markdowns. In keeping with new trends, you can find computer stationery for all your social correspondence at 9 cents a sheet or about $5 a pack (some with more than 25 envelopes); also supplies for memory books and scrapbook pages. Greeting cards at 2 for $1 generate the most traffic into the store, but don't overlook the gift wrap, party invitations, paper party supplies, stickers, gift items, ribbons, bows, and more. Occasionally, the company picks up discontinued merchandise from outside the company for its outlet division (I spotted inventory from Precious Moments, Anne Geddes, Telly Tubbies, and Figi frames on my last visit). Current keeps everyone in mind, so all occasions, ages, and styles are well represented.

DIDDAMS DISCOUNT PARTY HEADQUARTERS

215 Hamilton Avenue, Palo Alto. (650) 327-6204.
M–W 10–7, Th–F 10–8, Sat–Sun 9:30–5.
MC, VISA. Parking: street.
(Other store: 10171 South De Anza Boulevard, Cupertino.)

A great place for children's parties, but also reliable for all adult occasions! Balloon prices are really sharp. Theme parties a specialty; lots of hats, hostess servers, and party accessories. You may save considerably (up to 40%) on wedding invitations, depending on the size of your order and the processing time involved; appointments and a minimum $50 processing charge are required for this service.

THE PAPER OUTLET

Factory Stores at Vacaville, Vacaville.
(707) 449-3442. Daily. MC, VISA, DIS. Parking: lot.
(Other outlets: Folsom, Gilroy, Lathrop,
Milpitas centers.)
Stop by for giftwrap, gift boxes, ribbons, party
goods and decorations, greeting cards, invitations,
thank-yous, books, games, and puzzles, plus paper
products for the home and office at proper savings.
These are selected closeouts and seconds. The
wonderful stock of giftwrap (appears to be roll
ends from giftwrap departments) is hard to resist.

PAPER PLUS OUTLETS

1643 and 1659 San Pablo Avenue (north of
University Avenue at Virginia), Berkeley.
(510) 525-1799. M–Sat 10–6, Sun Noon–5.
MC, VISA. Parking: side lot.
(Other stores: 2114 Center Street, Berkeley;
1309 Castro, San Francisco.)
The store in Berkeley may be a bit of a mess, but
the other outlets are neat and tidy. You'll discover
satisfying bargains on discontinued and surplus
inventory from many sources including the well-
known Papyrus stores. There's a tantalizing selection of quality cards, giftwrap, and stationery at
up to 70% off retail prices. The unique giftwrap is
sold in single sheets; greeting cards, calendars,
books, frames, small children's toys, and all plush
animals are always 50% off. Photo albums, stationery in boxes, diaries, and guest books are
discounted. A complete party-goods inventory at
very competitive prices. You'll find boxes in any
size, even tiny boxes for your truffles! The store at
1659 San Pablo is devoted to seasonal specials
and is merchandised accordingly (some very special
Christmas and Chanukah merchandise). Great
source whenever you're planning theme parties
around holidays. Check the new sections featuring
ceramics and other fine art from local artists.

PAPER PLUS/PAPYRUS OUTLET

Factory Stores at Vacaville, Vacaville.
(707) 447-7924. MC, VISA, AE, DIS. Parking: lot.
A version of Paper Plus above, but under different ownership. Immaculate displays bear a strong resemblance to your neighborhood Papyrus store, except the merchandise is discontinued (not that you can tell). Cards of all kinds are always 50% off, bulk sheets of gift wrap are usually $1 each; there's oodles of little gift items and bargains at every turn.

PARTY AMERICA

1257 Marina Boulevard, Marina Square,
San Leandro. (510) 297-5110. Daily. MC, VISA.
Parking: lot.
(Other stores: Campbell, Dublin, Larkspur,
Pleasant Hill, Redwood City, San Jose,
Santa Clara, Santa Rosa, Union City.)
Party America stores sell paper products for parties, plus balloons, Wilton cake-decorating supplies, hostess servers, etc. Greeting cards are discounted 50% every day; wedding and party invitations from several catalogs at 20% discount. Good overall party resource.

PARTY CITY

1909 Mt. Diablo Boulevard, Walnut Creek.
(925) 945-8200. M–Sat 9–8, Sun 10–5.
MC, VISA, AE, DIS. Parking: street.
(Other stores: Dublin, El Cerrito, Sacramento,
San Lorenzo.)
One hundred and fifty stores around the country and growing. This is the first in the Bay Area, and the profile is similar to all the other party stores mentioned in this chapter. Good end-of-season half-price sales, frequent special promotions, and special discounts to local schools, caterers, restaurants, churches, synagogues, clubs, corporations, etc.

THE PARTY WAREHOUSE

221 Oak Street (at Third Street), Oakland.
(510) 893-1951. M–F 10–6, Sat–Sun 10–5.
MC, VISA. Parking: street.
(Other stores: Alameda, Daly City, El Cerrito, San
Bruno, San Francisco, San Leandro, San Mateo.)
The Party Warehouse discounts 20–50% on party
necessities: theme-party paper products, as well
as wedding, juvenile birthday, and baby shower
departments, which are quite impressive. Bargain
prices apply on giftwrap, ribbon, classroom
decorations, Christmas and other seasonal decorations. Additional discounts are available for
caterers, churches, and schools.

PAULA SKENE DESIGNS

1250 45th Street, Suite 240, Emeryville.
(510) 654-3510. First Sat of every month, 9–3.
Checks/VISA. Parking: street.
Paula Skene is a wonderful resource for premium-
quality and elegant stationery, sold in galleries,
museums, and fine stationery stores in the United
States and Europe. These are cards that people
do not throw away. Paula uses heavy, fine-quality
paper and creates designs of deeply embossed

and elegantly foil-stamped images that may require
as many as seven passes through the presses.
These cards are works of art, most worthy of framing. At the warehouse sales, the stationery is sold
for 50% off retail. Occasional cards are about
$1.75 each; boxed cards about $14 for 8; boxed
stationery (20–30 sheets) for $12; and enclosures
about 75¢ each. Not inexpensive (when compared
to the discount card and party stores), but a solid
value. You'll want to stock up and keep these
beauties on hand for classy correspondence. To
keep up with sale dates, make sure to have your
name added to the mailing list. *Note: Corporate
designs are a specialty.*

Wedding Invitations

Many of the stores listed above sell wedding
invitations from budget to midpriced books for
modest discounts, typically 20–25% off published
price lists. There are also many mail-order companies for invitations that advertise prominently in
bridal magazines. Most have 800 numbers, special
consultation lines, and unconditional guarantees.

If you requested information from each company, you could fill a shopping basket with packets that include sample invitations, catalogs, and complete instructions for ordering. Mail-order prices are considerably less than the prices listed in most midpriced books carried locally, but there is a definite difference in the quality of the paper. In other words, for half the price, you'll get half the quality. Depending on how one wants to allocate the money in a wedding budget, and how important the quality or image conveyed by choice of an invitation, the mail-order option may be an acceptable alternative to local stores. It's a very personal decision. I can guarantee that when it comes to the wording and many esoteric details of invitations, you'll wish you were sitting face-to-face with an experienced stationer.

Also See

Under Art, Craft, and Hobby Supplies:
AMSTERDAM ART

Under Food and Drink:
CENTRAL CASH 'N CARRY

Under General Merchandise—
Discount Stores, Liquidators:
ALL LISTINGS

Under General Merchandise—
Membership Warehouse Clubs:
COSTCO

Food and Drink

What was true thirty years ago is still true today: Savvy consumers can easily trim grocery bills by monitoring weekly ads for specials at local supermarkets. When prices are low, buy in quantity. If you have a freezer, stock up. Clip coupons, but only on products that suit your family's needs. Often coupons don't bring prices below store brands, or below featured specials on competing brands. Too often, they apply to products that have little nutritional value and offer "savings" on products you wouldn't buy otherwise. If it's convenient, shop warehouse supermarkets like Food 4 Less and Pak N Save. Costco and Sam's Club are obvious money-saving sources if you can handle the multiple or oversize packaging on most products.

Farmers' markets: Check local papers for announcements of seasonal farmers' markets. Produce fresh from the farm is usually—not always—offered at lower-than-supermarket prices.

(Many folks are more concerned about flavor and freshness than price.) Local farmers' markets are open year-round in many communities. Booths selling gourmet edibles (mustards, vinegars, baked goods, sausages, etc.), esoteric greens, specialty vegetables, and fresh cut flowers are delighting and expanding the bounty for shoppers. For a listing of Bay Area certified farmers' markets call (800) 897-FARM or (800) 949-FARM.

Bakery thrift shops: It's truly worthwhile to check the Yellow Pages for the bakery outlets close to you. Parisian, Oroweat, Langendorf, Kilpatrick, and many other bakeries maintain thrift stores to sell their day-old bread and freshly baked surplus. Savings range anywhere from 20–75% off retail. Buy a lot at one time; you can freeze whatever you don't use. My favorite? Oroweat/Entenmann's Boboli pizza breads sold half-price every day.

BEVERAGES & MORE

2900 N. Main Street, Walnut Creek.
(925) 472-0130. M–F 10–9, Sat 9–9, Sun 10–7.
MC, VISA. Parking: lot.
(Other stores: Albany, Colma, Mountain View,
Oakland, Pleasanton, Sacramento, San Francisco,
San Jose, San Rafael, Santa Clara, Santa Rosa or
call 888/77-BEVMO.)

Along with its competitive pricing, Beverages &
More offers a connoisseur's selection of wines,
organized by country and varietal—from box wines
to fine vintages. It would take you almost two
years to work through the beer selection alone if
you sampled a new beer every day. Conscientious
hosts who want to provide nonalcoholic drinks for
their guests have hundreds of choices, too. In the
"More" category are packaged specialty foods
including mustards, seasoning mixes, candies,
snacks, coffees, and teas. New deli counters are
satisfying the palates of gourmets with cheeses,
olives, meats, and sundry other offerings. Cigar
aficionados can count on a good selection. The
company's not timid about posting the prices of
local competitors for comparison. Join ClubBev
for special membership savings.

THE CANDY JAR FACTORY OUTLET

2065 Oakdale Avenue, San Francisco.
(415) 550-8846. M–W 8–4. Before major holidays:
M–F 8–4. MC, VISA. Parking: street.

The Candy Jar produces truffles for specialty
candy stores and upscale shops. If you're willing
to go off the beaten path to its plant, you can
save a little or a lot depending on what you buy.
Basic and deluxe truffles in more than a dozen
flavors sell for $1 each ($1.25 to $1.50 elsewhere).
In addition to truffles, it also sells oversize turtles
(nuts and caramel) and other heavenly chocolate
candies. The best everyday buys are on seconds
(small surface imperfections), closeouts, and overruns. After holidays you may find deep discounts
on packaged chocolates. Budget watchers can
buy truffles in any amount for a big event or wedding and handle all the packaging and wrapping
themselves, or the Candy Jar Factory will do the
packaging for you.

CENTRAL CASH 'N CARRY

190 Keyes Street (at Fifth), San Jose.
(408) 975-2485. M–F 7:30–6, Sat 9–5,
Sun 9-Noon. MC, VISA. Parking: lot.

(Other stores: 1315 16th Street, San Francisco; 1131 Elko Drive, Sunnyvale.)

Central Cash 'N Carry is another option for the party planner. You'll find restaurant-sized cans and jars of condiments, salsas, cheese sauces, and other sauces as well as ice cream toppings, punches, and syrups. Also many hostess and catering trays, bowls, and pans. Good paper party products, piñatas, and favors, too. This is a no-frills warehouse store with many institutional supplies. Delivery service available.

CHOCOLATE FACTORY OUTLET

1291 Fremont Boulevard (next to Fish Wife restaurant), Seaside. (831) 899-7963. M–Sat 9:30–9, Sun 12:30–5. MC, VISA. Parking: lot.

It's right out of *I Love Lucy*—chocolate tunnels and fast-moving conveyor belts. Pick up a plastic glove and a box or bag and ramble down the 40-foot chocolate bar. Choose your favorite chocolates: truffles, turtles, caramels, English toffee, nuts, chews, and more. When you're done and the box has been weighed, you'll pay $9.95/pound (close to wholesale). If you're going to hide in the closet to eat these treats, then maybe you'll settle for a ½-pound bag of "bloopers" for $3 when available. They may be ugly, misshapen, or stuck together, but they taste just the same. The diet-conscious may opt for sugar-free chocolates at $10.95/pound. Lovely hand-packed gift boxes and baskets available. Locals and visitors alike can tour the factory anytime, or arrange for special chocolate-making classes.

COUNTRY CHEESE

2101 San Pablo Avenue, Berkeley. (510) 841-0752. M–Sat 9–6, Sun 10–5. Cash/Check. Parking: street.

Domestic and imported cheeses, meat products, dried fruits, nuts and seeds, grains, spices by the ounce, and health food items at wonderful prices. You'll love the old-fashioned country store atmosphere, with bins for scooping out grains and rice. I've found some pricey ingredients, like dried porcini mushrooms, at decent discounts. Inquire about discounts for co-ops and volume orders.

GROCERY OUTLETS

2001 Fourth Street, Berkeley. (510) 845-1771. M–Sat 8–9, Sun 9–7. Cash/Check/Food stamps. Parking: lot.

(*Other stores: Antioch, Fremont, Hayward, Newark, Oakland, Petaluma, Rancho Cordova, Redwood City, San Jose, San Pablo, Vacaville.*) Specializing in closeouts, packaging changes, and surplus goods, Grocery Outlets offers a constantly changing inventory at up to 40% savings. Be prepared to buy whatever the company has captured from the marketplace. Dry groceries, frozen and refrigerated foods, health and beauty aids, wines and beers, housewares, and general merchandise are backed with a 100% money-back guarantee. You may find well-known and unfamiliar brand names, as well as I've-never-seen-that-before products. Some excellent buys on gourmet and diet frozen dinners, ice creams, seasonal items, juices, and snacks!

HARRY AND DAVID

Factory Stores at Vacaville, Vacaville. (707) 451-6435. Daily. MC, VISA, AE, DIS. Parking: lot. (Other outlets: Folsom, Gilroy, Napa, Petaluma centers.)
Harry and David is a catalog company specializing in gourmet treats. Each catalog's tempting selection of gift baskets may include cheeses, candies, fruit (fresh or dried), jams, and more. You'll find products from the catalogs at the outlets: snack foods, boxes of candy, baked sweets, very elegant tortes, luscious cheesecakes (a company specialty), or seasonal spiral-sliced hams and smoked turkey. All are sold at the stores for 20–50% off catalog retail. They are every bit as good, wholesome, and fresh as what you'd get by ordering from the catalog. Other catalog items include gifts, home decor, kitchen-oriented products, and garden items from the Jackson & Perkins catalog.

HERMAN GOELITZ—
JELLY BELLY VISITOR CENTER

2400 N. Watney Way, Fairfield. (707) 428-2838. www.jellybelly.com. M–F 9–5. MC, VISA. Parking: lot. (Other outlet: The Jelly Belly Store, Factory Stores at Vacaville.)
The Herman Goelitz candy factory in Fairfield is the company Ronald Reagan made famous. The company's visitor center has developed "major" entertainment and recreational value with delightful tours, a cafe, educational activity center, birthday party rooms, and jelly belly–shaped heli-pad

to greet any visitors arriving by helicopter. Those wanting to take home some "inventory" can buy the Belly Flops. These are jelly belly beans that didn't pass the test for perfect appearance because they were too big, too small, or joined together. Typically, a two-pound bag is $4, an additional bag is sold for a penny. Of course, purists can buy first-quality, full-priced candies.

JOSEPH SCHMIDT CONFECTIONS

3489 16th Street (at Sanchez, one block south of Market), San Francisco. (415) 861-8682. M–Sat 10–6:30. MC, VISA. Parking: street.
Joseph Schmidt makes premium chocolates sold at quality department stores. They're very expensive! A single truffle may sell for $2, or $25/pound and more at upscale stores. It's a lot more than See's candy, but less than Godiva and Teuscher premium candies. This small store serves as an outlet and a test market, and is always stocked with a tempting selection of truffles and other candies, like chocolate-covered nuts and the exceptional candy sculptures (many holiday-themed) that are Joseph Schmidt hallmarks. Depending on whose prices you use for comparison, you may be saving

25–50% off retail. Truffles in a tempting variety of flavors are just $1 each. The store is stocked with many appealing and unique gift-oriented candy assortments.

LETTIERI & CO.

410 East Grand Avenue, South San Francisco. (650) 873-1916. M–F 9–5. Cash/Check. www.lettieri.com. Parking: lot.
This company imports gourmet brands for delis, supermarkets, and gourmet food outlets. Specialties: olive oils, balsamic vinegars, pastas, fancy treats, desserts, jams, and syrups. Stock up on assorted bags of pastas for as low as 50¢/pound, panettone from $3.99 to $9.99, and balsamic vinegar of all ages with prices ranging from $1.99 to $13.95 a bottle. Most imports are from Italy, but you'll also find Austrian jams, Hungarian pickles, and various German treats. You'll pay more than wholesale, but quite a bit below retail. This small outlet is located next to the office.

PLUMPJACK WINES

3201 Fillmore Street, San Francisco.
(415) 346-9870. M–F 11–8, Sat–Sun 10–7.
MC, VISA, AE. Parking: street.
PlumpJack sells a surprising 150 wines under $10 and is committed to offering good values on all its wines, indicated by its printed "Compare Our Prices" list and price guarantee. The company specializes in Californian and Italian wines. You'll find familiar labels and vintners, as well as those more easily recognizable to connoisseurs. Call or stop by and you'll get help putting together a case of wine that should delight wine aficionados. A 10% case discount helps, too! Delivery free anywhere in San Francisco; UPS otherwise.

SAN FRANCISCO HERB CO.

250 14th Street (bet. Mission and South Van Ness), San Francisco. (415) 861-7174, (800) 227-4530.
M–Sat 10–4. MC, VISA, DIS. Parking: street.
Go to the San Francisco Herb Co. for ingredients! Open to the public, it's a wholesale distributor of gourmet spices, culinary herbs, nuts and seeds, medicinal herbs, organic herbs, potpourri ingredients and fragrance and essential oils. It does most of its business by mail and requires a $30 minimum to place an order—but there's no such requirement for outlet shoppers. You pay only one price: wholesale. Most products are available in 4-ounce and 1-pound sizes. Call for a free catalog with potpourri recipes.

SMART & FINAL

24601 Mission Boulevard, Hayward. (510) 733-6934.
Daily 9–9. MC, VISA, DIS. Parking: lot.
(Other stores: Twenty Bay Area locations—
see Geographical Index.)
Smart & Final stores offer a spic-and-span shopping environment along with a fairly complete grocery selection; institutional foods; paper, party, and janitorial supplies; business and office supplies; and extensive frozen food and deli departments. Prices are sometimes higher than warehouse clubs, but there's no membership requirement. Labels in English and Spanish on most products.

TRADER JOE'S

337 Third Street, Montecito Plaza, San Rafael.
(415) 454-9530. Daily 9-9. MC, VISA. Parking: lot.
(Other stores: Seventeen Bay Area locations—

see Geographical Index or call 800/ShopTJS.)
Just about everyone else stops by Trader Joe's to
load up on gourmet foods and condiments, bakery
products, cheeses, ready-to-serve wholesome gourmet specialties, wine, beer, health products, etc.
There's a wonderfully casual and friendly ambiance
to these stores, and prices are usually excellent on
the often exotic offerings highlighted in every
"Fearless Flyer" specials announcement. Some of
the foods will please health-conscious consumers
who want products without eggs, salt, sugar, MSG,
dairy, or preservatives. The wine selection is so-so
to superb; prices are excellent. Caveat: I wouldn't
buy a case without first trying a bottle.

WINE CLUB

953 Harrison Street, San Francisco.
(415) 512-9086, (800) 966-7835. M–Sat 9–7,
Sun 11–6. MC, VISA. Parking: lot.
(Other outlet: 1200 Coleman Street, Santa Clara.
800/678-5044.)
The wine connoisseurs I know have put Wine Club
on their list of sources thanks to its pricing and
selection. Anyone can shop and take advantage of
its low markups, about 6–12% above wholesale.

Budget shoppers can find a Chardonnay priced
under $5 or $10, while serious connoisseurs can
trim costs even when buying a world-class
Burgundy at $78. Wines come from all over the
world. If you're on the mailing list, you'll get "For
Wine Lovers," the monthly buyer's guide, which
lists most wines in stock followed by a designation
of its value and availability. You can follow up with
a phone order, UPS delivery, or local courier
service for a $15 flat fee for up to five cases.

Also See

Under Cosmetics and Fragrances:
CRABTREE & EVELYN, LTD. OUTLET

Under General Merchandise—
Discount Stores, Liquidators:
ALL LISTINGS

Carpets, Area Rugs, and Flooring

The evolution (some would say it's a revolution) of the carpet industry continues. On the manufacturing level, companies have merged and consolidated until the greater part of the market is controlled by just two companies. On the dealer level, buying groups have been formed (like True Value and Ace Hardware) to gain more leverage in buying. Through these alliances, they've combined advertising and marketing efforts. The major buying groups are recognized through their advertising as Trustmark and Carpet One and Carpet Max. Many local dealers have joined these alliances. While this is beneficial to the dealers, it does not allow consumers the wide latitude to comparison shop that they have enjoyed in the past. The Trustmark members are able to private-label their carpets, while Carpet One dealers sell carpets exclusively to their members. Price guarantees offered by members ensure that dealers are likely to keep pricing in line. Territories are protected to

further control competition. Recently, some dealers have made comparison shopping more confusing by breaking with industry standards and pricing carpet by the square foot rather than the square yard. (I think it's a clever ploy to make the carpet appear less expensive at first glance.) And major "big box" warehouse stores have added to the competitive marketplace pressure.

As a consumer, it is now more difficult to rely on brand identification and style names when making comparisons. To determine value, shoppers have to pay more attention to comparable qualities between carpets: the depth and density of pile, warranties and guarantees, stain-protection finishes, etc. When making comparisons, remember to multiply the square-foot price by nine to get the equivalent square-yard price when necessary, and be sure to note the type of padding and all aspects of installation, including removal and disposal of old carpeting. Make sure the bid is complete and that it includes all extras. Carpeting is often the single biggest investment you'll make in furnishing your home, so buy wisely!

Independent carpet stores and sources still abound, however, and these continue to offer exceptional values and selection. Certain stores specialize in buying overstocks and closeout patterns and colors. Some buy room-sized remnants or pieces from off-color dye lots. Others go in for bankrupt inventories. For these reasons, you can still save on your carpeting dollar.

When it comes to area rugs, there is a rug priced for you, whether you're a bargain hunter or rich and famous. New fiber developments and new looms driven by computer technology (the same concept as player pianos) have opened the market to everyone. Companies have also developed new rug sources in countries around the world, resulting in a broader range of rug prices. In addition, new channels of distribution have been opened within the U.S. so that rugs can be purchased at stores that run the gamut from mammoth

home improvement stores, warehouse clubs, and catalog companies to traditional specialty rug merchants and every retailer in between. In many cases, companies have developed special rug programs to sell to a particular type of retailer—thereby eliminating direct competition between various types of retailers. That makes it hard to comparison shop, because a rug shown at a major full-service retailer like Macy's is unlikely to be found at a discount store.

What counts most for many consumers shopping for an area rug is finding stores with a good selection from which to make a choice and a price orientation that suits a particular budget. A 9-by-12-foot area rug can be found for as little as $69 today. One thing that hasn't changed: today as yesterday, you get what you pay for. A higher price usually results in deeper pile, tighter weaves (or more knots or lines in handmade rugs), more complexity of pattern, better color development, and better fibers and finishes.

In this chapter I've included stores with selections oriented toward contemporary designs, casual decorative rugs, "new" rugs in reproductions of classic patterns, and transitional styles in both synthetic and wool fabrications in budget to better qualities. Before you buy an area rug, I recommend that you survey the marketplace with a visit to many stores. Once you've seen what the market has to offer, you'll be able to make a buying decision that reflects not only the aesthetics of your choice but the best price/quality/value equation for your budget.

Remember that it's a changing market. Always take your time, comparison shop, and consider all the factors. Be sure to check the listings in this book under Furniture and Home Accessories—Catalog Discounters, General Furnishings, and Furniture Clearance Centers. Many companies in these categories come through with exceptional prices on carpeting and area rugs.

General Carpets, Area Rugs, and Flooring

A & M CARPETS
98 12th Street (corner of South Van Ness and Mission), San Francisco. (415) 863-1410. M–Sat 9–5:30. MC, VISA, DIS. Parking: street.
This is a family-owned business that keeps prices down with its low-rent location and no advertising. The owners also take advantage of special opportunities to buy discontinued area rugs from many manufacturers. Prices start at $59.99 for a 6-by-9-foot polypropylene and top out at about $899 for a wool. (Excellent selection priced under $300.) The inventory is heavily oriented toward reproductions of Oriental-style area rugs, but there are some contemporary patterns. The selection also includes "art silk" (rayon blends) and berbers with fringe, but no sisals. Sizes from 2-by-4 to 9-by-12 feet. Good selection of inexpensive runners, even runners cut to size off a roll. Delivery anywhere in San Francisco for $25. If you're looking for "wall to wall" carpeting, check the rolls in the back for some good pricing.

CARPET SYSTEMS, INC.

1515 Bayshore Highway, Burlingame.
(650) 692-6300. M–F 8:30–5, Sun by appointment.
Cash/Check. Parking: street/rear lot.

This offbeat location south of the airport can be attributed to the fact that most of the company's business is done with commercial and property-management companies. However, consumers can cross the freeway for Carpet Systems' excellent pricing. The showroom is neatly organized and well stocked with sample books from major carpet mills. You can go budget or top-of-the-line, or choose a contract carpet for your home office. Prices quoted include normal pull-up and disposal of existing carpets, labor, padding, and sales tax. A 30% deposit is requested with your order, the balance paid at installation. Nice, low-key setting and accommodating staff. *Directions: From SF/101 south, take Millbrae exit east to Old Bayshore and turn right. Going north on 101, take Broadway/ Burlingame exit right to first light and turn left.*

CARPETS OF NEW ZEALAND

4075-A Sprig Drive, Concord. (925) 689-9665.
M–F 10–6. MC, VISA, AE, DIS, financing.
Parking: lot.

Most wool carpeting is imported, entailing heavy freight, customs, and distribution costs. Cavalier Carpets, the second-biggest carpet manufacturer in New Zealand, bypasses traditional distribution and sells directly to customers. Thus, prices on wool carpets here are competitive with quality nylon carpeting, e.g., Ultron or Antron. You'll pay about half the price of competitors' wool carpeting. To extend your choices, the company sells wool carpeting from other manufacturers, also well priced. Your choices in pads are extensive. All carpets are moth-proofed and naturally resist soiling. Of course, you can borrow samples. You can have area rugs made from simple berbers or from carpets with more elaborate designs. Also, if you're some distance from the store, you can have the carpeting shipped to a local installer. The store is located off Port Chicago Highway, near the old Price Club location.

CONTRACTORS FLOORCOVERING OUTLET

818 Main Street #3, Pleasanton. (510) 417-0272.
M–F 1–5 or by appointment. Cash/Check.
Parking: lot.

This doesn't look like your typical carpet store, and it's not. For one thing, without advertising and tucked away on the side of a building across from the historic Pleasanton Hotel, few would ever find their way to the door without a referral from a satisfied customer. Much of the owner's business is done with local developers (including upscale custom home developments cropping up in the hinterlands of southern Alameda County), with realtors preparing properties for sale, and with property managers. Anyone can stop in and go through the extensive selection of samples from major carpet, vinyl, laminate, and hardwood flooring companies. Prices for carpet, padding, and installation will appeal to the skinflint in all of us—with low overhead, markups are minimal. The owner's years as a sales representative for major carpet companies prove invaluable when it comes to discussing the merits of each carpet and its appropriateness for your installation. You can borrow samples and order dye-lot samples from the manufacturer. Shoppers are bound to appreciate the owner's low-key informality, which strikes just the right note for comfortable shopping.

HAL'S CARPET & VINYL

7804 International Boulevard at 78th Avenue
(formerly East 14th Street), Oakland.
(510) 632-1228. M–F 9:30–4:30, Sat 10–2.
MC, VISA. Parking: street.

Hal's location keeps overhead down; he also owns the building, employs no commissioned sales staff, and deals directly with each customer. His main clientele is apartment-building owners. Closeouts, mill drops, some seconds, and short rolls are sold at reduced prices for as much as 50% off original wholesale. You'll find moderate- to better-quality carpets among the mill rejects and special buys. Additionally, he stocks samples from major mills so that you can special-order carpeting in just the right color, style, and price range. Custom orders are sold for a minimal markup, and prices may vary with the type of installation and your skill at negotiating the lowest price after you've done some comparison shopping. Prefinished wood flooring from Bruce,

Anderson, and Hartco; vinyl flooring from Armstrong, Tarkett, Congoleum, and Mannington; and laminate flooring from Wilsonart is well priced. For a one-man operation, Hal's volume is impressive!

LAWRENCE CONTRACT FURNISHERS
470-B Vandell Way, Campbell. (408) 374-7590. T–F 9–5:30, Th until 8, Sat 9–3. MC, VISA. Parking: lot.
Lawrence Contract Furnishers is one of the best resources for carpeting, vinyl floor coverings, hardwood flooring, and hardwood flooring kits from more than eighty companies. You'll probably have to arrive first thing in the morning to pat all the samples, and if you work fast, maybe you'll be done by closing time. After you've chosen your carpet, you can start again if you're shopping for wallpaper, draperies, or furniture from well-known manufacturers. Lawrence's discount system earns you average savings of 25–35%. Check the catalog library for additional resources. Most wallpaper books are discounted 30%. You're pretty much on your own, because decorator services are not available at these prices. Three times a year Lawrence has clearance sales on showroom samples, with prices reduced an extra 20–30%. *Directions: To find this out-of-the-way showroom from the San Tomas Expressway, take the Winchester exit in Campbell, go south to Hacienda, turn left, then right on Dell. Lawrence's is on the corner of Vandell and Dell.*

PIONEER HOME SUPPLY
657 Mission Street (bet. New Montgomery and Third), Fifth Floor, San Francisco. (415) 543-1234, (415) 781-2374. T–F 10–5, Sat by appointment. Cash/Check. Parking: street/pay lots.
Taking one of the smallest markups around, Pioneer occupies a special niche in the marketplace, with pricing that its competitors are hard-pressed to meet. Amazingly, Pioneer has never spent a penny on advertising, depending instead on the loyal following it's acquired through more than forty years in business. The emphasis at Pioneer is now on carpeting and mattresses. The selection of carpeting and floor coverings is extensive. There's no push to trade up for bigger bucks and more profit. Just let them know your budget, and they'll point out the appropriate book, whether you're redoing an office with sleek

contemporary contract carpeting or playing it safe with a conventional plush. If you live in the hinterlands, carpeting can be ordered and shipped directly to an installer in your area. I know some busy customers who are so confident of Pioneer's pricing and integrity that when they need a new box spring and mattress set they just call and say, "Send a new set." If you're like most people, you'll want to bounce on the mattresses first. No problem; when you stop in you'll have a variety of major lines in several price ranges to choose from. Delivery and installation are provided. Peninsula residents can save a trip into the City by scheduling an appointment at Pioneer's studio showroom just off Hwy. 92. *Note: Pioneer is closed Monday, Saturday, and Sunday, and weekday hours may vary depending on this "mom's" busy schedule.*

RUG DECOR

Prime Outlets at Gilroy, Gilroy. (408) 846-1041. Daily 10–6. MC, VISA. Parking: lot.
This may seem an unlikely source for area rugs, but it merits a close look—and you'll have a thousand different choices. Mammoth Shaw Industries, the world's largest carpet manufacturer, owns

Rug Decor. With the company's vast resources it's able to showcase an extensive selection of new patterns, sizes, and types of area rugs. The selection is further extended by catalogs for special orders of rugs and lines that it has access to that are not carried as in-stock inventory. This includes the option of having a custom rug made to match fabrics or wallpapers. Prices on its area and accent rugs are very good. Savings may be minuscule on very inexpensive rugs where margins are slim, to quite substantial on the more expensive, higher end rugs where everyday prices equal the 40–50% off sale prices offered during special department store rug sales. With most rugs displayed from racks with moveable wings, viewing the selection is easy. You'll find a smattering of styles—classic Orientals, florals, contemporary, themed (sports, pets, wildlife, fishermen, planes, golf, etc.), machine made, hooked, handmade (tufted or knotted), braided, etc. Shaw supplies most of the machine-made rugs and has forged relationships with several major importers (Nourison, Capel, Couriston, Oriental Weavers) to provide the selection of handmade rugs. In-stock sizes range from 2-by-4 feet to 8-by-11 feet. For rugs approximately

5-by-8 feet, prices start at $49 for a single ply poly-propylene or $159 for a machine-made wool and top out at about $1,799 for a handmade wool. Some prices: Shaw 3-by-5-foot novelty accent rugs are always well priced at $59; Dhurries were priced at $149 as closeouts and a selection of Kilims were $399 (sizes on both groups approximately 5-by-8 feet). Of course, quality accounts for the difference in price. The good news is that there's something for every budget and a particularly good selection of rugs in the mid-range of $279 to $699. Many rugs are offered with continuity sizing. Rugs can be taken home for a 48-hour approval period. Before ordering a larger rug, it's wise to try out the smaller version. Then the larger size can be ordered and shipped directly from the factory. Shipping is free nationwide on anything bought or ordered from the store—a real benefit when buying rugs without the means to transport them home (no refunds on shipped rugs).

RUG DEPOT OUTLET

4056 Hubbard Street at 40th (across from Bay Bridge Shopping Center), Emeryville. (510) 652-3890. www.rugdepotoutlet.com. Daily 10–6. MC, VISA, AE, DIS, ATM. Parking: lot.

This is legitimate—a warehouse concept for a major importer of machine-made and handwoven area rugs that are typically sold to retailers—from giant discount box retailers to department stores to small specialty furniture stores. Using its exten-sive connections, company buyers are able to make special buys on large shipments of rugs just for the outlet to augment the smaller inventory of "leftovers"—discontinued patterns, rugs from canceled orders, and surplus inventory. Savings of more than 50% may be offered on many dis-continued rugs while the special purchase rugs lack the middleman's markup—a savings passed on to consumers. With 20,000 square feet of warehouse space to showcase its inventory, the outlet's selection is quite extensive. It's a self-service operation, so start off by checking the hanging racks of samples that show rug styles and patterns available, with tags denoting sizes avail-able in each pattern, fiber content, price, and location on warehouse floor. Prices range from $6.99 to $12,000 on rugs starting out at 2-by-3 feet, plus runners to 6-by-9 feet and larger. Rugs may originate from India, Turkey, China, Italy, Brazil, Belgium, and Germany and range from contemporary to traditional, from informal cotton scatter rugs to elegant and formal wool or heat-set polypropylene rugs. Be sure to check the weekly promotions on selected handmade and machine-made rugs.

STYLER'S FLOOR COVERINGS, INC.

2249 Grant Road, Los Altos. (415) 961-8910. M–Sat 10–5, W until 7. MC, VISA. Parking: lot.
You can relax here. The service is low-key, and the focus is on better carpeting (although you can buy budget, too), with some of the best brands coming from smaller mills on the West Coast. Markups are minimal, which leads to very competitive pricing. Major brands of vinyl flooring take care of baths and kitchens, and those prices are equally competitive. Large carpet samples and books can be borrowed for making sure that the color that looks so great in the store will look equally great at home; the lighting, wall color, and window

orientation in your home can produce striking color differences from store lighting. Styler's licensed installers will see that the job is done to the highest standards. Check the very competitive prices offered on Hunter Douglas blinds.

TRADEWAY STORES WAREHOUSE

350-A Carlson Boulevard, Richmond. (510) 233-0841. M–Sat 10–5:30, Sun Noon–5. MC, VISA, AE, DIS. Parking: lot. (Other store: 10860 San Pablo Avenue, El Cerrito; furniture only.)
If you're looking for good deals on carpeting, this gloomy warehouse for Tradeway Stores offers carpeting that has been written off as an insurance loss. Name-brand mills also dispose of overruns, excess inventories, seconds, and off-color carpeting. Stacked in rolls twenty feet and higher, the carpets will make you feel like you're walking through a mini Grand Canyon. I'm always impressed at the good buys on commercial carpets, which is why so many savvy architects and contractors make their way here. Prices are usually lower than original wholesale, and on the dogs that have been around too long, substantially lower. This is

strictly a case of "what you see is what you get." You'll be impressed by the many fine-quality rolls, yet bewildered by others that seem unlikely to ever find a permanent resting place. Although not the primary emphasis, special orders are possible on some lines. There are no custom orders. Padding is sometimes available below wholesale. Tradeway does not install, but will provide you with contractor references. All carpeting is ready for immediate delivery.

Remnants

CARPET CONNECTION

390 Bayshore Boulevard, San Francisco.
(415) 550-7125. M–F 9–5, Sat 9–3. MC, VISA.
Parking: street.
Carpet Connection has a particularly choice selection of remnants, including many that are very effective in contemporary decors. You'll find stain-resistant carpets plus 100% wool and woolex blends. In many instances, the remnant prices are below manufacturers' listed wholesale prices. Along with remnants, rolls of discontinued carpets

are priced with bargain hunters in mind. There is a minimum installation charge of $75, and binding is $1.25/linear foot.

DICK'S CARPET ONE & AREA RUG WAREHOUSE

36 Hegenberger Court, Oakland. (510) 633-9533.
M–Sat 9–6, Sun Noon–5. MC, VISA, DIS.
Parking: lot.
(Other store: 1065 Ashby Avenue, Berkeley.)
The carpet spectrum is covered, but the best values are found in the impressive selection of remnant carpets, from absolutely tacky to superb, and of course prices vary accordingly. What's nice about Dick's is that the remnants are in workable sizes, with many that will easily fit most room dimensions; there are even some large enough to cover two or three rooms. If you're inclined to buy a 6-by-9-foot rug in a midpriced ($200 to $500) or better range ($500 to $2,000), or if you're interested in larger sizes, Dick's offers an extensive and pleasing selection of rugs to review. Modestly priced polypropylene rugs start at about $200 for a 6-by-9-foot. The selection of rugs, from companies noted for innovative designs, cutting-edge fashion, or

beautifully rendered reproductions of classics in wool or better-quality synthetics, is worth a special stop. Delivery charges are reasonable, usually $15 to $25, depending on distance. *Directions: From Hwy. 880 take the Hegenberger Drive exit. Turn west towards airport. Left on first street (Hegenberger Loop), continue straight into parking lot.*

FLOORCRAFT
470 Bayshore Boulevard, San Francisco. (415) 824-4056. M–F 8–6, Sat 8:30–5, Sun 10–5. MC, VISA, DIS. Parking: street.
You'll find about 1,000 remnants in easy-to-see racks. Your best prices are on the "weird" sizes, because it's harder to sell a 7-by-20-foot rug than a standard 10-by-12-foot. Ditto for vinyl remnants. The selection covers about every type of carpet, including wool berbers, commercial carpets, graphics, loops, textures, and plush. Installation, cutting, binding, and delivery are provided. Kitchen remodelers will want to compare prices on Floorcraft's midpriced kitchen cabinets from Diamond, Omega, and Dynasty. You may be surprised to find that you'll save at least 10% off all those other "deeply" discounted prices

advertised everywhere else, and maybe more on custom orders. Expect at least 15% lower prices than the warehouse superstores on custom orders for tubs, faucets, and toilets from Kohler, Moen, and Delta.

JUST REMNANTS
900 Anderson Drive (at Belham just off 580 or 101), San Rafael. (415) 455-8882. Daily 10–5. MC, VISA, AE, DIS. Parking: lot.
Expect a fairly mainstream selection of carpeting styles and colors. All the remnants are displayed standing on end (like a forest of trees), making it easy to evaluate all the possibilities. These are all first-quality carpet remnants from major mills— generally overstocked carpets or discontinued colors, design groups, etc. Minimum size on remnants is 10 feet by 12 feet, but most are in the 12-by-16-foot to 12-by-25-foot range. Additionally, on any one day you're likely to find 30 to 50 rolls with over 50 yards remaining on the roll. (If you don't need the entire roll, the store is accommodating about cutting a smaller amount as long as the balance remaining is a saleable remnant size.) Each roll is tagged with the name of the mill,

carpet style, and color. Information on fiber content and finish is also available. The selection of commercial carpeting is most intriguing. This flat-surfaced carpeting is particularly appropriate for home offices and the rolling wheels of office chairs, or in family or children's rooms where a good play surface is important. There are always some executive/corporate-type patterns and colors. The commercial carpet remnants are typically priced at $8 to $9 a square yard (original wholesale pricing generally ranged from $16 to $24 a yard). Just Remnants buys remnants with a "minimum" 45-ounce weight—resulting in a good mid-range to better quality selection. The remnant pieces of berbers, plushes, textures, friezes, etc., are priced at about $11 to $12 a square yard— prices generally less than the original manufacturer's wholesale pricing. A smaller selection of remnants, geared for more temporary circumstances or apartment residents, is priced at about $6 to $8 per square yard. "Leftovers" are just that, odd sizes, smaller pieces, priced under $50 for dog houses, backs of vans, or whatever. Nylon constitutes the biggest part of the selection, but you may find olefin from time to time. The com-

pany is increasing its inventory of wool carpeting with an emphasis on wool sisals and berbers priced at $20 to $30 per yard. Unless you're a diehard do-it-yourselfer, you'll pay about $8 per yard for padding and installation (includes pull up and disposal of old carpet). Those temporarily nesting may want to have a carpet bound as a rug so it can be removed at a later date. This can be done for $1.50 per linear foot; serging and fringing are also available at reasonable rates.

REMNANT WORLD CARPETS

5158 Stevens Creek Boulevard (at Lawrence Expressway), San Jose. (408) 984-1965.
M–F 9–9, Sat 10–6, Sun 11–5. MC, VISA, AE, DIS. Parking: lot.
(Other store: White Road Plaza, 1054 S. White Road, San Jose.)

You'll find more than 2,000 remnants from leading mills at good prices and 400 rolls of carpet. Want a take-it-with-you rug? Have it bound to your specifications. If you lack the fortitude to lay it yourself, you can have it installed. You can also special-order carpets from samples at very nice discounts, or pick up a bound area rug or hall runner from this extensive selection. Finally, check the vinyl flooring in rolls and remnants.

WOOD BROS. FLOOR COVERING, INC.

221 N. 16th Street, Sacramento. (916) 443-2031. M–Sat 8:30–5:30. MC, VISA, DIS. Parking: lot. Wood Bros. has a huge discount warehouse with thousands of rolls of carpet and vinyl flooring from major manufacturers. The prices are already good, yet the staff is always willing to dicker a little. The best bargains are in the annex, where remnants are neatly organized by size up to 12-by-30 feet. Each piece is priced. (It drives me nuts when stores don't tag carpets, requiring you to ask for a price over and over again.) You'll be referred to licensed contractors for installation.

Helpful Hints

BERT'S CARPET WORKROOM

120 Mendell Street, San Francisco. (415) 641-8255. M–Th 9–4:30, F 9–3. Cash/Check. Parking: street. Stretch your decorating dollar by making the best use of remnants or old carpeting. Maybe you're cutting down wall-to-wall carpeting to use in a bedroom, or you have some good remnants left over from a new carpet installation and you want to make runners or small area rugs. Worst-case scenario—your dog has chewed the edges of your expensive Oriental carpet. Call Bert's, one of the few companies around that specializes in binding. Binding is $4/yard; serging is $6/yard; fringing is $6/yard and up. Ask about costs on carpet repairs or a full line of Oriental fringe. Also, serging and binding of sisal carpets.

Also See

Under Furniture and Home Accessories—Catalog Discounters:
ALL LISTINGS

Under Furniture and Home Accessories—Furniture Clearance Centers:
MOST LISTINGS

Dinnerware and Kitchenware

AUBERGINE

The Village at Corte Madera, Corte Madera.
(415) 924-0560. Daily. MC, VISA, AE, DIS.
Parking: lot.
(Other stores: 1311 Burlingame Avenue,
Burlingame, 650/343-1742; 2301 Stoneridge Mall,
Pleasanton, 925/829-6471.)
Looks can be deceiving. While you may not expect
to find bargains on name brands of dinnerware,
flatware, and stemware at a shopping mall or chic
main street store, Aubergine is the exception.
You can capture savings of 20–50% off retail on
famous names like Villeroy & Boch, Rosenthal,
Amalfi, Vietri, Yamasaki, Couzon, Sambonnet (plus
other names they'd rather I not mention) at its
three stores. At Aubergine, you don't have to
settle for the ordinary. The stores are filled with
carefully edited collections of dinnerware, flatware,
stemware, unique crafts, accessories, and home
accent pieces for casual and casually elegant
lifestyles. Even better, the dinnerware patterns are
available to take right out the door (gift wrapping
a nice bonus); however, flatware is by special order.

AVERY'S

3666 Stevens Creek Boulevard, San Jose.
(408) 984-1111, (800) 828-3797. M–Sat 10–6,
Sun Noon–5. MC, VISA. Parking: lot.
Bargains go hand-in-hand with extra-special
benefits at Avery's—courtesy strollers for the tots
and starched linen hand towels in the lovely rest
room. Avery's may have changed its pricing on
some categories to appeal to bargain hunters, but
it retains its lovely ambiance, fine selection of
giftware, tasteful merchandising, and gracious
service. The realities of the marketplace prompted
its new discount policy: 30% off retail on most
patterns of fine china (Noritake, Villeroy & Boch,
Wedgwood, Spode, Lenox, Fitz & Floyd, etc.);
25–30% off retail on stainless and silver-plate

flatware; 30–50% off on sterling flatware; and discounted stemware (excluding Waterford and Baccarat). A 50% discount applies to any leftovers, closeouts, whatever, found in its clearance room. Brides will want to register! Throw in its courtesy giftwrap, shipping, 800 number, and in-stock availability of most patterns and you end up with a full-price service and real values. Avery's is located behind Kiddie World at the back of the parking lot.

BIA CORDON BLEU OUTLET

867 American Street (off Industrial Road), San Carlos. (650) 637-8405. M–Sat 9–5. MC, VISA. Parking: lot.

This store serves as an outlet for plain and patterned Cordon Bleu porcelain dinnerware and bakeware. New inventory (overruns, discontinued patterns, slightly imperfect pieces) is added weekly, so you may want to visit more than once. Because the line is frequently featured in major store sales and promotions, the discounts vary accordingly, but you can count on 50% off "regular" retail—maybe more, in the case of missing lids and other such incomplete items. This outlet

also caters to restaurant chefs and gourmet cooks; professional equipment and kitchenware are discounted about 20% off retail (even Calphalon, Le Creuset, All Clad, and Cuisinart). Along with the more popular items, you'll discover hard-to-find baker's equipment, like oversized pie plates (up to 12-inch), along with cake-decorating supplies, gadgets, utensils, pot racks, knives, spring-form pans, and other kitchenware.

CHICAGO CUTLERY, ETC.

Prime Outlets at Gilroy, Gilroy. (408) 842-3810. Daily. MC, VISA. Parking: lot.

Whether you're cutting up tomatoes or a side of beef, you'll find a suitable knife at Chicago Cutlery at below department store sale prices. You'll also find Wagner cast-iron skillets, Magnalite professional cookware, Colonial candles, and lots of other goodies. Your best buys are the discontinued items and seconds (not functional flaws; usually discolored wood handles on the knives or minute scratches on the Magnalite pans).

COOKIN'

339 Divisadero Street (bet. Oak and Page),
San Francisco. (415) 861-1854. T–Sat Noon–6:30,
Sun 1–5. MC, VISA. Parking: street.
This fascinating store is piled, stacked, jammed,
and crowded with "recycled gourmet appurte-
nances," or, in plain English, used cookware. If
what you want isn't made anymore or you can't
locate it anywhere, it may be here. I'm not sure
Cookin' qualifies as a bargain store, because the
"old" things sometimes cost more now than they
did originally, and many secondhand items are
superior to the new stuff. The brands that made
up Mom's or Grandma's kitchen are still available,
but they're often made overseas and don't reflect
the same quality. If you want anything copper,
there's plenty. Cast iron, stockpots, bakeware, old
measuring cups and utensils, exotic pastry items,
molds, grinders, and more are sure to tempt.
Count on dinnerware, soufflés, casseroles, cus-
tards, coffeemakers, waffle irons, glassware, and
china. Not everything is old; occasionally there are
closeouts at 25–45% discounts. Love the expensive professional-grade French pastry molds, bags,
tips, and stuff for those Cordon Bleu recipes. If
you're cleaning out your kitchen or disposing of
an estate, call the owner, who's always on the
lookout for good stuff.

CORNING REVERE FACTORY STORE

Great Mall of the Bay Area, Milpitas.
(408) 934-9070. Daily. MC, VISA, DIS. Parking: lot.
(Other outlets: Folsom, Gilroy, Petaluma, Tracy,
Vacaville centers.)
Corning and Revere products are the emphasis at
this store: Visions cookware; Corelle dishes (open
stock and boxed sets); Pyrex everything; Corningware bakeware and separate replacement lids;
Revere bakeware and copper- and aluminum-
disk-bottom pots and pans. The big discounts
apply to Corning's and Revere's own lines, typically
20–60% off retail. The best buys are on 24- or
32-piece sets, such as Corelle and Corningware,
in plain boxes. Overall, you'll find the best markdowns at the separate clearance store in Vacaville,
where only discontinued products from Corning
and Revere are sold at minimum 50% discounts.

DANSK FACTORY OUTLET

1760 Fourth Street, Berkeley. (510) 528-9226.
Daily 10–6. MC, VISA. Parking: lot.
(Other outlets: Carmel; Napa Factory Stores,
Napa; Tahoe Truckee Factory Stores, Truckee.)
Dansk factory stores showcase all the products
made by this fine company. Its lines are particularly
appealing for their clean contemporary designs
and functionality. Prices are typically discounted
30–60% on discontinued groups and factory
overruns. The stores are fun to visit, beautifully
merchandised, and brimming with colorful, well-
priced bargains. My favorite Dansk purchase: the
18-piece wineglass set packaged in a handy box
with drawers that functions neatly as a storage unit.

DAVID M. BRIAN

1126 Broadway Plaza (at S. Main), Walnut Creek.
(925) 947-1991, (800) 833-2182. M–F 10–9,
Sat 10–6, Sun 11–5. MC, VISA, AE. Parking: lot.
(Other store: Bon Air Center, Greenbrae.
415/464-0344.)
I think of David M. Brian as the Gump's of Contra
Costa County and Marin. It's a pleasure to peruse
its elegant home accessories, decorative fine art,

giftware, dinnerware, kitchenware, and linens. It's
not a bargain store, but one bargain angle may
be of interest to you—30% discount on all sterling
silver and silver-plate flatware by Towle, Reed and
Barton, Wallace, International, Oneida, Gorham,
Lunt, and Kirk Stieff, with interest-free, easy payment plans. Another plus is that almost every
pattern is in stock. You'll also find 20–30% savings
offered every day on most informal and formal
china patterns. If you're buying a present, you'll
love the free giftwrap and free shipping within the
Bay Area—just another aspect of this first-class
store! Phone orders accepted.

FAMOUS BRANDS HOUSEWARES

Factory Stores at Vacaville, Vacaville.
(707) 451-2463. Daily. MC, VISA, AE, DIS.
Parking: lot.
(Other outlets: Gilroy, Tracy centers.)
Here you'll find everything Rubbermaid, closet
accessories and organizers, picture frames, bakeware, cookware, gadgets galore, potpourri, kitchen
linens, pots, pans, serving dishes and platters,
glassware, microwave cookware, laundry-room
necessities, giftware, and more. The store offers

promotional items, discontinued styles, closeouts, and regular merchandise at 20–70% discounts. It's a subsidiary of the Lechters stores.

FARBERWARE OUTLET

Factory Stores at Vacaville, Vacaville.
(707) 452-0533. Daily. MC, VISA. Parking: lot.
(Other outlets: Folsom, Gilroy center.)
You'll be blinded by the gleam of Farberware's stainless steel pots and cookware as you wander through this outlet. Discounts are 25–40% off on most items, but can go as high as 60% off retail. Farberware also makes small electric appliances, like toasters, coffeemakers, hand mixers, and teakettles, as well as mixing bowls, measuring cups, etc., all offered at minimal to large discounts. Millennium and Gourmetrix cookware is occasionally offered at modest discounts.

HEATH CERAMICS, INC. (FACTORY OUTLET)

400 Gate 5 Road, Sausalito. (415) 332-3732.
www.heathceramics.com. Daily 10–5. MC, VISA.
Parking: lot.
The Heath factory store could well be the focal point of a trip to Sausalito. Overruns and seconds

of tile for flooring, counters, and walls are available in extraordinary colors and textures at very worthwhile savings. The dishes and heat-tempered cookware that do not pass Heath's high standards are sold for 33% below retail prices. You'll find new glazes reflecting the latest looks in home decorating trends, plus a sushi line of square and rectangular plates and special one-of-a-kind decorated plates. These savings are apt to keep you coming back to round out your dinner settings, to buy gifts, to purchase tile for a remodeling project, or to introduce a friend to the experience.

HERITAGE HOUSE

2190 Palou Avenue, San Francisco.
(415) 285-1331. M–F 10–6, after 6 by appointment,
Sat 10–5. MC, VISA, AE, DIS. Parking: street.
Heritage House offers some special benefits that make it a solid alternative to the popular mail-order discount companies. First, the selection is distinguished by the many premium lines of imported European (some hand-painted) lines of china, stemware, and flatware and other lines that bear prestigious American designer names. Heritage House may be able to offer only minimal

(10–20%) discounts on these lines, but that's better than none at all (and many are not available through mail order). On the more mainstream lines sold in department stores everywhere, prices are sometimes a tad higher than many mail-order companies, but still very competitive. If you're adding to your patterns, the staff is helpful about advising you when the manufacturers have scheduled sales and special promotions, so you can time your purchases for maximum savings. Brides get very special treatment, with a complete registry program and a telephone registry program for out-of-area brides. Appointments are preferred for bridal consultations; with hundreds of patterns to choose from and combine, you'll appreciate the staff's expertise in helping you through the process of choosing the patterns you'll live with for many years. There are only two or three very upscale retail stores around the Bay Area that have a selection that rivals what you'll find here. Stop in too if you're shopping for tasteful gifts. The company has a most unlikely location: It's in an industrial park in the Bayshore area. Its modest exterior is in complete contrast to the beautiful showroom you'll encounter once you go through the doors. *Directions: From downtown, take the Army Street/Bayshore exit off Hwy. 101 to Bayshore. Turn left on Oakdale, right on Barneveld, and left on Palou.*

HOME ACCENTS
Great Mall of the Bay Area, Milpitas
(408) 934-9302. Daily. MC, VISA. Parking: lot.
(Other outlet: Gilroy center.)
Home Accents sells lots of one-of-a-kind giftwares, usually manufacturers' samples in crystal, china, silverplate, etc. (figurines, photo frames, candy dishes, candlesticks and the like), at 20–50% off retail. You'll also find displays of current silver, silver plate, and stainless flatware patterns from Towle, Wallace, and International Silver at 35 to 50% discounts, plus Gorham, Reed & Barton, Lunt, and Kirk Stieff competitively priced with the best mail-order companies. These companies make several qualities of silver-plated giftware and hollowware: a lot of budget-priced trays, bowls, and candlesticks that offer the gleam but may not have the weight or quality engraving found on the better groups in stock. Check for special promotions of one kind or another, offered every week.

JANUS

221 Main Street, Los Altos. (800) 697-3500.
M–F 10–6, Sat 9:30–5:30, Sun Noon–5.
MC, VISA. Parking: street/rear lot.

Use the Janus 800 number to take the legwork out of gift buying. Or stop in and find a beautiful store featuring fine china, crystal, flatware (stainless, sterling, and silver plate), and giftware, with a discount policy that rivals many of the best mail-order companies. A few patterns in a few lines are not discounted, but 20% discounts are offered on Jean Couzon stainless (no one else does that). Minimum discounts start at 20% off retail; some are around 40% and occasionally even more when manufacturers' promotions are added. Brands include Wedgwood, Christian Dior, Spode, Fitz & Floyd, Lenox, Noritake, Dansk, Villeroy & Boch, Royal Doulton, Reed & Barton, and other famous lines. Janus will ship anywhere!

THE KITCHEN COLLECTION

Factory Stores at Vacaville, Vacaville. (707) 446-7823. Daily. MC, VISA, AE, DIS. Parking: lot.
(Other outlets: Anderson/Shasta, Gilroy centers.)
The Kitchen Collection is a factory store for Wear-Ever and Proctor-Silex. Everything in kitchen essentials is covered, including other brands, like Meyer, Lincoln, Wilton, Anchor Hocking, Kitchen-Aid, and Hamilton Beach, all at a good price. There's a complete array of Wear-Ever pots and pans, pressure cookers, roasters, cake pans, and indispensable small electric appliances like toaster ovens, coffeemakers, juicers, popcorn makers, portable mixers, griddles, electric frying pans, woks, and Crock-Pots, as well as less essential but still useful devices. Sign up for the mail-order discount catalog.

LE CREUSET FACTORY OUTLET

Factory Stores at Vacaville, Vacaville.
(707) 453-0620. Daily. MC, VISA, AE, DIS.
Parking: lot.
(Other outlet: Gilroy center.)
Le Creuset cookware is exactly what you need for cooking comfort foods: stews and brews that need long, slow simmering or baking. If price has kept you away, check out the bargains on everything familiar (and unfamiliar) this company makes. First-quality pieces are discounted about 40%, seconds about 50%, and discounted pieces and

liquidations as much as 70% off retail. Don't pass up the other culinary accessories, like the never-fail screw-pull corkscrews, woks, and storage containers. Shop prime time every 4th of July and two weeks in December when big blow-out sales bring prices to buy-everything-in-sight-levels. Ships UPS anywhere!

LE GOURMET CHEF

Petaluma Village Premium Outlets, Petaluma. (707) 766-8893. Daily. MC, VISA. Parking: lot. (Other outlets: Folsom, Gilroy, Napa centers.)
An irresistible store for browsing, buying and, to a lesser extent, bargains. The latest in gourmet cookware, gadgets, and accessories is almost as tempting as the gourmet edibles in jars, packages, bottles, and boxes (sauces, mixes, jams, marinades, vinegars, etc.). Value-priced famous names: Cuisinart, Krups, Henkel, Chantal, Meyer, Circulon, Fagor, Rowenta, and Wagner cast-iron cookware. Give your kitchen a culinary update by selecting some new fine cutlery, gourmet cookware, microwave bakeware, glassware, small electronics, kitchen gadgets, or accessories (salt and pepper shakers, mugs, cleaning aids, etc.). Except for

kitchen gadgets and edibles, everything is priced at or below department store sale prices.

LENOX FACTORY OUTLET

Prime Outlets at Gilroy, Gilroy. (408) 847-1181. Daily. MC, VISA, AE, DIS. Parking: lot. (Other outlet: Vacaville center.)
A large, elegant, and well-stocked store with Lenox china, stemware, crystal, flatware, and giftware (vases, picture frames, candles, coordinating paper products, etc.). Because Lenox now owns Gorham, you'll also find stemware, flatware (stainless, silver plate, and sterling), and Gorham giftware. Prices are discounted 30–50% off retail. Everything is almost invisibly marked as a second, yet the merchandise may in fact be overstocks or closeouts. Some of the most popular patterns made by Lenox are sold on an open-stock basis. Phone quotes and orders are accepted on the store's inventory; however, no special discounts are offered on merchandise that may not be carried in the outlet. The outlet is now carrying Lenox lamps at about a 20–25% discount, more on seconds. Great monthly specials on selected inventory; major sales in July and December. UPS shipping anywhere!

MARJORIE LUMM'S WINEGLASSES

112 Pine Street, San Anselmo. (415) 454-0660.
E-mail: mlumm@wineglasseslitd.com. M–F 10–4,
weekends by appointment. MC, VISA, AE.
Parking: municipal lot.

The serious wine buff doesn't want cutwork or
ornamentation on glasses, obscuring the color
and clarity of wine. If you're as serious about your
wineglasses as you are about your wines, you'll
want to pay a visit to Marjorie Lumm's warehouse/
store. She has been at the helm of her own mail-
order glass company for thirty years. Most of her
glasses retail between $5 and $20 apiece. Bargain
hunters will want to scrutinize the seconds,
reduced 50% off retail. You may also find discontinued first-quality glasses sold at a considerable
discount. Glasses can be engraved for a modest
charge, and chipped or broken glasses can be
repaired. Call first about availability and store
hours. Write for Lumm's catalog: P.O. Box 1544,
San Anselmo, CA 94979.

MIKASA FACTORY STORE

1239 Marina Boulevard, Marina Square,
San Leandro. (510) 352-1211. M–F 10–9,
Sat 10–6, Sun 11–6. MC, VISA, AE, DIS.
Parking: lot.
(Other outlets: 280 Metro Center, Colma;
Anderson/Redding; Gilroy; Milpitas;
Napa; Petaluma; San Mateo; South Lake Tahoe;
Tracy; Vacaville centers.)

You have a chance to buy everything Mikasa here.
Because it makes more than 300 patterns of dinnerware alone, you know there's a lot you haven't
seen before. You'll also be energized by the
prices, a tempting 20–50% off retail. At the outlet
you'll find dinnerware; casual to fine china; casual
and formal stainless flatware; cookware, bakeware, and casseroles; canisters; crystal stemware
and giftware; linens; teakettles; vases; housewares; and more. Using Mikasa's special-order
desk is the best way to order additional settings
or pieces. UPS shipping available for normal
charges. Sorry, no giftwrap. Keep receipts for
exchange or refunds within 21 days.

NORITAKE FACTORY STORES

Prime Outlets at Gilroy, Gilroy. (408) 842-9559, (888) TABLEWR. Daily. MC, VISA, AE, DIS. Parking: lot.

The only outlet in California with more than 200 Noritake patterns of china, crystal, stemware, glassware, and giftware, plus dozens of boxed sets, may challenge your decision-making abilities and keep you browsing. Everyday savings on first-quality wares range from 30–65% off. Savings are less, of course, when prices are compared to sale events at Bay Area stores and to mail-order companies. Some patterns may not be familiar— it would be impossible to find a store that carries everything that Noritake makes. On special patterns or closeouts, make sure you buy everything you need. Beautiful store. Phone orders and UPS shipping.

ONEIDA FACTORY STORE

Factory Stores at Vacaville, Vacaville. (707) 448-5803. Daily. MC, VISA. Parking: lot. (Other outlets: Gilroy, South Lake Tahoe centers.)
You can't miss these stores, with their dazzling displays of silver-plated goods. You'll find over-runs, vendor returns, excess inventory, and some seconds in traditional silver-plated hollowware, stainless and gold-electroplate flatware, gift items, leaded crystal stemware and accessories, and melamine children's giftware. Expect 50–70% discounts off original retail. Tea sets, serving trays, casserole holders, picture frames, candleholders, most patterns of Oneida flatware, and food warmers are plentiful. Almost every item is available in prepacked gift boxes.

PFALTZGRAFF FACTORY STORE

Factory Stores at Vacaville, Vacaville. (707) 446-4984. Daily. MC, VISA. Parking: lot. (Other outlets: Gilroy, South Lake Tahoe centers.)
Factory-owned and operated, Pfaltzgraff Factory Stores offer the largest selection of Pfaltzgraff dinnerware and exclusive stoneware items made just for factory stores and catalog sales. Save 15% and higher on more than forty patterns with coordinating glassware, flatware, linens, and much more. Bridal and gift registry. Shipping available.

ROBIN'S NEST

116 E. Napa Street (just off the Plaza), Sonoma.
(707) 996-4169. Daily 10–6. MC, VISA.
Parking: street.

Going to the wine country? Then stop off here for kitchenware, giftware, and gourmet cooking accessories and foods for 15–50% off retail (selected markdowns to 60% off). The best buys are on closeouts and special purchases. Uncommon wares from local artisans are especially appealing.

ROYAL DOULTON

Factory Stores at Vacaville, Vacaville.
(707) 448-2793. Daily. MC, VISA, AE, DIS.
Parking: lot.
(Other outlet: Gilroy center.)

Slightly imperfect patterns of Royal Doulton, Royal Albert, and Minton china are sold at 40–70% discounts. Patterns not in stock can be special ordered and shipped to your home; recently discontinued patterns are sold at clearance prices. Beatrix Potter, Classic Pooh, Brambley Hedge, and Bunnykins giftware are sold at 20% discounts. Sorry, no discounts on Toby Jugs, Character Jugs, and Crinoline Ladies. You'll also find Royal Albert giftware and some crystal. Keep your eyes peeled for "extra specials" and markdowns around the holidays. You can special order anything in Royal Doulton, Royal Crown, or Derby. Don't worry about getting your china and giftware home: They ship via UPS anywhere, and most items are sold in gift boxes. Shop the warehouse sales in April, September, and December when special closeout inventory is shipped to the outlet for final disposal—lots of open stock dinnerware and boxed sets of crystal gifts and stemware.

TOSCANA CERAMICS

1301 17th Street (bet. Connecticut and Missouri streets), San Francisco. (415) 552-2118, (800) TOSCANA. www.toscanaceramics.com. M–Sat 10–6, Sun Noon–5. MC, VISA. Parking: street.

Toscana will be at a new location by January 2000. It must leave its SOMA location so the building can be converted to a high-tech facility. Its Web site is probably the best way to keep in touch if you're looking for Majolica tableware. Toscana's Majolica tableware, imported from Umbria and Tuscany, may reflect the art form of the Renaissance, but it meets current standards for food use.

Many shoppers consider Majolica wares somewhat expensive when confronted with the current pricing at specialty gourmet and gift stores or from catalog companies. Toscana's prices are 20–50% less than competitors' prices on most items. For instance, 1999 shoppers found an Umbrian Apothecary jar with portrait, 14 inches high, 7 inches in diameter at $185 ($275 in catalogs); a dinner plate in the popular Rooster design, Galletto Verde, at $34 ($48 in catalogs); a Raffaellesco 12-inch serving bowl at $80 ($120 elsewhere); a 17-inch serving dish at $78 ($155 elsewhere); a Geometrico 4-piece canister set at $375 ($500 elsewhere); and wine chalices at $35 were a bargain when compared to $55 at other stores. Antiquated designs that more closely represent the art form as it existed during the 14th and 15th centuries are available. They include reproductions of *piatti da pompa* (display portrait plates) that were produced in Umbria in the first quarter of the 16th century and large jugs and portage vessels painted in the *stile arcaico,* or archaic style, dating back to the 14th century. A bridal registry program is available on in-stock and eleven special-order patterns. Delivery takes about three months.

UNION STREET GLASS OUTLET

833 South 19th Street, Richmond. (888) 451-7752. Quarterly weekend sales. M–F 9–3 by appointment only. MC, VISA. Parking: street.

Union Street's Manhattan stemware design won the prestigious Niche design award in 1995. It's no wonder this line has become so popular with discriminating consumers. Its goblets, barware, bowls, and vases are elegant—and expensive: goblets retail for about $50 to $70 each. Each piece is hand blown, signed, and dated. It's hard to figure what makes a second, because subtle variations on each piece enhance and emphasize the handmade look. Most collections here are embellished with 23-karat gold that will not scratch or wear off. You can choose goblets that have jewel tones drawn through the stem and gold leaf permanently fused into the design. For maximum versatility, the clear glass and gold-leaf treatments are the ultimate in elegance. From my perspective, the seconds at $10 to $20 per stem, $5 to $10 for a piece of barware, paperweights for $10, and bowls and vases at $35 to $150 are genuine bargains. You'll want to have your name on Union's mailing list for advance notice of quarterly sales.

The sales have attracted quite a following, so plan on being an early bird to get first crack at the seconds.

VILLEROY & BOCH OUTLET

Petaluma Village Premium Outlets, Petaluma. (707) 769-9029. Daily. MC, VISA. Parking: lot. If you're cruising up Hwy. 101, take time out to visit the Villeroy & Boch Outlet, where shoppers delight in 20–75% discounts off retail (most dinnerware discounted at least 30% off retail every day). You'll find seconds and current pattern overruns. Villeroy & Boch company makes about sixty patterns; at the outlet you'll find about twenty-five, including many of its best-known patterns, like Basket, Petite Fleur, Mariposa, Botanica, Switch, Virginia, and its popular Christmas Naif pattern. You can buy a piece or a place setting from open stock. You're limited to the patterns in stock; no special orders for other patterns. However, you can call and order anything in stock and have it shipped UPS to your home. Villeroy & Boch also makes 24% lead crystal stemware. Prices on seconds and overruns range from $6 to $18.

VINEWARE POTTERY STUDIO & OUTLET

419 Allan Court, Healdsburg. (707) 431-8979. M–F 8–5, Sat 10–1. MC, VISA. Parking: street. Elaine Greene and Tina Duffy create distinctive handpainted pottery inspired by their vineyard and farmland surroundings. Their primary business is selling their special ceramic pottery to wine tasting rooms throughout California. Accordingly, many themes encompass vines, grapes, fruit, and olives in intricate and colorful designs. Prices at retail range from $25 to $200 and include platters, pitchers, jars, plates, bowls, cups—pieces that are functional but add decorative elements to kitchen and dining areas whenever they're not in use. A specialty is customizing colors to match whatever, even inscribing dates for wedding and anniversary gifts. At the studio outlet, prices are about half off, even more on occasional seconds. If you end up anywhere around the Plaza in Healdsburg, you're not far away—the studio is one and a half blocks off the Plaza. Too bad they're not open longer on weekends when many folks make their treks to the area.

WATERFORD/WEDGWOOD OUTLET

Prime Outlets at Gilroy, Gilroy. (408) 846-9488, (888) 668-9436. Daily. MC, VISA, AE, DIS. Parking: lot.

You can buy lots of beautiful things here, but not Waterford crystal stemware. Nearly perfect inventory from the more modestly priced Marquis collections and some stemware patterns that are made just for sale in the company's outlet store division are available at reduced pricing. The best buys are found on gift items (vases, bowls, lamps) and Wedgwood, Johnson Bros., and Franciscan patterns of dinnerware (equivalent to mail-order catalog prices). You're in luck if your pattern is on the seconds' tables where dishes are sold open stock for minimum 50% discounts. Order using the toll-free number and UPS shipping and you don't even have to leave your home.

Mail Order

Many mail-order companies offer the best of both worlds: good service and good prices on fine and everyday china, flatware (silver and silver plate), hollowware, crystal stemware, fine giftware, better jewelry, and collectibles. Check the back pages of almost any home magazine for starters. If a local retailer is having a special 40% off sale, then you may save just a few dollars. To avoid problems, keep careful records and copies of your order, ask for an estimated shipping date, and make sure you understand the company's return policy. There are trade-offs. For those starting or completing their own sets of china, crystal, or silver, there's no club plan to spread the payments without interest. On the plus side, you may avoid the California state sales tax (pending legislation); you can use toll-free 800 numbers to place your order; most companies have a national bridal registry; and shipping and insurance charges are very reasonable. The companies listed here have good track records. Each may have slightly different pricing, availability, and shipping charges, so it's a good idea to get on the mailing list of each.

BARRONS
(800) 538-6340; fax (800) 523-4456.
Bridal registry, fine china, crystal, flatware, collectibles, and giftware.

LANAC SALES
(800) 522-0047; fax (212) 925-8175.
Bridal registry, high-end patterns (Bernardaud, Haviland, Raynaud/Ceralene, Baccarat, etc.), gourmet cookware and electrics, giftware, and home accessories.

MICHAEL C. FINA
(800) BUY-FINA; fax (718) 937-7193.
Bridal registry, good prices, some hard-to-find (at discount) patterns in china and stemware, better housewares, and jewelry.

REPLACEMENTS, LTD.
1089 Knox Road, P.O. Box 26029, Greensboro, NC 27420. (800) 737-5223.
www.replacements.com. Daily 8–9.
MC, VISA, DIS. Parking: lot.
This company's small ads with convenient 800 phone number are ubiquitous on the back pages of national and regional shelter magazines. The ads hardly convey the scope of its operations. It has the largest inventory of discontinued and active china, crystal, flatware, and collectibles in the world. Tours are offered every 30 minutes of its 225,000-square-foot facility (the size of four football fields). There's only one way to really describe this tour: "WOW!" The tour reveals all aspects of the company's services: the mammoth warehouse with 50,000 shelves accommodating approximately 100,000 patterns and 5,000,000 pieces of china, crystal, flatware, and collectibles from more than 3,000 manufacturers; receiving, inspection, and identification department (more than 50,000 pieces received every week); restoration, cleaning, and repair department; the shipping department; and the 12,000-square-foot retail showroom and museum with over 2,000 rare pieces.

It's best to try replacing pieces before your patterns become too rare. If you can provide the name of your patterns (via phone, mail, or its Web site), the company will send a computer-generated list of every piece, with condition and price noted, that's currently available in its inventory. If you don't have the name, the company will send a brochure with pattern identification instructions. With your details and their expertise the mystery is soon solved—and at no cost. Don't toss that fork or spoon that tangled with the garbage disposal—most can be repaired for about $15 per piece in their silver restoration and cleaning service department. When discontinued patterns are no longer being produced, the remaining inventory is priced according to supply and demand, which usually translates into prices that bear little resemblance to the original prices. Most prices are at least double original costs and on very rare, collectible status patterns, the sky's the limit. However, it may be less expensive to add a few missing crucial pieces (plates, cups, or saucers), than to buy a complete new set of whatever.

There may be moneymaking potential in your china cabinets. Replacements, Ltd. also buys many patterns of china, crystal, flatware, and collectibles. Prices are based on current inventory levels and customer demand. Inquire through their purchasing department.

Most current running patterns are available. Prices are very competitive, but not quite as low as the prices at leading discount mail-order companies. However, those lucky enough to shop at its Greensboro showroom will find some exceptional prices on manufacturers' overruns and closeouts on all sorts of giftwares and tableware. Although you don't need to travel to Greensboro to take advantage of all this company has to offer, it's an intriguing destination in this part of the country. In fact, on Sundays, it's one of the few businesses open for business. It's about an hour from Raleigh/Durham and Duke University, and two hours from Charlotte.

ROSS-SIMONS
(800) 556-7376; fax (800) 896-9191.
Always my first choice for mail order. Most major brands, in-stock inventory, and bridal registry. Also fine jewelry, watches, nice giftware.

SMYTH
(800) 638-3333; fax (410) 252-2355.
Bridal registry; major brands of china, flatware, and crystal; jewelry; and watches.

THURBER'S
(800) 848-7237; fax (804) 278-9480.
Cover all your bases with this company's catalog.
Bridal registry and most mainstream china, flatware, and stemware patterns offered at discount.

Also See

Under Giftware and Home Decor:
ALL LISTINGS

Under Linens:
BED, BATH & BEYOND; LINENS 'N' THINGS

Under General Merchandise:
ALL LISTINGS

Draperies and Window Coverings

**AMERICAN DRAPERIES & BLINDS
FACTORY SALE**

*1168 San Luis Obispo Avenue, Hayward.
(510) 487-3500. Usually first Sat of May and Nov,
8:30–4:30. MC, VISA. Parking: lot.*
American makes draperies and blinds; twice a
year it opens its factory to the public to clear out
miscellaneous stock, draperies in discontinued
fabrics, production overruns, and odd sizes. Most
draperies are priced between $20 and $60, a
savings of 50–75%. Bring your required rod sizes
and lengths. Expect traditional, three-pronged,
French-pleated, lined/unlined draperies (double
fullness), fan-folded and ready to hang with hooks
inserted. You'll find a variety of colors, weaves,
textures, and weights. Extra-strong miniblinds and
verticals in alabaster and white are sold with a
lifetime warranty in the twenty most requested
sizes (custom sizes available, too). The sales
usually occur on the first weekends in May and
November. All sales final. Call anytime during the
year and ask to be put on the mailing list.

WELLS INTERIORS CLEARANCE CENTER

*41477 Albrae Street, Fremont. (510) 490-6924.
M–F 10–6, Sat 10–5, Sun 11–5. MC, VISA.
Parking: lot.
(Other stores: fourteen stores in Northern
California; check Geographical Index.)*
If you don't mind spending a little time scrounging
to unearth your bargains, Wells Interiors offers
hard-to-beat prices. This is where all the returns,
double orders, customer mistakes, factory mistakes, etc. are sent from nineteen stores. Sizes
and styles are limited, but even Wells' everyday
discount prices are drastically reduced. For example, vertical blinds for patio doors that would
normally sell for $80 to $200 go for $50 to $75.
Wood blinds priced normally at $50 to $200 per
window are $25 to $50 each. Keep your window

measurements in your wallet so you can shop if you find yourself in the area. Repair service is available here for most blinds and shades. The company manufactures its vertical blinds at this location—prices are very good! If you never get to the clearance center, stop by one of its fourteen Northern California stores. I have no trouble at all choosing Wells Interiors as a reliable source for value. I love the audacious signs posted in its stores comparing its prices to other local companies. *Directions: From Hwy. 880, take the Stephenson exit west. Turn left at Albrae, and follow around curve. Outlet faces highway.*

THE YARDSTICK
2110 S. Bascom Avenue, Campbell.
(408) 377-1401. M–Sat 9:30–6, Th 9:30–7:30,
Sun 11–5. MC, VISA, DIS. Parking: lot.
If you need draperies right away or you want luxury window treatments at budget prices, check the Yardstick. It usually has about 1,000 ready-mades (guaranteed 2½ fullness) from its own workrooms available for you to take home and hang. For better than budget, there's also a complete custom window-covering department using popular fabrics from Kravet, Duralee, Robert Allan, Richloom, and others. Discounts on custom-order fabrics only kick in on large orders, not hard to do with an extensive drapery or window covering project. Free in-home decorating service anywhere from San Francisco to Monterey—a convenient way to place custom orders on "hard" window coverings (vinyl shutters, miniblinds, verticals, etc. at very competitive prices). Kirsch and Graber drapery rods are always 25% off the manufacturer's list prices. Home-decorating services include furniture upholstering. DIYs should check the rolls of up-to-date, nicely discounted home decorating fabrics.

Also See

Under Fabrics—Home-Decorating Fabrics:
ALL LISTINGS

Under Carpets, Area Rugs, and Flooring—
General:
LAWRENCE CONTRACT FURNISHERS

Under Furniture and Home Accessories—
Catalog Discounters:
ALL LISTINGS

Under Furniture and Home Accessories—
General Furnishings:
IKEA

Under Linens:
MOST LISTINGS

Flower and Garden

AW POTTERY
601 50th Avenue, Oakland. (510) 533-3900. M–Sat 9–5. MC, VISA, AE, DIS. Parking: street. (Other outlet: 2908 Adeline Street, Berkeley. 510/549-3901.)
Those who must limit their gardening to container plantings will find pots for every situation at AW Pottery. It's been a fixture in Berkeley for years, but most shoppers have yet to discover its warehouse retail and outlet store in Oakland, north of the Coliseum complex. The company imports everything from tiny pots to gigantic vases and urns, from rustic earthenware to porcelain (most from its family-owned pottery studios in Malaysia and China). It supplies nurseries locally and around the country, national catalog companies, and florists, and also handles direct imports for megastore chains and warehouses.

At both locations, AW Pottery sells imports to consumers for about a 20% discount off prevailing retail. (Marked prices do not reflect the discount, which is given at the register.) For more impressive savings take a look at all the seconds and damaged pieces. If you can live with a chip or crack (from minor to major) then you can pick up pots for 70–80% off retail (prices on seconds generally range from 50 cents to $8). AW offers organized chaos; with so much inventory and so many types of imports—including teapots, small gift items, bonsai dishes and pots, and every variety of pot and urn imaginable (glazed, unglazed, porcelain, etc.)—keeping it all neat and tidy would keep the staff working twenty-four hours a day.

CALAVERAS NURSERIES

1000 Calaveras Road, Sunol. (510) 862-2286.
M–Sat 8–4:30, Sun 8–3. MC, VISA. Parking: lot.
This firm grows many of the plants that it sells
wholesale and directly to the public. Bring your
list and landscaping plans and buy everything you
need in one fell swoop at down-to-earth prices.
Prices in 1999 were as follows: 1-gallon shrubs
$4.40 and up; 1-gallon trees and vines $4.40
to $5.40; 5-gallon shrubs $12.40 and up; 5-gallon
trees and vines $21.75 and up; 15-gallon trees
$58 and up; and flats of ground cover $11.95 to
$16.95. Call first to make sure that what you want
is in stock. Delivery can also be arranged.

COAST WHOLESALE FLORIST

149 Morris Street, San Francisco. (415) 781-3034.
M–F 6–3, Sat 7–Noon. MC, VISA. Parking: lot.
One glance at the warehouse and you'll get the
feeling that they've scoured the forests and fields
for unusual dry flowers such as hydrangeas, along
with wreaths, oak leaves, pine cones, and more.
Garlic braids, unique baskets, gourds, pods, and
potpourri create a fragrant shopping environment.
Lots of decorative accessories for ornamenting

wreaths and arrangements, floral supplies, and
beautiful fancy ribbons are also available. Prices
are in line with other flower market vendors.

COTTAGE GARDEN GROWERS

3959 Emerald Drive, Petaluma. (707) 778-8025.
Mar–Oct, daily 9–5; Nov–Feb, daily 10–4.
MC, VISA. Parking: lot.
This nursery specializes in perennials, grasses,
clematis, herbs, and many varieties of new and
old antique roses. All plants are grown on the
premises, ensuring consistent care and quality,
as well as acclimation to the region. You'll find
more than 400 varieties (most offered in 1-gallon
cans). Prices are very reasonable—$5.49 each, or
choose any six for $31. The more common vari-
eties are also at the big discounters (Kmart, Home
Depot, etc.) at slightly lower prices, but Cottage
Garden's plants are fuller and healthier and get
my money every time. If you have your heart set
on a particular plant, call for availability and a list
of all the plants carried.

COTTAGE GARDEN PLANTS

2680 Franklin Canyon Road, Martinez.
(925) 946-9136. Sat 9–1. Cash/Check. Parking: lot.
This is a very different shopping experience. You'll drive down a quiet back road that leads to a lane that ends at Cottage Garden's 3-acre growing and selling area. There's also no phone on site, no comfort facilities, and only a cardboard table for transacting business. If you shop with kids, they'll love the chickens hopping freely around the plants. The owner, a landscape contractor, starts his plants from cuttings and seeds and specializes in both common and uncommon perennials, native grasses, woody ornamentals, and some trees. Rows and rows of plants (most in 1-gallon containers) are in various stages of growth. Unless you're really a plant pro, you'll need to wait for a "walk through" to identify the various plants, which are often not labeled. It's sometimes wet and muddy, so wear your oldest shoes. Type-A people might want to bring the morning paper to make the wait for service easier when too many customers show up at the same time.

The prices: Most perennials are $3 (1 gallon); woody ornamental shrubs, $3.50 (1 gallon); 15-gallon trees, $35 to $40; trees in 24-inch boxes, about $120. Plants include six to seven varieties of daylilies, penstemon, yarrow, cone flower, rud-beckia, salvia, agapanthus, amaryllis, cranesbill (true geraniums), verbenas, potato vine, clematis, hibiscus, sedum, lirope, camellias, scented barberry, dianthus, cotoneaster, butterfly bush, Mexican evening primrose, Japanese maples, crepe myrtle, bushes and trees, and more. The plants are "acclimated" (grown in the open) and are less likely to incur transplant shock. Finally, many customers have extended existing plantings (unusual varieties) by bringing in cuttings from their gardens for propagation. *Directions: From Hwy. 4 take the Alhambra Avenue exit south, turn right/west (about 300 feet) onto Franklin Canyon Road. Drive 1.7 miles, turn right on Wolcott Lane, look for signs.*

FLOWER OUTLET

5758 Shellmound Street, Emeryville.
(510) 450-1350. www.floweroutlet.com.
M–Sat 9–6, F 9–6:30. MC, VISA. Parking: lot.
(Other outlet: 6131 La Salle Avenue, Oakland.)
East Bay shoppers don't have to cross the bridge
to find super buys on fresh-cut flowers. Just take
the Powell Street exit east off Hwy. 80 to the first
light, turn right, and head for the orange building
behind Lyon's restaurant. This good-sized shed-
type building is filled with buckets of flowers and
some house plants. The company supplies many
flower kiosks in supermarkets and other retail
operations with ready-to-go bouquets and
bunches of individual blooms. It keeps a fresh
stock of flowers for sale to the public at nicely
discounted prices. Usually in stock: roses,
Casablanca lilies, tulips, alstromeria, carnations,
mums, baby's breath, foliage, greenery, orchid
plants, dried flowers, and more. Regulars compete for the not-quite-as-fresh blooms put out in
special markdown buckets. Inquire about flowers
for weddings or other special events (bouquets
or centerpieces) and monthly floral design work-
shops. Accommodating staff.

FLOWER TERMINAL

Sixth and Brannan Streets, San Francisco.
Hours vary, generally M–F 2 a.m.–2 p.m.,
Sat hours for a few vendors 8–Noon. Cash/Check.
Parking: street/lot.
Several wholesale nurseries are located in this
block, selling cut flowers, houseplants, greenery,
and floral supplies to the trade and the public.
Don't expect information or advice. Vendors have
neither the time nor the personnel for retail services. You are required to pay sales tax, unless
you have a resale number. Highlights: Ira Doud
and Floral Supply Syndicate are headquarters for
ribbons, decorations, wrapping paper, wreaths,
and other fixin's for holiday decorating, floral
displays, or table decorations. Silver Terrace is the
largest of several vendors selling cut flowers,
foliage, and plants. While prices aren't "wholesale" to the public, many items are simply not
sold elsewhere at retail. From October through
Christmas, anxious shoppers crowd these dealers
to get a head start on their holiday decorations.
Note: Only people with resale numbers are
allowed to park in the lot in the early morning
hours, and street parking can be a real problem!

FLOWERS FAIRE

360 Bayshore Boulevard, San Francisco.
(415) 641-7054. M–Sat 8:30–6:30, Sun 9–5.
MC, VISA. Parking: street.
People who live and work in this area stop by here to pick up roses, tulips, or tasteful mixed bouquets. For decades, this quick-service, budget-priced operation has specialized in carry-away bouquets. You'll get more blooms for the buck here than at your local supermarket. Flowers Faire offers several reasonably priced packages for weddings based on the use of seasonal flowers—and additional savings if it doesn't have to deliver. You can have it your way, but some flowers will cost more. If you become a frequent customer, you'll want to pick up a discount card.

NOR CAL POTTERY PRODUCTS

2091 Williams Street, San Leandro. (510) 895-5966.
M–F 10–4. Cash/Check. Parking: lot.
Nor Cal is an importer and distributor of pots and planters. It also imports many unique pots and planters used by landscape architects and interior designers. Because most of its pots are terra-cotta imported from Italy, a fair amount of seconds are accumulated—damaged in shipping, with cracks or chips. These seconds are usually 50% off retail. Occasionally, special pots get damaged, and then prices may be dropped to 75% off retail. There are bargains aplenty. You'll want to poke around each stack and pallet of pots, but ignore the excess first-quality inventory, also stacked outside, at full retail. At times, I've spotted fairly large terra-cotta pots (seconds) priced at $5 (well below wholesale). If you approach Nor Cal with an "I'll take pot luck" mind-set, you'll probably be more than satisfied. *Directions: From Hwy. 880, take the Marina exit west. Turn right at Merced, left on Williams.*

ORTIZ POTTERY OUTLET

123 S. Capitol Avenue, San Jose. (408) 347-9217.
M–Sat 9–6, Sun 9–2. MC, VISA, AE. Parking: lot.
This old house has been converted into pottery paradise. Inside and out, you'll find this outlet offers pallets, tables, and stacks of pottery containers, such as Italian terra-cotta, Gainey ceramics in more than fifty colors, and Mexican and Chinese pottery. These are closeouts and seconds at nicely discounted prices. Inventories from other

manufacturers produce an ever-changing selection. Look for statuary items, such as fountains and birdbaths. Catalogs are on hand for special orders on some pretty upscale Italian pots, patio statuary, and garden accessories.

POTTERY OUTLET

15715 Hesperian Boulevard, San Lorenzo. (510) 481-1902. M–W 9–5, Th–F 9–4, Sat 10–5, Sun 11–5. MC, VISA. Parking: street/lot.
When warm weather rolls around and you're in a potting mood, you'll find good buys on an ample selection of planters and pots. The store carries first-quality bargains in closeouts, and direct purchases at discount prices—a consequence of its wholesale business. A 6-inch standard clay pot sells for about 99¢. You'll find standard terra-cotta pots, Mexican clay pottery, Malaysian pottery, handthrown ceramic stoneware, South Sun's collection of antique painted pottery, and more. Seconds in every category are reduced 50% and more. Sometimes the pottery yard is overflowing, sometimes it's practically bare.

R. ELEMENTS FACTORY OUTLET

938 Tyler Street, #104, Benicia. (707) 746-0235. Sat & Sun 10–4, weekdays by appointment. MC, VISA, AE. Parking: street.
"What's wrong with this?" That's the first question you're likely to ask when looking at the half-priced seconds at R. Elements factory outlet of home and garden decorative accessories. The selection of wall plaques, statuary, candle holders, sconces, and fountain water sculptures have a rustic finish that camouflages most minor imperfections to all but the company's quality-control team. All the products at R. Elements are made out of a cast stone material, in etched or antique finishes, that holds up perfectly indoors and out. Bright green stickers identify the seconds in the factory outlet. Large and small wall plaques are priced at $20 or $12; candle holders and sconces are typically about $15. To drown out traffic noises or the neighbors, pick up a fountain water sculpture (priced without pump) at $55 to $65 when available as a second.

The original fantasy garden sculptures (13 to 15 inches tall) that are the company's claim to fame are a departure from most traditional garden sculptures. Inspired by the owner's interest in science fiction and fantasy novels, the sculptures are presented as benevolent ancient souls with names like the Watcher, Gatekeeper, Guardian, Star Gazer, Grounds Keeper, and Knight Gardener. Occasionally available as seconds, they're priced from $25 to $45. The finials at $7 are popular finishing details for garden fences, spa and tub enclosures, or as an architectural decorative accessory for bookcases or tabletops. *Directions: Exit East Second Street from Highway 780. Go south to Military East, turn left. At split, go right on Grant, right on Polk, left on Tyler. Contact: Dan Rider (707) 746-0235.*

REMEMBER WITH FLOWERS
24901 #B Santa Clara Street (off Jackson and Hwy. 92), Hayward. (510) 784-8990. M–F 9–7, Sun 9–6. MC, VISA. Parking: lot.
(Other store: 1553 A Street, Hayward.)
Remember with Flowers is a clearinghouse for fresh-cut flowers, selling surplus inventory from the Flower Market and local growers every day. Flowers are graded for shipping (1–5); Remember with Flowers buys flowers that have passed their

tolerance for cross-country shipping (a 3 grade), but they're not bloomed-out or tired. All flowers are sold in bunches of ten or two dozen stems, the wholesale norm. Shop prepared to select the best of what's available. You may find freesias, chrysanthemums, hybrid lilies, alstromeria, roses, and baby's breath at 20–25% off the price of the supermarket. About ten months out of the year, you can count on medium stem, pastel roses sold for $11.99 for two dozen. If you're buying a lot, you'll save even more taking advantage of special offers—buy two bunches for the price of one, buy two and get the third one free, etc.

A. SILVESTRI CO. FACTORY SECONDS
2635 Bayshore Boulevard, San Francisco. (415) 239-5990. www.asilvestri.com. M–Sat 8:30–5, spring and summer Sun 10–4. MC, VISA. Parking: lot.
Anyone navigating the roads to reach the Cow Palace or 3Com Park has probably noticed the displays of concrete statuary at the A. Silvestri showroom—a large complex that's been a fixture in the area for years. Indoor and outdoor architectural fountains, planters, benches, statues,

religious figures, columns, bird baths, fish ponds, mantels, balustrades, and garden ornaments in many guises attract buyers from all over. Bargain hunters will want to check out the seconds selection, where anything from Silvestri's vast inventory may end up, particularly if it's cracked, chipped, oversprayed, or just real old. Prices are reduced by about half on these rejects. Some cracks can be easily camouflaged using a product like Bondo, a body filler for cars. Some buyers will feel that the cracks just add an antique authenticity to the piece. In any case, it's up to each buyer to decide if they can fix or live with the imperfections. Fountains will not include pump elements, but these can be purchased. Some exceptionally large seconds may be located in other parts of the showroom or yard. No delivery is provided on seconds, a consideration when buying a very large or heavy piece. Check in between November 15th and 30th for Silvestri's yearly clearance sale and extra discounts.

SMITH & HAWKEN OUTLET

1330 Tenth Street, Berkeley. (510) 525-2944.
M–F 9:30–7, Sat 9:30–6, Sun 10–6.
MC, VISA, AE. Parking: lot.
Smith & Hawken's outlet is partitioned from its very attractive full-service retail store and nursery. It has a separate entrance and offers merchandise in garden furniture, distinctive gift and dinnerware items, garden tools, plant food and fertilizers, fireplace tools, garden books, some apparel, and much more in the way of esoteric gardening and decorative items. Some merchandise may be slightly damaged or irregular, but most is discontinued catalog inventory reduced 25–75% off retail. *Note: I've found that hours change from time to time, so call first.*

SONOMA COMPOST

550 Mecham Road, Petaluma. (707) 664-9113.
Daily 8:30–3:30. Cash/Check. Parking: lot.
Give your soil an "organic" boost by adding some compost—or in gardener's terms, add some "Black Gold" to your soil. To save about half the cost of other private compost providers around the Bay Area, take the do-it-yourself approach by

driving up to the Sonoma Compost Yard. You can do it the hard and messy way by taking shovel in hand and filling your own bags (up to 2 cubic feet) and pay just $1 per bag, or buy and fill one of their bags for $1.50. Come with a pickup truck, load up the truck bed and you'll pay $12 per cubic yard (1999 prices). Price breaks are offered for larger orders and delivery is available. On 22 acres at the central Sonoma County Landfill, the County's organic "leftovers" are sorted, shredded, moistened, screened, piled, tossed, aerated, tested, and sniffed over a three-month period before the compost is ready to sell. The final product is basically free of weed seeds, pathogens, and pesticide residues—all destroyed during the carefully monitored composting process when temperatures reach more than 140 degrees Fahrenheit for 10 days or longer. Compost is the lifeblood of organic agriculture. It provides a number of important nutrients and minerals needed for vigorous production. Rather than depleting soils of nitrogen after several months as some urea-fortified products do, Sonoma Compost will generally release its nutrients over an extended period. Make no mistake, this may be a recycled product, but the end product is of premium quality. This was the first operation in the state to be recognized for product quality by the California Compost Quality Council. Call for availability—occasionally contractors or landscapers with stadium-sized projects scoop up all the day's available compost. Make it a family outing. The kids will be fascinated by the big equipment moving compost around the facility, and there's a notable demonstration garden.

SSILKSS

635 Brannan Street, San Francisco. (415) 777-1353. M–Sat 8–5. MC, VISA. Parking: lot.

Ssilkss, an importer, wholesaler, and manufacturer of artificial trees, stocks an impressive inventory of silk flowers, plants, and trees and offers the same discounts to everyone. Ssilkss makes a variety of artificial trees up to twenty-five feet tall: ficus, palms, flowering trees, and bonsai. Complete your presentation with baskets and dried material to coordinate with the silk flowers and greenery. Christmas starts in August here, with an extensive display of Christmas trees 4 to 15 feet tall and grapevine reindeer up to 6 feet tall.

SUNFLOWER WHOLESALE FLORAL SUPPLY

1243 Boulevard Way, Walnut Creek.
(925) 947-0543. M–Sat 9:30–5:30. MC, VISA.
Parking: lot.

East Bay floral designers and wanna-bes flock to this upscale operation to get the very best in floral supplies. Since opening its operation to the public, word has spread that this is the place to go for inspiration and unique and high-end flowers and fixings. Amid the abundant floral displays are sample arrangements created by Sunflower's talented in-house designers that reflect the latest trends and sophistication in flowers, colors, and foliage. If you're clever at duplicating but short-changed in creativity, you'll welcome the ideas that are provided. If you're lazy or in a rush, you can buy the ready-to-go arrangements, which are very reasonably priced, considering the level of originality. I found the prices competitive to sometimes a bit higher than some vendors at the San Francisco Flower Mart, but you get so many extras at Sunflower: excellent customer service and free advice, unique blooms (dried, paper, and silk), beautiful ribbons (silks, French-wired, and other high-end exotics, which can be quite pricey), distinctive containers and objects for showcasing your arrangements (baskets, bowls, bird cages, papier-mâché boxes, twig chairs), wreaths made from out-of-the-ordinary materials, and some elegant home accessories (window boxes, stands, statuary, topiaries, pots, vases, etc.). I saw many things that I haven't seen at other floral supply outlets, which is what makes this company so special.

There is a two-tiered pricing structure. Wholesale buyers must have a valid California resale license, and the general public pays the listed retail price (with additional discounts for quantity purchases). Hands-on classes with an emphasis on basic floral design techniques are offered throughout the year for a modest fee. In addition, free floral demonstrations by in-house and guest designers are frequently offered, particularly during the fall and holiday open houses. Martha Stewart would love this place!

Also See

Under Art, Craft, and Hobby Supplies:
ANGRAY FANTASTICO

Under Home Improvement:
HOME DEPOT

Under General Merchandise—
Membership Warehouse Clubs:
COSTCO

Furniture and Home Accessories

In this chapter, I've separated the listings into logical groups. All the stores mentioned offer substantial savings. Some have large showrooms with backup warehouse stock, allowing you to buy furniture directly off the floor, while others may have minimal or no stock on display and do most business through catalog orders. A few are clearance centers for full-service retail stores. When stores have focused on a particular category of home furnishings, e.g., office or baby furniture, I've created a separate section for them.

It's important to understand the system when buying furniture. When you place a custom order (as opposed to buying in-stock inventory), you usually have to wait anywhere from a few weeks to several months for delivery. The store you're buying from often has no control over turnaround time. For instance, the fabric you've chosen for a new sofa may be out of stock at the factory, or delivery may be delayed until the manufacturer schedules another production run. Often the store won't be aware of these problems until the piece is ordered from the manufacturer. Once the furniture arrives, there may be additional delays if freight damage has occurred or the piece must be "finished" or "deluxed." It's hard to fathom how a china cabinet can be sent without shelves or hardware, but it does happen. When something goes wrong, it may seem to take forever to sort everything out. In most cases, the only way the store can alleviate the aggravation is to keep you informed. Patience is required when placing a custom order, whether you're trying to save a few hundred dollars or several thousand dollars on your furnishings.

Catalog Discounters

The businesses in this section sell furnishings primarily from manufacturers' catalogs rather than from in-house stock. They offer some of the best alternatives to high retail prices. The operations I have listed are all similar, in that they take a small markup. Many eliminate costly services and forgo advertising. Some of these places have no furnishings at all to show; others have quite a few. Buying furniture this way will usually enable you to save 20–40%. The discounts offered by these stores differ by degrees. Some offer little more than a very low price, while others combine a high level of service and design support with slightly higher prices. I'm confident that you'll be able to find the store that most fits your needs among the ones I've listed. Most have no credit plans other than MC or VISA. These stores may also focus heavily on two or three categories of furnishings. Therefore, I've cross-referenced them under the carpets, appliances, and draperies sections, or in instances where I felt it was more appropriate, I've placed the stores' listings in those categories. Note the cross-references to consider all your options.

ALIOTO & ASSOCIATES
644 Third Street West, Sonoma. (707) 996-4546. M–Wed 9:30–5, Th–Sat by appointment. Cash/Check. Parking: lot.

Alioto & Associates maintains a low profile compatible with Sonoma's pastoral image. Although the exterior resembles a new apartment house, the showroom is quite lovely. You'll find several room groupings complete with tasteful accessories providing a tempting assortment of furnishings from the manufacturers the store represents. Showroom prices reflect the manufacturers' suggested retail listing; you'll have to ask for the discount price. Of course, you can buy off the floor, but chances are you'll end up purchasing from the store's catalog resources. Alioto has an extensive selection of wallpaper books (average 25% discount); carpet and flooring (vinyl) samples from leading manufacturers; window treatments (blinds, pleated shades, woven woods); and fabric samples for draperies and upholstery. Alioto works with new homeowners and remodelers at the blueprint stage to help them avoid expensive mistakes. It controls costs by operating with a minimal markup, doing business on a cash basis, and being family owned. Using its interior design service, you can completely decorate your office or home. In addition to most major brands of high-end furniture, it can also order some "restricted" brands, although the discounts may be less. Phone quotes are given if you can provide all the specifics.

DAVID MORRIS CO.

1378 Sutter Street (bet. Franklin and Van Ness), San Francisco. (415) 346-8333. M–F 9:30–5:30, Sat by appointment. MC, VISA, 30- to 90-day interest-free payment plans. Parking: street.
You'll see just a few sample pieces of furniture on the floor, but David Morris offers good savings on custom orders from major catalogs. The store does a tremendous carpeting business and works closely with insurance companies on replacement claims. If carpeting is your top priority, you'll want to settle down with sample books from just about every carpet company. Inquire about Karastan and its Persian and Chinese carpets. Selecting new draperies or window treatments is a piece of cake. If you must see before you buy, you can arrange a preview trip to the Furniture Mart. David Morris

also sells well-known brands of kitchen and laundry appliances. You'll save 30% on almost all purchases, including freight and delivery.

DEOVLET & SONS

1660 Pine Street (bet. Van Ness and Franklin), San Francisco. (415) 775-8014. M–Sat 9–5. MC, VISA. Parking: street/pay lots.
This store has been around for more than fifty-five years, and for good reason. The grown-up children of its original customers now get the same good values, prices, and service that their parents received years ago. You may have to ask someone to turn on the lights on the second and third floors for a good look at the bed, dining, breakfast, and living room furnishings. You'll find displays of very moderately priced goods in upholstered lines and case goods for the bedroom and dining room, plus major lines of kitchen and laundry appliances (including Wolf, Viking, Gaggenau, Dacor, General Electric, KitchenAid, and Sub-Zero), and vacuum cleaners. The store leans toward traditional and includes Victorian-inspired reproductions in upholstered furniture and case goods, and many oak pieces. It can usually offer immediate delivery on

appliances and bedding. You'll find excellent prices on its large selection of carpets from several major mills, and count on a 25–30% discount off retail.

EASTERN—THE FURNITURE COMPANY

1231 Comstock Street, Santa Clara.
(408) 727-3772. www.easternfurniture.com.
M, T, Th 9:30–8; W, F, Sat 9:30–5:30; Sun Noon–5.
MC, VISA. Parking: lot.
Eastern has 50,000 square feet, featuring galleries by Century, Hickory-White, Bernhardt, Natuzzi, and Harden. Other manufacturers the store represents include Vanguard, Sherrill, Hancock & Moore, Hickory Chair, Lane, Hekman, Customcraft, Rowe, Kincaid, Maitland-Smith, and many more. You'll find leather furniture, youth furniture from companies like Lexington and Stanley, mattresses from Aireloom, recliners from Braddington-Young, plus many informal dining sets and occasional tables, carpeting, oriental rugs, and wall and window coverings. Filling in the spaces are upholstered sofas, chairs, sectionals, entertainment centers, and accessories. The backup inventory in the nearby warehouse may save you a possible three-month minimum wait. You can special order mer-

chandise from the approximately 200 manufacturers Eastern represents. Prices are often considerably less than full-service retail stores on most furniture lines carried. Beautiful showroom with elegant displays. Interior designers on staff.

GALLERY WEST

1355 Market Street (at Tenth Street),
San Francisco Furniture Mart, San Francisco.
(415) 861-6812. T–F 9:30–4:30, Sat 10–4.
MC, VISA, financing. Parking: validated basement garage weekdays, street on Sat.
At Gallery West you'll have access to the wholesale showrooms of the Western Merchandise Mart. Browse through manufacturers' catalogs of sofas, chairs, bedroom and dining room pieces, occasional tables, lamps, accessories, draperies, window coverings, carpeting, and vinyl or hardwood flooring. Serious customers get to view possible selections in Mart showrooms in the building or at Showplace Square. The staff can provide complete design services at no extra cost when combined with major purchases. The usual discount reflects 25–40% off the prices in conventional retail stores. Look for these lines offered at special discounts:

Highland House and Designer Gallery Ltd. (upholstery), Hekman Furniture, Sumpter Cabinet and Howard Miller (clocks, curios), and James Moder crystal chandeliers. Delivery is extra. You'll have to stop at the desk in the main lobby to get the okay to visit the Gallery West showroom. This building is not open to the general public.

GIORGI BROS.
212 Baden Avenue, South San Francisco.
(415) 588-4621. M–Sat 9–6, F 9–9.
MC, VISA, DIS, financing. Parking: street/lot.
Giorgi Bros. is not an elegant store. To earn that description, it would have to carpet, paint, and triple its space to provide room for lovely vignettes that would do justice to the furnishings it sells. As it is, the store is usually crammed with about one hundred sofas, approximately fifty bedroom and fifty dining room sets, entertainment cabinets, grandfather clocks, mattresses, appliances, floor coverings, chairs, occasional tables, and more. Its buyer does an impressive job selecting fabrics for the upholstered pieces on the showroom floor. Additional inventory is kept in a nearby warehouse, helpful if you're in a rush. If you want to select your own upholstery pattern or finish, you can custom order through the catalogs. Across the street in the annex are informal kitchen and dining sets, children's furniture, and other articles. A showroom just a half block away showcases even more furniture. You'll see moderate- to high-end lines like Century, Hickory-White, Flex Steel, Bernhardt, Wexford Collection, Pennsylvania House, Lexington, Hammary, Weiman, Pulaski, Classic Leather, Stanley, Lane, Hekman, Harden, La Barge, Burton James, Borkholder, Henkel-Harris, Hancock & Moore, Hickory Chair, and dozens more. Tags list Giorgi's discount price (at least 33% off prevailing retail), plus manufacturer's name and model number. With all this emphasis on its classy furniture selection, it's easy to overlook the appliances, home electronics, and floor coverings (carpet, vinyl, laminate) at very competitive prices. Inquire about the in-home custom drapery and window covering service (shutters too) that requires an appointment. The new parking lot across the street from the main store allows for leisurely shopping.

HOME CATALOG CENTER

1901 Camino Ramon, Danville. (925) 275-8145.
T–Sat 10–6, Sun Noon–5. MC, VISA. Parking: lot.
An extension of the Home Consignment Center next door, this no-frills store for catalog orders is convenient if you can't find consignment furnishings. Check the showroom samples representing many of its catalog resources to judge quality, finishes, seat comfort, etc., and then sit down at a table and start your research. When you place your order, you should be able to save 30–50%. A 25% deposit is required with the order, the rest on delivery. Many well-known and mainstream manufacturers of dining, bedroom, upholstery, etc. are represented. Space at the catalog tables may be hard to come by on weekends when it seems everyone wants to shop, so try for weekdays if your schedule allows. First 25 miles of delivery is free.

HOUSE OF VALUES

2565 S. El Camino Real, San Mateo.
(650) 349-3414. T–Sat 9:30–5:30, F until 9.
MC, VISA. Parking: street.
Just when I think I've seen everything at House of Values, I'm directed out the door and down the street to the next showroom. There's an outstanding selection of furnishings that reflect all the latest design trends (including new shabby-chic slip-covered upholstery and Shaker-style pine, maple, and cherry tables and cabinets). My comparison surveys earned it high marks on pricing and values. Although it sells no carpeting or draperies, its in-store selection of fine-quality bedroom and dining room furniture, entertainment cabinets, occasional tables, lamps, upholstered goods, brass and iron beds, and mattress sets is quite extensive. Some famous names: Century, Hickory-White, Harden, Bernhardt, Burton James, Hekman, Garcia Imports, La Barge, Highland House, Lexington, Stanley, Lane, and more. House of Values takes one of the smallest markups around—a reason so many people drive miles to shop there. If you find the perfect piece on the floor, it's yours as soon as delivery can be arranged. You can custom order "designer lines" of furniture from its catalogs or showrooms at Showplace Square and designer fabrics by the yard for your own home-decorating projects. Need help? Then you'll appreciate the interior design service available at no extra charge. Worth a visit from anywhere in the Bay Area.

THE INTERIOR WAREHOUSE

7077 Village Parkway, Dublin. (925) 829-7280, (800) 547-8614. T–Sat 11–4 or by appointment. MC, VISA. Parking: lot.

This charming catalog furniture buying service has several choice pieces of upholstered furniture on its floor; hundreds of furniture catalogs; fabric, flooring, and carpet samples; window treatment displays; and wallpaper books. Even better, it's comfortable. The sales staff is friendly, knowledgeable, helpful, and very low key. Members of its entourage include Henry Link, Bernhardt, Pulaski, Lane, Hickory Tavern, Hekman, Fremarc, Dino-Mark Anthony, Brown Jordan, Cavalier, Chapman, Weiman, La Barge, Habersham Plantation, McGuire, Stanley, and many more. The discounts on these lines are 20–40% off most retail pricing. On wallpaper and fabrics in sample books, discounts are 15–30%, or occasionally more when the manufacturer is having a special promotion. The store's drapery and upholstery swatch selection is one of the finest in the East Bay. Carpeting is sold for 10% over cost. Custom wood shutters are 30% off! Resident designers can provide in-home consultations at approximately $60/hour.

Directions: From Hwy. 680 (north of 580 interchange) take the Alcosta exit east of Village Parkway, and turn right.

JOHN R. WIRTH CO.

1080 Terra Bella, Mountain View. (408) 736-5828. T–Fri 10–6, Sat 10–4. MC, VISA. Parking: lot.

Southern Peninsula residents stretch their home-furnishing dollars on living room, dining room, bedroom, and outdoor patio furniture and accessories by shopping this low-profile discounter. You can spend hours eyeballing fabric swatches for draperies or upholstery, carpet samples (including area and Oriental), vinyl or hardwood flooring samples, even custom kitchen cabinets. You can also place orders for wallpaper. Wirth can handle any window covering or treatment, including shutters. For additional choices on home furnishings not in the showroom, you can go to catalogs. The salespeople are experienced, helpful, and not pushy. The prices on furnishings (including freight and delivery) are discounted on the average about 35%. *Note: No phone quotes, sales usually final, full payment expected before delivery. Directions: Heading south on 101, take* the Shoreline exit west. Terra Bella is the first street on the left; go one and a half blocks.

MILLBRAE FURNITURE COMPANY

1781 El Camino Real, Millbrae. (650) 589-6455. T–F 10–6, W until 9, Sat 9–5. MC, VISA. Parking: street/city lot (side of building).

To be in a position to provide good value, it helps when you own your own building and warehouse. That way, you have the space to take advantage of special discounts on volume purchases when manufacturers make their offers. Millbrae Furniture fits the bill on both counts. Millbrae manages to cram in a good selection of furniture, appliances, bedding, carpets, and window coverings making it a one-stop resource for consumers. On the first floor you'll find upholstered goods and the appliance department, which showcases its upscale Sub-Zero, Dacor, and Wolf lines, plus other consumer favorites. Go up to the second floor to bounce on the beds and check the dining and bedroom groupings. Finally, explore the basement for recliners, leather furniture, and children's furniture. You can buy moderately priced furniture right off the floor, or mosey over to the back room, where there are cabinets full of manufacturers' catalogs that provide additional resources. On most items the savings run about 30% off prevailing retail prices; however, appliances are 10% over cost. Like most discounters, this store rarely advertises but does a steady business based on referrals.

NORIEGA FURNITURE

1455 Taraval Street (at 25th Avenue), San Francisco. (415) 564-4110, (800) 664-4110. www.noriegafurniture.com. T, W, F 10–5:30; Th 1–9; Sat 10–5. MC, VISA, DIS. Parking: street.

Noriega Furniture is appealing for its beautiful showroom, personal service, and decorator consultants. Its specialty is expensive high-quality furniture, and its manufacturers' catalogs offer furniture, carpets, draperies, wallpaper, beautiful artwork, and accessories at savings of at least 20% and as much as 40%. Noriega is the oldest Stickley dealer in California and features Arts and Crafts lamps and pottery. It's also one of the only resources in the Bay Area discounting Lladro as well as Waterford and Lenox lamps. You can purchase European, American, and Oriental reproductions and accent pieces; distinctive accessories, and original oil paintings, engravings, and prints. Overall, you'll be dazzled by traditional furnishings from companies like Stickley, Kindel, Karges, Henredon, Guy Chaddock, Hickory Chair, Hancock & Moore, Karastan, and others. If you need help, Noriega's decorators will go to most Bay Area communities with samples. Located in the Sunset/ Parkside district, one mile north of Stonestown shopping center. If you can't make it to the store, check out their comprehensive Web site.

R & R FRENCH BROS.

333 Alabama (at 16th Street), San Francisco. (415) 621-6627. M–F 9:30–6, most Sats 10–3. MC, VISA. Parking: street/lot.
French Bros. is an excellent resource for home furnishings, floor coverings, mattresses, and window coverings at very special discounts. Furniture selections can be made from its library of catalogs or by personally escorted visits to the Western Merchandise Mart and showrooms at the Showplace Square Design Center. Visits are arranged by appointment. Here's a partial list of the manufacturers represented: Stanley, Bernhardt, Pulaski, Lane, American Drew, BarcaLounger, Henredon,

Coleman of CA, Baker, Bassett, and Lexington. The extensive carpet and vinyl flooring selection includes a wide range of residential and contract carpeting. As it is displayed gallery fashion, you won't have to exhaust yourself hauling heavy sample books around. Finally, prices are right on target for bargain hunters.

WESTERN CONTRACT INTERIORS

1702 Park Avenue, San Jose. (408) 275-9600. M–F 8:30–5:30, Sat 11–3. Cash/Check. Parking: lot.
If you're past the start-up phase of furnishing your home and are in search of quality furnishings at significant savings, you'll be in good hands here. When you want to sit down and get serious with your queries, I suggest making an appointment. Western's lovely showroom has sample pieces of furniture for starters and tasteful accessories, but it's hardly representative of the total resources available. You can order window coverings, mattress sets, carpeting, ergonomic chairs, and furniture for any room in the house. Western is an authorized Herman Miller dealer which allows individuals to buy famous designs such as the Aeron chair and the Charles Eames Collection at

contract prices. They also specialize in home office furnishings. Space planning is available. Expect to save 25–40% off full service retail store prices on most lines. Many Silicon Valley executives have ordered ergonomic seating and office products for their offices, then go one step further and have their homes furnished by the residential side of the business.

Also See

Under Carpets, Area Rugs, and Flooring— General:
LAWRENCE CONTRACT FURNISHERS

Under Fabrics—Home-Decorating Fabrics:
FURBELOWS

General Furnishings

If you're into dollar-wise decorating, there are familiar stores all around the Bay Area that offer stylish furnishings and accessories at "getting started" prices. Stores like Cost Plus and Pier 1 offer low-cost furnishings—kitchen sets, informal chairs, tables, and sofas, plus the accessories and accent pieces to fill the empty spaces in your rooms. The Bombay Company is an excellent resource for accent pieces and accessories for those in the traditional mode.

BENICIA FOUNDRY & IRON WORKS, INC.
2995 Bayshore Road, Benicia. (707) 745-4645. www.beniciafoundry.com. M–F 9–6, Sat 9–5, Sun 11–5. MC, VISA. Parking: lot.
This company is a major manufacturer of metal beds sold to famous stores around the country. Everything is made by hand using traditional craft techniques. Traditional to contemporary styling is offered in a variety of finishes. The company is careful to avoid conflict with the retailers that sell its beds: No special or custom orders can be placed, nor does it sell anything from its current

wholesale catalog inventory. However, when orders are cancelled, a bed is returned by a retailer, or there is some imperfection in a finished bed, it is sold for a substantial savings: 35–50% off original retails. The selection is limited in terms of style, finish, and size, but it is worth a visit to see this unpredictable mix of "leftovers." You may find complete beds, a headboard only, canopy styles, daybeds, etc., in twin, full, queen, or king sizes. Recently, the company has expanded its manufacturing to include a very nice line of garden furniture and accessories made from cast aluminum and finished with a durable baked-on polyurethane powder coating. These are Victorian and classic designs of patio tables and chairs, lampposts, urns, planters, mailboxes, settees, benches, and more. Prices are very reasonable. Delivery provided for a fee.

BUSVAN FOR BARGAINS

900 Battery Street, San Francisco. (415) 981-1405. M–Sat 9:30–6, Sun Noon–6. MC, VISA, revolving charge. Parking: street and pay lots. (Other store: 244 Clement Street, San Francisco.) Although not your typical furniture store, Busvan

carries almost anything in its somewhat tired but too busy to remodel store: furniture, rugs, pianos, antiques, paintings, books, bric-a-brac, and office furniture. The main floor is filled with new, discount-priced upholstery and mattress sets at excellent prices. Its newest focus is on deep-seated upholstery from some of the state's better-known manufacturers that are using Busvan to expand their sales. The top floor is crowded with bedroom, dining room, and accent furniture in the budget to moderate price ranges, and occasionally some exceptional one-of-a-kind accent pieces (trade samples). Nestle your preteen or adolescent in style from its expanded selection of bedroom groups. Busvan offers a sea of RTA (ready-to-assemble) or lifestyle furniture, especially desks, bedroom pieces, computer furniture, bookcases, and entertainment centers. Its solid-pine unfinished furniture is priced to make other stores blush. Opportunistic buys lead to an eclectic selection of floor samples and factory closeouts. The basement features used furniture at rock-bottom prices. Although the staff is friendly and helpful, the size of the store makes it primarily self-service. All sales final. Reasonable delivery charges, or bring your own van; Busvan will pad your furniture and stash it in or on your vehicle for free.

COMMINS DESIGN GROUP

990 Grant Street, Benicia. (707) 745-3636. M–Sat 10–5, Sun Noon–5. MC, VISA, AE. Parking: lot. Commins' warehouse showroom in Benicia is an extension of its furniture manufacturing and design company. The company sells direct to consumers out of its impressive selling space at its factory. For contemporary furnishings that embrace classical design elements, a trip is mandated. Everything speaks of nature and the organic, with elegant faux finishes on all the pieces. The spotlight is on dramatic chests, étagères, entertainment cabinets, wall units, consoles, bedroom systems, and glass-top tables with architectural pedestal bases. The many accessories on hand are from local artisans and importers, selling for appreciably lower prices than elsewhere. Altogether, this upscale collection of distinctive furniture and accessories is in no way ordinary or predictable. You can acquire prototype samples, buy pieces off the floor, or opt for a custom design that allows you to choose the color of the finish and possibly some design modifica-

tions at no extra charge (or a very modest one). In this way you'll save about half of what you would have paid a designer or showroom (but this doesn't mean things are inexpensive). Also, glass tops for anything at really good prices.

COTTAGE TABLES CO.

550 18th Street (off Third), San Francisco. (415) 957-1760. T–Sat 1–5. MC, VISA. Parking: lot. Tony Cowan builds superior-quality tables in the old tradition—from solid wood using dowel-and-glue construction. Each table is custom-made. A table that you buy from him will become a family heirloom. There's no inventory on hand, other than several sample tables to show the quality of his work, some style variations, and the woods and finishes used. A reasonably formal, solid cherry plank table 36-by-72 inches was priced at $2,200; a country pine table 33-by-60 inches was $1,200. You can have tables made in maple, walnut, pine, cherry, or oak; in styles conveying a contemporary, country, traditional, or transitional feeling; with any of a variety of leg styles; and you can add a silverware drawer for about $150. Tony does not make chairs, but keeps several on hand that he can order for you from manufacturers' catalogs. He sells the chairs at cost, which amounts to almost a 50% discount to you—a nice accommodation for his customers. A 50% deposit is required with your order.

ENGLISH GARDEN FURNITURE & LIGHTING

128 Mitchell Boulevard, San Rafael.
(415) 492-1051. M–Sat 10–4, Sun 11–4
(call to verify). Cash/Check. Parking: lot.
English Garden Furniture captures the look of Victorian garden furniture. It duplicates elegant designs from the 1700s to today in cast aluminum or in wrought aluminum (with cast aluminum seats that need no cushions). The pieces will last for years. The tables, chairs, and benches in these historical patterns reflect charm and grace and beautifully enhance traditional decors and gardens. The company has built furniture for the Embassy Suites Hotels and many historical mansions, gardens, and other public places. It also serves discriminating consumers who want good value and good design that's out of the ordinary. Once you understand the quality of this furniture, the prices appear reasonable. When it comes to top-of-the-line garden furniture, you can find similar styles in each of the three major manufacturers' lines. A chair from English Garden Furniture at $195 is comparable to one that may be priced closer to $700. Charming dining sets (table and four chairs) in various patterns are available for $795 to $1,300. Tables are sold in small dimensions or large. The chairs and chaise longues are popular with city residents who want balcony furniture that is heavy enough to withstand wind and attractive enough to blend visually with interior room decors. The company also excels in its selection of garden benches, light fixtures, chandeliers, lampposts, urns, authentic French doors, and anything custom you might desire. If you've passed the plastic-and-webbing stage and you're willing to invest in a lifetime set of garden or patio furniture, then you may want to consider this source before making any final selections.

FURNITURE EXPRESS OUTLET

667 Folsom Street (bet. Third and Fourth streets), San Francisco. (415) 495-2848. M–F 11–7, Sat 10–6, Sun Noon–5. MC, VISA, AE. Parking: street.
Folks on the prowl for inexpensive furnishings will find most of what they need right here. There are easily assembled computer workstations, desks, TV carts, dressers, bookcases and shelving units, microwave/utility carts on casters, solid maple tables, affordable dressers and pine bedroom furniture (finished and unfinished) for teen or children's rooms, and home entertainment centers (as low as $39). This is not forever furniture, but the overall quality/price/value equation is solid and the prices are very appealing for budget decorating. Those getting a little ahead can step up in quality with the newer contemporary pine, maple, and aluminum pieces so popular with the hip high-tech crowd. Prices on many pieces were about 30% below those in a local department store "sale" ad posted on the wall. Everything is sold in boxes. Delivery can be arranged.

IGUANA AMERAMEX

301 Jefferson Street (at Third Street), Oakland. (510) 834-5848. www.iguana-mexico.com. Daily 10–6. MC, VISA. Parking: street.
(Other stores: Sacramento, Santa Rosa, Walnut Creek.)
In its 45,000-square-foot store, Iguana Ameramex sells furniture and home accessories imported from Mexico. The outstanding prices offered on almost all its inventory can be attributed to strategies that lead to savings in shipping (a significant overhead cost) and buying directly from manufacturers, craftspeople, and artisans, thereby eliminating middleman or distributor costs. The furniture, sold directly to the public, is similar to many collections of furniture showcased in several local furniture specialty stores and similar in design to furnishings being shown in well-known catalogs like Pottery Barn and Robert Redford's Sundance catalog.

The furniture has broad cultural appeal. It's most often made from pine and reflects the design roots of Mexico's colonial past. It's appealing to those who are trying to achieve a more relaxed and informal environment for their homes. The rustic nature of the wood and finish allows these pieces to blend nicely with furniture defined as Southwest, country, or traditional. Prices here are often 15–50% less than comparable styles in other stores or catalogs. Armoires in various configurations and sizes are priced from $350. There's an array of furniture for many uses—armoires, occasional and dining tables, chairs, consoles, headboards, dressers, buffets, china cabinets, library units, chests, benches, etc.—crowding the huge space.

There's an intriguing selection of folk art, tabletop accessories, distinctive glassware (margarita glasses, etc.), hand-cast pewter tableware, Contera (carved stone) table bases and pedestals, and some Talavera ceramics in myriad designs from the Guanajuato, Michoacán, and Dolores Hidalgo regions. Rustic, bisque-fired architectural pots in a variety of sizes and finishes are scattered throughout the store. Pottery prices are about half off the prices of other retailers.

IKEA
Shellmound Avenue, Emeryville. Phone: Pending. M–Sat 10–9, Sun 10–7. MC, VISA, AE, DIS. Parking: lot.
What do I think of IKEA? If it weren't a privately owned company, I'd gather up all my spare dollars and buy stock in this dynamic and innovative retailer. Kudos to Emeryville for wooing this international giant into its corner of the Bay Area. I've shopped IKEA in Southern California, New York, and in other countries, and even though the store had yet to open before I went to press, I can attest to the great design and solid values waiting for Bay Area shoppers on opening day.

IKEA's furniture-at-factory-prices business approach cuts out the second-biggest cost to every furniture retailer: distribution. By offering all case goods in flat packages, which are warehoused and picked up by consumers on site, the stores offer instant gratification with the majority of its products. With no shipping, storage, or assembly charges to pay, IKEA is able to pass along considerable savings—many estimate about 30% less for like products from traditional retailers. However, don't think you're stuck doing the assembly routine. IKEA offers delivery and assembly for additional charges. Its affordable, well-designed products appeal to a younger crowd with its updated, Scandinavian designs, yet customers of all ages fill the stores and shop enthusiastically.

IKEA stores are bright, well organized, exhilarating, and fun to shop (they have a buzz and energy that could make millions if it could be bottled and sold to other retailers). Shop IKEA for every room in the house—for furniture, bedding, linens, accessories, rugs, lighting, wall decor/frames/ pictures, window coverings, storage products and solutions, decorative hardware, dinnerware and kitchen everything, even European-style kitchen cabinets and countertops in many finish options. IKEA's children's home furnishings department will be a winner with parents and kids—furniture is designed to grow with kids (a baby changer converts into bookcases), unfinished wood and storage products are served up for youngsters from birth to age 7. IKEA catalogs that showcase all its products are likely to end up in tatters by

the time you've thumbed them a dozen times. People have been known to call and order a complete new kitchen from the catalog.

LAMPS PLUS FACTORY OUTLET

15928 Hesperian Boulevard, San Leandro.
(510) 278-5307. M–F 10–9, Sat 10–6, Sun 11–6.
MC, VISA, AE. Parking: street.
(Other stores: Pleasant Hill, Sacramento,
San Francisco, San Jose, San Mateo, San Rafael.)
Lamps Plus benefits from volume purchasing power (a thirty-eight-store lighting superstore chain along the West Coast and the largest specialty lighting chain in the country). It offers a lot, and while it can't be all things to all people, it comes close. I spotted the ordinary, ho-hum, and familiar styles seen in most home-furnishings stores, and some extraspecial lamps and fixtures. In a competitive market, Lamps Plus offers consistently low everyday pricing, and at its clearance center in San Leandro, some exceptionally good buys.

At the San Leandro store, 30–50% of the display space is devoted to clearance inventory. Take notice of the tags and you'll be able to sort the regular merchandise from clearance merchandise. Black-and-white tags denote regular-priced merchandise with everyday pricing; yellow-and-white tags indicate that the item is "reconditioned"— it may have small cosmetic flaws on the finish, or it may have required reconditioning at the factory to repair any functional problem. These are all sold with the company's 100% satisfaction guaranteed policy, which applies to all its merchandise. Red-and-white tags represent closeouts or discontinued products from its own line of lamps from other Lamps Plus stores, or from factories anywhere in the world (these last products may or may not have been sold in a Lamps Plus store previously). The company uses its connections in the industry to make good closeout buys for its clearance centers and passes the savings along to customers.

The clearance inventory changes from month to month, reflecting whatever "buys" the company has garnered from its suppliers. There may be some delightful surprises from time to time, when exceptional values are captured. When the item is unique to the clearance center, savings may be from 10–60% off Lamps Plus original prices or estimated retail value. Can't complain about these manufacturers: Koch & Lowy, Halogen, Westwood, Fine Arts, Geo. Kovacs, Stiffel, and ceiling fans from Casablanca and Hunter. Lamps Plus can also special order fixtures from catalogs. Finally, it has about the biggest array of replacement lamp shades I've spotted in the Bay Area.

NATIONAL MATTRESS CLEARANCE CENTER
15430 Hesperian Boulevard, San Leandro.
(510) 481-1623. M–Sat 9–6, Sun Noon–5.
MC, VISA, DIS. Parking: lot.
National, in business for sixty-nine years, has such a large collection of mattresses and box springs that it could host a slumber party for hundreds. Its huge mattress department has two sections. First, you'll find new Simmons, Sealy, Serta, and Spring Air mattress sets at about 20% below the advertised department store "50% off" sales. Every manufacturer offers price groups ranging from budget to ultrapremium. So wherever you fit, you'll be sure to find a terrific value. You can do even better if you're willing to consider mattresses from the "as is" area. That is where you'll find legitimate factory seconds and mismatched

sets. Defects or flaws are carefully pointed out and explained when you're making a choice. Some flaws are obvious, but many are not. Factory seconds also carry a warranty, but for a shorter time. I spotted a top-of-the-line, king-sized set priced at half National's discount, first-quality price. Mattresses can be purchased without box spring units.

RONEY'S FURNITURE

14000 Washington Avenue, San Leandro. (510) 352-4074. M–Sat 9:30–7, Sun 11:30–6. MC, VISA, DIS. Parking: lot.
Roney's warehouse (a former National Guard armory) is stuffed. The emphasis is on traditional or transitional furniture from major manufacturers. If you need it yesterday, you can buy sofas, chairs, and tables; living room, bedroom, and dining room furniture; and entertainment cabinets, recliners, lamps, and accessories right off the floor. Some of the most popular lines in furniture are ready to go—lots of weekend country collections and better reproductions of the classic Arts and Crafts styles. Prices are nicely discounted, whether you buy a piece off the floor or opt for a custom catalog order. Whether you're buying your first piece of furniture with a minimal budget or upgrading, Roney's offers many options for most budgets. Expect a small delivery charge. If you're in the mood for a good browse with the hope of finding a great bargain, give Roney's a whirl; you're sure to become a regular. Sunday's are busy—it's take-a-number-time. Do yourself a favor and shop during the week.

SLEEP SHOP LTD./KIDZ & TEENZ LTD.

1530 Contra Costa Boulevard, Pleasant Hill. (925) 671-9400. www.sleepshopltd.com. M–F 9:30–9, Sat 9:30–6, Sun 11–6. MC, VISA, DIS. Parking: lot. (Other stores: Antioch, Dublin, Walnut Creek.)
This very complete store makes a profit through volume sales rather than high markups. A diverse selection of brass and iron beds (at least thirty-six models) and daybeds (about twenty-four models) are available from Elliotts, Wesley Allen, Fashion Bed Group, and Elm Creek. Sleep tight on mattress sets from Simmons, Serta, Chattam & Wells, and Spring Air that are always available at less than department store sale prices. Sleep Shop aggressively discounts special buys and mattress

sets with discontinued covers. Delivery charges are minimal. If your tots are ready to leave their cribs, check out the extensive selection of juvenile and teen furniture in the Kidz & Teenz Ltd. department. With eighteen vignettes and more than sixteen bunk beds on display, you can find just the right look to suit your child's personality. Parents appreciate that many companies are offering suites of furniture with classic and clean lines that can leave home with the kids when they set up their own households. Stanley, Camelot, My Room, Treadwood, Boyd, Silver Eagle, Vaughn, and Tempo are companies making the grade at Kidz & Teenz Ltd. Special orders may take a few extra weeks or months, but the prices discounted at least 30% make the wait worthwhile.

STANFORD FINE FURNITURE & DESIGNS

6925 Central Avenue, Newark. (510) 745-9962. M–F 8:30–4:30. Cash/Check. Parking: lot.
If you want to achieve a designer look in upholstered furniture without designer prices, go where designers go: Stanford Designs. This company makes its own lines of sofas and does a lot of custom work. (Loved the new shabby-chic style, a slightly loose slipcover over a muslin-covered sofa.) There are several ways to get a deal at Stanford. First, sample pieces can be purchased off the factory salesroom floor. Next, you can go back to the warehouse and check the inventory of discontinued fabrics. Pick your sofa, sectional, sleeper, or chair style, your fabric, and your quality—you'll get such a deal! Pay extra and you can have coil-spring construction, down pillows, and so on. Otherwise, Stanford uses kiln-dried hardwood frames, double bracing, HR 30 foam cushions with a ten-year guarantee (even the best companies often use only 1.85-density foam), and lined skirts. Shopping this way takes a little initiative. If you're trying to achieve a certain look, bring in a picture, find the fabric, and prepare yourself for extra customization charges. Services also include reupholstery and slipcovers. You'll still come out way ahead. A 50% deposit is required with the order, balance before delivery.

TRADEWAY STORES

10860 San Pablo Avenue, El Cerrito.
(510) 529-2360. M–F 9–6, Sat 9–5:30. MC, VISA.
Parking: street.

At Tradeway you'll find discounts on high-end pieces and some fairly ho-hum furnishings. It has contracts with several manufacturers like Thomasville, Dixie, Hammary, Broyhill, Universal, American Drew, Lexington, Bassett, American of Martinsville, Drexel-Heritage, Kincaid, Miles Talbott, Berkline, and others. When furniture isn't delivered to a retailer for whatever reason, the manufacturer avoids shipping it back across the country by redirecting it to Tradeway. Everything is "detailed" (repaired) if necessary and then priced at about 40–50% off original retail. Anything marked "as is" has been part of a redirected inventory. Savvy shoppers case the store frequently to latch onto the unusual high-end designer pieces that show up from time to time. Other furniture lines are also stocked as needed to balance out this unpredictable incoming inventory. For the most part they're budget- to moderately priced lines of upholstered furniture; dining and bedroom furnishings are also discounted. The furnishings are jammed haphazardly into several rooms on two levels. If you're looking for farmhouse-style kitchen tables, inexpensive dinettes, recliners, bunk beds, student desks, or family room sofas, Tradeway has lots of potential. Also a good selection of bedroom and dining room furniture. Delivery on purchases of more than $750 is free from San Leandro to Vallejo; otherwise delivery is priced according to distance.

THE WOODEN DUCK

2919 Seventh Street, Berkeley (Ashby exit off Hwy. 80, left at first stoplight). (510) 848-3575.
www.thewoodenduck.com. M–Sat 10–6,
Sun Noon–5. MC, VISA. Parking: lot.

The Wooden Duck offers consumers good value and new options in buying furniture. The store is a showcase for an intriguing array of new reproduction pine furniture (some made from old wood), old pieces from Indonesia (many 95 to 100 years old), new teak garden furniture, new and old boxes and trunks, and other surprises that come with each new shipment. This company is reflective of a recent trend where many antique dealers and stores noted for selling reproductions are buying up furniture in former colonies in lieu of buying from Europe due to price and supply considerations. New sourcing is occurring in Vietnam (French), India (English), and Eastern Europe as well as Indonesia. The Wooden Duck is both a retailer and wholesaler of furniture, and its warehouse-styled store is set apart by its extensive selection of imports and lower pricing. Some new reproduction pieces (chairs, armoires, tables, etc.) are made from pine, finished with a coat of wax to achieve a light honey color. They closely resemble furniture associated with the English country pine look. The pine bedside tables, bedroom dressers with curved fronts, and small consoles were priced about 20–25% lower than other stores in the area. Another customer-pleasing category is the teak garden furniture, similar to styles shown in many high-profile gardening catalogs. These garden benches, tables, and chairs were 30–50% lower in price than similar catalog versions. The new teak furniture is made from plantation teak grown specifically for furniture making. Those looking for a table for a kitchen or dining room, and wanting a piece with a bit of history, should take a look at some of the Wooden Duck's old teak tables. Keep in mind that these teak tables bear no resemblance to the teak furniture sold as Danish Modern (so popular in the 1950s and 1960s). Furniture manufactured in Indonesia in the nineteenth and early twentieth century was made to suit the tastes of European settlers or government officials (primarily Dutch or British colonials). The old teak pieces, usually tables and assorted cabinets and armoires, resemble the vintage oak and mahogany furniture typically associated with antiques from England and Western Europe. When the original finishes have been obscured with use, the Wooden Duck has had the tables refurbished with a shellac-based French polish which results in a lovely patina. These old pieces have been purchased from buying expeditions to small villages throughout Indonesia. The tables are priced according to quality of finish, size, thickness and cuts of wood, and condition and generally range from $450 to $900. Most tables are made without nails and joined with mortise-and-tenon joints. Some pieces do reflect an "ethnic" and Asian influence, but most are decidedly European in design with classic styles familiar to consumers. Wooden Duck is expanding its inventory and developing new sources, so it is a store that bears watching. Its corner location is easy to spot—there's always a display of furniture set outside the entrance to catch the eyes of passing motorists.

ZEBRA

727 East Francisco Boulevard, San Rafael. (415) 453-6078. M–F 10:30–6, closed Tuesdays; Sat 10–5, Sun Noon–5. MC, VISA, DIS. Parking: lot. You'll find an updated collection of rustic and country-style pine plus an eclectic selection of slipcovered sofas and chairs and an inspired global collection of accessories. Working with a smaller markup, everything is well priced in the modest-to midprice range of furniture lines. Some collections are imported directly from Mexico, others originate from smaller West Coast companies. The store is fun, catering to those who don't want the usual, same old stuff. Customers can find beds and bedroom furnishings; tables, cabinets, and occasional pieces for the dining room; living room pieces; and entertainment systems, wall systems, stereo cabinets, TV stands, and bookcases, priced about 25% below competitors. Many lines are transitional and reflect the informality that many

are seeking for family living. All furniture is assembled and can be purchased right off the floor for immediate delivery. You can special order other options from manufacturers' catalogs. This is a good place for younger couples getting started and anybody who wants good value.

Also See

Under Carpets, Area Rugs, and Flooring— General:
PIONEER HOME SUPPLY

Under Linens:
DREAMS

Mattress Buyers Beware

Beware the mattress "discounters" that have proliferated around the Bay Area. Ads promising hard-to-believe prices are most often a lure to an aggressive bait-and-switch sales pitch. It seems that some sales personnel have the attitude, "If you can't sell them, insult them." Mattress sets from major manufacturers sold at these outfits are often made expressly for the discounters. From my comparisons, you can buy better quality and receive greater value when purchasing a mattress set from the sources listed here. Hints for savvy shopping: When you canvass the market for mattress sets, you're likely to end up very confused by the many names from the same manufacturer you find at different retail stores. Large stores and chains with volume accounts usually pick their own names for the manufacturers' groups they buy; they may also decide upon special fabric patterns and colors for the ticking. Most independents will sell mattress sets with the manufacturers' original names. By carefully studying the components displayed in a manufacturers' cut-out samples—the number of coils; turns and gauge of the coils; weight, thickness, composition, and layers of the cushion elements; type of suspension system; and relative price range—you'll soon figure out that a specific manufacturer's Pontiac Supreme at Store A is equivalent to Buick Ultra at Store B and on a par with Oldsmobile Maximum at Store C. Many manufacturers have enlarged the selection at the high end of the market, offering mattresses with more design and comfort features, and accordingly higher prices.

Baby and Juvenile Furniture/ Equipment—New and Used

You might as well decide where to shop for baby furniture and equipment on the basis of convenience and selection, unless you want to go endlessly in circles, comparing prices to save a few bucks. It's a very competitive market—kept that way by manufacturers who closely control distribution of various style groups to selected retailers. The opening of baby "superstores" has increased the pressure on independents. They've responded with more service, expert advice, and pricing that keeps them in the game. The stores in this section are all very competitive and noteworthy for keeping prices as low as possible. I've included stores that also sell quality used furnishings, along with the new. Other Bay Area resources for budget- to moderately priced baby furniture and equipment: Toys 'R' Us, Wal-Mart, Kmart, and Costco.

BABIES 'R' US

4990 Dublin Boulevard, Hacienda Crossings, Dublin. (925) 875-0350. www.toysrus.com. M–Sat 9:30–9:30, Sun 10–7. MC, VISA, AE, DIS. Parking: lot.
(Other store: 865 Blossom Hill Road, San Jose, 408/281-1710.)
After visiting these stores you'll wonder how the independent specialty stores can survive the awesome competition in price and selection. New parents will be overwhelmed with the selection of "everything" that baby needs (and probably doesn't need), while grandparents will wonder how they ever managed without the paraphernalia that is de rigueur for today's parents. The selection is all encompassing, with choices that range from budget to best no matter what you're shop-

ping for. The baby gift registry (that can be accessed through its Web site) allows you to gift shop for anyone, anywhere in the country.

BABY DEPOT

Great Mall of the Bay Area, Milpitas. (408) 934-0454. Daily. MC, VISA, AE, DIS, layaway. Parking: lot.
(Other stores: located within Burlington Coat Factory Stores at Westgate Mall, San Jose; across from Southland Mall, Hayward.)
A subsidiary of Burlington Coat Factory, it occupies a large space within Burlington stores. Shop for an impressive selection of merchandise geared toward the needs of newborns to kids age 14. Whether you're setting up a nursery as a first-time parent, buying back-to-school clothes for a second grader, picking up toys for a birthday party, or finding the best breast pump, car seat, or stroller, you'll find selection and good prices. Everything is backed by a "lowest price" guarantee.

BABY SUPER—ROCKERWORLD & FURNITURE FOR KIDS

1523 Parkmoor Avenue, San Jose.
(408) 293-0358. M–W, Sat 10–6; Th, F until 8:30;
Sun Noon–5. MC, VISA, layaway. Parking: lot.
Almost supermarket-sized, this store is great for
one-stop shopping. It offers an extensive selection, both in quality and quantity, of baby and
toddler equipment and furniture for tots and the
juvenile market. Buy everything you need for the
first eighteen months: infant clothing, diapers,
blankets, cribs, high chairs, Portacribs, adult
rockers, playpens, car seats, and more. There's a
complete furniture selection for infants through
teens. Crib suites (cribs, dressers, changing
tables, etc.) and youth furniture add up to one of
the best selections of furnishings found anywhere
in the Bay Area. Stanley, Pali, Vermont Precision,
Ragazzi, Legacy, EG, Morrgeau, Baby Dream,
Childcraft, Play Space, Morigeau, and Vermont
Tubbs are some of the lines. Furniture prices
are nicely discounted. The selection of Dutailier
rockers and gliders is appealing. They're great all
the time, for anyone. Be sure to check the Baby
& Kids Bargain Warehouse, where discontinued
merchandise, floor samples, and more budget-
priced lines of goods are sold.

BABY WORLD

5854 College Avenue, Oakland. (510) 655-2950.
www.babyworldusa.com. M–F 10–6, Sat 10–5,
Sun Noon–5. MC, VISA. Parking: lot.
Baby World provides new and used children's
equipment, furniture, and toys. There's a wide array
of riding toys (try to leave without one if you're
shopping with your toddler). The playthings range
from popular classics up to the latest in high-
demand amusements. This is an excellent source
for grandparents who need to set up a baby
room. The selection of cribs, playpens, bassinets,
high chairs, and car seats is quite extensive. The
prices are great!

KIDS AGAIN

6891 Village Parkway, Dublin. (510) 828-7334.
M–Sat 10–5, Th until 7, Sun Noon–4. MC, VISA.
Parking: back lot.
Kids Again, a store with multiple personalities,
sells new brand-name lines of baby and youth
furniture at discounts up to 30% off retail. After

browsing through its floor inventory of infant, child, and teen furniture, extend your options even more by turning the pages in manufacturers' catalogs. Special orders involve a few months for delivery, but you'll end up delighted with your savings. Several popular lines of crib and juvenile bedding (sheets, bumper pads, dust ruffles, quilts, shams, etc.) can be ordered from catalogs at 10–25% off suggested retail. Kids Again is also a consignment store—a big one. Buy or sell your children's clothing (sizes 0–10), toys, furniture equipment, or your still-wearable maternity clothing. The Fashion Court is set aside for consignment clothing for women, with an emphasis on better-quality, classic, casual, career, and special-occasion clothing. All that grown-up furniture from Furnish Again (page 280) is from Kids Again's recent expansion into consignment furnishings for adults.

LULLABY LANE & KIDS FURNITURE CLEARANCE CENTER
570 San Mateo Avenue, San Bruno.
(650) 588-7644. M–F 10–6, W until 9,
Sat 9:30–5:30, Sun 11–5. MC, VISA, DIS.
Parking: free rear lot or street.
(Other stores: Kids Furniture [juvenile only],
532 San Mateo Avenue; Lullaby Lane,
556 San Mateo Avenue, San Bruno.)
Opened in 1947, Lullaby Lane is now three separate operations. The first stop for bargain hunters is its clearance center, where closeouts, floor samples, and discontinued and slightly damaged items are sent over from its two other stores and sold for up to 50% off regular store prices. Grandparents can shop the clearance center to pick up a used crib (buy or rent) for when baby comes visiting. Next, the main store, a few doors away, at 556 San Mateo Avenue, has an extensive selection of baby "everything." Think you can save more elsewhere? Take Lullaby Lane up on its offer to meet any price. Kids Furniture, just a few doors from the main location, is filled with nicely discounted juvenile furniture.

Also See

Under Furniture—Catalog Discounters:
ALL LISTINGS

Under Furniture—General Furnishings:
IKEA

Under Recycled Apparel:
GENERAL INFORMATION

Furniture Clearance Centers

**CORT FURNITURE RENTAL
CLEARANCE CENTERS**
*2925 Mead Avenue (off Bowers), Santa Clara.
(408) 727-1470. www.cort1.com. M–F 10–7, Sat
10–6, Sun 11–5. MC, VISA, AE, DIS. Parking: lot.
(Other stores: 1240 Willow Pass Road, Concord;
5757 Stevenson Blvd., Newark; 416 El Camino
Real, San Bruno; 1830 Hillsdale, San Jose.)*
Sometimes you need budget-priced furniture ASAP!
Cort's "retired furniture" goes on sale when a line
has been discontinued from its rental inventory or
the pieces are too tired to pass muster with rental
customers. In either case, you'll save 30–70%. The
rental business has gone upscale, so the better
the quality and condition of the item, the higher
the price. Sofas, lamps, mattresses, pictures, and
just about anything Cort rents might be found, but
no appliances other than TVs, VCRs, and microwaves. When used rental inventory is scarce, Cort
makes special purchases of discontinued and
excess inventory from furniture manufacturers and
buys wholesale trade showroom samples to keep
the clearance centers well stocked (prices nicely
discounted). Most furnishings come from midprice
manufacturers. You'll also find office furnishings.
Delivery is extra.

THE FUTON SHOP FACTORY OUTLET
*2150 Cesar Chavez Street (formerly Army
Street, between Hwy. 101 and Third Street),
San Francisco. (415) 920-6801.
www.thefutonshop.com. M–Sat 10–5, Sun 11–5.
MC, VISA, AE, DIS. Parking: street.*
Futons have gone mainstream. The frame styling
is more sophisticated, and fabrics used for covers
reflect au courant design trends and may also
be the same as fabrics on popular upholstered

furniture lines. The Futon Shop has grown with consumers' acceptance of futons, with twenty-two specialty stores and this one clearance center. At any one time you'll find two to three dozen discontinued futon frames, slightly damaged floor samples (usually finish flaws or scratches), and out-of-box frames. Savings are 20–50% off original retail. The best deal here is on the closeouts on futon covers, usually marked down to 40–50% off original retails. Futon mattresses, usually floor samples, are sometimes reduced about 30%. Tables and other accent pieces and closeouts from the Futon Shop stores fill the spaces around the warehouse floor and add to your bargain options. Delivery is available for an extra charge.

LIMN EXTRA

290 Townsend Street, San Francisco.
(415) 543-5466. M–F 9:30–5:30, Sat–Sun 11–5:30.
MC, VISA, AE. Parking: lot.
Limn is a specialty-furniture retailer whose fur-nishings reflect best-quality European manufac-turers, including more than 500 Italian and other European firms often found in *Metropolitan Home*. Its style is classic contemporary, design oriented, and appeals particularly to architects and a younger, affluent clientele. The Townsend Street retail showroom is filled with distinctive and unusual furnishings. Many of the contemporary pieces provide the eclectic note needed to spark a ho-hum room. All this superior design comes at a big price, which is why it's worth checking Limn Extra—a separate 5,000-square-foot area that takes all the main showroom's discontinued samples, color changes, and slightly damaged merchandise. Selected furnishings are carried here to offer options for price-conscious customers who may not be able to afford the regular showroom inven-tory. Limn Extra offers savings on upholstered furniture from the main showroom, plus lighting products and accent pieces (distinctive chairs, tables, tabletop accessories). Savings range from 15 to 50%. Delivery service available.

MACY'S FURNITURE CLEARANCE CENTER

1208 Whipple Road (1.2 miles east of Hwy. 880),
Union City. (510) 441-8833. W–Sun 11–6.
MC, VISA, AE, Macy's charge. Parking: lot

The Bay Area's biggest furniture clearance center is enormous, with a truly impressive selection of merchandise lined up row after row in a spartan warehouse. The clearance center is kept filled with "leftovers" from Macy's Northern California furniture and rug departments. The leftovers represent many aspects of furniture retailing—canceled orders, floor samples, customer returns, damaged or slightly soiled pieces, surplus inventory, discontinued merchandise, and furniture pieces or groups with missing components. That's great for consumers who can expect 50% markdowns on the furniture as soon as it hits the floor. Just about everything that goes through the Macy's furniture pipeline might show up in the clearance center—modestly priced promotional furniture lines to distinctive pieces from its high-end designer lines. Depending on your furniture-buying savvy, you may or may not recognize the lines and labels that include Wexford, Lee Industries, Miles Talbot, Agnes Bourne, Henredon, Riverside, Stanley,

Bernhardt, Ralph Lauren, National Mt. Airy, and others. It's not always possible to identity the manufacturer, but as long as the piece suits your needs and the price is right, who cares?

Make what you will of these choices: dining tables without chairs; dining chairs without tables; table bases without glass tops; glass tops and glass shelving without bases; ottomans without chairs; loveseats without sofas; sectional pieces; china cabinet tops without bases (many people use these as bookcases); and orphan mirrors. All this translates into some of the best buys at the clearance center—up to 70% off original retails—and a wonderful opportunity for clever and resourceful shoppers who can adapt the "limitations" into something that works at home. To round out the picture: count on row upon row of sofas and occasional chairs in a vast array of styles; plus recliners and a you'll-find-something selection of leather sofas and chairs. There's also formal and informal dining furniture, entertainment centers, bedroom furniture, beds, mattresses and boxsprings, and assorted odds and ends. If home is where the office is, you'll find complete desk and computer stations—and challenges for utilizing many orphan modular components.

Maybe the best reason to shop the clearance center is to survey the vast selection of area rugs reduced 30–70% off original retails. More than 400 room-size rugs are hanging for easy browsing before you start flipping rugs from stacks on the floor. Rugs cover the gamut, from machine-made and budget-priced to classy handmade rugs with bargain prices topping out around $2,000. Shop smart with swatches for matching and measurements of spaces, and be prepared to make buying decisions on the spot. The bargains won't wait for wishy-washy shoppers. Delivery is very reasonable. In 1999, it was a $65 charge for delivery to your address (no matter how many pieces were in the delivery order). Delivery routes throughout the Bay Area are computer managed for efficiency and cost savings, but delivery is usually completed within a week or two at most.

Office Furniture

BERKELEY OUTLET
711 Heinz Avenue, Berkeley. (510) 549-2896. T–Sat Noon–6. Cash/Check. Parking: street, limited on-site.

This outfit gives new meaning to being "tucked away." It's piled and jammed with office furnishings that range from old and ugly to nearly new and up-to-date. Bay Area corporations rid themselves of used office furniture by selling to companies like this one. Because it buys in huge lots and provides no services, prices are very low for better-quality pieces like heavy-duty file cabinets from insurance companies (they take a lot of use). You'll spot brands like Steelcase, General Fireproofing, Knoll, Allsteel, Art Metal, Herman Miller, Hayworth, and Hamilton. Most of the items are geared for offices or businesses where real work is done, rather than providing front-office glamour or image. Customers are referred for delivery services.

BIG MOUTH

1129 Airport Boulevard, South San Francisco. (650) 588-2444. www.bmof.com. M–F 8:30–5:30, Sat 11–3. MC, VISA. Parking: lot.

With a name like Big Mouth you might expect lots of fast talk and hustle; instead you'll find seasoned experts who buy used office furniture at a bottom price and pass on the savings to you. If you need top-notch, fire-safe, lockable files with full suspension, there's always a good selection on hand. You might be surprised that used file cabinets are sometimes as expensive as new, until you realize that there's a wide range in quality and durability. It's easy to find a new four-drawer cabinet for around $100, but chances are it does not compare to a used commercial-quality one. Check in for desks, chairs, tables, and lots of odds and ends. Good deals are frequently offered on slightly damaged new desks. If you must have new furnishings, a visit can be arranged to a wholesale distributor to make your selection; Big Mouth will place the order and give you a very substantial discount. Extra discounts for large lot orders.

THE DESK DEPOT

89 Pioneer Way, Mountain View. (415) 969-3100. M–F 9–6, Sat 10–5. MC, VISA, AE, DIS. Parking: lot.

This place specializes in used office furniture. You can also buy computer furniture, partitions, chairs, coat trees, wholeboards, school desks, and wastebaskets. Some new pieces are stocked at 20–40% off list price.

INTERIOR MOTIONS

1460 Park Avenue, Emeryville. (510) 653-6100 ext. 103. E-mail: intmot@ccnet.com. M–Sat 8–4:30. MC, VISA. Parking: street.

If you're operating in the home office mode, at some point it just makes sense to get your space configured for maximum efficiency. In an ideal world, that means esthetically pleasing, high-quality, durable furnishings usually costing far more than most want or can afford to pay. With some compromising, it's possible to meet most of those goals by shopping at places like Interior Motions, where there's always a stash of quality used office furniture. Interior Motions configures and installs modular panel systems for its corporate customers. As a byproduct of this primary business, a large quantity of used corporate office furniture is acquired. The furniture is generally of a higher commercial quality, which is most desirable when it comes to specific items like filing cabinets. Many of the pieces (three- or four-drawer lateral files) are not readily found in the typical discount office furniture selection at warehouse clubs or mass merchandisers.

Buying used has its drawbacks. Some filing cabinets are in industrial colors—black or institutional gray. There may be small dents, finish imperfections, etc. Yet, all is not lost. Interior Motions acquires many pieces in like-new condition that result in still-a-bargain-but-higher selling prices. Stick with the cosmetically impaired and the staff freely offers helpful suggestions on applying your own remedies to improve the appearance. Interior Motions has a good selection of desks—from oversize wood executive suite beauties, to smaller metal institutional versions and everything in between. Commercial quality most often translates into roller-bearing drawers and dovetailed drawer construction on the wood pieces.

Occasionally, you'll find older desks and desk chairs with real character and personality—as if they've come right off the set of *Masterpiece Theater*. Those interested in setting up a modular arrangement to use as a combination desk and computer station can consider the selection of used modular components generally resulting in a high-tech look. The assortment of tables and conference tables can serve multiple uses inside or outside an office environment. Look for stools or steno, stacking, reception area, and ergonomic office/desk chairs that run the gamut from peon to presidential in quality, style, comfort, and features. Because the company also buys inventory from offices going out of business (liquidations) there's often a smattering of other office accessories that might prove useful to home office situations. Prices in the warehouse vary according to condition, quality, and manufacturer. Used furnishings are a fraction of new prices. Two-drawer through five-drawer vertical files range in price from $39 to $110; lateral files start at $85. Desks range from $50 to $500. Delivery can be provided at a reasonable price, starting at $30. Interior Motions also sells new office furniture (suitable for Fortune

500 corporations to one-man operations). Prices are competitively priced with most other Bay Area suppliers, and in many cases much less.

JUST CHAIRS CLEARANCE OUTLET

525 Fourth Street (near Bryant), San Francisco. (415) 543-5575. www.justchairsauction.com. M–Th 9–5:30, F 9–5, Sat 10–4. MC, VISA. Parking: street.

If you spend long days at the computer and your back is sending pain messages, it may be time for a new chair. Chairs are a specialty here—chairs to address the ergonomic needs of the users and chairs designed to eliminate work-related back, neck, and wrist disorders. Major corporations have utilized this store's expertise in selecting proper seating for their workforces. Increasingly, Just Chairs is serving the home-office market. Anyone working from the home has the same requirement for appropriate seating as corporate employees (maybe more so, because there's no one to pay compensation for time off or downtime due to back, neck, or wrist disorders). If you've underestimated the difference a chair can make in comfort and efficiency, you'll quickly see the light after sitting in a variety of ergonomically designed chairs. As with all specialized products, the more features and technology involved, the more expensive the item. Custom-configured chairs (for height, weight, use, etc.) from the retail showroom can cost from $500 to $1,500. In a separate room behind its second-floor showroom, Just Chairs' clearance outlet offers consumers the chance to buy better-quality office and work chairs at discounted prices. Expect 30 to 40 different chair styles priced from $98 to $395 (retail values from $130 to $550). Some of these chairs are not seen in the retail marketplace, because they are primarily sold through contract design companies. In addition to clearance inventory from its showrooms, some chairs represent special purchases from manufacturers that regularly do business with Just Chairs. The fabrics may have been discontinued; an order may have been canceled, leaving the manufacturer in a bind; or the manufacturer may simply wish to clear out excess inventory. The selection usually includes basic computer chairs, multi-use computer chairs, executive multi-use chairs, comfortable conference chairs, stacking chairs, reception or guest chairs, and occasionally some stools. Features may include tilt and swivel, pneumatic seat-height adjustment, and adjustable armrests. If you take your chair away in a box, you'll save on the modest assembly charge. Those from out of the area can buy online by checking the company's Web site, updated daily, that lists clearance chairs and prices.

RUCKER FULLER OFFICES TODAY

750 Brannan Street, San Francisco.
(415) 431-9919. www.ruckerfuller.com.
M–F 8–5. MC, VISA. Parking: lot.
If you're starting business in a day or two, don't worry; whiz by, do your shopping, and arrange for immediate delivery. There's also a large selection of used stock. The savings on the samples and closeouts range from 40% off retail to below cost. The used furniture is priced according to condition and original price; save 40–60% off original cost. There's an expanded selection of home-office furniture, computer furniture, and lots of desks, credenzas, files, tables, and chairs for any use. Need to rent? You can—everything from panel systems to complete wood offices. Delivery will cost. You'll rejoice when you find the parking lot behind the store.

SAM CLAR OFFICE FURNITURE

1221 Diamond Way, Concord. (800) 726-2527.
www.samclar.com. M–F 9–6, Sat 10–4.
MC, VISA. Parking: lot.
(Other stores: 6801 Dublin Boulevard, Dublin;
341 13th Street [bet. Webster and Harrison],
Oakland; 2502 Channing Avenue, San Jose.)
Some of the office furnishings in Sam Clar's used department may be a little dated, but they're functional and cheap. Others are nearly new, with today's business looks, but of course they're more expensive. Everything is priced and, for the most part, firm (but negotiable). Many customers head right for the new factory closeouts (desks, files, and more) unloaded by major manufacturers and priced for beginning entrepreneurs. You can often save by combining new merchandise from the main floor with used furniture pieces. Nice selection of ensembles that work well in a home-office environment, especially when sharing space with guest or other family-use rooms.

Also See

Under Office Supplies:
ARVEY PAPER CO.; OFFICE DEPOT;
OFFICEMAX; STAPLES

Under Furniture and Home Accessories—
Catalog Discounters, Clearance Centers:
ALL LISTINGS

Under General Merchandise—
Membership Warehouse Clubs:
COSTCO

Used/Consignment Furniture

Used furniture stores have been around forever, but there's a new way to buy used furniture— from consignment stores that specialize in selling furniture and home accessories. These stores have struck a responsive chord with shoppers. They are a boon for consumers who lack the time and inclination to canvass garage sales and thrift stores, attend auctions, or search through classified ads—for many, the potential for greater savings does not make up for the time involved. On the other side, those redecorating or downsizing their households with furnishings too good to give away may want to consider consignment shops as a viable alternative to garage sales or classified ads.

Generally, consignment furniture stores are very discriminating. They're willing to take furniture in good condition that still has consumer appeal. Antiques, heirlooms, old pieces with personality, and fine-quality furniture from recognized manufacturers top their most-wanted lists. Some stores do accept pieces that may be somewhat dated, reflecting furnishing trends throughout the last 30 years, because those pieces are often good candidates for painted or faux finishes. A run-of-the-mill dining room set of fairly recent vintage (1970s pecan finish or 1980s bleached oak) can be transformed with a little paint, ingenuity, and new seat covers.

Store owners will want to discuss your piece in detail before accepting it on consignment. A picture of the item is very helpful. Most shops will also accept fine collectibles, art, chandeliers, and home-accessory items (lamps, area rugs, etc.). Upholstered pieces must be really special and in top condition to attract the interest of consignment store owners. Any documentation that can be provided on the history of a piece is a benefit. Some of the smaller shops maintain a photo gallery or album to show pieces that are available for sale but not on their showroom floor. (This often applies to large pieces that are awkward to move from the seller's home.) In that case, the shop acts much like a broker, bringing buyer and seller together.

The furniture owner (consignor) and consignment shop typically split the selling price. The division depends on each store's policy, which is spelled out in advance. Some may give a greater share to the consignor, but levy a floor charge for showing the piece in their store. Generally, store owners work closely with clients to set prices. Setting a realistic price is the best means to arriving at a timely sale. It's important to understand the store's policy regarding price reductions or whether it will accept or present offers for less than the original asking price. Consignment periods may range

from 30 to 90 days before the furniture must be removed from the floor. Owners unwilling to reclaim the furniture are usually offered several options—drastically reducing prices, donating the pieces to charity, or in some cases, allowing the store to auction the merchandise. There are treasures to be found in all these stores.

Because consignment stores share so many similarities, I'm providing a just a brief profile of the stores listed below to avoid being redundant. Keep locations of these stores in mind and allow a few minutes for a quick stop whenever you're driving through the area.

CONSIGNED FURNISHINGS CO.
150 Longbrook Way, Suite D, Pleasant Hill. (925) 798-8556. M–Th 10–6, F–Sat 10–8:30, Sun Noon–5. MC, VISA. Parking: lot.
Tasteful interior that's neat and clean. Appears to show more old pieces and antiques, along with mainstream furnishings. While the older pieces have the most personality, there's also a selection of recently owned upscale furniture. Also, a consignment fine-jewelry department.

CONSIGNMENT PLUS
HOME FURNISHINGS, INC.

1299 Parkside, Walnut Creek. (925) 927-6600.
M–Sat 10–6, Th until 8, Sun Noon–5. MC, VISA.
Parking: lot.
(Other store: 4250 Rosewood Drive,
Rose Pavilion Shopping Center, Pleasanton.)
These stores stand out in the crowd, with 29,000 square feet of showroom space that has all the amenities of upscale furniture stores. The large space, lighting, and carpeted floors are very effective in displaying the furnishings and accessories that consumers all over Contra Costa County have placed on consignment here. The overall selection is quite diverse, with furniture from every design period—traditional, Arts and Crafts, Oriental, contemporary. Consignment Plus can also assist buyers with their in-house furniture replacement service known as "FurnishZing." The Walnut Creek store features a large selection of fine jewelry on consignment.

Consignors receive 60% of the final selling price. Merchandise that has not sold in 30 days will be marked down 20%, and after 60 days another 20%. Furniture pick-up and delivery is available for reasonable charges. Items can be brought directly to the showroom. The Walnut Creek location is two blocks north of Ygnacio, one block east of North Main.

CORNUCOPIA

1444 South Main Street, Walnut Creek.
(925) 256-4486. M–Sat 10–5. MC, VISA.
Parking: street.
You'll be helping out the Wellness Community (a support network for people fighting cancer) with your purchases, consigned furniture, or donations. Furniture shows to advantage in this charming cottage with real-life room settings. Consignors claim 60% of the selling price and the remaining 40% supports the charity. Progressive markdown policy.

COTTRELL'S

150 Valencia Street, San Francisco.
(415) 431-1000. M–F 9–5:30, Sat 9–4:30.
MC, VISA. Parking: street.
The interior is gloomy and the dust level is high, but there's a vast inventory, ranging from new to almost ancient furniture—some good, some downright ugly, and most well priced. With a little inventiveness, those willing to take paintbrush to wood may end up with a real conversation piece. Delivery in the city is free on purchases of more than $100.

FURNISH AGAIN

6891 Village Parkway, Dublin. (925) 828-7334.
M–Sat 10–5, Th until 7, Sun Noon–4. MC, VISA.
Parking: lot.
A separate but integral part of the Kids Again family (listed under Baby and Juvenile Furniture/ Equipment, page 267). Furniture for grown-ups (living room, dining room, bedroom, accessories, etc.) on consignment.

HOME CONSIGNMENT CENTER

1901-F Camino Ramon (near Costco), Danville.
(925) 866-6164. M–Sat 10–6, Sun Noon–5.
MC, VISA, ATM. Parking: lot.
(Other stores: 400 Main Street, Los Altos;
1888 South Norfolk Street, San Mateo;
600 El Paseo De Saratoga, Saratoga.)
Home Consignment has the size and space to handle lots of furniture. Trucks deliver new "old" furniture twice a day. There's usually some new furniture from model homes, and occasionally new furnishings from trade showrooms. All items are priced as if they were used, even though many items are new. You can expect prices anywhere from 35 to 75% off original retails. The consignor receives 60% of the selling price. Not sure? Each store offers a 24-hour hold, plus a 24-hour home approval. Shopping on weekends is a bit more hectic, but workers are available to handle loading and unloading. Consignments are accepted every day. A fine-jewelry department is staffed with an experienced jeweler, and cases are full of beautiful jewelry. Delivery is extra; also charges for consignment pickups.

JUDITH FROST AND COMPANY

67 Encina Avenue, Palo Alto. (650) 324-8791.
T, W, Sat 10–4, and by appointment. Cash/Check.
Parking: street.

This is a somewhat elitist collection, with prices that range from five dollars (on accessories) to thousands, showcased with real panache. Count on a nice selection of old pieces, antiques, occasional chairs, new and used sofas, and Oriental accessories. Upon completion of a sale, the consignor receives 60% of the price.

NATIONAL FURNITURE LIQUIDATORS

845 Embarcadero, Oakland. (510) 251-2222.
M–Sat 10–5, Sun 11–4. VISA, MC, AE, DIS.
Parking: lot.
(Other stores: 1110 Van Ness Avenue [at Geary],
2301 Mission Street [at 19th], San Francisco.)

Major hotels renovate their guest rooms every few years, not because the furniture is worn out, but to give their guests fresh, up-to-date surroundings and to keep up with the competition. The furniture that is being replaced by San Francisco tourist hotels, boutique hotels, and hotels noted as luxury out-of-town escapes—names well known to Bay Area residents—is resold by National Furniture Liquidators. The furniture from the better hotels is generally high quality, has been well maintained, and usually has been put only to light use, because tourists and business travelers tend to be out and about, not sitting around in their rooms.

Scout here for furnishings for vacation homes or primary residences—extra chairs, tables, lamps, sofas, sofa beds, bedroom furniture, armoires, and desks. The selection of furnishings is ever-changing. Pricing is determined by condition and is also affected by supply and demand. Prices do change on individual pieces and are frequently reduced when the company is overstocked. Lamps are often priced at $5 to $25, occasional chairs at $25 to $65, bedroom furniture from $25 to $125. Check the walls for framed pictures, mirrors, and artwork.

National has a split personality of sorts. In addition to its hotel furniture, it also sells samples from wholesale/trade showrooms at the San Francisco Merchandise Mart and new budget-quality furniture to those who may have little money to spend but still prefer to buy new furniture. Shoppers should also expect to find some pieces that are a little tired (priced accordingly), but there's more than enough tempting and attractive furniture and accessories to justify a visit.

POPIK FURNITURE CO.
935 Main Street, Redwood City. (650) 368-2877. M–F 9–5:30, Sat 9–5. MC, VISA, AE, DIS. Parking: street.
The children and grandchildren of Popik's original customers have sustained this business for sixty years. The original family is still at the helm, supplying Peninsula shoppers with new and used furniture. Furniture is bought outright, and then most pieces are spruced up in the refinishing shop in the back of the store. At first glance it may not be obvious that much of the furniture is used. It's unlikely you'll find antiques, but many pieces are definitely vintage. If you're set on finding a piece to slipcover, stencil, or personalize with a faux finish, this is a good place to start. After fifty-four years, the interior of the store is a little tired, and furniture is crammed throughout. New furnishings and bedding are geared for the budget crowd rather than an upscale market, but the

prices are all nicely discounted. Free delivery. If you have furniture to sell, call to schedule a home evaluation (no tired sofas wanted).

Also See

Under Furniture and Home Accessories—Clearance Centers:
ALL LISTINGS

Giftware and Home Decor

ANNIEGLASS SECONDS OUTLETS

109 Cooper Street, Santa Cruz. (831) 427-4260.
M–Sat 10–6, Sun 11–5. MC, VISA. Parking: street.
(Other outlet: 310 Harvest Drive [corner Riverside],
Watsonville, 831/761-2041 ext. 21.)

The Annieglass Roman Antique collections of slumped glass dinnerware and serving pieces with 24K gold or platinum bands have become industry icons. The company's fame and fortunes have grown with each introduction of a new and innovative contemporary design. Though contemporary in style, the sculptural, textured glassware is designed to blend with traditional china. Much of the collection is modeled after shapes found in nature—fish, flowers, shells, leaves, rocks, rippling waves. Some pieces are elegantly frosted while others are bright and whimsical in spirit. Annieglass makes wonderful gifts! Shop either of the company's seconds outlets and you'll save 40–60% off retail. Seconds are gift-worthy, no chips or cracks, but may have nonconforming shapes or surface imperfections. The selection in the outlets is sometimes inconsistent, with varying quantities of styles and collections, and your favorites may be missing altogether. It's not hard to refocus and find something that's too good to pass up. Regulars return time and again to complete sets of dinnerware. There's also the option of buying first-quality pieces at full retail prices. The Watsonville outlet usually has greater quantities of whatever pieces are available as seconds; however a visit to the Santa Cruz outlet fits nicely into family excursions to Santa Cruz.

CLAY ART CERAMICS OUTLET

239 Utah Avenue, South San Francisco.
(650) 244-4970. Th 1–4. Cash/Check.
Parking: street.

Clay Art/About Face makes ceramic masks, banks, and housewares (teapots, cookie jars, salt-and-pepper sets, mugs, tissue dispensers, candle-sticks, and chip 'n' dips), sold through gift shops around the country. The decorative ceramic masks are made in about seventy images, including the company's original limited editions. They can get very expensive with the addition of feathers, jewels, or other design elements. The tabletop and home accessories collections combine functional creativity with sophisticated whimsy. Lots of animal motifs. Everything in the seconds room is discounted about 50% off wholesale, and the flaws are no big deal (usually painting defects).

COHN-STONE STUDIOS

5755 Landregan Street, Emeryville.
(510) 654-9690. M–F 10–5:30 (closed 1–2:30).
MC, VISA. Parking: street.
The artists at Cohn-Stone studios have earned a reputation for quality and design. Their contemporary handblown glassware, distinctive bowls, vases, paperweights, and plates have been exhibited in some of the nation's top galleries and fine arts specialty stores. Save 50–75% on seconds that may have a bubble or a scratch; they may be too big or too small, experimental, or discontinued. There's a

good range of gift-priced beauties from $12 to $200, although some very special pieces may be priced from $300 to $750. Anything made by Cohn-Stone is destined to be a tasteful, timeless gift or a wonderful accent for your home. All sales final.

COLLECTIBLES OUTLET, INC.

1899 W. San Carlos Street, San Jose.
(408) 288-6027. M–F 10–6, Th until 9, Sat 10–5,
Sun Noon–5. MC, VISA. Parking: back lot/street.
For classy collectibles, you can't do better than the Collectibles Outlet. Here are just a few of the names: Hummel, Lladro, David Winter and Lilliput cottages, Precious Moments, Royal Doulton, Nao, Swarovski, Armani, Crystal World, Disney, Fenton Glass, Harmony Kingdom, Nadal, Boyd Bears, and many other brands of status bears and dolls (Madam Alexander, too)—and more! Naturally, your first question should be, "Are these authentic?" The answer: Yes! The proof: the registered trademark on each piece. Even though most of the inventory is discounted starting at 20% off retail, prices may be as much as 40–70% off original retail on special purchases and closeouts. The Collectibles Outlet is simply marvelous!

COUROC FACTORY STORE

501 Ortiz Avenue, Sand City. (831) 899-5479.
M–F 10–5, Sat 10–3. MC, VISA, AE. Parking: street.
When in Carmel or Monterey, make a beeline
for the Couroc Factory Store, about five minutes
away. This classy giftware (mainly bowls, trays,
and serving pieces) is unique for finished designs
hand-inlaid into a secret-formula phenolic resin
compound, then buffed to the singular luster of
satin blackness characteristic of Couroc products.
The line is popular with tourists who seek tasteful
mementos of California visits; natives may find
all the designs appealing. Prices on seconds are
35–50% off retail. Expect to spend $27.50 to $75
for trays, depending on size. Group tours of the
factory can be arranged in advance.

CRATE & BARREL OUTLET

1785 Fourth Street, Berkeley. (510) 528-5500.
M–Sat 10–6, Sun 11–6. MC, VISA, AE, DIS.
Parking: lot.
Picture what you find in Crate & Barrel's lifestyle
stores: bright, contemporary, functional home
accessories. Out-of-season, discontinued, and
occasionally damaged goods are sent to the
outlet from the full-service retail stores. Discounts
are 20–70% off original retail, although many
discounts are in the more modest 25–30% range.
Check every nook and cranny of this colorful and
creatively merchandised outlet. Crate & Barrel's
popular basic stemware and barware are carried
at retail store prices. Returns and exchanges.

DESIGN STUDIO AND GALLERY

6604 San Pablo Avenue, Oakland. (510) 594-9034.
M & W 10–5, or by appointment. MC, VISA.
Parking: street.
Darin Tennesen creates steel sculptures that have
been sold through the Guggenheim Museum
gift shop, at trendsetters like Barney's NY, and in
many fine contemporary art galleries and stores.
She works with an arc welder and uses various wire
brushes and grinders to create beautiful etched
steel vases and slender sculptures. The vases are
flat, but look three dimensional and can stand
alone or hold flowers from a glass vase attached
directly behind the piece. The vases in 5- to 45-inch
versions run $45 to $215 in galleries. At the studio
outlet, the vases and many other designs sell for
about 40% off as seconds, prototype samples, or

just-for-fun pieces. Depending on the quality of the seconds, prices may go even lower, but nothing looks bad. If you have all the vases you'll ever need, then consider picture frames, clocks, bookends, figurative sculptures, lamps, and abstract wall art—all elements of her line that may show up in the seconds or closeout selection. Look for the sign "Steelworks" and you've found a path to some wonderful, at times whimsical gifts or artware for the home.

DOLCE MIA HANDMADE FRAMES & COLLECTIBLES

1805-B Clement Avenue, Alameda.
(510) 814-0440. M–F 8:30–5. MC, VISA.
Parking: lot.

It's unlikely you'd just happen on Dolce Mia's outlet on the second floor of this large building; it's a bit removed from the rest of Alameda's shopping action. However, its shelves are jammed with photo frames, serving trays, accessory boxes, coasters, and framed mirrors. The company's products are made using a decoupage process finished with an extremely thick, smooth epoxy resin. The resin imparts a certain luxury to the

design beneath, resulting in a fresh, contemporary product from this traditional process. It may be difficult making a choice from the more than 60 styles of frames. The designs address many themes—sports, vacation, travel, geography, romance, florals, foliage, kids, even traditional Victorian relief solid color designs. It's a cinch finding a frame for a particular personality, interest, or occasion. In the outlet, samples, returns, seconds, prototype samples, and discontinued designs are priced at a minimum of 50% off retail. 3½-by-5-inch and 4-by-6-inch frames are outlet priced at $15; 5-by-5-inch and 5-by-7-inch frames are $20. Framed mirrors (15-by-17-inch or 17-by-20-inch) are typically priced at $42 or $58 at half off; serving trays are about $42 (retail $80 to $90). In late 1999, botanicals, Western tots, cabin, and pin-up guys and gals were popular design themes. If you're a do-it-yourselfer, the leftover unfinished pine frames with wide, flat, approximately two-inch borders, priced at $6, will bring to mind many possibilities.

EVANS DESIGNS GALLERY

1421 Lincoln Avenue, Calistoga. (707) 942-0453.
M–F 10–5, Sat–Sun 10–6. MC. Parking: street.
Evans Designs produces designer vases and art
pieces in raku, a firing process in which exotic
finishes are achieved by pulling pieces directly
out of a yellow-hot kiln. Evans's gallery is filled
with one-of-a-kind prototypes, seconds, and
overruns at clearance prices. The 40–90% markdowns vary with the status of the pieces. Evans's
art evolves with design trends. Newer pieces and
color palettes are continually being developed.
The latest? The new blown-glass line, Fusion Z,
that's very au courant with its bubbles and lines
that are a natural result of the creative process.

GIFT OUTLET

1455 E. Francisco Boulevard, San Rafael.
(415) 256-1884. M–F 12:30–4:30. MC, VISA.
Parking: street.
Look for the bright banner on the outside of the
new Gift Outlet when tooling down 580 in San
Rafael. Whiz off the freeway for a look-see and
you'll find a colorful selection of storage products,
decorative accessories, and unique lighting
products for home and home office. The outlet is
the repository for all the leftovers—discontinued
product lines and often just discontinued colors of
the ongoing basic collections—all priced at
wholesale or less. The line is designed by a local
company with a reputation for designing and
manufacturing clean, structured, simple, and
functional products from natural-fiber materials.
Many of its products are made from pandan, a
plant in the aloe family. The pandan is processed,
dyed, and then woven—resulting in sturdy finished
products with the appearance of woven seagrass.
In the marketplace they serve as an alternative to
wicker or rattan baskets, especially for those with
a more contemporary or Zen orientation. Whether
you're shopping from a gift angle or just accessorizing or organizing your spaces, you'll find lots
of possibilities. At outlet prices expect picture
frames at $4 to $8; portfolios at $10; tote bags at
$9; and waste baskets at $9. Boxes in many shapes
(cubes, ovals, rectangles, rounds) range from $4
to $18. Boxes can be purchased individually or as
nested sets. Round hat boxes in 12-inch, 14-inch,
and 16-inch sizes are $12 to $18 individually. Stack
three for a statement, use just one for a great gift

and gift box, or store just about anything at all to keep clutter at bay. Colors can add a little zip to your rooms or offices—purple, citron, hunter green, red, blue, bright yellow, slate, and black were in the discontinued category at this writing.

Check the shelves and tables for some of the company's more recent design innovations made from wood or wood and bamboo combinations; also galvanized metal candleholders, lamps, and napkin ring sets. The boxes, home office accessories (pencil holders, desk or letter trays, file holders), and bowls help create work spaces with a clean Zen-type appeal. Occasionally, the accent string lighting sets for enhancing patios, gardens, and parties are available. Design themes run from wacky to sophisticated. Expect some surprises from whatever odds and ends need to be cleared from the warehouse. Just to keep you coming back, some discontinued inventory from other small manufacturers will share shelf space with appropriate bargain prices.

JUDIE BOMBERGER, INC. SECONDS OUTLET

65-J Hamilton Drive, Novato. (415) 883-3072. www.judiebomberger.com. M–F 9–5. MC, VISA, AE. Parking: lot.

Judie Bomberger manufactures a line of whimsical contemporary crafts for the home that sell in galleries and gift stores around the country. Some of her most popular pieces are the rusted metal sculptures mounted on a rod for garden staking. The dancing ladies, cats, and assorted winged critters are classified as seconds when they have a touch too much rust. Most people don't quibble when that translates to prices discounted 50%, ranging from $7 to $90 (most at $12 to $45). The fanciful and carefree indoor metal sculptures (mounted on rods attached to stands) are painted with layers of bright acrylic coatings—each piece has a character all its own. Reproductions of original watercolors are mounted and ready to hang. The seconds may have small dents at the edge or an almost imperceptible surface scratch. These are priced as seconds, at $17 to $35. Look for little treasures like magnets for $1 or hand-painted pins for $7.

KAY YOUNG GLASSWARE OUTLET

2025 Clement Street, Alameda. (510) 523-1082.
First Saturday every month 10–4.
MC, VISA, AE, DIS. Parking: street.

If you don't watch the calendar, you may miss the
monthly opening of the Kay Young's Glassware
Outlet and that would be a shame if you're an
aficionado of contemporary glassware. The Kay
Young signature collection (painted with metallic
and glass enamel paints) is noted for its use of
strong and cheerful colors with bold patterns
evocative of modern art: dots with spirals, squig-
gles, and swirls. The plates, bowls, platters,
goblets, and cups convey "unique" whether they
are sitting on a display shelf or serving a special
dinner. All colors work in rhythm with each other
and coordinate in beautiful place settings.
Though the company is young, Kay Young wares
sell in over 400 retail stores throughout the U.S.
and Canada including the American Craft Museum
in New York. On the first Saturday of each month,
the seconds and discontinued designs are priced
at 20–50% off regular prices at the outlet.
Additionally, marked down "as is," clearance, and
closeout items from her elegant Studio Gallery
retail store on Park Street in Alameda are included
in every monthly opening. The seconds have
minor paint or finish imperfections—too minor for
most to detect. Pricing: at retail, mugs and stemware range from $30 to $48 each; dinner plates
are $50; bowls in four sizes (from 4 inches to 11
inches) range from $20 to $76.

LUNDBERG STUDIOS

121 Old Coast Road, Davenport. (831) 423-2532.
Daily 10–5. MC, VISA, AE, DIS. Parking: street.

Lundberg Studios is the recognized leader in
Tiffany art-glass reproductions. Pieces sell in fine
galleries and world-renowned stores. A Lundberg
paperweight retails for $200 to $400, a Tiffany-
style lamp also in the hundreds! At any time in the
studio there are usually seventy-five to a hundred
seconds that are discounted about 50%. Lamps,
paperweights, vases, crystal, and glass perfume
vials may have minor flaws, or they may be
discontinued. In exchange for the seconds' low
prices you may have to forgo Lundberg's prestigious signature. If you are an art-glass collector,
the trip to Davenport will be worthwhile.

MASLACH ART GLASS STUDIO & SECONDS STORE

44 Industrial Way, Greenbrae. (415) 924-2310. W, Th, F Noon–5. MC, VISA. Parking: street.
The elegant displays in this outlet showcase the many original pieces produced by Maslach. The goblets are very popular, when they're being produced. What's not readily apparent is that most of these beauties are seconds reduced about 25–50%. Maslach's distinctive marbles, a great favorite with collectors, are priced from $10 to $90 at retail, and happily, much less as seconds. You may find paperweights, bowls, sculptures, and new designs. The designers are constantly innovating and creating new treasures. Just about anything will qualify as a beautiful gift. Great wedding presents!

NOUROT GLASS STUDIO

675 E. H Street, Benicia. (707) 745-1463. M–Sat 10–4, Sun Noon–5. MC, VISA. Parking: street.
Works by Nourot are in the collection of the Corning Museum of Glass. If you would like to own a museum-quality piece of art glass that is individually crafted in the ancient tradition, be sure to get on the Nourot mailing list for special promotions, when selection is best and bargains abound. Special sales events are scheduled on the weekend before Mother's Day, the second weekend in August, and the first weekend in December. Retail prices are steep, but the quality is impeccable. Sale prices reduced 50% make them more affordable.

ONE HALF

1837 Polk Street (near Jackson), San Francisco. (415) 775-1416. T–Sat 11–6, Sun 11–5. MC, VISA. Parking: street.
Count on each visit to One Half for an eclectic mix of giftwares, decorative home accessories, and an ever-changing and unpredictable assortment of discontinued, surplus, or, occasionally, slightly imperfect merchandise. The two owners have more than 40 years of combined experience in the giftware industry as importers, product representatives, and retailers. All this adds up to a lot of connections, too—to other importers, manufacturers, and sales reps from dozens of companies who are all too happy to send their excess inventory of whatever classification to One Half. Pricing is

simple: everything is half off retail. The selection typically includes a selection of cookwares, molds, and decorative wall accessories—often discontinued lines from wholesale gift showrooms; dinnerware and serving pieces; small accent rugs (salesman's samples); a wall of cookbooks, coffee table books and similar nonfiction specialties; very high-end journals and photo albums made with acid-free papers; lines of paper goods—boxes, gift bags, journals covered with mulberry paper; greeting and note cards; global imports in all categories; aluminum wares; and a popular line of cosmetic pouches, bags, totes, and carry-ons made from space-age mesh fabrics and usually sold through status stores. Check every nook and cranny, and maybe you'll see stashes of ceramics, gift enclosures, rubber stamps, bath and body products, candles, toys, fun flannel pajamas, and tabletop linens. However, a month from now the whole scene will have changed, so be decisive when you spot a good buy. Shoppers may recognize the names of some of the companies supplying the outlet; however, don't expect to find current merchandise that's being sold in retail stores. The trade-off for half-off savings is merchandise that's

from a previous market season and therefore old to the manufacturer or sales rep. In addition to the actual finished products or merchandise, many small companies would just as soon clear space by selling the leftover components used in making their products. That includes fabrics, trims, ribbons, charms, ornaments, buttons, embellishments, millinery silk flowers and leaves, and other goodies. Crafters can find some very original fixin's for their own projects. All sales final.

R. STRONG GLASS STUDIO & GALLERY
1235 Fourth Street (at Gilman), Berkeley.
(510) 525-3150. T–Sat 11–4:30. MC, VISA.
Parking: street.
Randy Strong designs and creates distinctive handblown goblets, vases, sculpture, marbles, and paperweights, many of which have 22K gold leaf fused to the glass. His unique works are seen at fine exhibitions, galleries, fine stores, and in arts and crafts magazines. Prices at the studio's gallery are 20–75% off regular retail prices. The outlet's prices range from $10 to $58 for goblets and paperweights (seconds); special sculptures and platters can cost more (first-quality pieces are

also available at slightly higher prices). R. Strong's handblown hollow and solid crystal and gold hearts and dichroic hearts make wonderful romantic gifts for many special occasions. The studio also features some special works by other artists including handmade glass beads and jewelry at reduced prices. The main entrance to the studio is on the side of the building.

SAN FRANCISCO MUSIC BOX COMPANY OUTLET

Great Mall of the Bay Area, Milpitas. (408) 956-9427. Daily. MC, VISA, AE, DIS. Parking: lot. (Other store: Vacaville center.)
You'll love the melodic greeting from dozens of music boxes when you enter this outlet, which serves as a combination clearance center and retail store. Not everything is discounted—look for tags or display signs with red dots to zero in on the special discounts. Music boxes come in any number of surprising configurations: figurines, water globes, stuffed animals, masks, trinket boxes, picture frames, watches, ornaments, and more. Don't worry, closeout or discontinued merchandise will be in working condition.

SMYERS GLASS STUDIO

675 E. H Street, Benicia. (707) 745-2614. M–Sat 10–4 (May through December, Sun Noon–5). MC, VISA. Parking: lot.
Smyers Glass is known throughout the country for its fine handblown stemware. A favorite of young brides and those who love to entertain, Smyers glass is sold in fine stores such as Neiman Marcus, Gump's, and Nordstrom. In addition to his handblown stemware, Stephen Smyers creates beautiful paperweights, bowls, vases, and perfume bottles. Seconds in the studio sell for 50% or more off retail. Special sales the first weekends in May and December offer exceptional buying opportunities.

TAKAHASHI HOME DECOR OUTLET

235 15th Street (corner of Kansas), San Francisco. (415) 552-5511. E-mail: takatradco@aol.com. M–Sat 9:30–5. MC, VISA, AE. Parking: street.
For bargains on home accessories, check out the clearance corner at Takahashi, a fifty-year-old San Francisco company that imports high-quality decorative and practical items for the home from Japan. It wholesales its line to prestigious catalog houses—Horchow, Charles Keath, Ballard Designs,

Smithsonian, Winterthur, and many others. Famous gift stores also carry the Takahashi line, and many of the products selling in its outlet remind one of a familiar piece seen before, elsewhere. A space has been set aside inside the beautiful retail/wholesale gallery for the clearance outlet, where first-quality samples and discontinued or surplus inventory are sold at 50% discounts off retail prices. New pieces are added to the outlet selection almost daily. Majolica fruit plates and pictures, English teatime sets, French-style planters, an enormous selection of bathroom sets, and an even larger choice of fine mugs are always in evidence. Depending on when you shop, you may also find small porcelain jewelry boxes, picture frames, magnets, mama-san aprons, place mats, vases, cookie jars, celadon dinnerware, etc. Many items are one-of-a-kind; others are available in unlimited supply. Design collections are versatile, with some reflecting the subtle quality of Japanese design, others replicating traditional European and English designs, plus some hard-to-find masculine styling and even children's storybook-inspired dishes. Good values may be found on the showroom inventory of Japanese painted screens, scrolls, wooden panels, architectural trim, urns, Tansu and other accent pieces, and textiles.

TUESDAY MORNING

239 Third Street, Montecito Plaza, San Rafael.
(415) 453-9816. www.tuesdaymorning.com.
All stores: M–Sat 10–6, Th until 8, Sun Noon–6.
MC, VISA, DIS. Parking: lot.
(Other stores: Danville, Fremont, Pleasanton, Sacramento, San Mateo, Saratoga, Sunnyvale, Walnut Creek.)

Texas-based Tuesday Morning has built its success and reputation on the uniqueness and quality of its inventory. Prices are promised to be 50–80% off original retail on excess inventories from manufacturers around the world. If you currently shop at other discounters, like T.J. Maxx or Marshall's, the prices on some merchandise may be merely competitive, or they may be much better. Everything is relative! The company's opening "events," held four times a year, draw shoppers attracted by the prospect of buying both the expected and unexpected: Oriental rugs; crystal and silver-plated giftware; housewares;

porcelain lamps; bed, bath, and table linens; paper products; Christmas and holiday paraphernalia; baskets; children's toys and apparel; men's furnishings; even some furniture. You'll see some very famous names attached to the inventory. Everything is first quality. Wow! Cash refunds and returns allowed. Selections vary from store to store. Special shopping opportunities are offered to selected mailing-list customers (big spenders). Opening events scheduled generally for mid-February or March, May or June, mid-August or September, and mid-October to December.

WE'RE ENTERTAINMENT

Prime Outlets at Gilroy, Gilroy. (408) 848-4311.
Daily. MC, VISA, AE. Parking: lot.
(Other store: Great Mall, Milpitas.)
The company licensed to sell this whimsical giftware sends its closeouts and discontinued inventory to this store. Calvin and Hobbes, Curious George, Star Trek, Star Wars, Winnie the Pooh, the Pillsbury Dough Boy, Harley-Davidson, Elvis, Coca-Cola, and Mickey Mouse and other Disney friends are just a partial list of famous icons found on the novelties, music boxes, ties, magnets, key chains, T-shirts, caps, boxers, etc. There are no discounts on the current, first-quality merchandise, but look for the closeouts marked down 30–40% making it tempting to stock up on a bag full of little gifts for friends and family members of all ages.

ZELLIQUE ART GLASS

701 E. H Street, Benicia. (707) 745-5710.
M–Sat 10–4. MC, VISA. Parking: street.
Zellique offers handblown art glass designed by Joseph Morel. If you don't mind a slight imperfection that you probably can't even see, then you'll save about 50% off retail. The collection includes paperweights, perfume bottles, bookends, vases, individual sculptures, bowls, and lamps. For the best selection, schedule a visit when Zellique, Smyers, and Nourot join forces for special open-house events on the weekend before Mother's Day and the first weekend in December. Get on their mailing list for these special events.

Also See

Under Family Apparel, Men's & Women's
General Clothing:
THE BIG FOUR

Under Jewelry and Watches:
CRESALIA JEWELERS

Under Dinnerware and Kitchenware:
ALL LISTINGS

Under Furniture and Home Accessories—
General Furnishings:
IGUANA AMERAMEX

Under Furniture and Home Accessories—
Used/Consignment:
ALL LISTINGS

Under Linens:
**BED, BATH & BEYOND;
LINENS 'N' THINGS**

Under General Merchandise:
ALL SECTIONS

Under Special Sales and Events:
ALL LISTINGS

Home Improvement

When it comes to home-improvement projects, it's hard not to mention HomeBase and Home Depot. These two warehouse stores dominate the market with vast selection and deep discount pricing. Similar in operation, they offer an in-depth selection of everything you need to build and fixture a home from the blueprint stage to the final step of landscaping and fencing. Most consumers are satisfied with the overall quality offered in the selection of products. However, if you're looking for more luxurious and expensive products, you may have to use specialty sources and forgo any hope of a bargain. Considering the sheer number of people who besiege these stores every day, both companies do a fair job with service, but they'd have to triple the staffing to provide the one-on-one attention that most of us would like. To that end, each company offers many special events for do-it-yourselfers. Think of these stores when buying plumbing, fencing, paint, tools, lighting fixtures, lumber, paneling, windows, sprinkler systems, hardware, garden equipment and supplies, window blinds, flooring, kitchen and bath cabinets and fixtures, electrical supplies, patio furniture, barbecues, and more, more, and more.

BLACK & DECKER

Factory Stores of America, Vacaville.
(707) 453-1256. Daily. MC, VISA. Parking: lot.
You'll discover that Black & Decker makes lots of helpful and innovative gadgets and Handy Andy aids, in addition to its well-known line of tools and garden equipment. Everything in the outlet is priced at least 25% off retail. (The company sets prices to undersell its competitors.) You'll see "service products" (reconditioned items that carry a full two-year warranty and often are sold at 50% off retail), blemished cartons, and discontinued models. It may be worth a visit to buy a new cordless drill, palm grip sander, router, Workmate,

variable speed drill, power miter saw, circular saw, Groom 'N' Edge garden trimmer, buffers, hedge trimmer, or One Touch lawn mower. Black & Decker has also introduced many new garden products like sun catchers, manual garden tools, and garden stones.

BUILDING RESOURCES
701 Amador Street, San Francisco. (415) 285-7814. Daily 9–4:30. MC, VISA, AE. Parking: lot.
At first glance this looks like a junkyard, but savvy artists, fixer-uppers, and bargain hunters look closer and see lots of cool stuff for recycling or adaptive reuse: doors, windows, pipe, tubs, sinks, plumbing fixtures, lighting, cabinet hardware, cabinets, remnant pieces of vinyl flooring (or new carpet), lumber, and other materials removed from buildings that have potential for reuse. This is a nonprofit waste diversion program to promote recycling and to reduce landfills. To that end, they try to capture goods before they hit the landfills and in the process save many businesses and folks from dump charges. Donations come from manufacturers and distributors too, so occasionally you'll see new tile, flooring, or other building products

(often seconds or slightly imperfect). You can donate too, but there are some restrictions: no scrap wood, used carpets, appliances, toilets, single-pane aluminum frame windows, water heaters, or just plain junk. Building Resources is not the dump! As the new kid on the block, prices here provide options for many shut out by the highfalutin prices at other recyclers. Folks here are friendly and helpful; they even keep a wishlist for hard-to-find items. Zero in on the old grain elevators, they're right underneath. A tyrannosaurus rex keeps watch from the yard (a donation, of course).

C. H. BULL
233 Utah Avenue, South San Francisco. (650) 871-8440. M–F 8–5. MC, VISA. Parking: lot.
C. H. Bull and its Western Hardware division are major suppliers of tools for line workers, electricians, auto mechanics, carpenters, iron and steel workers, and manufacturing and industrial plants in Northern California. They are a great favorite with woodworkers. These tools are industrial-rated and may cost more than home-rated tools, even at discount. However, prices here are substantially discounted from manufacturers' lists. On products

that serve both the industrial and home markets—Stanley tapes, vise grip sets, block sanders, saws, hammers, and other hand tools—prices are competitive with the warehouse stores. Western has no sales gimmicks or loss leaders, just low dealer prices every day. Located off Airport Boulevard, about one block from Costco.

CALDWELL BUILDING WRECKERS

195 Bayshore Boulevard, San Francisco.
(415) 550-6777. M–F 8:30–4:30, Sat 9–4:30.
MC, VISA. Parking: street.
Caldwell Building Wreckers recycles building materials and offers new distributors' closeouts, plus seconds and liquidated stock. It's a labyrinth stocked with new and used building materials. I was impressed with the variety in the hundreds of new windows and doors (exterior and interior). You'll discover well-known brands in wood frame windows and patio doors, most dual glazed. Also check out the decorative molding. You can go basic and budget-quality, or trade up to something really upscale. Either way, you'll be saving considerably. You can trim your building costs by buying recycled lumber, plywood, beams, mirrors, used bricks, cobblestones, occasionally slabs of granite and marble. The lumber is fully dried, avoiding the twisting that occurs later if it's too green. Also, Caldwell can custom cut special beams or sizes for you. I can't get too excited about used toilets, sinks, or bathtubs (unless they're Victorian style), but they're in stock, too. Delivery can be arranged.

DESIGNER'S BRASS

280 El Camino Real, San Bruno. (415) 588-8480.
M–F 10–5, Sat 9–5. MC, VISA, DIS. Parking: lot.
Check out Designer's Brass if you're replacing nondescript bath, kitchen, or door fixtures. With luck you'll find something you like among the many discontinued bathroom and kitchen faucets, fancy front-door locks, and indoor knobs, all deeply discounted. If you buy regular inventory, discounts vary with the amount of sale ($100 and more) and according to what line you buy and how much you buy of it. This outfit carries status brands that ordinarily cost far more than the budget-to-moderate models at HomeBase, etc. Very nice selection of the latest in kitchen and bathroom fixtures and accessories (pulls and knobs for cabinet doors).

DURANT CERAMICS

253 S. 25th Street, Richmond. (510) 620-0200.
www.durantceramics.com. M–F 9–5, Sat 10–3.
MC, VISA. Parking: lot.

The name Durant Ceramics is new, but anyone who shopped Norstad Ceramics over the years will see that nothing has changed. The original owners have retired and the business is now owned by a long-time employee who continues the tradition. Durant, like Norstad, produces distinctive, beautiful, and functional stoneware planters, tableware, and vases, plus bath, kitchen, vegetable, and bar sinks that are handcrafted from stoneware clay fired to approximately 2,400 degrees. Each piece is hand-thrown and decorated; therefore, each is different. Dinnerware, platters, and baking and serving dishes appeal to those shopping for contemporary aesthetic designs. The sinks and stoneware are typically sold through architects and specialty tile and bath showrooms. Bargain hunters check the Richmond showroom for seconds that may have slight color imperfections or something as minor as a pinhole in the glaze. These are visual flaws that don't impair product integrity. Discounts on seconds are 25–40% off retail. Catch sales in April and early December, when everything is reduced 25% and seconds are reduced an additional 40%.

ITALICS WAREHOUSE SALES

1476 66th Street (west of Hollis, south of Ashby),
Emeryville. (510) 547-1872. Fri 10–4, most Sat
9–2 (by appointment T–Th). Cash/Check.
Parking: street.

Today's homeowners are taking tile from the entryway down the hall and into all rooms of the house. New sizes and grout colors that camouflage soiling add to tile's appeal. Its only drawback? The price—combined with the cost of installation—is out of range for many homeowners.

Italics, with a focus on high-end tile, opens its warehouse every Friday for bargain shoppers. Most of its selection is imported from Italy. The designs are reproductions of natural stone—marble, slate, limestone, granite, patio terra-cotta, etc.—all suggesting the look usually associated with Mediterranean villas, one of the hottest trends in the past few years. Tiles for other applications include wall tiles in glossy or satin finishes, bright or neutral colors, and sizes from 6-by-8 inches to 8-by-13 inches. Japanese porcelains in a rainbow of pastels or solid colors are good choices for countertops. Take a peek at the company's classy retail showroom (a half-block away, on the corner of 66th Street and Hollis) to see how these products will appear in actual installations. Friday warehouse openings allow bargain hunters a chance to eyeball the inventory close-outs, overstocks, and odd lots, which may be reduced 30–50% off the showroom's retail prices. Don't expect fancy displays at the warehouse; most tiles are sitting in boxes, with a few sample tiles for viewing. The fixings—setting thinsets, mastics, and grouts—are available for do-it-yourselfers. Although Italics does not provide installation services, the store may be able to put you in touch with tile contractors.

KEN'S SUPERMARKET OF GLASS AND MIRROR
2905 Senter Road (at Lewis), San Jose. (408) 578-5211. www.strukture.com/ken'sglass. M–Sat 9–5, closed W. MC, VISA. Parking: lot.
Ken offers great prices because he cuts corners: no secretary, virtually no overhead, no delivery, no installation, no cutouts on glass or mirrors (although he will trim edges to size), and a cash-and-carry policy. Ken stocks first-quality glass and mirrors, as well as seconds with a substantial price differential, in all sizes and shapes. He has a good selection of precut sizes of glass and mirrors for shelving, picture frames, rounds for tabletops, and mirrored closet doors. Look for bronze and clear beveled mirrors. Check all his bargains before deciding; you'll find many price options (40–80% discounts), whether you're covering an entire wall with mirror or simply replacing a broken window.

THE KITCHEN TABLE
151 Third Street, San Rafael. (415) 453-2662. M–F 9–4, Sat 9–2. Cash/Check. Parking: street.
This small shop is hardly more than a shed. The floor is covered with sawdust (you may be too by the time you leave), and the smell of glue per-

vades. You'll see work in progress: butcher-block tables and countertops being built. Each butcher-block item is made to the customer's specifications. Drawers, knife racks, wine or glass racks, shelves, microwave platforms, and more can be made to accessorize the tables. Because they're handmade, you won't find the uniform edges and perfectly finished surfaces typical of mass-produced butcher-block products; these are more like antiques. They're finished in your choice of oil or urethane. Custom services are usually costly, but not here. You may save 40–60%, depending on where you do your comparison pricing. A table 48 inches long, 24 inches wide, 4 inches thick, any height, runs $200; one 27 inches long, 18 inches wide, 4 inches thick is $90. Orders can usually be filled in a couple of weeks. Call for a phone quote.

LUMBER LIQUIDATORS
1061 Eastshore Highway, Albany. (510) 524-7800. M–F 8–5, Sat 10–4. MC, VISA, AE, DIS. Parking: lot.
If you're ready to scrap that wall-to-wall carpeting for hardwood flooring there's a way to trim costs. Lumber Liquidators (with several successful outlets in New England) opened its first Bay Area operation in 1999. Its winning formula for low prices follows a familiar path for discounters. Buy right, in quantity, keep overhead costs low, and pass on the savings to consumers. Lumber Liquidators goes directly to the mills and purchases truck-loads of flooring products at a time (from 16,000 to 60,000 square feet). The inventory may be current or categorized as liquidated, discontinued, or surplus. Prices generally range from 99 cents to about $4.75 a square foot (on a prefinished select cherry). The flooring is ready to take right out of the warehouse. Samples from the warehouse are propped against the walls of the small showroom/ office—about 50 different species and styles of flooring from oak to exotic imports, including some laminates and engineered wood floorings. In 1999 white oak, red oak, cherry, maple, and many exotics in unfinished hardwood flooring were priced from 99 cents a square foot; prefinished hardwood flooring in oak, maple, birch, ash, and cherry started at $2.75 per square foot; laminates and engineered floorings (good over slabs) in maple, cherry, oak walnut, heat pine, and beech were priced from $1.99 per square foot.

Of course, you'll have to choose from what's there—the widths, grade/quality, and wood species—but if you stay flexible, you'll save money. Someone on a really tight budget might opt for red or white oak in short-length bundles in a lower grade (more knots, more grain and variation in color) for 99 cents a square foot. Once installed, the effect is rustic. With more money, maybe the quartersawn oak, ash, or maple at $3.30 per square foot, prefinished ash (3¼-inch width) at $3.60 a square foot, or the engineered natural beech (7½-inch width) for $2.75 per square foot will seem just perfect. Some caveats. No installation is provided, but referrals are made to flooring installers. Delivery is extra. New shipments arrive weekly, so don't give up if you strike out on the first visit. Finally, estimate carefully. On some inventory, once it's gone, it's gone forever.

MAJOR LINES

235 Bayshore Boulevard, San Francisco.
(415) 647-9066. M–F 8–5, Sat 9–4. MC, VISA.
Parking: lot.

Look for the "As Is" area in the warehouse for the bargains. If you're clever you can do a lot with the options available at Major Lines, wholesale distributor for Merillat and other lines of kitchen and bathroom cabinets. The Merillat line offers standard features like roll-out trays, a furniture-quality finish, and wipe-clean interiors. There are several styles of doors, finishes, and wood species available. The bargain angle starts when you enter the warehouse, where discontinued (some just with style modifications), slightly damaged, or otherwise marked-down cabinets are shown. At times, you may find enough cabinets in one style to completely outfit a kitchen or bath. More often, you'll find just a cabinet or two for the utility room, small bath, etc. Prices are about half off contractor pricing. All sales final.

MCINTYRE TILE CO. SECONDS

55 W. Grant Street, Healdsburg. (707) 431-7468.
Every other Wed 9–1. MC, VISA. Parking: street.
McIntyre Tile is sold directly through architects
and interior designers. Its handcrafted, high-fired
stoneware and porcelain tile is available in many
beautiful colors, at about $12/square foot. Call
and request a selection of samples in your color
range. If you see one you like, inquire about its
seconds, which are more than half off (about
$3.50/square foot) and may be off-color or slightly
warped, but otherwise structurally sound. Allow
plenty of time to pick and poke through the
seconds. Be sure to call ahead for open days and
hours. Get on its mailing list.

THE MOULDING COMPANY

2310-D Bates Avenue, Concord. (925) 798-7525.
M–F 7–5. MC, VISA. Parking: lot.
(Other store: 3233-A De La Cruz Boulevard,
Santa Clara.)
East Bay consumers should stop by this warehouse
(wear a sweater on cold days) to select moldings
or decorative trims. Most moldings (crown, base,
casings, cove, etc.) are available in finger-jointed
pine (paint grade), stain grade, and primed. A few
moldings are stocked in oak, while other woods
are available by special order (including mantels
and columns). Sorting out the choices is made
easier by reviewing the company's six-page catalog,
which illustrates the type, dimension, and style of
its molding. (This will be mailed on request.) The
company supplies many smaller establishments with
molding for resale, sells to many contractors, and
offers consumers pricing that's substantially lower
than the local home-improvement superstores.
My comparison surveys revealed savings of about
35–40% on average. You can send your contractor
in to make purchases, or, if you're a determined
sort, do it yourself. It's not that hard to do if you
plan each cut carefully and practice first on an extra
length of molding. If you're doing several rooms,
an investment in a chop saw makes the whole
enterprise easier. Delivery is free in Contra Costa
County and to other areas on larger orders.
Location: Bates is off Port Chicago Highway.

POST TOOL & SUPPLY

800 E. Eighth Street, Oakland. (510) 272-0331.
M–Sat 8–5, Sun 10–3. MC, VISA, DIS.
Parking: street.
(Other stores: Modesto, Sacramento, San Carlos,
San Francisco, San Jose, San Rafael, Santa Rosa,
Stockton, Vallejo.)

Post is all set up for serious tool users, offering high-quality brands: Milwaukee, Skil, Hitachi, DeWalt, Ryobi, Porter-Cable, Makita, and others. You'll usually find drill presses, bench grinders, table saws, hand tools, jacks, vises, wrenches, socket sets, electric tools, air tools, electric saws, lathes, and tool boxes. Everything is fully guaranteed and comes in the original factory packaging. Prices are sometimes a tad higher than at Home-Base or Price/Costco, but the trade-off is expanded selection, customer service, and support.

R.V. CLOUD

1217 Dell Avenue (Irrigation) and 3000 S.
Winchester (Plumbing), Campbell. Irrigation,
(408) 374-8370; Plumbing, (408) 378-7943.
M–F 8–5. MC, VISA. Parking: lot.

When landscaping your yard and installing a sprinkler system, stop by R.V. Cloud, a major wholesaler of irrigation supplies for contractors and perfect for do-it-yourselfers. Do everyone a favor and do some homework first; the staff is busy! You can buy pipe, fittings, sprinkler heads, timers, regulators—in short, everything you need. You'll pay about 10% more than contractors, which will save you about 20–30% off the prices at building-supply stores. The plumbing department is through a separate entrance at the other end of the building. You can order plumbing supplies, water heaters, pumps, and bathroom, kitchen, and laundry fixtures (toilets, sinks, tubs, and faucets) from catalogs. Kohler, Price Pfister, Moen, Delta, Grohe, and others are stocked. R.V. is a good source for high-end fixtures. Keep an open mind and you may find really special prices on discontinued fixtures that offer quality you probably can't afford if you buy current stock.

Special plumbing fixtures for the handicapped can be ordered. The quality ranges from standard to superlative. The merchandise comes in sealed boxes, so be sure to research style and color selections before coming in. Local delivery can be arranged for a nominal fee. *Note: R.V. is not open on Saturdays.*

RAFFLES FANS

1244 Fourth Street (corner of Fourth and C), San Rafael. (415) 456-6660. M–Sat 10–5:30. MC, VISA, AE, DIS. Parking: street, lots.
Raffles specializes in ceiling fans and offers everything savvy value-conscious shoppers need: expertise, good service, and competitive prices. Raffles sticks with the proven leaders in the field: Casablanca, Hunter, and Emerson. Prices range from $89 to $1,099. Most sales fall in the $189 to $339 range. It's important to evaluate first what charges are involved in installation, particularly if a new ceiling outlet must be put in. When shopping around, be sure to compare apples to apples: Some stores may quote prices that do not include fan blades, a light fixture, or fitting. Raffles offers good discount prices up front and stands behind

its prices with a guarantee "to meet or beat any advertised or written quote."

STONELIGHT TILE CO. SHOWROOM AND YARD

609 South First Street, San Jose. (408) 292-7424. Hours: Most Sat 10–1, weekdays by appointment. Cash/Check. Parking: lot.
For over 80 years, Stonelight Tile has manufactured hand-glazed ceramic tiles boasting hundreds of custom colors and designs. Its list of clients is impressive—from movie stars to royalty, and famous buildings like Hearst Castle and the Monterey Bay Aquarium. Overruns of custom colors and an assortment of hand-molded, hand-painted tiles are available at 20–50% off the custom order prices which range from $7.50 to $50 a square foot. Run-of-kiln field tiles and some trim pieces are also on hand. A minimum quantity of seconds suitable for mosaic projects are sold by the piece (50 cents to $1 per piece). Quantities vary, but it is possible to do a kitchen, bath, or entryway with overruns (especially if you're open to mixing and matching and being creative about working with what's in inventory).

TOOLS & MORE!

Prime Outlets at Gilroy, Gilroy. (408) 842-1992.
Daily. MC, VISA, AE, DIS. Parking: lot.
Just the ticket, "Tool Time" folks. This is an
outlet for the Tool Warehouse chain, out of Troy,
Michigan, and generally unknown to West Coast
shoppers. While shopping partners are cruising
through the apparel outlets, spend some time
looking at all the gadgets, tools, doodads, and
other clever goodies that make up this store.
Some interesting stuff: 8-foot garden windmills;
hand tools; assorted power tools, including cordless drills (minimum to maximum powers); pocket
torches; magnifiers; clamps; levels; talking alarm
clocks; lighted screwdrivers; videos; polishes;
grout coatings; and altogether lots of things you'd
expect to see in a catalog geared for basic, innovative, and original handyman/woman helpers.
Prices are discounted 30–70% off the Tool Warehouse retail prices.

Getting the Job Done— Helpful Hint

THE TRADES GUILD

Alameda County, Contra Costa County, Marin
County, Peninsula, South Bay, and San Francisco
County. (888) 733-3739.
The Trades Guild is a free consumer referral
service that specializes in the building trades, so
if you're unsure of the type of worker you need,
it can help. Everyone who calls speaks to a real
person (no voice mail) who will talk to you about
your job, then refer you to several members in
your area who do the type of work you need. In
addition to the contractor names and telephone
numbers, the Trades Guild will also relay comments about the contractor from his/her previous
customers. The guild continuously solicits feed-
back about its members through postage-paid
opinion cards that are sent to consumers who use
the service. Contractors referred by the Trades
Guild must meet strict membership criteria before
they can be referred to the public. Contractors
must be licensed by the state and bonded. The

guild verifies all insurance information, checks for complaints on file with various consumer agencies, requires a personal interview at the contractor's place of business, and requires five written references from previous customers. There is no charge to consumers—the service is supported by membership dues. The next time you need a carpenter, tree trimmer, painter, carpet installer, landscaper, plumber, electrician, or someone for earthquake retrofitting, give the guild a call. This service provides a peace-of-mind alternative to plucking names willy-nilly out of the yellow pages.

Also See

Under Carpets, Area Rugs, and Flooring—General:

FLOORCRAFT

Linens

General Linens

BED, BATH & BEYOND

555 Ninth Street, San Francisco. (415) 252-0490.
M–F 9:30–9, Sat 9:30–7, Sun 10:30–7. MC, VISA.
Parking: lot.
(Other stores: Dublin, Oakland, San Mateo,
Santa Clara, Santa Rosa.)
Humongous superstores that have gone far beyond
the original focus on linens. Of course it has bed
linens from brand-name manufacturers, even some
designer lines. Prices are discounted 20–40% on
current, first-quality merchandise every day. You
can give the bathroom the once-over, too. You'll
find a wonderful collection of closet organizers
and gadgets. Don't miss the housewares and
kitchen department. Farberware, Fitz & Floyd,
Mikasa, Rubbermaid, and Copco are a few of the
lines in dinnerware, cookware, and accessories.
Lots of giftwares and decorative home accessories.

All the stores are beautifully merchandised and
well stocked, although sometimes it takes a ladder
to reach the nearly ceiling-high shelves.

DECORATOR'S BEDSPREAD OUTLET

5757 Pacheco Boulevard, Pacheco.
(925) 689-3435. M 10–7:30, T–Sat 10–6,
Sun Noon–5. MC, VISA, DIS. Parking: lot.
(Other store: Fair Oaks.)
Here's a selection of bedspreads, goose-down
comforters, daybed ensembles, Dacron-filled
comforters, decorator pillows, and dust ruffles,
offering depth and variety to suit almost everyone's taste and needs (there are many high-quality
bedspreads for upscale shoppers). If you're also
covering windows, consider ready-made draperies
at prices lower than major-store sales. On regular,
first-quality merchandise, you'll save approximately 25% off prevailing retail. On custom orders
you can save 30–40%.

DISCOUNT DEPOT

2020 San Pablo Avenue, Berkeley.
(510) 549-1478. M–F 10–7, Sat–Sun 10–6.
MC, VISA, AE, DIS. Parking: lot.
(Other stores: 520 Haight Street and 1620 Polk
Street, San Francisco; Futon Discounters,
920 San Pablo Avenue, Albany; Futon Depot,
Westgate Shopping Center, San Jose.)

Discount Depot comes in handy for new Cal students building their nests. They can pick up affordable linens and simple furnishings, a discount-priced futon and frame (budget to better versions), or a carton containing one of the contemporary RTA furnishings that make up much of the inventory. Usually a screwdriver is the only tool needed to put together a computer desk, end or coffee table, cart, bookcase, small eating table, etc. Find starving-student discounts on pillows, tablecloths, sheet sets, towels, and throw rugs. Mattresses and box springs from Serta and Simmons are discount priced for those who prefer traditional sleeping modes. Delivery can be arranged for about $25 to areas within a reasonable distance of each store.

DREAMS

921 Howard Street (at Fifth Street), San Francisco.
(415) 543-1800, (800) 419-1200. M–F 10–6:30,
Sat 10–6, Sun Noon–5. MC, VISA, AE, ATM.
Parking: street.

For starters, Dreams is a great place to shop for down comforters and other down products (feather beds, pillows). Because most comforters are made on-site, you can specify the weight of the fill, the design stitch, and the covering fabric, allowing you to buy budget to top quality. The price you pay for whatever you choose results in excellent value and solid bargains. There's also a ready-to-go selection. You can decide on the type of down fill by examining the various down products on display. More information is provided by the staff on fill power and loft, and on the thread count and fiber detail for the covering. You can also bring in your down comforter or cushions to be cleaned and renovated by Dreams' German down-cleaning plant, which gently refluffs old down as it cleans. The service department can replace or repair your comforter cover (pillows too) and add or delete fill for reasonable charges. Dreams offers a nice selection of domestic and imported bed linens in cotton, Egyptian cotton, flannel, satin, and jersey knits. There's a very nice discount fabric selection for making duvet or futon covers (seamstresses on-site work with amazing speed). If you need odd-size linens or bed coverings, bed skirts, shams (any kind of bedding accessory), or window treatment, your problems are over. Making custom slipcovers has become a specialty—use the store's fabric on your furnishings and you're likely to save a little more. You can have old cushions cleaned and refurbished here. Dreams also sells competitively priced mattress sets and brass and metal beds (including daybeds) —all nicely discounted.

LINEN BARN
Petaluma Village Premium Outlets, Petaluma.
(707) 773-1755. Daily. MC, VISA, AE, DIS.
Parking: lot.
(Other outlet: Gilroy center.)
It's easy to describe Linen Barn—ditto, ditto, ditto, all the other national discounters profiled. Most major lines of linens are represented in bed and bath selections, at similar discounts. There are also displays devoted to bath accessories, kitchen linens and kitchen doodads, cleaning products, picture frames, and some decorative accessories. It's worth a look-see—I spotted some patterns and a few lines that didn't show up elsewhere.

LINEN FACTORY OUTLET
475 Ninth Street, San Francisco. (415) 431-4543.
T–Sat 10–4. MC, VISA, DIS. Parking: street.
Linen Factory Outlet is connected to Western Linen, which sells textiles for kitchen, bed, and bath to department stores, hotels, restaurants, caterers, and small specialty stores. Being small, it can fill orders for special sizes that are often hard to buy from manufacturers. You'll find irregulars, overruns, and discontinued items from its stock. Among them are the classic bistro-check tablecloth in many colors and European damask tablecloths/napkins in 100% cotton. Look for imported items, such as famous British woolen blankets, 100% pure merino wool blankets from Australia, 100% alpaca wool throws from South America, and high-end flannel bed linens. Each Saturday there are several items on special.

LINEN FACTORY OUTLET

508-L Contra Costa Boulevard, Pleasant Hill.
(925) 827-0255. M–F 10–8, Sun 11–6:30.
MC, VISA, AE. Parking: lot.
(Other stores: 1001 Clement Street and
Westlake Shopping Center, San Francisco.)
When you've been in the business for more than
two decades, you make connections that lead to
the unpredictable inventory and good buys that
show up almost weekly at these discount stores.
These simple, no-frills stores offer everything from
budget to best (often seconds with cosmetic
flaws), at prices that should make other discounters
blush—budget-quality sheets sets, twins to kings
from $14.99 to $34.99 and better-quality sets
priced from $19.99 to $49.99. You'll find labels
too! Utica, Martex, Sanderson, Royale, Crown
Crafts, Charisma, and some you've never heard
of. Maybe you'll find pillowcases for $4.99 a set,
twin single sheets $2.99, queens single at $7.99,
or comforters at $19.99 (all sizes). This outfit does
a great job with ready-to-hang window coverings—tab curtains, sheers, laces with matching
valences, and three styles of drapes in 21 different
sizes. Kirsch rods are always 20% off.

LINENS 'N' THINGS

Great Mall of the Bay Area, Milpitas.
(408) 934-9288. Daily. MC, VISA. Parking: lot.
(Other stores: Citrus Heights, Pleasanton,
Roseville, Sacramento, San Jose.)
Bigger is better—especially as represented
by Linens 'n' Things' superstore concepts. This
powerhouse national chain (more than 140 stores)
offers 20–50% discounts off department store
prices every day and backs them up with a price
guarantee. Its stores stock a wide selection of
linens in every category for the home. That's
just the beginning, because the stores go on to
provide picture frames, framed art, everything
for entertaining, kitchenware (pots, pans, dishes,
cutlery, etc.), small electronics, organizers, and
tasteful home accessories and accents. It relies on
some of America's leading companies to keep
customers happy: Braun, Cuisinart, Calphalon,
Krups, Farberware, and linens from Laura Ashley,
Croscill, Waverly, Martex, Bill Blass, Adrienne
Vittadini, and others. It's not hard to duplicate a
picture-perfect bedroom with the coordinated
groups of upscale linens in very current patterns.

PAPER WHITE LTD. WAREHOUSE SALES

769 Center Boulevard, Fairfax. (415) 457-7673.
Quarterly sales. MC, VISA. Parking: lot.
The linens from paper white ltd. convey a romantic and nostalgic theme. The company designs and imports a high-end line in pristine white linen, linen/cotton blends, and luxurious Italian cottons. Many groups are lovingly trimmed with hand-made lace, embroidery appliqués, or cutwork. It's not hard to find linens that are similar to this line at much lower prices, but close inspection will reveal the difference—finer fabrics, superior embroidery, and designs that reflect owner Jan Dutton's discriminating design talent. If you're on paper white's mailing list, you'll get sale invitations that will lead to 40–60% markdowns on discontinued items, slightly soiled, or (insignificantly) flawed but always lovely linens. For the bedroom, you'll find duvet covers, window panels, dust ruffles, pillows, bedcovers, and shams; for the dining room, place mats, tablecloths, and napkins; plus home accessories, aprons, pillows, etc. Other treasures can be found in a special selection of christening gowns to last through several generations, and accessories for babies.

Call or write for a sale notice (usually in March, May, September, and December).

SPRINGMAID WAMSUTTA FACTORY STORES

Prime Outlets at Gilroy, Gilroy. (408) 847-3731.
Daily. MC, VISA, AE, DIS. Parking: lot.
(Other outlet: Vacaville center.)
These outlets have not gone highfalutin like so many discount linen stores. You'll find real old-fashioned bargain-basement prices in a no-frills ambiance. As a manufacturer, the company makes linens under many different labels—Eddie Bauer, Lands' End, Liz Claiborne, Martha Stewart, Bill Blass, and others that end up in the outlet as seconds, discontinued patterns, and overruns. Of course, that's in addition to all the Springmaid and Wamsutta labels from budget to very best. As leftovers of one kind or another, it's not always possible to pick up a whole matching kit and kaboodle, but wander around and you can probably put together a suite of linens (from bed skirts to window coverings) combining prints and solids from various bargain tables.

The very best buys come from the center aisle "end-of-the-line" tables, where all kings (including high-end sheets originally priced at $50) are $10.99, all queens are $8.99, and twins are $3.99. Other promotions produce $50 Elite 250-thread-count queen flat sheets reduced to $18.99, selected comforters (with posh labels) in all sizes at $20, and bed skirts priced from $6.99. Even more to my liking, you don't have to buy a packaged set, especially nice if you're transforming sheets into another decorative project. Also, great pricing on window treatments, shams, duvet covers, down comforters, children's bedding sets (many movie and cartoon characters), and bath collections. Seniors shop on Tuesdays for an additional 10% discount, and everyone can pick up a frequent buyer card for a 15% discount on the next purchase after spending $150.

STROUDS

500 El Camino Real, Menlo Park. (650) 327-7680, (800) STROUDS. M–F 10–9, Sat 10–7, Sun 10–6. MC, VISA, AE, DIS. Parking: lot.
(Other stores: Corte Madera, Dublin, Newark, Pleasant Hill, San Francisco, San Jose, San Mateo, Sunnyvale, Walnut Creek. Outlets: Strouds Super Outlets in Tracy, Vacaville centers.)

Strouds is a specialty off-price linen operation that offers top-quality products at decent discounts on virtually everything for bed (including down comforters), bath, kitchen, and dining room. The selection includes current colors and styles (many top-of-the-line). Using its special order program, you can coordinate wallpaper, window coverings, and accessories with your linen selections. In-home service for custom window coverings. The Super Outlets in Vacaville and Tracy offer moderately priced linen lines, more special promotions, closeouts, and irregulars unique to those outlets. Also, clearance inventory from its full-line stores at great prices. Return policies are very liberal.

Linens

313

WARM THINGS FACTORY STORE

180 Paul Drive (Terra Linda Industrial Parkway),
San Rafael. (415) 472-2154. M–Sat 10–5,
Sun Noon–5. MC, VISA. Parking: lot.
(Other stores: 16 Town and Country Village,
Palo Alto; 6011 College Avenue, Oakland;
3063 Fillmore, San Francisco.)
Everything from budget to best means everyone
has warm and cozy nights! Warm Things provides
all you need to know about loft, fill power, fabric,
and design variables, plus good value. Its selection includes its top-of-the-line, European-style
baffle construction in channel or box designs;
100% cotton cambric covers (230- to 360-thread
count); and for lean budgets, light- and medium-
weight goose-down comforters. Everything at
the Warm Things factory stores sells for 40–50%
off its catalog prices. Warm Things also sells down
pillows, featherbeds, boots, goose-down bath-
robes, wool mattress pads, slippers, many styles of
down jackets, and throws. Duvet covers are available in many fabrics, including damask, sateen,
flannel, denim, and vegetable-dyed cotton.

Mail Order

Because of shelf and display space limitations,
local stores are limited in providing all your
options for accessorizing. The companies listed
here offer discounted prices, ranging from modest
to very impressive, on a wide selection of linens in
all quality ranges for children's and adults' rooms.
You're much more likely to see everything available in a particular pattern. You'll also find many
esoteric bedding accessories and hard-to-find
products. Call and request a catalog.

TOUCH OF CLASS *(800) 457-7456*
THE LINEN SOURCE *(800) 431-2620*
DOMESTICATIONS *(800) 746-2555*
THE COMPANY STORE (DOWN SPECIALTY)
(800) 356-9367

Also See

Under San Francisco's Factory Outlets
and Off-Price Stores:
ESPRIT OUTLET

Under Family Apparel, Men's & Women's,
General Clothing:
THE BIG FOUR

Under Furniture and Home Accessories—
Catalog Discounters, General Furnishings,
Clearance Centers:
ALL LISTINGS

Wallpaper

I'm all for saving money, but if you're going to use a local store's wallpaper books, do the right thing and give it your business. It's very expensive for independent dealers to maintain an inventory of hundreds of wallpaper books for customers. Your local store may indicate when sales are likely to occur, so saving money becomes a matter of timing if you can't use the resources listed below. Also check the listings under Furniture and Home Accessories—Catalog Discounters, General Furnishings; Fabrics; and other cross-references listed here for stores that maintain an extensive selection of wallpaper books and then sweeten the process with nice discounts.

THE WALLPAPER CONNECTION
3124-D Crow Canyon Place, San Ramon.
(925) 275-8055. M–Sat 10–6, call for Sun hours.
MC, VISA. Parking: lot.
This charming, cozy, boutique-like wallpaper and home-decorating store has bins full of wallpaper (many with matching borders) discounted 25–75% off retail ($10.99 to $15.99). After you see those, spend some time leafing through the library of books from companies that read like a Who's Who of wallpaper; you'll save 20–35% on those offerings. Companion fabrics are discounted 15–20% off list. If Waverly and other fabric companies are your choice, you can also order comforter ensembles, draperies, and window treatments at 20% savings. If you need window coverings, bedding treatments, or a chair reupholstered, take a gander at the fabric swatch books. You'll save a little to a respectable amount, depending on what you're ordering. Miniblinds and shades are competitively

priced with the "big boys." With a new custom line of upholstery covers, they've covered all the bases.

WALLSTREET FACTORY OUTLET

2690 Harrison Street (near 23rd Street),
San Francisco. (415) 285-0870. T–Sat 10–6.
MC, VISA, AE. Parking: street.

This is the city's best resource for wallpaper at bargain prices. In the front, about 1,000 current wallpaper patterns are stocked in bins at 40–50% off retail book price. About 500 borders and 75–100 companion fabrics are stocked as well. Check the back room for overruns and discontinued patterns at even greater discounts. Wallstreet stocks 500 wallpaper books for special orders at 30–50% discount. Its lovely displays and mockups help customers picture the finished room (its emphasis is on coordinating papers, fabrics, and borders). For best results, come with an open mind and prepare to be versatile. You can borrow samples for evaluation. If you start your decorating project with the wallpaper choice first, it's a cinch to coordinate the other elements.

Also See

Under Fabrics:
FURBELOWS

Under Carpets, Area Rugs, and Flooring—
General:
LAWRENCE CONTRACT FURNISHERS

Under Furniture and Home Accessories—
Catalog Discounters:
THE INTERIOR WAREHOUSE;
JOHN R. WIRTH CO.; NORIEGA FURNITURE

Flea Markets

Attending flea markets has become a national weekend pastime. Here are some of the better-known markets in the area, held regularly throughout the year. Other markets occur on some other basis, maybe monthly or annually, and can be fantastic sources of bargains because they aren't as well attended as the listed ones. Check your local paper for notices of these events. Best bets: The San Jose Flea Market is the largest and maintains a reputation for the most reliable selection of everything from A to Z. In Cupertino, De Anza's reputation has grown with its size and consistent roster of better vendors of arts, crafts, collectibles, jewelry, and generally great stuff. The Foothill College Flea Market is distinguished by the number of artists and artisans who regularly offer some very original wares, while many hope Treasure Island's Flea Market will eventually attract the high-end and eclectic goods associated with the defunct Marin City Flea Market.

ALEMANY FLEA MARKET
100 Alemany Boulevard, San Francisco.
(415) 647-2043. Sun 8–3. Parking: lot.
Admission: free.
Early birds hit this market to nail down good buys on antiques and collectibles. Lots of funky booths for vintage clothing and household goods.

BERKELEY FLEA MARKET
Ashby BART Station Parking Lot (Adeline and Ashby), Berkeley. (510) 644-0744. Sat–Sun 8–7. Parking: free. Admission: free.

CAPITOL FLEA MARKET
3630 Hillcap Avenue (Capitol Drive-In), San Jose. (408) 225-5800. Th–F 7–5:30, Sat–Sun 6–5:30. Parking: lot. Admission: 50¢ Th, $1.25 Sat, $1.50 Sun (children under 11 years free).

CHABOT COLLEGE FLEA MARKET

2555 Hesperian Boulevard, Hayward.
(510) 786-6918. Third Sat each month 8–4.
Parking: free. Admission: free.

DE ANZA COLLEGE FLEA MARKET

21250 Stevens Creek Boulevard, Cupertino.
(408) 864-8946. First Sat every month 8–4.
Located in campus parking lots B and C;
over 850 vendors. Parking: $3. Admission: free.

FOOTHILL COLLEGE FLEA MARKET

12345 El Monte Road (corner Highway 280),
Los Altos Hills. (650) 948-6417. Third Sat every
month 8–3. Parking: $1. Admission: free.
Noted for its antiques and collectibles, art, fine
arts, plants, toys, books, jewelry, household items,
clothing, etc. Benefits Foothill Theatre Guild.

MIDGLEY'S COUNTRY FLEA MARKET

2200 Gravenstein Highway South (off 101, west to
Sebastopol 5 miles), Sebastopol. (707) 823-7874,
(800) 800-FLEA. Sat–Sun 6:30–4:30. Cash only.
Parking: free. Admission: free.

NAPA-VALLEJO FLEA MARKET AND AUCTION

303 Kelly Road (off Highway 29, halfway between
Napa and Vallejo), Napa. (707) 226-8862.
Sun 6–5. Parking: $2. Admission: free.

OHLONE COLLEGE SUPER FLEA MARKET

43600 Mission Boulevard, Fremont.
(510) 659-6285. Second Sat each month 8–4.
Parking: $1. Admission: free.

SAN JOSE FLEA MARKET

1590 Berryessa Road, San Jose. (408) 453-1110.
W–Sun dawn to dusk. Cash only. Parking: pay lot.
Admission: free.
The largest flea market in the United States,
with the largest number of regular vendors,
offering a smattering of everything from clothes
to furniture. Plants, pottery, toys, flowers, T-shirts,
and children's apparel are very popular. Don't
miss produce row!

SOLANO DRIVE-IN FLEA MARKET

Solano Way and Highway 4, Concord.
(925) 687-6445. Sat–Sun 7–4. Parking: free.
Admission: Sat 25¢, Sun $1.

TREASURE ISLAND FLEA MARKET

Avenue of the Palms, Treasure Island.
(415) 255-1923. Parking: $5. Admission: free.
The view alone is worth the trip, but chances are
you will find some great deals on food, antiques,
crafts, collectibles, flowers, and standard flea
market goods. Promising!

General Merchandise

Discount Stores

In many cases, you don't have to drive miles out of your way to go bargain hunting. Throughout the Bay Area, discount stores like Target, Wal-Mart, Payless, and Kmart do a respectable job of pricing merchandise lower than full-service retail stores. They're good for all types of merchandise, particularly housewares, giftware, consumer electronics, jewelry, toys, and sporting goods. They cover almost every area except major home furnishings and larger appliances. They are very competitive with each other, so comparison shopping pays off if you take the time to check catalogs before you buy.

Liquidators

Small liquidators abound all around the Bay Area, selling novelties, food items, health products, paper and party supplies, household goods, baskets, toys, whatever. So it's hardly worth the time and expense of driving out of your way to shop at any particular one. These places often have names like "$1.99," "Everything's a Buck," or, my favorite, "98 Cents Clearance Center Stores." Some stay strictly within the bounds set by their names; others have prices much higher than the names would suggest. By all means, cruise through the aisles of these stores if it's convenient. You may find some real deals, but sometimes you'll leave thinking it's all a bunch of junk.

CLOSE-OUT CENTER

4665 Clayton Road, Concord. (925) 687-7628.
W–Th 10–6, F 10–7, Sat 9–6, Sun 11–6.
MC, VISA, DIS. Parking: lot.

Choose this destination for some exceptional treasure hunting. It's a new concept, taking inventory on consignment from importers, distributors, manufacturers, closeout dealers, retail stores, and manufacturers' reps. These leftovers are priced at least 50% off original retails. The allure is the sheer unpredictability of any week's selection, but it usually includes minimal to maximum amounts of the following: paper goods, sundries, apparel, teacher's aids and supplies, gifts, basketry, ceramics, picture frames, food, garden goodies, pet supplies, baby necessities, silk flowers, books, games, toys, and whatever the company has negotiated to take on consignment. Don't come with a list, just prepare to buy what strikes your fancy and pushes your bargain buttons. The Close-Out Center is a bit removed from Concord's main retail districts near highways 24 and 680. *Directions: Take the Treat Boulevard exit east from Highway 680, drive about five miles and turn right on Concord Avenue.*

MACFRUGAL'S

200 Serra Way, Milpitas. (408) 946-9605.
M–Th 9–9, F–Sat 9–10, Sun 10–7.
MC, VISA. Parking: lot.
(Other stores: Nineteen Bay Area locations.
Call 800/800-9992 or check Geographical Index.)

MacFrugal's is strictly bargain basement. It buys carloads of closeout merchandise and sells at deeply discounted prices (40–70%). Goods include such diverse items as candles, linens, toys, books, housewares, giftware, and clothing. A great selection of Christmas ornaments and goodies is stocked every year.

Membership Warehouse Clubs

Almost everyone has a cluster of cards in their wallets, but probably none is more valued than a membership card to Costco or Sam's Club. By now thousands of Bay Area consumers of all economic and social levels have discovered the delights—and the hazards—of shopping at a warehouse club. Nearly everyone has a tale to tell along the lines of "I just went in to buy toilet paper and came out with a new TV" or, in other words, "Every time I shop, I end up spending an extra $100 to $200 on completely unplanned purchases." It's hard to resist the prices and the tempting selection of new items. "Grazing" down the aisles tasting vendors' new products guarantees that you'll leave with a full stomach and cart. Each club provides an extensive variety of consumer goods (electronics, computers, apparel, books, food, beauty items, tires, housewares, giftware, fine jewelry, watches, tools, etc.) and office and institutional products, but don't expect an in-depth selection of anything. Each company makes buys at prices that allow it to undersell the competition. The trade-off: Many items are sold in extra-large

quantities or packaged as multiples—a disadvantage for some individuals or small families. Surprisingly, the clubs manage to capture a fair amount of high-demand merchandise. At times, I've spotted Reebok, Adidas, and Nike athletic shoes, Dooney & Bourke and Liz Claiborne handbags, Guess? jeans, Rolex watches, Cross or Montblanc pens, Waterford crystal, and other items from consumers' "most wanted" lists. Each club continues to innovate and expand its offerings. Call for membership requirements. See the Geographical Index for the Costco or Sam's Club locations near you.

Special Sales and Events

AMERICAN INDUSTRIAL CENTER SALE

2325 Third Street (bet. 20th and 22nd streets),
San Francisco. Sale info: (415) 621-1920.
First Sat in Dec 9–4. Cash/Check. Parking: street.
Every year this cavernous industrial building, the
American Industrial Center, opens its doors to
the public for a most unusual sale opportunity.
It's the place to go if you want to scope out some
unique bargains. Plan to spend a few hours walking
the halls, keeping your eyes posted for balloons,
sandwich boards, and signs to lead you to the sale
participants. Each year the traffic increases as word
spreads that this is the only opportunity one has
to buy certain very upscale merchandise. Because
of market sensitivity, I can't mention companies
by name, but I can give a few clues to the types
of merchandise that you can find. For starters: an
expensive line of handknit sweaters for women
and men; several fashion jewelry manufacturers
(lines that sell under the glass at posh stores);
home accessories, including many sold through
national catalogs and at chic and trendy special
boutiques locally; bath and body products (many
in elegant packaging); fashion hats; and several
charming lines of children's apparel. It's a different
environment, yet rest assured that security guards
are on hand to ensure your comfort and safety.
The sale is usually held on the first or second
Saturday in December. Sign up on someone's
mailing list so that you'll get sale announcements
for future sales. I'd start at the 2325 entry on Third
Street (corner of 20th). Look for sale flyers that
identify the participants and spaces where the
doors will be open for your shopping adventures.

CELEBRATION FANTASTIC CATALOG OUTLET SALE

Sales held in San Francisco. For address and
dates in July and November–December,
call (800) Celebrate. MC, VISA.

Celebration Fantastic, a San Francisco–based catalog company, usually schedules two sales a year of discontinued, slightly damaged, overstock catalog inventory and samples. The catalog is devoted to presenting an uncommon and unique selection of gift merchandise themed around ALL of life's special occasions. Sale prices are typically 50–75% (except for Limoges boxes) off catalog retails. Expect festive and whimsical home decor: cookie canisters, candy dishes, mugs, pitchers, framed art, novelty accent rugs, small accent furniture pieces, holiday-themed decorative pillows, nutcrackers, collectible dolls, Christmas decorations and ornaments (many desirable collectible lines), plus painted trays, books, games, etc. Also, baby and children's gifts; women's apparel and accessories (usually some Michael Simon sweaters); and men's gifts, boxers and ties, great unisex novelty T-shirts, and more. Collectors will appreciate the Limoges boxes reduced by 25–30%. For several years the company has taken over a space at 899 Howard at the Yerba Buena Center for its sale events. Each sale is set up in just a few days, so the overall effect is organized chaos—tables overflowing with piles of stuff, big boxes filled

with soft goods. However, the regulars don't care and plunder through the store with a surgeons's eye for an opportunistic buy—maybe an adorable devil's baby suit for Halloween, a musical carousel for the holidays, or a slightly damaged limited-edition holiday ornament. The sale, which usually starts in November right after Thanksgiving, usually lasts until the end of December. Summer sales are scheduled for one or two days only.

CONCOURSE SAMPLE SALES

The Concourse, between Seventh and Eighth streets, Brannan and Townsend, San Francisco. Info: (415) 490-5800. Sat–Sun Thanksgiving weekend; one Sat in June. Cash preferred/Checks okay with many participants. Parking: pay lots. Admission: $3.

Tenants of the Gift Center and Fashion Center and many importers, distributors, manufacturers, and designers rent booth space at the Concourse for these mammoth events. Some participants never show up anyplace else to sell their samples, overruns, or leftovers. Each sale is frenzied from the moment the doors open. The inducement for consumers? Wonderful prices, usually 50%

off original retail. Categories of merchandise: apparel for the whole family; body, bath, and beauty products; baskets; giftware; silk plants; fashion jewelry; leather goods; household goods; stationery; holiday decorations; home accessories; and more. Watch the *Chronicle* and *Examiner* for sale announcements and clip the $1-off coupon for admission.

CYCLAMEN SECONDS SALES

1311 67th Street, Emeryville (510) 597-3640.
Occasional weekend sales. Cash/Check.
Parking: street.

From a small factory in Emeryville, Cyclamen produces a free-spirited line of high-fired stoneware that's sold to many posh specialty gift stores and upscale catalogs. Food and gourmet publications choose the tableware and bakeware with its distinctive retro-inspired freeform shapes and imaginative colors to show off its recipes and tablesettings. At occasional seconds sales (at least twice a year in June and November) you'll save 30–80% off retail on seconds and first-quality discontinued colors or shapes. Cyclamen's hybrid line of dinnerware and gift accessory pieces is

expensive—oversized plates sell at retail for about $38 each (seconds for $20), the mugs from $26 to $34 ($14 as seconds). Many Cyclamen pieces do double duty as functional food servers and decorative art pieces. The "Cyclamen Cooks" line features refrigerator-to-oven-to-table bakeware in a popular Forma pattern. It's microwave and dishwasher safe and easy to clean. Seconds in large lasagna dishes sell for about $42 ($82 retail), pie plates about $20, and you can fill cupboard spaces with several sizes of oval bakers and bread bakers.

You may have to be a bit of a scavenger when trying to put together placesettings from the Forma, Stella, and Galla collections. Don't sweat matching up the various elements; instead, follow recent tableware trends and combine colors or patterns creating your own original place settings. Some will gravitate towards glossy finishes, others will find satisfaction in the matte finishes. Add more interest with the bas-relief detailing on some pieces, and shapes that include square dinner and serving plates and out-of-the-ordinary narrow platters. The colors are terrific—many pastels, plus stronger colors like plum, Chinese red, royal, mango, persimmon, orange, blue, yellow, and combinations of colors in some patterns. The various platters, servers, pitchers, bowls, and mugs are chameleon-like, blending easily with traditional and rustic settings as well as modern, retro, and contemporary settings. Send a postcard or give them a call to add your name to the mailing list.

DESIGNERS' WAREHOUSE SALE

414 Lesser Street (66th Avenue exit from Highway 880), Oakland. (510) 434-1600 (extension 24 for directions). One-day sales in July and December. Cash/Check. Parking: lot.

The Designers' Warehouse Sale is organized by a group of young, progressive design and manufacturing companies with closeouts, one-of-a-kinds, scratch and dents, overstocks, and samples to unload. About twice a year they gather at this warehouse to achieve critical mass—presenting the public with a great variety of uncommon and very desirable merchandise. The sales are usually scheduled for just one day in July and in December. Many have learned to schedule weekend activities around these sales so they won't miss an opportunity to buy normally expensive department and specialty store designs (including some very fine lines normally sold through museum gift shops) at wholesale prices or less. The just-getting-started-crowd can really stretch their home-furnishings budgets and gift-buying dollars.

Participants do vary from sale to sale, but a core group provides the nucleus that attracts the crowds. In this group one company is known for old-fashioned forever-quality combined with simple modern styling in its line of hand-forged iron furniture and accessories (coat racks heavy enough to withstand a family's load of outerwear, slightly imperfect tendril shelf units with forged steel finials and natural steel shelves, glass-topped coffee tables with heavy steel bases, clocks with hand-welded numbers on the faces and more). Another company brings its light young designs of contemporary imported metal and wood furniture at very affordable pricing (shelf units, beds, tables, chairs, and more); a maker of contemporary lighting is a frequent participant (lamps, sconces, chandeliers) with innovative metal mesh, dupioni silk, or parchment shades combined with metal bases or forms; discontinued styles and colors, overstocks, and returns priced at 50–70% off retail ranging from $20 to $200. Industrial design is the inspiration for a collection of lamps, waste bins, picture frames (slight imperfections save you more than 30%), unique umbrella floor lamps, and machined aluminum table lamps, plus the famous bean-bag-base lamp. Others that often participate bring functional and contemporary storage and accessory products (wastebaskets, picture frames, cases, boxes, metal house numbers, knobs, cabinet hardware, framed mirrors, etc.). A few participants offer a different kind of merchandise—semi-precious stone and sterling silver handcrafted designer jewelry (sold under the glass at status stores) priced at 60% off at $15 to $200; another sells pewter Judaica—a collection of picture frames, mezuzahs, and jewelry. Many recognize the line incorporating chunks of colored glass, twisted copper wire, and dropped crystals on candlesticks, napkin rings, photo frames, and vases. Many shoppers are delighted to discover products that are pictured on the pages of their favorite mail-order catalogs. Call the number above for dates and directions.

EMERYVILLE SHOPPING HIDEAWAYS

Free maps available at the AMTRAK Station, Powell and Landregan, Emeryville. Stroll starts Friday, Saturday, and Sunday Thanksgiving weekend and continues Saturday and Sunday the first weekend of December. 10–5.

The Emeryville Shopping Hideaways event showcases the many designers, wholesalers, manufacturers, artisans, etc. who have facilities or studios in the area. The mix is unusual and eclectic. After picking up a map, you'll need your car to navigate the area. You may find sophisticated and contemporary men's ties; fine art glass (very fine vases, paperweights, bowls, etc.); wonderful hand puppets and stuffed animals; fun-themed string lights and night lights; contemporary glass oil-burning lamps; table linens; women's artwear and accessories; silk sachets, pillows, ribbons, and handcrafted personal accessories; fine-quality fashion jewelry, notecards, and handcrafted gifts; and assorted other gift merchandise. Altogether, twenty-five to thirty-six individual companies open their doors for this popular event. *Directions: Take the Powell exit east from Highway 80 to start the stroll. Parking is readily available throughout the area.*

FIRELIGHT GLASS SECONDS SALE

844 Doolittle Drive, Oakland. (510) 652-6731.
Daily 11–5 (Fri before Thanksgiving until Dec 23).
MC, VISA. Parking: lot on side of building.
Firelight Glass puts on a glow every year. The
warehouse is always well stocked with tables of
contemporary, clear-glass, oil-burning candles.
It's a breathtaking display! I'd have to describe
the quality-control inspectors at Firelight Glass as
"picky, picky, picky" because I can't spot the flaws
that make up the seconds sold at this annual
factory sale. As seconds the candles are priced at
30–40% off (most at 40%), from $9 to $50. Many
styles are offered in graduated sizes. Pick up just
one, or a trio for a more dramatic display. I find
these to be wonderful all-purpose gifts, and,
generally speaking, they're appealing to almost
everyone. Buy some just to tuck away for a little
gift for some person or occasion later in the year.
Go all the way and buy a small or large bottle
of clean-burning Firelight lamp oil. The candles in
cylinders, rounds, triangles, prisms, squares, cubes,
obelisks, and other artful shapes (like the new
side-filling chimney lamps) come with a lifetime
Fiberglass wick. Some candles are sold as sets
with incentive pricing (usually three candles in
graduated sizes), although these candles can be
purchased individually. Whatever you buy, you'll
appreciate the careful packing and boxing done
at the counter. Add wrap and ribbon, and your
gift is ready to go. *Note: These boxes will not
withstand the stress of shipping or mailing.* Store
is closed on Thanksgiving. *Directions: Traveling
north or south on San Pablo Avenue, turn east on
43rd Street. Go to Adeline, turn right, then turn
left on 42nd Street. This company is located south
of Powell Street off Highway 80.*

FURNITURE MART SAMPLE SALES

1355 Market Street (at Tenth Street), San Francisco.
*(415) 552-2311. One-day Sat sale dates
announced in May and Nov, 9–5. MC, VISA, AE.*
Parking: pay garage off Market. Admission: $6.
It's hard to get past the desk and into the showrooms at San Francisco's Furniture Mart, but the
doors open wide to the public during sample sales
twice a year. The Mart has over 300 showrooms
in two buildings (one ten-story, one eleven-story).
The Mart reflects the entire spectrum of home
furnishings and accessories—from tacky to terrific,

from budget to best. Approximately eighty showrooms participate in each sale. Prices are close to wholesale, possibly less on some items. Expect to find a little of every category: area rugs, upholstered furniture, case goods (dining, bedroom, occasional tables), lamps, lighting, pictures, mirrors, and great home accessories! Delivery service is available at extra cost. Watch the *Chronicle* and *Examiner* for sale announcements, or call to have your name put on the mailing list for sale notification.

GIFTCENTER SAMPLE SALES

888 Brannan Street, San Francisco.
(415) 864-SALE. Dates: Sat sales in early Nov;
usually in May before Mother's Day.
Admission: $3. Parking: street or pay lots.
Tenants of the Giftcenter combine with other manufacturers' reps, importers, and distributors to present a tantalizing shopping excursion. Booths and tables are set up on four levels of the Giftcenter; you won't want to leave until you've canvassed each floor. Fashion jewelry, women's designer clothing, giftware, housewares, linens, bath and body products, kitchen items, novelties,

picture frames, and gifts for any occasion are on display. Check the Pink Section of the *Sunday Chronicle/Examiner* for sale announcements and $1-off coupon for admission.

MELISSA'S EXCELLENT CLOTHING SALES

(415) 456-3050 for location and dates of
Bay Area sales. MC, VISA.
Started initially as a means to help children's manufacturers from around the state sell leftover inventory, the sale events have taken on gigantic proportions, expanding to include women's and men's clothing. If you hear a different name when you call to add your name to the mailing list or get information, don't worry, that means that the enterprising owners have finally settled on a more "grown up" name for their business. Sales are held about 15 to 18 times a year, usually at the Hall of Flowers in San Francisco's County Fair Building, or in Marin at the Marin Civic Center or San Rafael Community Center. Each sale has a different theme or demographic. It may focus on inventory from 6 to 15 children's manufacturers at one sale, contemporary women's apparel from small Los Angeles manufacturers at another, or

showcase the leftovers from just one big private label company/store or manufacturer. Bottom line, what keeps people lining up are the 50–80% reductions on everything. It's a given that you shop opportunistically with an eye to buy whatever makes sense, knowing sizes, colors, and styles may be limited on the past season or current over-runs, seconds, samples, etc. The system works for everyone—many of the vendors don't have out-lets or the wherewithal to have sales of their own, and consumers get some terrific deals.

NOMADIC TRADERS WAREHOUSE SALE

1385 Ninth Street, Berkeley. (510) 525-5854. Daily 10–5. Special factory sales, two weeks in June and from Friday after Thanksgiving until Dec 31, closed Christmas. MC, VISA. Parking: street. The focus at these semi-annual sale events is on clearing out surplus inventory of the sweaters, women's casual sportswear, hats, accessories, and other goodies that Nomadic Traders sells to cata-log companies and many stores catering to the outdoor industry. World travelers and all-around casual dressers can update their wardrobes with easy-fitting coordinates and cool summer dresses

(in June). Winter collections feature fleece, chenille, and corduroys with the same chic styling. Made locally and in Bali, the clothes have a familiar look—loose, unstructured, oversized, and contemporary. Wonderful fabrications in rayon, fleece, and knits in rich colors and prints are dis-counted 30–60%. Winter collections of sweaters are made in and imported from Uruguay, Peru, China, Nepal, and other foreign locales. Original knits in natural fibers translate ethnic traditions into contemporary designs. Look for great colors (and neutrals); interesting designs and patterns; and light, medium, and heavyweight versions in many hand-knit and hand-loomed, primarily unisex styles. Pick a cardigan, pullover, or vest. Discounts at the sale are 25–60% off retail on current and past-season styles. Pick up a pair of warm socks, a knit cap or hat, mittens, a scarf, or a blanket—other items imported by the company sometimes include holiday ornaments and deco-rative accessories.

PALECEK WAREHOUSE SALE

350 Carlson Boulevard, Richmond. Sales in late March every year. MC, VISA. Parking: lot/street. Send announcement request to Palecek Warehouse Sale, PO Box 225, Richmond, CA 94808. Palecek, the country's largest designer and importer of crafted accessories and woven rattan furniture, opens its warehouse to the public once every year in late March for a mammoth sale much anticipated by hordes of shoppers—early birds primed for their annual grab-and-go marathon. The incentive? 50–70% savings on the company's discontinued styles or finishes, samples, and slightly damaged goods. Each year the inventory is a reflection of how the company continues to diversify its product lines (that's what keeps the faithful coming back).

Can you have too many baskets? Not according to Palecek. They've got baskets in all sizes, many finishes, and with or without handles (for Easter or every day). Plus, large baskets for logs, trees, plants, or for stashing books; baskets for bathroom storage, hampers, and waste baskets; and some very interesting display baskets. Pricing can go way past bargain basement (even at great discounts) on the wicker furniture or wicker and combinations wood/glass/iron and updated painted finishes— occasional and dining chairs, tables, hampers, plant stands, magazine racks, and love seats (sometimes cushions too). Some of the most desirable sale inventory comes from the company's new design collections: accessories and accessory furniture pieces from the Norman Rockwell, Carole Endres folk art, and China Bay British Colonial collections.

SAN FRANCISCO BAY AREA BOOK FESTIVAL

Fort Mason, San Francisco. (415) 487-4550. Generally one weekend in October. 10–6. Admission: adults $5 (good for both days), children 18 and younger free. Parking: street/pay lots. The small press revolution started in the Bay Area. That's evident when you peruse the booths at the book festival, where small presses showcase the fruits of their labors. Book lovers appreciate the opportunity to see many titles that they may overlook when browsing through local bookstores. Mainstream publishers and local independent stores participate as well. Bargain hunters can fill their book bags with good deals, as most participants offer modest to maximum discounts on many of the titles in their inventories. Books run the gamut of topics from A to Z (children's books included). Authors' readings and appearances, combined with book-related events, contribute to the appeal of the festival.

SONOMA SAMPLE SALES

574 First Street East, Sonoma. (707) 996-5278. Sales in spring and fall. MC, VISA. Parking: lot. Four times a year at the Sonoma Women's Club (just a short block off the historic Sonoma Square), ladies line up early in the morning to be first in the door to grab fashions from the racks of samples— all priced at wholesale or less—from about 20 manufacturers' apparel representatives. Each rep usually handles several lines. There are two three-day sales in spring, two in the fall. Each is season-specific and all merchandise is new in the size 6–12 range (a few reps send large size samples in 1X–3X). When women see something they like, the only way to determine whether it will fit is to try it on, because fit and sizing vary greatly. No size problems on the handbags and accessories. Every sale offers up a mixed bag of dress-up

fashions, loungewear, sleepwear, dresses, pants, tops, skirts, etc. Some names on the roster of labels: Carol Anderson, Wild Rose, Willow, Rialto, Karavan, P.A. Company, Auditorium, Chava Sweaters, Tru Supply, Nomad, New Aura, Garron, Bila, Johnny Was, Misty Harbor Coats, Dumas jackets, and Barganza handbags. Call or send a card to Sonoma Sample Sales, 526-B West Napa Street, Napa 95476 to get on the mailing list for future sale dates.

WATSONVILLE FACTORIES' SALE

Information (800) 833-3494, or www.santacruzca.org. Typically, Saturday and Sunday before Mother's Day, and first weekend of December (or weekend after Thanksgiving weekend). Twice a year it becomes obvious that a lot of interesting things are being made in Watsonville, belying the area's image as a place where things grow just from the ground. Plan on an underground shopping excursion to the dozen or so manufacturers that open their doors to the public to sell their discontinued, surplus, sample, and slightly imperfect inventory—and leave with treasures. You may even find the CEOs manning the cash registers. Some possibilities for your gift and personal shopping: how about art-image umbrellas (sold in museum stores) from Salamander Graphics, or their potholders, very funny hats, computer mouse pads, and pillows? Smith & Vandiver's fine natural-ingredient personal care, bath, body, and aromatherapy products are priced at wholesale or below, up to 90% off. Think gift baskets and you won't leave without a few dozen salts, soaps, oils, and gels; home fragrance products including candles, glassware, baskets, display pieces, and more. Crafters or any fabric fanatic will head first for Nomi Fabrics, the decorator fabric manufacturer that normally sells only to the trade. Natural silks, linens, velvets, and high-quality cottons that are hand-painted, screened, stenciled, and dyed for use in upholstery, drapery, and accessories sell for $40 to $150 per yard at retail (you won't pay anywhere near that). $300 pillows are usually under $150. Pick up a stash of candles from Hi-Lite Candles (buy seconds or returns for black-out duty, others for "company's coming"). You can also find some fancy lingerie, elegant glasswares from Annieglass, and wonderful craftsman-style lamps. Maps are available at each factory to get you around the area. There are two separate clusters of companies. One cluster, near the Municipal Airport, has manufacturers within walking distance of each other. *Directions: Simply exit Highway 1 onto Highway 129 or 152 and follow the event signs. Call or visit the Web site to get up-to-date information.*

Sporting Goods

BENT SPOKE

6124 Telegraph Avenue, Oakland.
(510) 652-3089. T–F 11–6, Sat–Sun 11–5.
MC, VISA, DIS. Parking: street.
The owners travel the state buying used bikes
from various law-enforcement auctions. That must
account for the wide variety of "wheels"—with
little girls' pink bikes, tricycles, three-wheel bikes,
and mountain, hybrid, and road bikes filling up all
the space in this store. Some bikes look like they've
spent time languishing outdoors at the mercy of
the elements, while others are spiffy and like new.
Prices start at $19 for kids' bikes, about $30 for
adults. Bikes are reconditioned, and better bikes
have a limited warranty. Budget-priced mass-
market bikes (those sold at Kmart, Toys 'R' Us,
and other big chain stores or warehouse clubs)
are not warranted. Look around for special deals
on new closeout models from manufacturers like
Redline BMX, Jamis, Bianchi, Diamond Back,
Onivega, and Nishiki. No bikes are bought directly
from consumers. Good resource for families!

DEMO SPORT

1101 E. Francisco Boulevard, San Rafael.
(415) 454-3500. www.demosport.com. Sat–W
10–6, Th–F 10–8. MC, VISA, AE. Parking: lot.
(Other store: 1690 Tiburon Boulevard, Tiburon.)
Demo Sport rents and sells top-of-the-line snow skis
and snowboards for discount prices. Customers
have the opportunity to try before they buy. Major
brands include Burton, Rossignol, Salomon, and
Nordica. Full ski and snowboard repair services
are available, plus outerwear, sports racks, racquet
stringing, and a used equipment exchange program. During the summer, Demo Sport switches
gears to rent and sell in-line skates, wakeboards,
and water skis. Major brands include Rollerblade,
Hyperlite, Liquid Force, KD, and H.O. When you're
ready to buy, you'll save about 20–50% on snow

skis and boots; 10–30% on snowboards and outer-wear; 20–30% on waterskis and wakeboards, wetsuits, vests, and accessories. In-line skates and accessories are 10–15% off. Count on 15–20% discounts on quality sunglasses from Oakley, Arnette, Smith, Revo, Ray-Ban, and Maui Jim.

FRY'S WAREHOUSE SPORTS

164 Marco Way, South San Francisco.
(650) 583-5034. M–F 9:30–6, Sat–Sun 10–5.
MC, VISA, AE. Parking: street.
(Other store: 1495 E. Francisco Boulevard,
San Rafael.)

The sporting goods market is pretty competitive, especially on golf equipment. However, I find that Fry's offers value, selection, and discounts on better pro-shop lines of shoes, clothing, and equipment that give them a little edge. Slip into shoes from Nike, Adidas, Wilson, K-Swiss, Foot-Joy, Reebok, or Dexter. Also, tennis equipment from Wilson, Lynx, Power Bilt, Ping, Dunlop, Spalding, Hogan, MacGregor, Mizuno, Titleist, Cobra, Ram, Callaway, Daiwa, Cleveland, Yonex, and Taylor Made. These are not seconds or closeouts. While a discount operation, it provides

tennis racket stringing and free club fitting with its golf-swing computer.

GUS' DISCOUNT FISHING EQUIPMENT

3710 Balboa Street (bet. 38th and 39th Avenues),
San Francisco. (415) 752-6197.
www.citysearch.com/sfo/gus co. M–Sat 8–5.
MC, VISA. Parking: street.

If words like crocodile, pencil popper, or super-duper mean anything to you, read on. Gus' Discount Fishing Equipment is an experience! The prices entice regulars to stop in almost daily on their way to the water to see what's new. Serving as a West Coast wholesale distributor for Master, Rapala, Cossaks, Trophy, Dot Line Nets, and Abu Garcia, Gus' also buys factory overruns, salvage losses, and inventory from liquidations. Everything is discounted 25–60% off original retail. You'll find equipment for salmon, trout, freshwater, saltwater, and surf fishing. The terminal tackle selection deserves careful scrutiny. Check the lures from Luhr Jensen, Bass Buster, Hopkins, Diamond Gigs, and Panther Martin. All rods and reels are guaranteed. Keep warm and pick up a new vest, sweatshirt, or jacket from the sportswear corner.

KARIM CYCLE

2800 Telegraph Avenue, Berkeley. (510) 841-2181. www.teamkarim.com. M–Sat 11–6, selected Sun Noon–5. MC, VISA, ATM. Parking: street.

This company's location close to the Cal campus is a definite advantage. Students come in to buy a bike when the semester begins and often return at the end of the year to sell it back. The company is careful to protect the integrity of its business. The seller's personal identification is required for all transactions, and Karim clears all bike registrations with local police departments. The selection covers bikes of all descriptions: mountain, road, hybrid, three-speed, and a few children's and tandem bikes are usually in stock. Prices are set according to condition and usually offer 40–60% savings off original retail. Karim usually has a recent inventory printout with descriptions and prices of better bikes. Mountain bikes start at $199; otherwise expect to spend $99 to $1,000 (on top-quality bikes). Before putting the used bikes out for sale, each is reconditioned and further supported by a thirty-day free service policy for any adjustments. You can save time by previewing the used bike inventory from Karim's Web site.

Karim also sells new bikes and always has several deeply discounted closeout models in stock from well-known manufacturers. If biking is not your thing, you can rent or buy in-line skates and new and used snowboards. Finally, you often can trade in your old bike on a new and better model. Located three blocks north of Ashby at Stuart.

NEVADA BOB'S DISCOUNT GOLF

1975 Diamond Boulevard, Concord. (925) 680-0111. M–F 9:30–8, Sat 9:30–6, Sun 9:30–5. MC, VISA, AE, DIS. Parking: lot. (Other stores: Belmont, Fremont, Modesto, Rohnert Park, Sacramento, San Jose, San Leandro, Stockton.)

With more than 300 franchise stores, Nevada Bob's has considerable volume purchasing power. It will also beat any verifiable price on current pro-line equipment. Each store's experienced, professional staff ensures that customers are fitted for their build and ability. Along with balls, bags, carts, accessories, and extras, shoes at 30–50% discounts deserve your attention. Give the apparel racks the once-over and you're sure to end up looking like a golf pro at nicely discounted prices.

NORDICTRACK "FACTORY DIRECT"

Prime Outlets at Gilroy, Gilroy. (408) 842-4721.
Daily. MC, VISA, AE, DIS. Parking: lot.
(Other outlet: Great Mall, Milpitas.)
The company sends its reconditioned equipment, overruns, closeouts, and past-season models to its factory store, and showcases first-quality equipment there as well. Current season, first-quality equipment is full priced. The best buys are found on reconditioned equipment and discontinued models, where markdowns can exceed 40% off original retails. Shop for fitness and exercise equipment, cross-country skiers, treadmills, strength-training equipment, and abdominal exercisers.

NORTH FACE FACTORY OUTLET

1238 Fifth Street, Berkeley. (510) 526-3530. M–Sat
10–7, Sun 11–5 (extended holiday hours). MC,
VISA, AE, DIS. Parking: street.
(Other store: 1325 Howard, San Francisco.)
The North Face manufactures high-quality outdoor equipment and colorful, long-lasting sportswear. Prices start at 20% off retail and dive from there. These price reductions are applied to seconds, overruns, and discontinued items. Casual tops, pants, shirts, sweaters, etc. for men and women (some unisex) can be classic or colorful. You'll find Gore-Tex and other high-tech fabrics in the company's outdoor clothing, rainwear, and skiwear. North Face backpacks, sleeping bags, lumbar packs, tents, and duffels are always in good supply and reduced 20–40% off. You'll even find hiking boots discounted. Soft luggage, carry-ons, and business cases made from sturdy cordura nylon are appropriate for both a Manhattan boardroom and a Jumla yak caravan. Get on the mailing list for the outlet's biggest sales.

OUTDOOR OUTLET BY ANY MOUNTAIN

2990 Seventh Street (at Ashby), Berkeley.
(510) 704-9444. www.anymountaingear.com.
M–F 10–9, Sat 10–7, Sun 11–6.
MC, VISA, AE, DIS. Parking: lot.

Any Mountain has twelve big retail stores and this outlet right next to its distribution center. This is where retail store closeouts, clearance, and surplus inventory ends up at the end of the season. Even though the outlet is well arranged and merchandised (it's a neat looking store), you won't find the same up-to-date inventory and full technical support of its full-service, full-price stores. Discounts generally range from 20–40% off retail, sometimes more. The company also doesn't miss an opportunity to pick up manufacturers' closeouts from its regular vendors. Selections vary by season. Shop spring and summer and you'll see tents, camping gear, sleeping bags, hiking boots, backpacks, rafts, ski twins, etc. Winter comes with skis, snowboards, snowboard boots, and the like. In-line skates, high performance shoes for outdoor activities, and lots of accessory items for every category keep shoppers shopping. A very extensive selection of specialty apparel for men and women and a smaller selection for children take up about half the store. Marmot, Mountain Hardware, Columbia, and Burton are just a few of the labels. You don't have to be a mountain man or ace skier to appreciate the apparel. Many lines serve a crossover market—travelers and anyone wanting well made, functional, quality casual sportswear (many lines featuring high-tech fabrics and style innovations). You've got seven days for returns and refunds.

PLAY IT AGAIN SPORTS

1601 Contra Costa Boulevard, Concord.
(925) 825-3396. M–F 10–7, Sat 10–6, Sun 11–5.
MC, VISA. Parking: lot.
(Other stores: Alameda, Campbell, Fremont, Los Altos, Pleasanton, San Bruno, San Francisco, San Rafael, Santa Rosa, Sunnyvale.)

At Play It Again Sports, most of what is sold is used; each Bay Area store may have a different mix of merchandise. Prices on used goods are discounted about 50% off original retail. You can buy, sell, trade, or consign equipment for football and soccer (including shoes), golf, street hockey, baseball/softball, and racquet sports; roller skates and Rollerblades; exercise equipment and weights; and water, downhill, and cross-country skis. No weapons or bowling balls. The store is geared mainly to weekend athletes and beginners (children or adults) rather than the serious sportsperson. Brands would be midpriced if sold new. The stores carry some new merchandise and samples. I suggest that hard-pressed parents give this outfit the once-over. And call before coming in, especially if you're bringing something to sell or consign. The staff keeps a list of special requests and will notify you when or if the merchandise comes in.

SPORTMART
1933 Davis Street (Westgate Center),
San Leandro. (510) 632-6100. M–Sat 9:30–9:30,
Sun 10–7. MC, VISA, DIS. Parking: lot.
(Other stores: Concord, Daly City, Emeryville,
Milpitas, Sacramento/Roseville, San Jose,
San Mateo, Santa Rosa, Sunnyvale, Vacaville.)
These stores offer a great selection of bikes ($60 to $400); equipment for skiing, bowling, tennis, golf, water sports (skis, Boogie boards), fishing, and camping; sports and workout apparel; shoes for every sporting activity for the whole family;

and exercise equipment. You'll find brand names, a wide range of prices representing budget to better in the lines carried, and an in-depth selection that far surpasses almost all competitors. Each category is well supported with an endless array of accessory items. My comparisons show that Sportmart trims prices to beat the competition from a little to a lot every day. Competitors' loss leaders may undersell it on occasion, but its price guarantee takes care of that. Very accommodating return and refund policy.

WILDERNESS EXCHANGE
1407 San Pablo Avenue, Berkeley. (510) 525-1255.
www.wildernessexchange/citysearch.com.
Sun–W 11–6, Th–F 11–8, Sat 10–6.
MC, VISA, DIS. Parking: lot.
Wilderness Exchange serves backpackers, climbers, mountaineers, campers, and cross-country skiers. It sells closeouts, sales rep's samples, blems, and overstock from more than thirty outdoor companies at discounts of 15–40% off retail. Another angle: About 20% of the inventory is used (high quality, cleaned, and reconditioned if needed), most often sold for at least 50% off original retail. Buy, sell, or

trade your way to good deals. Call to inquire about availability of any specific item or brand of equipment you have in mind.

About Bikes—Strategies for Buying New Bikes

Once you understand how distribution works, you'll see why it's very difficult to select any particular bike retailer as a source of bargains. Bike manufacturers protect their markets by creating a carefully balanced network of dealers, ensuring that each store is able to serve a particular market area profitably. To that end, manufacturers suggest a minimum selling price for the dealers. In the Bay Area, it appears that most dealers sell bikes at the "minimum suggested price." Therefore, the market is very competitive, with no one dealer offering substantially lower everyday prices. Of course, each store holds a few sales during the year, but if a dealer holds too many, or attempts to lower prices too much, other dealers complain to the manufacturer, and the offender is in jeopardy of losing the line. So everyone plays along. Because the Bay Area is considered a year-round market, you don't have the predictable end-of-

season blowout sales prevalent in ski equipment. Also, because the bikes are expensive, dealers control their inventory so that they can offer a good selection without becoming overstocked. If you're buying a better bike for off-road or heavy street use, you'll want to spend at least $300 to get reliable components. Each step up—to $500, $700, or higher—buys you better braking, shifting, frame materials, etc. Choosing which brand to buy is a very subjective decision. If you're in a good shop, the staff will spend time determining your anticipated use, where you'll be using the bike, perhaps even what trails you plan to ride on, and then you'll need to try several bikes to see how they handle. To buy at a bargain, first spend time evaluating the various models, make your decision, and then watch for a sale. Another option: cycling or bike publications for mail-order companies. Many have discounted prices, but you'll have to forgo after-purchase service and support, something you may regret.

If you're not interested in the better bikes, you won't have any problem finding bikes in the $100 to $300 range. Sportmart, Wal-Mart, Toys 'R' Us,

Kmart, Price/Costco, Sears, Play It Again Sports
(used), and others are likely resources. Don't
overlook classified ads or sheriff's department
or police auctions. Refer to listings in this section
that profile the best sources for used bikes—
a good alternative when money's tight and for
many out-of-state students who need a bike just
for the school year.

Also See

Under General Merchandise:
ALL SECTIONS

Toys

BASIC BROWN BEAR FACTORY

444 De Haro Street (off 17th Street), San Francisco.
(415) 626-0781. www.basicbrownbear.com.
M–Sat 10–5, Sun Noon–5. MC, VISA, AE, DIS.
Parking: street.
Basic Brown Bear is now a factory-direct company
that provides wonderful tours and experiences for
children and their parties. It made its reputation
years ago when it made and distributed a line
known for the quality of its plush fabrics and the
appealing personalities of its critters. Life is
simpler for the owner now dealing direct and
you'll still find B.B. Bear, Beary God-Mother, and
FOBs (friends of bears) like Chocolate Moose and
Mother Goose. Prices range from $5 to $250
(a gigantic, fully jointed grizzly bear with leather
paws), but the median price is $25 to $30. You
may want to return with your children at another
time for a captivating tour and bear-making
(kiddies can choose to fill their own baby bears).

Call for tour information for individuals or groups.
Lots of fun!

FOLKMANIS

1219 Park Avenue, Emeryville. (510) 658-7677.
www.folkmanis.com. M–F 9:30–4:30. Cash/Check.
Parking: street.
This factory-second store features some of the
most creative puppets on the market—weird and
wonderful animals, from cuddly to creepy. Poor
puppets. Some are flawed, discontinued, or production samples, but these lovable creations offer
hours of entertainment for the child in all of us
because of their appealing, lifelike appearance.
Just try to resist the new "robins in a nest" or
"mice in a box" or the cockroaches, dinosaurs,
dragons, otters, dogs, bears, and more. They're
far superior to the typical puppet; in fact, they
look more like stuffed animals. Witches and other
extraordinary folks are also part of the family.

Prices on seconds with minor flaws range from $5 to $25, at about 50% off retail.

LAKESHORE LEARNING MATERIALS

1144 Montague Avenue, San Leandro.
(510) 483-9750. M–F 9–6, Sat 9–5, Sun 11–5.
MC, VISA, AE, DIS. Parking: street.
Lakeshore Learning Materials supplies teachers and educators (preschool and elementary grades) and nursery school and day-care operators with educational toys, games, teaching materials, books, play equipment, and more. Parents are free to shop for their children and find bargains in Lakeshore's large clearance center in the back. Stop by for 25–75% savings on overstocked, discontinued, returned, and slightly damaged items. You'll find a constantly changing selection of toys, teacher's aids, and equipment. I noted many books (some teachers' copies with answers), clear plastic boxes for treasures, little nylon backpacks, even classroom tables, large activity carpets, and miscellaneous small toys. Pick up a catalog when you enter the retail showroom, because many catalog items are not displayed.

SANRIO SAMPLER

Factory Stores of America, Vacaville.
(707) 447-3721. Daily. MC, VISA. Parking: lot.
If you've got little girls, chances are you've had to buy from Sanrio's popular "Hello Kitty" line of novelties, school supplies, party goods, lunch boxes, stationery products, cosmetic and beauty sets, craft sets, and other goodies. Sanrio Sampler offers 50% savings on many discontinued items. About 40% of the store is discount—it annoys me to no end that the rest is at full price. If you stick to the marked-down merchandise you can stock up on birthday party presents that will save you expensive last-minute sorties to local stores.

TOY GO ROUND

1361 Solano Avenue, Albany. (510) 527-1363.
M–Sat 10–5. MC, VISA. Parking: street.
A consignment and resale store that's well stocked with toys, Barbies, books, records, videos, games, tapes, and even skates for budget-strapped parents. Nice preschool selection of developmental toys, new wooden toys, and a wall of books priced to gladden the hearts of parents of budding bookworms. Consignments accepted 10–12 daily.

TOYS UNLIMITED/KB TOYS OUTLET
Factory Stores of America, Vacaville.
(707) 448-7314. Daily. MC, VISA, DIS.
Parking: street.
(Other outlets: Anderson/Redding, Folsom,
Gilroy, Petaluma centers.)
Toys Unlimited and KB Toys, now consolidated,
constitute one of the country's largest toy firms,
selling large quantities of closeout inventory from
a wide variety of toy makers, including Mattel,
Fisher Price, Hasbro, Tonka, and Playskool. There
are typically about 1,300 toys: dolls (including
Barbie everything), action figures, die-cast
collectibles, some ride-ons, games, big box toys,
seasonal specialties, and gazillions of other little
goodies in stock at any one time. Stop by for little
treasures or big-ticket items. Prices are kept low
because there is no advertising of individual
brands or stores.

Also See

Under Recycled Apparel:
GENERAL INFORMATION

Under Furniture and Home Accessories—
General:
IKEA

Under Furniture and Home Accessories—
Baby and Juvenile Furniture/Equipment:
ALL LISTINGS

Under General Merchandise:
ALL SECTIONS

Outlet Center Shopping

Approach shopping at outlet centers with the right expectations and you'll come away satisfied. If you're unrealistic and expect wholesale pricing or 50% discounts everywhere you shop, then you'll wonder what all the fuss and hype is about. Many stores offer discounts that I can only call modest. If you find that prices are just as good at department store sales—well, maybe they are. Yet each manufacturer's store offers far more of its own lines than you'll ever see in any one store, so your choices are much greater. Combined with the overall aspect of value pricing, and the concentration of so many attractive factory and off-price stores in one location, it's hard to spend a few hours shopping without leaving with several bags of good buys. Finally, there are usually several exceptional tenants at each center whose discount prices will more than satisfy your thriftiest inclinations.

Unlike conventional malls, outlet malls are usually located away from urban areas to avoid placing manufacturers in competition with retail stores that sell their products. Many manufacturers benefit greatly from their outlet stores. They can make more money selling their merchandise directly to the public than selling it to an off-price retailer or discount store. As department stores have moved heavily into developing their own private-label lines and direct-import programs, many manufacturers have been propelled into the outlet business to maintain their profits and production. Outlet centers have popped up all over Northern California. These are typically destination centers— at a comfortable distance from the major retail stores and shopping malls in the Bay Area, but close enough for a day's outing of shopping thrills, savings, and fun!

A word about timing: Just like every kind of retailer, outlet tenants have special sales that pile savings on already discounted merchandise. Holiday weekends or any national holiday where substantial numbers of people have a day off are prime time for a day of outlet center shopping. Individually, some outlets have their own timetable for special sale markdowns or events. Unless you've ensured that your name is on the store's mailing list, you may never get the word on these special sales. Fortunately (for those concerned about mailing lists and junk mail in general), most companies are very proprietary about their mailing lists.

For a complete profile of the outlet stores found in the centers closest to the Bay Area (and in most outlet centers around the country), refer to the individual listings under the appropriate category.

Greater Bay Area Outlet Centers

*For a listing of stores in each center,
see Geographical Index.*

Anderson/Shasta
PRIME OUTLETS AT ANDERSON
*1856 State Highway 273, Anderson.
(530) 378-1000. www.primeoutlets.com.
M–Sat 9:30–8, Sun 11–6;
winter M–Sat 9:30–6, Sun 11–6. Parking: lot.*
A good stopover on your way north on Highway 5.
Closest Polo/Ralph Lauren Factory Store. *Directions: Eight miles south of Redding. From Highway
5 North: Anderson-Factory Outlets Drive exit;
from Highway 5 South: Factory Outlets Drive exit.*

Folsom
FOLSOM PREMIUM OUTLETS
*13000 Folsom Boulevard, Folsom. (916) 985-0313.
www.chelseagca.com. M–Sat 10–9, Sun 10–6.
Parking: lot.*

Charming and appealing villagelike complex and
a convenient detour for Tahoe travelers. More
than 70 stores. Famous labels: Nike, Jones New
York, Off Fifth, Carter's Childrenswear, and more.
*Directions from Bay Area: Highway 80 to Highway
50 to Folsom Boulevard exit, turn left.*

Gilroy
PRIME OUTLETS AT GILROY
*681 Leavesley Road, Gilroy. (408) 842-3729.
www.primeoutlets.com. M–Sat 10–8, Sun 10–6.
Parking: lot.*
Located 30 miles south of San Jose. More than
150 factory stores. Famous labels: Ann Taylor
Loft, J. Crew, Gap, Lenox, Nautica, Versace,
Polo/Ralph Lauren, Waterford/Wedgwood, Bose,
Anne Klein, Nike, Birkenstock, Etienne Aigner, Liz
Claiborne, Kenneth Cole, and more. *Directions:
From 101 South, take the Leavesley exit left.*

Milpitas

GREAT MALL OF THE BAY AREA

447 Great Mall Drive, Milpitas. (408) 956-2033; tours: (800) MALLBAY (625-5229). www.greatmallbayarea.com. M–F 10–9, Sat 10–8, Sun 11–7. Parking: lot.

The 1.5 million-square-foot project (the former Ford Motor plant) includes 9 anchors and 185 specialty retailers (primarily off-price tenants and manufacturers' outlets). Famous labels: Off Fifth (Saks Fifth Avenue Outlet), St. John, Mondi, Gap Outlet, Donna Karan, bebe, Florsheim, Carter's Childrenswear, OshKosh B'Gosh, Calvin Klein, London Fog, and more. *Directions: Located off 680 and 880 at the intersection of Montague Expressway and Great Mall Parkway.*

Napa

NAPA PREMIUM OUTLETS

629 Factory Stores Drive, Highway 29 and First Street, Napa. (707) 226-9876. www.chelseagca.com. Daily 10–6. Call for extended seasonal hours. Parking: lot.

An outdoor center in the heart of the wine country, with more than 40 factory-direct stores. Famous labels: Ellen Tracy, Karen Kane, Cole-Haan, Tommy Hilfiger, Nautica, Timberland, TSE, BCBG, Dockers, Kenneth Cole, Calvin Klein, and others! *Location: At the intersection of Highway 29 and First Street.*

Pacific Grove

THE AMERICAN TIN CANNERY PREMIUM OUTLETS

125 Ocean View Boulevard, Pacific Grove. (408) 372-1442. www.chelseagca.com. Sun–Th 10–6, F–Sat 10–8. Parking: lot.

A lovely, airy, enclosed shopping outlet mall with more than 50 tenants. Famous labels: Anne Klein, Carole Little, Jones New York, Woolrich, and more. *Directions: Easy access from Highway 1, Pacific Grove exit. Follow signs to Cannery Row and Aquarium. American Tin Cannery is one block past the aquarium.*

Petaluma

PETALUMA VILLAGE PREMIUM OUTLETS

2200 Petaluma Boulevard N., Petaluma. (707) 778-9300. www.chelseagca.com. M–Sat 10–8, Sun 10–6. Parking: lot.

A village-themed outdoor center with more than

50 factory stores. Famous labels: Ann Taylor, Petite Sophisticate, Off Fifth, Villeroy & Boch, Brook Bros., Joan & David, and more. *Directions: From 101, take E. Washington Street to Petaluma Boulevard, turn right.*

San Leandro
MARINA SQUARE
Marina Boulevard West at Fwy 880, San Leandro. M–F 10–9, Sat 10–7, Sun 11–6. Parking: lot.
Very convenient outlet/off-price center located in the middle of the Bay Area. Famous labels: Ann Taylor Loft, Talbots Outlet, Eddie Bauer, Nordstrom Rack, Mikasa, and more. *Location: Next to Freeway 880 at the Marina exit East.*

St. Helena
ST. HELENA PREMIUM OUTLETS
3111 N. St. Helena Highway, St. Helena. (707) 963-7282. www.chelseagca.com. Daily 10–6, seasonal hours vary. Parking: lot.
A small center, distinguished by its status tenants—Donna Karan, Movado, Coach, Brooks Bros., and others. *Location: On Highway 29, one mile north of St. Helena.*

Tracy
PRIME OUTLETS AT TRACY
1005 Pescadero Avenue, Tracy. (209) 833-1895. www.primeretail.com. M–Sat 9–8, Sun 10–6. Parking: lot.
Just an hour east of the Bay Area, on the road to Yosemite, with over 40 shops: Sony, OshKosh B'Gosh, Jones New York, Bass, and many more. *Directions: From 205, exit at MacArthur Boulevard.*

Vacaville
FACTORY STORES AT VACAVILLE
321-2 Nut Tree Road, Vacaville. (707) 447-5755. www.factorystores.com. M–Sat 10–8, Sun 10–6. Parking: lot.
Halfway between San Francisco and Sacramento. More than 120 stores in this center. Famous labels: Lenox, Gap, Nike, Mikasa, Le Creuset, Royal Doulton, Johnston & Murphy, Naturalizer, Etienne Aigner, and more. *Directions: From 80 East: take 505/Orange Drive, exit at Orange Drive, turn right to access center entrance. From 80 West: exit at Monte Vista Avenue, first right onto Monte Vista, left at Nut Tree Road.*

Glossary of Bargain-Hunting Terms

Whenever an item is for sale to the public at 20–50% under retail, common sense tells you there must be a reason. I have tried in each entry to give you an explanation; the answer generally falls into one or more categories described by the following terminology used in retailing.

discontinued or manufacturer's closeout: Apparel or products that are no longer being manufactured. In most instances this does not affect the merchandise, but if parts may need to be replaced, it could cause a problem.

floor sample: A model displayed in the store.

freight damage: Even if only one or two items in a shipment are broken, burned, chipped, or marred, for insurance purposes the entire lot is designated "damaged." This merchandise may be noticeably damaged; often, however, it is actually in A-1 condition but was part of a large shipment that met with physical mishap.

gray market: Also known as "parallel importing." Refers to the overseas purchase of foreign goods by independent companies who are not authorized U.S. dealers for those goods. The goods are then sold in the United States by off-price and discount retailers who compete with the owners of the U.S. trademarks for those goods. Not having to pay for service, warranties, or advertising, the gray-market merchants can undercut the prices of the U.S. trademark owners.

in-season buying: Whereas most retailers buy preseason, a discounter will often purchase in-season, relieving the manufacturer of merchandise that is old from a manufacturer's standpoint but still new to the public.

irregular: Merchandise with minor imperfections, often barely discernible.

job lot: Goods, often of various sorts, brought together for sale as one quantity.

jobber: A person who buys goods in quantity from manufacturers or importers and sells those goods to dealers.

keystone: Traditional retail markup. Based on the wholesale price being doubled, i.e., a $50 wholesale price results in a retail price of $100.

knock-off: A copy of a popular design. These may be nearly authentic renditions or shabby imitations. Some manufacturers and designers make their own knock-offs in different or lesser-quality materials for off-price stores and chains.

liquidated stock: When a company or business is in financial trouble, the stock it has on hand is sometimes sold to merchandisers at prices much lower than retail in order to liquidate the assets of the company.

loss leader: An item purposely priced low (sometimes at a loss) to get you into the store.

odd-lots: A relatively small quantity of unsold merchandise that remains after an order has been filled.

off-price retailing: The sale of major-brand merchandise at reduced prices.

open stock: Individual pieces of merchandise sold in sets, which are kept in stock as replacements.

overruns: An excess of products, similar to surplus and overstocks, but generally due to a manufacturer's error.

past-season: Goods manufactured for a previous season.

retail: The selling of merchandise directly to the consumer.

returns: Orders returned to the manufacturer by retail stores because they do not arrive on time. Fashion discounters are able to buy this merchandise below cost from the manufacturer.

samples: An item shown by the manufacturer's representative to the prospective merchandiser/buyer for the purpose of selling the product.

seconds: Merchandise with more-than-minor flaws, which may affect the aesthetic appeal or performance of the product.

surplus overstock: An excess quantity, over and above what is needed by the retailer.

wholesale price: The cost of goods to the retailer, except in discount shopping, when consumers can buy at or near this price.

wholesale to the public: This term is often used inappropriately by discounters. From my perspective, "wholesale" is the price the seller pays for the merchandise. If that same price were passed on to the consumer, a discount retailer would make no profit. When a discounter is able to buy merchandise for less than the manufacturer's original published wholesale price (at liquidations, end-of-season closeouts, etc.), it is possible for the discount retailer to add a markup and sell the merchandise for the original wholesale price or for even less.

Store Index

Store Index

Store Index

357

Store Index

363

Geographical Index

Subject Index